You don't have to be a [   ]
to get professional results from home craftsmanship if you know

HOW TO WORK WITH TOOLS AND WOOD

In this compact all-inclusive book, two experts have gathered together all the basic principles you need to know—plus hundreds of shortcuts and techniques used by carpenters to make working with hand and power tools easier for you.

Here is a reference book and home study course that takes you step by step to mastery of skill in the use of every woodworking tool. In addition to the selection of the proper tools and lumber, it shows you with easy-to-understand instructions and illustrations how to turn out a satisfactory professional-looking piece of work with the least effort, how to fix things around the house, and finally how to plan and complete dozens of projects, from making furniture to finishing a basement.

Most important of all, this book helps you have fun while you work because it shows you how to work surely and safely and productively—doing the right things in the right way to produce results of which you will be proud.

HOW TO WORK WITH TOOLS AND WOOD is a greatly expanded and revised version of the book of the same title originally published by Stanley Tools and reprinted by Pocket Books.

HOW TO WORK WITH TOOLS AND WOOD

Edited by
ROBERT CAMPBELL
and
N. H. MAGER

Illustrated

PUBLISHED BY POCKET BOOKS NEW YORK

HOW TO WORK WITH TOOLS AND WOOD

Stanley Tools edition published 1952

POCKET BOOK edition published March, 1955

28th printing..................December, 1975

This edition of *How to Work with Tools and Wood* is newly revised and enlarged from the original edition published by Stanley Tools.

L

This original POCKET BOOK edition is printed from brand-new plates made from newly set, clear, easy-to-read type. POCKET BOOK editions are published by POCKET BOOKS, a division of Simon & Schuster, Inc., 630 Fifth Avenue, New York, N.Y. 10020. Trademarks registered in the United States and other countries.

Standard Book Number: 671-80244-5.

Printed in the U.S.A.

CONTENTS

CHAPTER ONE
Anyone Can Work with Tools and Wood...................... 1

CHAPTER TWO
First Tools First.. 3

CHAPTER THREE
Achieving Skill with Your Tools................................... 35

CHAPTER FOUR
From Plan to Product.. 111

CHAPTER FIVE
Finishing up the Project.. 124

CHAPTER SIX
Choosing the Wood.. 131

CHAPTER SEVEN
About Putting Pieces Together....................................... 141

CHAPTER EIGHT
Holding the Pieces Together... 183

CHAPTER NINE
Sharpening the Tools... 218

CHAPTER TEN
Some Fancy Touches... 237

CHAPTER ELEVEN
Portable Power Tools, the Energy Savers....................... 244

CHAPTER TWELVE
The Portable Drill.. 248

CHAPTER THIRTEEN
Power Saws... 266

CHAPTER FOURTEEN
Portable Power Sanders.. 279

CHAPTER FIFTEEN
The Router.. 288

CHAPTER SIXTEEN
The Matter of Safety.. 319

CHAPTER SEVENTEEN
The Finishing Process.. 322

CHAPTER EIGHTEEN
This Will Be a Bench.. 347

CHAPTER NINETEEN
Things around the House.. 367

CHAPTER TWENTY
Two Basic Techniques.. 381

CHAPTER TWENTY-ONE
Working Drawings for 37 Things to Build........................ 386

APPENDIX
Working Drawings for Five Things to Build.................... 465

INDEX.. 473

HOW TO WORK WITH

TOOLS and WOOD

CHAPTER ONE

Anyone Can Work with Tools and Wood

Perhaps you have read, with a little laugh, the famous advertisements: "You too can learn to play the piano"—or to paint, or write . . . or do anything else that you just know you can't learn to do.

The surprising thing is that in spite of ten thumbs, more or less, you can learn to do many things you never thought you could. Certainly *anyone* can learn to work well with tools. Of course, your skill will come quickly or slowly depending on your talent and your determination to develop your abilities But there is no reason why anyone without serious physical impairments cannot do a creditable job while working with tools. Some skill, a lot of care, and a good design can provide for your home many things that will give you the threefold satisfaction of seeing your own handiwork, of providing the unique thing most suited for your needs, and of knowing that it cost you only a small fraction of what the same object would have cost in a retail store. But even more important, you will find that the making—the sweat and tears and frustrations—will give you the ultimate joys that come only from a satisfying hobby: the satisfaction of creating a fine thing with your own skills.

Craftsmanship is a combination of knowledge of how to use tools and skill in using the hands. An old cabinetmaker or carpenter knows more about using tools and wood than he could possibly teach. These tricks are a part of his day's work. They come from many hours of cut and try, trial and error. But you can start today and in half an hour learn all by yourself many fascinating things about tools and wood. If you take a plane to a piece of white pine, you will soon discover that when you attempt to push the tool against the grain, you don't make a smooth cut, but when you push the plane with the grain, you do. With a sharp plane, the cut is almost as smooth as if you had used sandpaper.

1

The other factor in craftsmanship is skill with the hands. To become a skilled workman in wood requires practice, for two reasons: (1) you learn to handle tools delicately and firmly, as a pianist learns to strike the notes on his keyboard to produce precisely the effect he wishes; (2) you learn by trial and error the best ways of using your hands.

No book can possibly give you all the tricks of good carpentry. They have to be learned at the bench. But this volume will give you fundamentals that will enable you to get the most fun out of your tools and to achieve the most skill, to find relaxation from the stress and strain of a busy day, and to add to the richness of your life.

Working with tools and wood is a hobby packed with romance and tradition. There is a special kind of delight in making the sturdy colonial furniture in the same way that early American settlers did. The craftsmanship of Chippendale, Hepplewhite, Duncan Phyfe, and other masters takes on new meaning as you strive to reproduce their work. Every kind of wood that you use has a charm and story of its own, and the tools that you use have a history that extends back to crude implements used many generations ago.

There are unlimited interesting possibilities in woodworking. In this book, we try to give you the fundamentals to help you start on the right track. It may be that wood carving, reproducing antiques, making model boats, trains, or airplanes, building furniture for your home . . . will catch your fancy. No matter if you make one or many kinds of things, every article you make is a new and complete diversion. Into it will go your thought and your individuality, all of which help to identify that article as distinctly yours. In detail, it will be unlike anything else, for it is rare that two pieces of handwork are ever exactly alike.

Begin in a modest way. Each new experience and success will inspire your ambition to go on to a greater degree of accomplishment. Your appreciation of woodworking as a hobby will grow in proportion to your effort. Your workshop will become a happy haven in which you can relax from everyday care and work.

Remember that the full extent of enjoyment you obtain from any hobby depends on the amount of your own personality you put into it. The result of your effort will reward you ten times over.

CHAPTER TWO

First Tools First

Even before you decide what you want to make, you will need some basic tools. Most of these you will probably have picked up through the years to meet emergency needs around the house—a hammer, a screwdriver, pliers, and perhaps half a dozen more. But as you progress in home carpentry, you will find use for many more sophisticated tools.

If you expect to take your carpentry seriously, do not make the mistake of buying low-priced, inferior tools. Poor tools make a poor workman; they often just do not do the job. If cutters will not hold a keen edge, you may become discouraged and blame yourself when the trouble is really a poor tool. Parts will break at just the wrong moment. A dull edge will require more pressure than you should exert. Altogether, a good tool is a good investment in facility, durability, workmanship, and long-term economy. It will pay dividends for many years. Good craftsmen need good tools. Even an experienced person cannot expect to do a good job with inferior tools.

If you want to select your own individual tools instead of a set, you'll find on the following pages a list of the primary tools you should have. Start with the first ten or more, then add to your tool collection as you find need for more specialized aids.

For your first set of tools, you will certainly need a nail hammer, a crosscut saw, a jack plane, a rule, a square, four or five screwdrivers, a hand drill, one or two chisels, a bit brace and several auger bits, a marking gauge, nail sets, a Surform surface-forming tool, an oilstone and oiler, and pliers. For work a bit more complicated, you should have a bit gauge, a block plane, a ripsaw, a woodworking vise, a backsaw, a coping saw, a knife, a file, an awl, a countersink, perhaps a spokeshave.

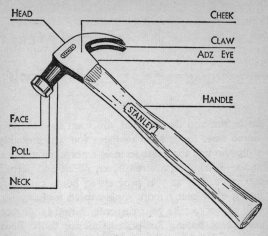

The illustration is of hammer; Stanley No. 52 Bell Face, 16 oz. The weight is of the head only.

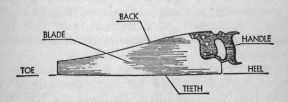

The size of a saw is determined by the length of the blade in inches. Some popular sizes are 24 inches and 26 inches.
The coarseness or fineness of a saw is determined by the number of points per inch.
A coarse saw is better for fast work and for green wood.
A fine saw is better for smooth, accurate cutting and for dry, seasoned wood.
5½ and 6 points are in common use for ripsaws.
7 and 8 points are in common use for crosscut saws.
Saw teeth are set; every other tooth is bent to the right and those between to the left, to make the kerf wider than the saw.
This prevents the saw from binding in the kerf or saw cut.
Quality saws in addition are taper ground, being thinner at the back than at the toothed edge.
Keep saw teeth sharp and properly set.

There are many other good tools you will need in time, but let us start with these.

Your first step in creating a good piece of craftsmanship in wood is measuring and marking properly. To help you mark accurately, you have access to half a score of time-tested tools with adaptations for almost any marking problem.

These include—

Measuring Tools

BENCH RULE

The illustration is of Stanley Rule No. 34¼V-12″

1. *The basic rule, or bench rule.* Select one made of hardwood, with graduations of common fractions (halves, quarters, eighths, sixteenths) of inches. Look for easy visibility and markings that reverse on opposite sides. (Recommended: Stanley No. 34¼V.)

2. *The Zig-Zag rule with an extension slide.* This is the carpenter's folding wood rule and when extended is 6 feet long. Markings should be in inches and common fractions. The brass extension slide makes it possible to take an inside

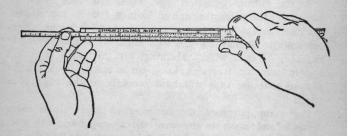

zig zag extension rule

The zig zag extension rule is particularly useful for inside measurements. The reading on the extension is added to the length of the opened rule.

measurement in a single step. The strength of the joint should be an important factor in your choice. (Recommended: Stanley zig-zag Extension No. X6LG.) The zig-zag rule is useful for taking or laying off long or short measurements. It is stiff enough to measure across horizontal openings. Care should be taken in opening folding wood rules to avoid damage to joints and sticks.

ZIG ZAG RULE

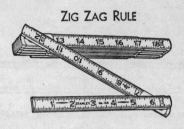

The illustration is of Stanley rule No. 106-6'

FOLDING RULE

The illustration is of a 2-ft. rule.

3. *The flexible-rigid steel tape.* These are made in 6-, 8-, 10-, and 12-foot lengths, and in ½-inch and ¾-inch widths. The most useful for the home carpenter is 10 feet long. (Recommended: Stanley PL 10, with a blade ½ inch wide, or PL 312, ¾ inch wide.) Markings are graduated in inches and in common fractions. Look for a sturdy hook on the end so that the tape will hold properly at the edge of a board.

For many purposes, the flexible-rigid steel rule is more versatile and easier to use than the zig-zag rule. The steel tape is less cumbersome than the zig-zag for the average handyman and is available in longer lengths. This gives a greater range of measurement and lessens the chance of error. Wearing quality, markings, and visibility are important

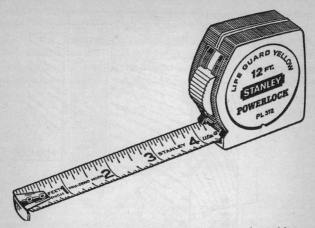

elements in selecting a tape. Black numbers and markings on yellow blades provide greatest legibility.

For long wear, select a tape rule with a polyester film bonded to the blade. This finish guards against abrasive wear, rust, and acids. The better tapes are also equipped with a lock that holds the position of the blade and prevents inaccuracies due to slipping. When the blade is unlocked, a spring rewinds the tape into the case.

For long measurements, select a steel tape ⅜ inch wide and 50 feet long. It is graduated in feet and inches (sometimes in tenths of a foot) and is marked with prominent figures. It is wound on a spool that is manipulated by a folding handle. A small ring is attached to the end of the tape so that it may be easily held or made fast to a stationary object. It is carried in a leather case. (Recommended: Stanley No. MY50.)

4. *The steel square* is a right angle of steel about ⅛ inch thick and marked with graduations and special tables. The body is 24 inches long, and the tongue is 16 inches long. The steel square was designed principally for measuring distances between studdings in a house construction, but it is now a basic tool for any carpentry project.

Just as making or measuring a straight line is the function of a rule, the function of the square is making an angle. Nothing is more disheartening than a lopsided piece of work. Many modern squares mark decimal fractions as well as the

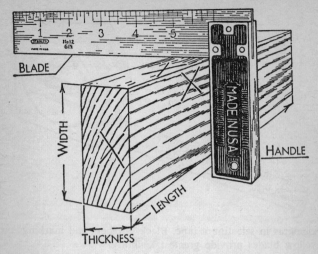

Stanley No. 12TS Try square in position to test smoothness of wood surface.

conventional halves, quarters, eighths, and sixteenths of an inch. (Recommended: Stanley No. R 100.)

5. *The try and mitre square* is the basic tool for checking the squareness of a board. An L-shaped tool, it usually has a steel blade 6 or 8 inches long and a handle 4 or 5¼ inches long. A 45-degree bevel on the handle helps to lay out mitre joints. (Recommended: Stanley No. 1-8 inch.)

Try squares come with blades 4 inches to 12 inches long. They are also used for testing and marking boards for cutting, planing, and fitting. For larger pieces, the steel square serves better. (Recommended: Stanley No. 12-6 inch.)

6. *The combination square* is a try square with a sliding head and a steel body. It is a Try Square, Mitre Square, Level, Plumb, Depth Gauge, and Scriber all in one tool. (Recommended: Stanley No. 122.)

7. *Wing dividers,* or the compass, are used to mark arcs and circles, to transfer exact distance from a rule to the work, or divide distances accurately along a straight line. (Recommended: Stanley No. 58.)

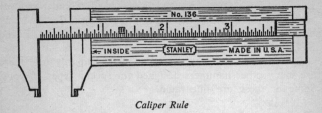

Caliper Rule

8. *Caliper rules* come in several sizes, each of which is designed to make accurate inside and outside measurements. It is also particularly useful for measuring diameters of dowels, rod stock, pipe, and other round stock. (Recommended: Stanley No. 136R.)

9. *A depth gauge* is a thin ruler with a movable clamp to mark the distance on the gauge. It is used to measure the depth of a hole.

The Hammer

Since your childhood you have probably thought of a hammer as just a hammer, although you must have seen scores of different shapes and styles. When you select your first hammer as a tool, you will notice several things that you probably took for granted before.

The shape of the hammer head, for instance. A bell-faced hammer has a slightly convex face. It is preferred as a "first" tool because with it a nail can be driven flush with the wood without leaving hammer marks even if the striking angle is not exactly perpendicular. A flat "plain-faced" hammer is preferred for rough work when it is not important if some hammer marks appear on the surface. Some hammer faces have cross-checkered grids that prevent slipping, but often show on the wood.

The claw of the hammer may be straight or curved. The straight claw is best for ripping boards apart; the curved claw is better for removing nails.

As for the material, drop-forged steel heads are best. Cast heads are dangerous; they may chip or break, with considerable hazard to the user. It is important to select a good tempered-steel hammer that has been treated for professional use. Handles are made of hickory with or without rubber grip, and are securely wedged in the head. Tubular steel or solid steel shafts with rubber grip are also preferred by many wood-workers. (Recommended: Stanley Nos. RG1½ and ST1½.)

In addition to the hammer you will ordinarily use, there are many other hammers designed for special types of work. Some of these are illustrated.

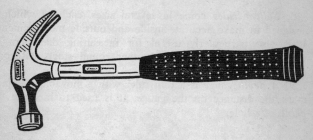

Curved Claw Nail

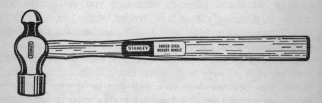

Ball-peen

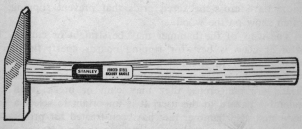

Machinist's Riveting

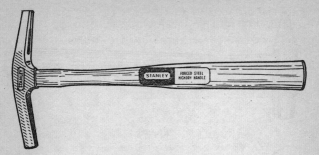

Upholsterer's (for tacking)

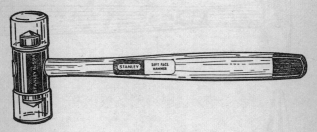

Soft-face

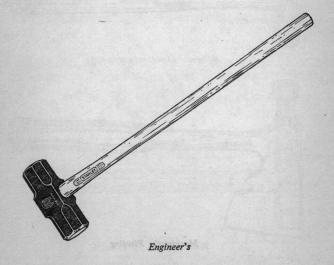

Engineer's

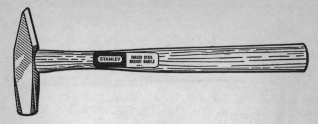

Riveting

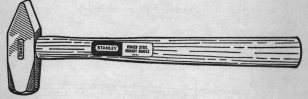

Blacksmith

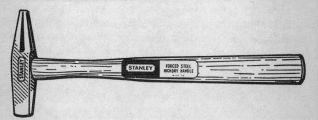

Billposter's (with magnetic tip)

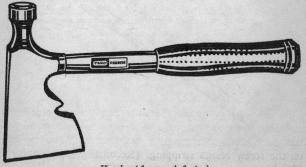

Hatchet (for rough facing)

The Level

The spirit level is a simple device to tell you whether a surface is exactly horizontal (level) or vertical (plumb). Level vial is a sealed, slightly crowned glass tube incompletely filled with a liquid (usually alcohol, which has a low freezing point), it has an air bubble that comes to the top when the level is held horizontally. Markings on the tube indicate whether the bubble is in the exact center. The vial is housed in a squared board up to four feet in length. Some levels have more than one tube located at various points, usually in pairs. Levels are also made of iron, aluminum, magnesium, and various other metals as well as laminated, warp-proof materials, and are available in lengths of 12 to 48 inches. For the average woodworker, Stanley No. 313-24 inches is recommended.

The Marking Gauge

The marking gauge is designed for measuring and marking lines parallel to a planed face or edge. Usually made of wood, but sometimes of metal, it has an 8-inch beam usually graduated up to 6 inches. A sharp scribing spur is located near one end at the zero point. The distance is marked off and set with an adjustable sliding head that can move up and down the beam. The head is tightened by a thumbscrew to set the distance from the pin, or spur. The head is then placed on the smooth surface and the spur will scratch a line parallel to the edge of a board at the distance set.

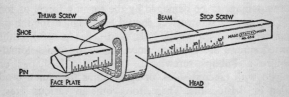

Because the gauge is exposed to heavy wear, and often to moisture, it should be made of fine-grained hardwood with a rustproof metal facing and a brass screw. A coarse thread on the screw resists stripping. (Recommended: Stanley No. 61G.)

Metal gauges have greater durability and often are equipped with a roller cutter wheel instead of a spur. These should be plated to prevent rust.

The Screwdriver

Everyone has used a screwdriver, but most woodworkers use it without thinking much about it. Driving a screw into wood is a simple operation, but it can be frustrating and damaging if the proper screwdriver is not used or if the tool is mishandled.

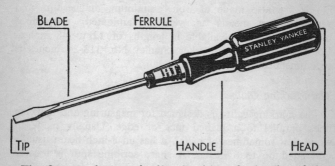

The first requirement is that the driver fit the slot of the screw in shape, width, and length. A screwdriver blade that is too wide will tear the wood of a countersunk screw; one that is too narrow will not provide the proper leverage and may damage the head of the screw. A properly designed screwdriver has a width and thickness slightly less than standard screw slots and is so proportioned that it will not cause damage or be damaged by the turning force, or torque.

The tip of a screwdriver should be designed for the particular screwhead on which it is used. (See p. 15.) Although slotted screws are most common, some are cross-slotted and require a Phillips screwhead. Others are U-shaped or V-shaped with tapered sides, or special tips for clutch heads or Allen or Bristo slots. These, too, come in various sizes, and although an off-size may sometimes suffice, it is best to match tip with slot. A good selection of screwdrivers includes a No. 1 with a ⅛-inch blade, a No. 2 with a ¼-inch blade, a No. 3 with a 5/16-inch blade, and a No. 4 with a ⅜-inch blade, two sizes of Phillips screwdrivers, a short or stubby driver handy for cramped quarters, and a Z-shaped offset

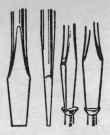

Select a screwdriver of length and tip fitted to the work.
Screwdrivers are specified by the length of the blade.
The tip should be straight and nearly parallel-sided. It should also fit the
screw slot and be not wider than the screw head.

If the tip is too wide it will scar the wood around the screw head.
If the screwdriver is not held in line with the screw it will slip out of the
slot and mar both the screw and the work.

If the tip is rounded or beveled it will raise out of the slot, spoiling the
screw head. Regrind or file the tip to make it as shown above.

screwdriver for other difficult positions. The stubby screwdriver is available with a light- or a heavy-duty tip. Offset
screwdrivers are made in four sizes, with ratchet or non-
ratchet handles.

For extensive or difficult work, two effort savers are available—the spiral driver, which turns under pressure, and the
driver that comes as a bit for a brace, particularly useful
for large screws. A ratchet driver has a handle that can turn

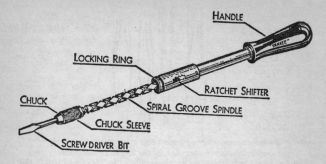

The illustration is of "Yankee" Spiral Ratchet Screwdriver No. 130A

the screw in either direction. Special insulated blades, magnetic blades, and lighted blades are made for electricians and other special types of workers.

Appreciation of the importance of a proper tip should be sufficient to prevent abuse of the screwdriver as a prying device, a scraper, or an awl. A tip that has lost its shape for any reason can be reground on a wheel and filed to the original shape and taper. The end should not be overheated in grinding; an occasional dip in water will prevent this. And for obvious reasons, the end should not be ground too thin. The tip should be square and straight.

The Awl

This sharp-pointed tool has a host of uses in the workshop, from marking fine work to making small pilot holes for nails, screws, and brads.

The illustration is of Stanley Awl No. 7A

The awl has a hardened, round steel blade, tapered down to a small point. The blade is fastened securely in handle to withstand twisting and light rounding. (Recommended: Stanley No. 7A.)

The Saw

The saw serves many purposes. A careful workman will select the saw that does the job most effectively and with the least effort.

Six types of saw are particularly useful in a home workshop: (1) the hand ripsaw; (2) the hand crosscut saw; (3) the compass or keyhole saw; (4) the coping saw; (5) the backsaw; and (6) the hacksaw. These differ in shape, length, number and position of their teeth, and the curvature of the back.

There is much more to the blade of a saw than meets the unpracticed eye. The metal should be of tempered spring steel so that the teeth may be filed and sharpened. The edge with the teeth is slightly thicker than the rest of the blade, to give firmness at the cutting edge. The handle should be made of a hardwood, shaped to provide a good handhold, properly fastened with brass rivets and finished to protect against deterioration. Each of these characteristics changes the usefulness of the tool. Thus a skewback blade, with a slight curve at the end, is more flexible than a straight backsaw.

But the important element in a saw blade is the number, size, shape, and direction of its teeth. The teeth are set alternately in opposite directions to give a cut wider than the blade itself. Otherwise the blade would bend in the cut (the kerf). How much the tool should be bent depends on the type of wood to be cut; the softer and wetter the wood, the wider the cut (kerf).

A good saw should be flexible. One veteran shopper always bends the blade back so that the end almost touches the handle. When it springs back, the saw should be perfectly straight. If it is wisely chosen, a steel saw will give a long, clear ring if the blade is snapped. The cutting edge should be thicker than the top edge. The blade surface should be ground and polished.

The Crosscut Saw

The crosscut saw is designed for cutting across the grain of the wood. Its teeth are small knives set parallel, far enough apart to keep the saw from binding. The crosscut saw does 75 per cent of its cutting on the downstroke and 25 per cent on the upstroke.

A saw with coarse teeth cuts faster than one with close teeth, and it is especially suitable for thick boards, for it does not clog as easily. For most home work a blade with 7 to 8 points to the inch is satisfactory. But if fine work or joinery is to be done, 10 points an inch will do a better job. The number of points is usually stamped on the heel of the blade. Small, fine-tooth crosscut saws, called panel saws, are used for extremely fine work.

Blade lengths vary from 20 to 28 inches, but for home carpentry a 26-inch blade will be the most satisfactory, unless a major project is to be undertaken. (Recommended: Stanley 1526.)

Crosscut saw teeth are like knife points. They cut like two rows of knife points and crumble out the wood between the cuts.

The Ripsaw

Ripsaws, used for cutting along the grain of the wood, will meet less resistance and thus have larger and fewer teeth than the crosscut—usually from 5½ to 6 points to the inch. The teeth are slanted at almost 90 degrees so that wood fibers can be ripped as well as cut. For cutting thick stock, a coarser tooth is required—for thin stock, a fine tooth. Because each

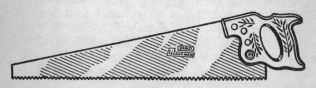

tooth rips, no bevel is required on the edge of the tooth, as it is on the crosscut saw. Carpenters compare the ripsaw with a row of chisels pushing forward. (Recommended: Stanley 1527.)

The Keyhole Saw

The compass, or keyhole, saw has a narrow, tapered blade so that it can fit into narrow spaces. Some types come with three or four alternate blades that can be substituted to meet the requirements of the particular cut: there may be ripsaw blades and blades for crosscut work. Because of its flexibility, the compass saw is particularly useful for cutting along curved lines. This saw is also often used for short cuts, or to finish off a long cut as well as for fine irregular sawing. (Recommended: Stanley 175C.)

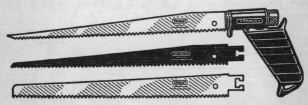

Stanley Keyhole Saw No. 175C

The Coping Saw

The coping saw is a small tool, a saw blade set in a steel frame. It is sometimes called a jig saw. The blade is removable and can range in thickness from a threadlike wire to ⅛-inch width. The blade is therefore fragile and should be used only on thin wood. When an interior cut is to be made, a hole is drilled, and the blade is threaded through the hole and then attached to the frame. On the frame are pawls with slots into which the blade fits. Usually the blade can turn in the frame. Blades can be flat or spiral: the spiral blade has the advantage of being able to cut in any direction without turning.

For vise work, the teeth of the coping saw should point toward the handle, but on work supported by a saw horse, it is best to have the points turned away from the handle.

Compass or keyhole saws are used to cut curved or straight-sided holes.

Coping saws are used for light inside cuts.

The Backsaw

The backsaw is a thin crosscut saw with a reinforced back to provide rigidity. It is usually a crosscut saw, 10 to 20 inches in length and with 10 to 14 teeth to the inch. For short, precise cuts, as in mitring, it is the best tool to use. (Recommended: Stanley No. 1514.)

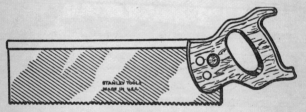

The backsaw is a thin crosscut saw with fine teeth, stiffened by a thick back. A popular size is 12 inches with 14 points per inch. It is used for fine accurate work.

The Hacksaw

The hacksaw is a fine-toothed saw used for cutting metals. You will find it useful in your home workshop when you must shorten a screw or bolt, when you must cut off or through a nail, and when a piece of pipe or hardware must be made to fit. (Recommended: Stanley No. 408.)

The Mitre Box

If you expect to do any amount of mitring—that is, sawing at an angle—a mitre box will be a big timesaver. Guides on the mitre box can be adjusted so that a backsaw will cut at

any angle from 45 to 90 degrees to any desired depth. Care should be taken that the stock does not shift during the cutting, and that the saw does not either touch the front or pull out of the rear guide. Duplicate pieces can be easily cut merely by adjusting the length rod.

Frames from 4 to 12 sides can be cut by referring to the proper angle, often indicated on the mitre box itself.

In sawing, always start on the outside of a mark. A crosscut saw has a kerf of almost 1/16 inch, and a rough edge will require some additional smoothing. (Recommended: Stanley No. 60MB.)

Braces and Bits

The ratchet-action bit brace is a tool that has almost been replaced by the electric drill. But for some purposes it is still an essential tool. Large holes—those more than ⅜ inch in diameter—are almost universally made with brace and bit. It is still best for careful work where plenty of working space is available. For close work, where there is no space to swing a brace, the ratchet bit brace is used. A cam ring regulates the direction of the turn. When the cam is turned to the right, the bit cuts into the wood; when the cam is turned to the left, the motion is reversed.

The bit brace has a chuck that holds the bit. To place a bit into the chuck, hold the shell firmly and turn the brace handle. This widens the jaws to receive the tapered shank of the bit. Reverse the process to tighten the jaws. (Recommended: Stanley 923.)

Bits

A variety of bits is available for your use with a brace drill. Each does a special job in a special material.

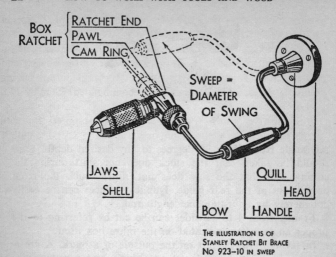

BOX
RATCHET
{ RATCHET END
  PAWL
  CAM RING

SWEEP =
DIAMETER
OF SWING

JAWS

SHELL

QUILL

HEAD

BOW   HANDLE

THE ILLUSTRATION IS OF
STANLEY RATCHET BIT BRACE
NO 923–10 IN SWEEP

The shank of a drill or bit for a bit brace has a tapered or square tang. Automatic drills require a straight-shank twist drill or bits with slats ground on the shank.

Bits also vary in coarseness of the screw, sharpness of the spur (which touches the wood directly after the screw), angle of the cutting lips, width of the throat, and style of the shank (which fits into the chuck).

The auger bit is most commonly used with bit and brace for drilling holes in wood. They are available in short lengths of 5 inches (dowel bits), medium length of 8 inches, and long (ship bits) from 18 to 24 inches in length. Use the shortest bit practical for the job you are doing. Auger bits also vary in style of twist: the solid center or single twist is strongest and fastest to work, and is preferred by most carpenters. The double-twist bit is designed for slower but more accurate drilling and is especially popular for doweled joints. The bits available for the brace are discussed in the section on using tools. (See p. 93.) (Recommended: Stanley No. H 1227.)

The expansive bit is also used in a bit brace and has a tapered square shank. It has a screw point on the cutting end that pulls the bit into the work. Cutters used permit boring holes 7/8- to 3-inch diameter. (Recommended: Stanley No. 71AB.)

Screwdriver bit has a regular or cross-pointed tip with tapered square tang to fit bit brace chuck. (Recommended: Stanley No. 26.)

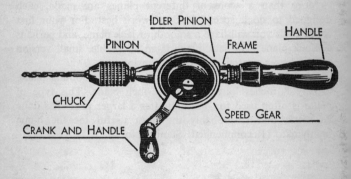

The Hand Drill

The hand drill serves many purposes for which the bit brace would be a poor substitute. Drill points used in the hand drill come in sets of eight sizes—in 1/64-inch diameters from 4/64 (1/16) inch to 11/64 inch. The drill is placed in the chuck by holding the chuck shell and turning the crank forward to open the jaws. The hand drill is used for rapid drilling of small holes.

To drill a hole, first make an impression in the work with an awl. Keep the drill vertical or the hole will be enlarged. The depth of a hole can be regulated easily by cutting a wooden gauge to measure the portion of the drill that is to remain above the hole. (Recommended: Stanley Hand Drill No. 610.)

The Plane

The plane is used for two purposes: (1) to bring woodwork down to finished size, and (2) to smooth off rough surfaces. Planes differ in construction, size, weight, length, and width and type of blade, depending on the way they are to be used. The chief advantage of a large plane is that it keeps the cut true—that is, is straight.

More than a score of different planes are made, each designed to do a special kind of work best. For your first set of tools you will have a smooth or jack plane, and perhaps a block plane. The jack plane is an adaptable, small version of the larger professional plane, the jointer.

Smallest and lightest of the planes is the smoothing plane, usually 8 inches long with a 1¾-inch blade. This type of plane is often used for finishing after a larger plane has done its work, and is probably the most useful for the home handyman. (Recommended: Stanley No. 4.)

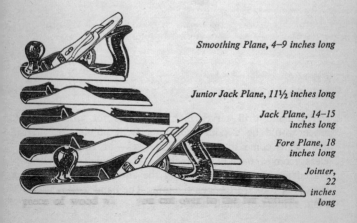

Smoothing Plane, 4–9 inches long

Junior Jack Plane, 11½ inches long

Jack Plane, 14–15 inches long

Fore Plane, 18 inches long

Jointer, 22 inches long

*A short plane follows the shape of the wood as a small boat
rides over the waves and into the hollows between.
A longer plane does not follow the hollows.*

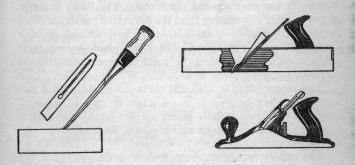

*A plane is a chisel blade with a guide to regulate the cut.
Iron and wooden planes are fundamentally similar. Improved
material, shape, and adjustments make the iron plane preferable.*

A jack plane is used to plane the edges of a rough board
and prepare it for final truing up with a fore or jointer
plane. (Recommended: Stanley No. 5.)

The jointer is usually 20 to 24 inches long, with a blade
of about 2½ inches wide and is used by professional carpenters for long boards to produce straight edges on such
objects as doors and flat boards that are to be joined together.

One size smaller is the fore plane, about 18 inches long,
with a blade 2⅜ inches wide. For home use, the most satisfactory tool is a smaller version, the jack plane, about 14

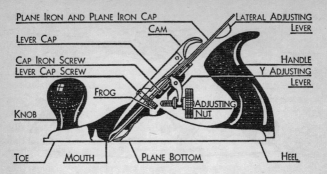

inches in length. (Recommended: Stanley No. 5.)

Another type of plane you will find useful is different from the others. The block plane is used to smooth end grain, especially for beveling and chamfering. The blade is set at a lower angle (12 degrees from the horizontal) than the other planes (20 degrees from horizontal) because end grain is much more difficult to cut. The block plane is small and light enough to be held in one hand. (Recommended: Stanley No. 9½.)

The rabbet plane is a special plane designed to cut a rectangular recess or groove on the edges or ends of a board. Several variations of this plane are available—the duplex, cabinetmaker's, and bench rabbet planes, each of which cuts a special kind of groove.

The duplex rabbet plane has unique flexibility. It has two seats for the plane iron—one seat for the ordinary cutting of a rabbet, the other for close corners or perpendicular cutting. Special adjustable guides make it easy to cut the right width. A spur on the rear seat (which can be raised when not required) is used to score the fibers when cutting across the grain. (Recommended: Stanley No. 78).

A cabinetmaker's rabbet plane has a bullnose that permits it to be used close to an obstruction for stopped rabbet (one that does not extend to the end of the board) and is especially useful for fine work in which extreme accuracy is essential. An adjustable throat opening is set narrow for fine work, opened for coarse work.

The side rabbet plane is used for smoothing sides of a groove, or for trimming dadoes or moldings. This device contains two small adjustable knives on the sides, facing in opposite directions so that cutting takes place on both the forward and the backward strokes. By reversing the plane, the left and the right side may be trimmed. Some side rabbet planes have a bullnose, which allows the plane to cut very close to an obstruction. (Usually both blades are then set in the same direction.) (Recommended: Stanley No. 79.)

The router plane is used when a dado or groove has been sawed or cut out. Giving the groove a smooth finish presents some problems for the ordinary plane, and a router plane is used for this purpose. This tool has L-shaped cutters that in appearance resemble an offset screwdriver. These cutters are attached to a cutting post and extend below the surface of the board on which the plane rests. Cutters may face either front, for ordinary planing, or back, for bullnose work.

Like other planes, the router plane has adjustments to control the size of the shaving, the size of the cut, and the depth of the cut. A small rectangular version of the router plane is also made for inlay work, lock plates, small dadoes, and various model-making tasks. (Recommended: Stanley Nos. 71P and 271.)

These are not all the planes available to the home carpenter. Other planes are used for special types of work, but usually used only by the professional or the advanced hobbyist.

The Spokeshave

The spokeshave is a sort of two-handled plane with a short bottom and a wide throat particularly suited for ir-

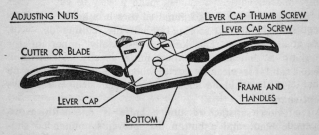

The spokeshave is practically a plane with the bottom short enough to follow curves.
The blade or cutter of the iron spokeshave is sharpened like a plane.

regular or curved surfaces. The handles permit the tool to be guided more accurately than the ordinary plane for cutting curved surfaces. Many variations of the spokeshave make it convenient for special types of work. Models come with a straight or curved bottom. (Recommended: Stanley No. 151SS).

Chisels

Chisels are made with beveled edges to cut into wood more readily. The cabinet, or pocket, chisel, with a somewhat shorter blade, is used for careful work where extreme accuracy is required. The butt chisel, with the shortest blade, is used for sinking hinges, butts, and the like.

Chisels are made in width from ⅛ to 2 inches. (Recommended: Stanley No. 60-1-inch blade.)

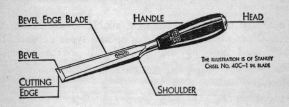

BEVEL EDGE BLADE   HANDLE   HEAD

BEVEL

CUTTING EDGE   SHOULDER

THE ILLUSTRATION IS OF STANLEY CHISEL NO. 40C-1 IN. BLADE

The Knife

The utility knife finds a hundred uses in a home workshop for cutting shingles, scoring asphalt tile, cutting dry wall, trims, and others. The knife is especially important for marking a thin line on wood more exactly than with a pencil, and for cleaning areas where the chisel cannot be used. The knife blade should be of good steel and always kept sharp.

The most satisfactory utility knife is one with a retractable blade and a button that prevents unintended sliding. The blade should be adjustable in two or more cutting positions so that a small cut or groove can be made without using the entire blade. Some knives have a hole in the handle for convenient hanging. Other models can be converted into scrapers for removing paint or stickers, and some others have substitute saw blades. (Recommended: Stanley No. 99.)

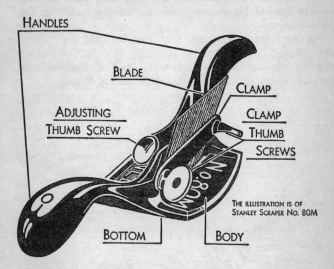

The Cabinet Scraper is used for the final smoothing before sandpapering. It removes the slight ridges left by the plane. It is also used to smooth surfaces that are difficult to plane because of curly or irregular grain.

"Surform" Tools

Many shaping and smoothing operations are performed by a new tool manufactured in a variety of shapes. Known as Surform Tools, they are used for shaping, trimming, and forming wood, plastics, and soft metals.

With a surface that looks a little like a roughened colander and a little like a file, Surform tools have many tiny cutting teeth which work like individual planes.

One Surform tool is in the shape of a file (Stanley 295), with a flat-blade surface. The front of the tool has a ribbed section that permits use of the tool with both hands. It is used in place of a rasp. A similar instrument, cylindrical in shape (Surform Round File, Stanley 297), is used for enlarging holes.

For shaping large flat surfaces, a Surform tool comes in

the shape and style of a plane (Stanley 296). A pocket Surform plane, 5½ inches long, is useful for trimming rough
edges on the job. (Recommended: Stanley No. 399.)

All Surform tools have replaceable blades, both flat and
curved. Special blades are made for cutting metals in the
same fashion.

An appropriate Surform tool can be used for almost
any shaping problem and is especially valuable for pattern
making, shaping a chair or table leg, or finishing any
intricate shape, from a gunstock to a mirror frame.

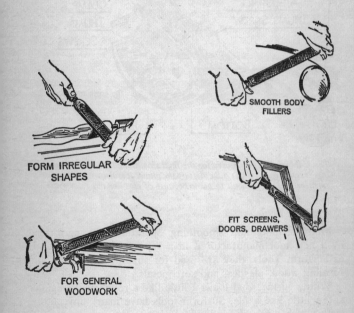

FORM IRREGULAR
SHAPES

SMOOTH BODY
FILLERS

FIT SCREENS,
DOORS, DRAWERS

FOR GENERAL
WOODWORK

Shaper Tool

This is similar to a Surform Tool, used for final speed
shaping. It forms, trims and smooths wood and plastic, and
works particularly well on metal. Straight or half-round
blades are used, and are replaceable. (Recommended: Stanley
No. SF490.)

Wood Files and Rasps

For smoothing edges and small shaping problems, the wood file is an essential tool. Files come in lengths from 4 to 14 inches. The cut of a file—that is, the angle and spacing of its teeth—determines how it can best be used. Single-cut files have teeth running diagonally in parallel lines; double-cut files have two sets of crossing parallel lines, making a grid. Files are classified as coarse, bastard, second, and smooth—each representing a smaller distance between the lines and therefore creating a smoother finish on the work. The distance between the lines of teeth is also proportional to the size of the file, so that smaller files have closer lines that permit smoother finishes. Rasps, which have deeper, coarser cuts than files, have triangular teeth rather than the parallel lines of the file.

The shape of the file is designed to fit the space in which it must work. The blade may be flat, half-round, round, triangular, or square. The shape may vary—it may be blunt or it may taper. (The taper permits the cutting area to increase gradually and permits working in smaller grooves.)

The Vise

Fastened to a bench, the vise is a tool that will hold a piece of work rigidly while it is being worked. Essentially two parallel iron jaws, it must be heavy enough, strong, accurately fitted, and easily worked.

The iron vise has solid metal jaws with a wide throat opening to allow as much working room as possible. The vise is opened and closed on a screw bar, which should be kept well lubricated. A 3½-inch opening is sufficient for ordinary jobs. The vise should extend just far enough from the bench to which it is securely bolted so that the backsaw can clear it and stock can be gripped securely.

Most jaws have roughened inner edges that may damage wood or soft metals. Such jaws can be covered for such work.

The wood vise that provides a larger holding surface is usually made as part of the workbench. (Instructions for making such a vise appear on page 365.)

When you start a home workshop, you may wonder what tools you should purchase first. To help you make a selection, we have compiled a list showing the tools you will need during various stages of woodworking. All of them are available from your hardware dealer, who will undoubtedly be most helpful in advising you in your selection.

The expense of setting up a good home workshop will not be too great if you begin with a minimum set of primary tools. Other tools can be added as your skills develop and your projects become more complex.

Be sure you buy good, brand-name tools. A tool that is designed right and made right will give you confidence while you use it and will do better work for a longer time. Manufacturers put their names on quality tools with pride, and they make every effort to guard against defects in material and workmanship. The assurance of quality is well worth small differences in price. Good tools, like old friends, wear well. Select your tools carefully, and gradually add to your set as your needs increase.

Primary Tools

Tools starred (*) in the list at the end of this chapter are recommended for those living in an apartment who want just a few tools for repairs and such simple projects as putting up hooks and rods, and perhaps an occasional shelf. The rest are tools that the serious hobbyist will want to own.

Keeping Your Tools Properly

Needless to say, your tools will last longer, in working condition, if you keep them properly. And you will find your tools more useful if you maintain them in an orderly fashion, readily available.

For most purposes, a peg board over your workbench is the handiest, most available place to keep your tools. Nails, screws, and small hardware can be kept in plastic boxes or in small jars. A common trick is to nail the screw tops of jars to the bottom of a shelf. In this way when jars are screwed in place, the contents are easily visible, and after selections have been made, they can easily be returned to storage.

Tools that are not regularly used should be kept in a toolbox or on a separate tool panel. The toolbox is the old-fashioned receptacle used primarily by those who carry tools from place to place. It should be made of half-inch hardwood stock. The cover usually holds the saw in a stationary rack and the inside should provide space for a nail box and screw containers. (Instructions for making your own toolbox will be given later.)

The tool panel is a larger version designed to fasten to the wall near the workbench. Slots are provided for saws, and screw eyes or hooks are used to hold chisels, screwdrivers, and other small tools. (Some designs include a silhouette of the tool to simplify returning tools to their proper place.)

	Stanley No.		*Stanley No.*
*1 Nail Hammer 13 oz......	52	1 Coping Saw, with extra saw blades.............	..
1 Combination Square 12"...................	122	1 Screwdriver, small 3" blade	4595
*1 Screwdriver 4" blade ...	20	1 Screwdriver, large 6" blade	20
1 Marking Gauge	65G	1 Screw Holding Screwdriver, 6"...........	415
1 Jack Plane 14"........	5	1 pr. Dividers 8"........	58
or		1 Smooth Plane 9" (or 8" No. 3).............	4
*1 Junior Jack Plane 11½"................	5¼	1 Steel Square 24" x 16"..	R100
1 set (13 pcs.) Auger Bits ¼" to 1"...........BXD32½ (Russell Jennings)		1 T-Bevel 8" blade	18TB
1 Ratchet Brace 8" sweep	923	1 Cabinet Scraper	80M
or 10" sweep	923	1 Burnisher	185
1 each, Chisels, sizes ¼", ⅜", ½", ¾", 1", 1¼"...	60	1 "Surform" Plane	296
1 Combination Oilstone fine and coarse 8" x 2" x 1".................	..	1 "Surform" File	295
1 Oiler	..	1 Half Round Cabinet Rasp 10".............	..
1 each Nail Set 2/32" and 4/32" tips	11¾	1 Half Round Cabinet File 10".............	..
*1 Brad Awl 1½" blade....	..	1 Smooth Mill File 10"...	..
1 Rule 2' folding	..	1 Auger Bit File	..
*1 Rule 8' Pull-Push.......	PL8	1 Slim Taper Saw File 8".	..
or		1 Round Bastard File 10".	..
1 Rule 6' Zig Zag ....126 or 106		1 Flat Bastard File 10" ...	..
*1 Hand cut off Saw 26"— 8 pt.	1526	6 File Handles for above .	..
1 Hand rip Saw 26"—5½ pt.	1527	1 Wire Filecard	..
or 24" may be desired	..	1 "Yankee" Automatic Drill	41Y
1 Hand Backsaw 14"—13 pt.	1514	1 "Yankee" Spiral Screwdriver	130A
1 Knife	99	1 Expansive Bit, large size, capacity ⅞" to 2½" with extra cutter (Russell Jennings)	71A
1 Block Plane 6"	9½		
1 Auger Bit Gauge	47		
*1 Screwdriver 6" small blade	4595	1 each Bit Stock Drill with square shank, 1/16", 3/32", ⅛", 5/32", 3/16", 7/32"...............	..

Stanley No.   *Stanley No.*

*1 Hand Drill ¼" chuck... 610
*1 pr. Combination Pliers
    6" 1500
*1 Woodworker's Vise..... 700
    Work bench, equipped
    with woodworking vise,
    practical sizes:
    60" long x 24" wide x
    32" high............... ..
    52" long x 22" wide x
    32" high............... ..
    42" long x 22" wide x
    32" high............... ..
 3 Gouges, outside bevel,
    ¼", ½", 1" ....
 1 Half Hatchet SH1½
 1 Nail Hammer 7 oz. 53
 1 Nail Hammer 16 oz. .. 51½
 1 Riveting Hammer 4 oz. . 230
 1 Level 24" 313
 1 Draw Knife 10" ....
 1 Ripping Bar 18" 118
 1 Jointer Plane 22"   7
    or Fore Plane 18" ...   6
 1 Rabbet Plane 78
 1 Router Plane 71P
 1 Plumb Bob 171
 1 Saw Set 42SS
 1 Keyhole Saw 175C
 1 pr. Tinner's Snips 10" .. ..
 1 "Yankee" Vise with
    swivel base 1992A
 1 Pipe Wrench Stillson
    type 14" ....
 1 Monkey Wrench 8" .... ..
 1 Open end Wrench 8".... ..
 1 Putty Knife 1540
 1 Scratch Awl 6B
 1 Spokeshave 151M
 1 Spokeshave convex
    bottom ....

 1 each Straight Shank Car-
    bon Drills for hand drill,
    1/16", 5/64", 3/32",
    7/64", 4/32", 9/64",
    5/32", 11/64" ....
 1 Countersink ¾" (for
    Bit Brace) 139
 1 Countersink — Round
    Shank (for Hand Drills). 137
 1 Mallet 3" face ....
 1 Dowel Jig with 6 guides . 59
 2 Screwdriver Bits 5/16",
    ⅜" 26
 1 Electric Grinder 7" x 1"
    wheels for plane irons and
    chisels and general grind-
    ing, 110 A.C. 60 cycles .. 697
    or Grinder H634
 1 Electric Drill ¼" Chuck . H81
 1 pr. Trammel Points 4TP
 1 Soldering Iron, electric . 435
 1 Caliper Rule, 1' 36½
 1 Cold Chisel ¾" 745
 1 Mortise Gauge 90G
 1 Center Punch 5/64" tip . 10¾
 2 Cornering Tools ....28 and 29
 1 Hammer Ball Peen 12 oz. 309
 1 Hammer, Upholsterer's 601
 1 Mitre Box with 26" saw 2246A
 1 Hack Saw adj. and 12"
    blades 408
 1 Dovetail Saw 6" blade .. ..
 1 Glass Cutter
 1 Bench Duster
 2 C Clamps 4"
 2 C Clamps 8"
 2 Adjust. Hand Screws 6"
    Jaws
 2 Adjust. Hand Screws 8"
    Jaws
 2 Adjust. Hand Screws
    10" Jaws
 2—4' and 2—6' Bar Clamps

CHAPTER THREE

Achieving Skill with Your Tools

There are, of course, in everyday use hundreds of tools which have not been described but with which you can become acquainted quickly and easily at your hardware store. There you will see, for instance, hammers of every type . . . innumerable files and rasps. There are axes and mauls, mallets and sledges. Each of them, of course, has some special use of its own, a technique that develops quickly when the need arises and you have work for the tool to do.

A few hints, however, are of great importance to the amateur shopworker. Consider using a hammer. Some people work for days attempting to learn how to drive nails quickly and efficiently, though that is a simple skill that you can easily learn. (See illustrations on pp. 36, 37.)

In driving nails, steady the nail with the left hand, and with the right hand grasp the hammer handle firmly near the end of the handle. Deliver the blow using three fulcrums—the wrist, the elbow, and the shoulder. How much muscle of each of these is to be used depends on the strength of the blow to be struck. Don't try to drive a brad with a sledge hammer!

Start the blow with the head of the hammer squarely on the nail. Draw back the hammer, then tap the nail lightly with a wrist movement. This helps give you proper aim and holds the nail in place during succeeding blows. Never use the cheek of the hammer for driving: the face has been specially processed for striking. Continue to hit the nail with a wrist motion, with elbow motions, then with wrist, elbow, and shoulder motions until your eye has adjusted to proper aim. Be careful to strike the nail squarely on the head. A glancing blow is never good; the hammer may slip and dent the wood, or the nail may bend.

Your next problem is to drive a nail into the board without leaving a mark. A bell-faced hammer has a slightly con-

Grasp the hammer firmly near the end.

The blow is delivered through the wrist, the elbow, and the shoulder, one or all being brought into play, according to the strength of the blow to be struck. Rest the face of the hammer on the nail, draw the hammer back and give a light tap to start the nail and to determine the aim.

vex face, so that a perfect hit will ensure a minimum contact. But the instrument you will use for fine work is the nail set, which is used to drive the nail below the surface of the wood. Finishing nails should be driven all but flush with the wood and then set below the surface.

If a nail should bend while you are driving it, remove the nail with the claw end of the hammer. Draw the hammer back only to a vertical position; drawing it further may mar the wood. Where marring may be a problem, place a strip of wood under the hammer head, both for protection of the face of the wood and to attain better leverage.

Small nails can be held by piercing them through a piece of light cardboard that can be held comfortably. Another type

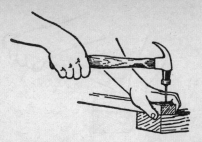

Always strike with the face of the hammer. It is hardened for that purpose. Do not damage the face by striking steel harder than itself. Do not strike with the cheek, as it is the weakest part.

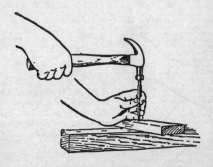

Use a nail set to drive nails below the surface of all fine work. To prevent the nail set from slipping off the head of the nail, rest the little finger on the work and press the nail set firmly against it. Set nails about 1/16 inch below the surface of the wood.

of nail holder is made by attaching a pencil clip to a nail set. A small brad can be held between the clip and the base of the nail set just as it might be held by a pair of pincers.

If hardwood resists a brad, a hole can be drilled using as a bit a beheaded brad or a needle cut above the eye. Dipping a nail in paraffin will help it enter hardwood more easily. Some home carpenters store paraffin in a hole drilled in the handle of a hammer, into which hot paraffin has been poured.

Using a nail set requires a technique that will prevent creating a big hole. Hold the nail set firmly in the left hand, between thumb and forefinger, with the hand resting on the wood. Press the nail set onto the head of the nail and strike it, checking the position before each blow. This is particularly

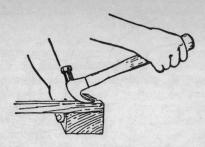

To draw a nail: slip the claw of the hammer under the nail head; pull until the handle is nearly vertical and the nail partly drawn.

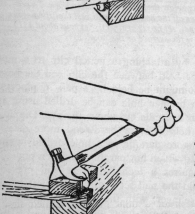

If the pull is continued, unnecessary force is required that will bend the nail, mar the wood, and perhaps break the hammer handle.

Slip a piece of wood under the head of the hammer to increase the leverage and to relieve the unnecessary strain on the handle.

important when driving nails in moldings, into corners, or when toe-nailing.

A little plastic wood or putty can be used to fill the nail hole after setting the nail below the surface. Plastic wood is available clear or in wood-grain colors. It dries quickly. It is applied with the fingers or with a putty knife in layers, then is sanded when dry.

If plastic wood is not available, wood putty mixed with water can be applied. Before this is used, the surface should be shellacked so that it does not stain. The putty is mixed with water and some stain and is applied in layers to a level slightly higher than the surface. After two hours it dries sufficiently to be sanded down.

There is no secret in pulling a nail. Grasp the hammer firmly and tilt it forward with the claws away from you. Work the hammer claws about the nail with a very slight sidewise movement of the hammer for a secure grip. Then give a firm, steady pull until the nail is withdrawn. In drawing an extra long nail, place a small block of wood under the head of the hammer. This gives greater leverage in pulling and protects the wood from injury.

There is, as a matter of fact, even a trick in using the wiggle nail or corrugated fastener. This device can be used for tightening up loose joints or cracks in chairs, tables, screen doors, window frames, flower boxes, and other similar things around the house. It is a nail that has a good deal of strength for holding two surfaces together side by side. The wiggle nail should be driven by light blows with a medium-weight hammer. Each blow should be evenly distributed over the top or driving end so that it drives the nail in evenly. It must also be driven on a surface which does not vibrate so you may have to put something heavy behind or under the work to brace it.

Small nails can be secured by placing them into a piece of light cardboard which can be held comfortably and removed after the nail has taken hold. Another type of nail-holder is made by attaching a pencil clip to a nail set. A small brad can be held between the clip and the base of the nail set, just as it might be by a pair of pincers.

If hardwood resists a brad, a hole may be drilled first, using a needle or a beheaded brad as a bit.

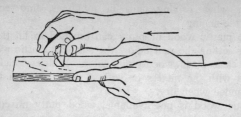

Lay the beam flat on the wood so the pin drags naturally as the marking gauge is pushed away. No roll motion is necessary. The pin and line are visible at all times.

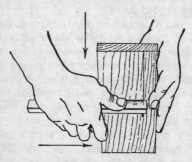

To make a gauge line push the gauge forward with the head held tight against the work edge of the wood. The pressure should be applied in the direction of the arrows.

Using the Marking Gauge

The marking gauge is designed to help you make accurate lines parallel to the edge of a board. An ordinary wood gauge is about 8 inches long, with a scribing spur near one end. A sliding head can be moved along the body and clamped with a thumbscrew at any point. In selecting a gauge, look for one made of hardwood protected with a brass head or metal. A special double-bar gauge with two spurs is made for marking a mortise. The gauge is set once, and the spur on each side is used in turn to indicate the mortise area.

Lay the gauge against the wood to be marked in such a way that the spur is at draw cut angle to the work being scribed. Grasp the gauge with the fingers over and around the head, the thumb extended along the side of the beam.

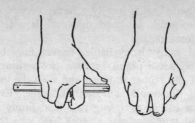

*Hold the gauge as you would a ball.
Advance the thumb toward the pin so as to distribute the pressure evenly between the pin and the head.*

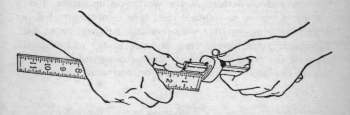

*Set the marking gauge by measurement from the head to the pin. Check
the measurement after tightening the thumbscrew.*

Engage the spur by means of a slightly rotary pressure of
the gauge. Holding the gauge at a slight angle, with the spur
pointing away from the direction in which the gauge will be
moved, make a line by pushing the gauge with pressure in
two directions—forward to mark the line, and sideways to
keep the head tightly against the guiding edge.

Care must be taken that the spur is not broken. When
the gauge is not in use, move the head along the beam until
it rests against the spur and lock it there with the thumbscrew.
Use a file to sharpen the spur. The spur should project about
1/16 or 3/32 inch. Don't tighten screw too tightly. It will
wear out the thread in the wood.

When the mark is to be made more than 6 inches from
the edge of the board, another type of gauge—the panel

gauge—is used. This is merely a larger version of the every-day marking gauge. A good substitute is a set of trammel points for long gauges.

When no gauge is available, fingers may be used as a guide. Merely set a pencil between two writing fingers with the point at the proper distance and slide the knuckles along the edge of the board at a constant angle. Even more accurate is the use of a zig-zag rule held firmly with the left hand at the board edge and a pencil held with the right hand at the end of the zig-zag rule.

Most marking gauges are graduated to 1/16 inch, but some have no markings at all and have to be set with a ruler.

Using Tapes

The kind of measuring tools you will need depends on the size and the nature of the work you undertake. For a big job, a 50- or a 100-foot steel tape is necessary, but for most jobs, a 6-, 8-, 10-, or 12-foot tape rule will do as well. Most tape rules have a ring or hook at the end that will catch at the point from which the measurement is taken. If this is not secure, drive a tack or nail onto the spot so

"Pull-Push" Rule.

The flexible "pull-push" rule measures regular and irregular shapes and permits inside measurements to be read by adding two inches to the reading on the blade.

that the tape does not slip and give you an inaccurate measurement.

Here are some hints on using the metal tape:

Use a helper to hold the free end of the tape.

Make sure that the tape is not kinked.

Read the measurement, and know definitely whether the graduations are in inches or in tenths of feet.

Do not read 6 for 9, or vice versa.

Keep a metallic tape dry and clean.

Be sure to check the zero point of the tape. Some tapes have the zero mark at the end of a ring, others a short distance from the end.

Whenever a tape is not in use, keep it wound within its cover.

A steel tape should not be used to measure around corners. It is easily kinked and must be protected from falling objects.

Pencils and Rules

Carpenters use several types of pencils: common lead, hard lead, and the regular carpenter pencil. The one most widely used is the flat, hard lead pencil about 8 inches long. For use in rough work, the pencil should be trimmed so that about ¼ to ⅜ inch of lead protrudes from the wood sheath. In finished work the pencil should be trimmed so that ⅜ to ½ inch of lead is exposed and the lead sharpened to a long, flat point. When marking, the pencil should be tilted away from the guide so that the lead will mark close to the edge of the guide. If the pencil becomes wet, the glue that holds it together may fail and render the pencil useless.

In measuring with a rule, it is best to hold the rule edgewise for accuracy. When it lies flat there is a tendency to lose accuracy because of the thickness of the rule and the angle of vision. Another factor that sometimes throws off your markings is the width of pencil marks, especially if one measurement is taken from another in a long series. For greater accuracy, use a knife or an awl to mark the dimensions. Of course, do not mark a piece of work in this way if it will show in the finished surface and there is danger that the mark will create a blemish.

Marking for saw cuts should make provision for the kerf, or width of the saw blade. Sawing is always done on the waste side of the cutting line so that sufficient stock remains to allow the end to be finished with a plane, a file, or sandpaper.

Using the Saw

Sawing a board in two or sawing the end off with a cross-cut saw is probably the most common chore in carpentry. There is only one way to proceed to start a line correctly. Grasp the handle of the saw firmly with the right hand, with the thumb and the index finger touching the side of the handle. Now draw the saw up at least one and probably several times, with the thumb of the left hand guiding the blade on the wood where the cut is to be made. It should be drawn up slowly and carefully at exactly the point at which you wish the cut to begin. If you try to do it quickly, the saw will jump and present you with a cut thumb rather than a cut board. Repeat this upward motion several times. Never try to start the cut by pushing down on the saw instead of pulling up. Before you may push down you must have the little guiding cut in the edge of the board. It is this down-stroke that does the actual cutting when you are going full blast.

Another thing: a saw has thickness of its own. You therefore do not start in the middle of the line; you have to start outside of it. Saw roughly near this line, on the waste side, leaving the line on the board to be cut to exactly with the plane in the finishing that follows rough cutting by the saw.

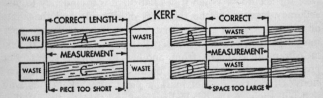

Be sure to saw carefully on the waste side of the line as at A and B. Saw-ing on the line or on the wrong side of the line makes the stock too short, as at C, or the opening too large, as shown at D.

Hold the saw very firmly after you have established the preliminary cut. If the blade moves off the line, bring it back with a twist of the handle. If you hold it loosely, it is very difficult to saw on a straight line, and your arm becomes tired very quickly. As you push down, the saw bites in beautifully, and if you hold it firmly and give a little pressure to the blade, it makes a firm, fairly rapid movement. Now the cut will start easily and nicely. The blade must be started vertically—at a right angle to the board—to make a square cut. You can easily catch on to this if at first you carefully sight above and to one side as soon as your cut is started, or test the angle with a try square. Because it is often difficult to judge the angle of the blade while working, some carpenters mark a 45- and a 90-degree angle and other markings on the face of the blade, or attach to the handle (with a brass nut and a long screw) a small hardwood block similarly marked.

A long, slow, easy stroke is best, moving the saw from the top to the hilt, putting pressure only on the downstroke, with the board held firmly. The teeth of the saw do not have a chance to do their real work unless you hold the blade at approximately 45 degrees to the surface of the board.

When cutting difficult portions, guide the blade, using the stronger part of the blade near the handle, but avoid hitting the pawls. Try to face in the direction of the cut.

Be careful not to force the blade if it sticks. If there is resistance, take short back-and-forth strokes to loosen the blade and to enlarge the kerf. At the end of the cut, be sure

ABOUT 65°

ONE INCH
8 POINTS PER INCH, 7 TEETH

15°   45°   SET   SET
60°

Crosscut saw teeth are like knife points. They cut like two rows of knife points and crumble out the wood between the cuts.

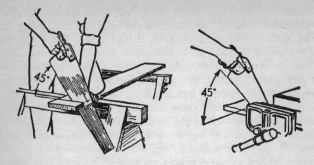

About 45 degrees is the correct angle between the saw and the work for crosscut sawing.

The coping saw is used to cut irregular shapes and intricately curved patterns in thin wood.

The backsaw is a thin cross-cut saw with fine teeth, stiffened by a thick back. A popular size is 12 inches with 14 points per inch. It is used for fine accurate work.

to provide support for the waste, and shorten your cutting strokes. Have your saw checked for set and sharpness.

If you are sawing a long board stretched between two sawhorses, or kitchen chairs, you must hold up the weight of the board with your left hand as you approach the finish of the cut. The weight of the board closes the kerf on the saw. Moreover, if you do not hold it up, a piece of wood can break off before the saw finishes the cut, and leave you with a piece of wood that you will have to glue back in place.

Nobody can enjoy working with wood until he understands how to use tools in relation to the grain. It is not good practice to cut with the grain with a crosscut saw; the ripsaw works much more rapidly in that case. The first thing that any good worker with wood does before he touches a tool to wood is to examine the grain. He does it so automatically that if you asked him if he had looked to see which way the grain runs, he probably would say "No." But rest assured that he knows.

Practically everything that grows has a grain. You will find it in beefsteak, in leather, in a grain of wheat, or, of course, in a piece of wood. It is always more difficult to cut or smooth across the grain than it is with the grain.

The crosscut saw is made to cut across the grain. Its teeth are small and are filed to a point. They literally score two knifelike lines and grind the wood between into granules. The ripsaw, on the other hand, cuts through more as a chisel does. The teeth of both saws are alternately bent, or set, one to the left and one to the right—which ensures a kerf, or cut, wide enough to keep the saw from bending.

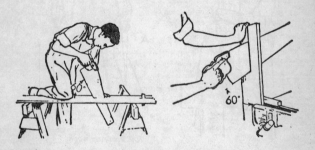

About 60 degrees is the correct angle between the saw and the work for ripsawing.
Ripsaw teeth are shaped like chisels. They cut like a gang of chisels in a row.

When a thin piece is to be cut from an end of stock, it is difficult to guide the saw accurately. A piece of waste stock placed under the cut will serve to guide the saw.

Circular cuts are usually made by boring a hole with a brace and bit or drill, then enlarging it with a compass or a coping or a saber saw. If much of this work is to be done, as in cutting a straight cut through floors, it is a good idea to round the end of a crosscut saw, extending the teeth so that they form a semicircle. This can be used to cut directly on the floor without drilling. A similar effect can be obtained by bolting half a blade from a circular saw to the base of a steel strip or old saw.

If the saw cut is to be of limited depth, make a fence of two thin strips of wood slightly longer than the saw blade. Bolt these strips together and slip the blade between them, allowing the blade to extend to the exact depth of the cut. Then tighten the bolts and saw. The fence will prevent the saw blade from cutting too deep.

A knothole is best filled by cutting a diamond-shaped hole around it and cutting similar wood with approximately the same grain to fill it. The diamond shape provides maximum glue area.

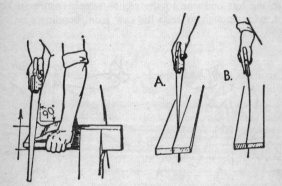

Start the saw cut by drawing the saw backward. Hold the blade square to the stock. Steady it at the line with the thumb.

A. If the saw leaves the line twist the handle slightly and draw it back to the line.

B. If the saw is not square to the stock, bend it a little and gradually straighten it. Be careful not to permanently bend or kink the blade.

Using the Backsaw

Mitring operations require careful, precision cutting that is best done with a backsaw. (Recommended: Stanley No.

1514.) To start a backsaw cut, make a slight groove along the cut on the waste side, then make a kerf on the waste side of the mark. Make sure to check the accuracy of the angle of the line, then hold the backsaw along the whole length of the cutting line. It is best to support the board being cut with an underlying board of scrap wood.

After using the saw, wipe the blade carefully with an oily rag to prevent rusting. Do not cut through nails (use a hacksaw for this) or sheetrock or painted lumber (use an old saw for these).

Using the Plane

Almost everyone will tell you that using the plane is probably the most fun in woodworking. A plane is simply a chisel held in a metal base so that you can use both hands and work much more rapidly, taking off at each stroke a very thin shaving. Using a plane, you begin to feel the real joy of carpentry; the smell of the wood rises in your nostrils; beautiful curling shavings rise from the blade; the surface behind the plane (provided you are planing with the grain, as you should be) is smooth and slick.

Before adjusting the plane, inspect the blade. You will notice that by removing the lever cap, the blade can be readily removed. Screwed on the blade is a cap iron that should rest slightly in back from the cutting edge on the unbeveled side. The cap iron acts as a shaving deflector. The sharp edge of the cap iron and the small flat surface that bears next to the cutter should lie tight along the entire width of the blade when they are screwed together. This prevents shavings from working between them.

In putting the blade back in the plane, be sure to have the cap iron uppermost and on the unbeveled side of the blade. Replace the lever cap, locking it with the small cam at the top.

If you do not have a good milled surface for planing an edge square to the working face, you will want to adjust your plane for planing a working face square.

With the left hand, hold the plane by the knob at the front end, bottom side up, with the bottom or sole level with the eye. With the right hand, move the adjusting lever to the right or left until both corners of the blade project from the throat the same distance. Then turn the adjusting nut

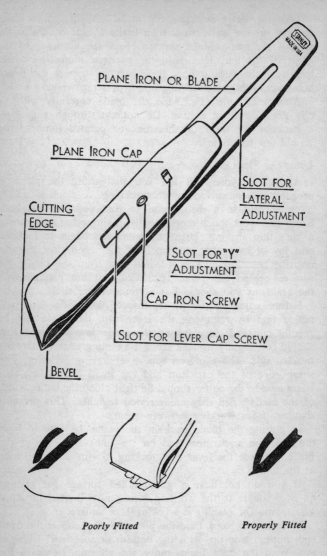

PLANE IRON OR BLADE

PLANE IRON CAP

SLOT FOR LATERAL ADJUSTMENT

CUTTING EDGE

SLOT FOR "Y" ADJUSTMENT

CAP IRON SCREW

SLOT FOR LEVER CAP SCREW

BEVEL

Poorly Fitted   *Properly Fitted*

Edge of plane iron cap must fit tight to prevent shavings from wedging under it, piling up, and choking the plane.

To put the plane iron and the plane iron cap together. 1—Lay the plane iron cap on the flat side of the plane iron, as shown, with the screw in the slot. 2—Draw the plane iron cap back. 3—Turn it straight with the plane iron.

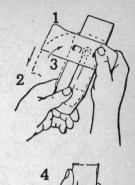

4—Advance the plane iron cap until the edge is just back of the cutting edge of the plane iron. The plane iron cap must not be dragged across the cutting edge.

The plane iron cap should extend 1/16" back of the cutting edge for general work. On cross-grained or curly wood, it should be as near to the cutting edge as possible.

5—Hold the plane iron and the plane iron cap firmly and tighten the screw to hold the two parts together.

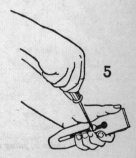

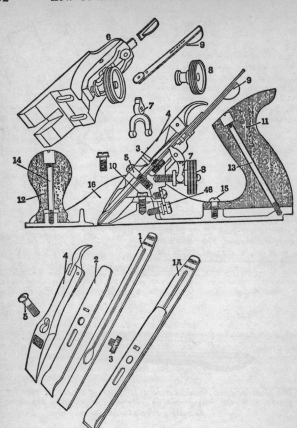

1A Double plane iron	*9 Lateral adjusting lever*
1 Single " "	*10 Frog screw*
2 Plane iron cap	*11 Handle*
3 Cap screw	*12 Knob*
4 Lever cap	*13 Handle bolt & nut*
5 " " screw	*14 Knob bolt & nut*
6 Frog complete	*15 Handle screw*
7 Y adjusting lever	*16 Bottom*
8 Adjusting nut	*46 Frog adjusting screw*

1.

To put the plane together lay the plane iron, bevel side down, on the frog. Be sure the roller on the lateral adjusting lever, the end of the Y adjusting lever, and the head of the plane iron cap screw are correctly seated.

2.

Slip the lever cap under the lever cap screw and press down the cam. If the plane iron is in the correct position, the cam will easily snap in place. If the cam will not snap in place easily, slightly loosen the lever cap screw.

If the plane iron is not firmly held when the cam is in place, slightly tighten the lever cap screw.

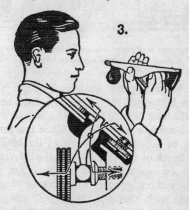

3.

The plane iron is pushed out when the adjusting nut moves out toward the handle.

The plane iron is drawn in when the adjusting nut moves in toward the frog.

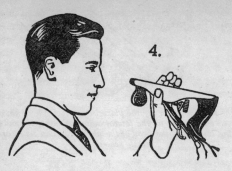

To adjust for the evenness of the shaving, sight along the bottom of the plane and move the lateral adjusting lever toward the right or the left.

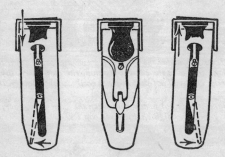

Knob, lever cap, and plane iron cap removed to show the action of the lateral adjusting lever.

until the blade slightly projects through the throat and beyond the bottom of the plane. This may be determined by touching the sole lightly across the throat with the fingers. A common mistake is to set the blade too far out. All plane blades can be adjusted for length of the blade, which determines the depth of the cut. If you take off very thin shavings not thicker on one edge than on the other, you will obtain best results without gouging the work or clogging the throat of the plane with shavings.

Another adjustment that should be made on most planes is for the throat opening. The throat opening is the distance between the blade and the front edge of the opening; this determines how long a shaving will run without being broken, and, thus, how smooth the cut will be. The finer the planing, the narrower the throat should be. The adjustment is made by moving forward or backward the frog supporting the blade.

The more nearly horizontal a blade, the less is the resistance of the wood to it. Thus end-grain planes are set at a low angle. Larger planes usually have blades set at a fixed angle.

When beginning to plane, take a firm position in front of the bench or table, with one foot forward. Make certain that the work to be smoothed is held securely—either clamped in a vise with the board butting against a stop of wood tacked onto the bench, or with the board clamped to a sawhorse. Position the board so that it can be planed with the grain.

Now check the depth and straightness of the plane blade. Hold the plane with both hands, the left hand on the knob for controlling direction and the right hand on the handle for powering the plane. Press on the knob when you begin the stroke; then exert equal pressure on both knob and handle. As you finish the stroke, lighten the pressure. A common fault is dubbing, or rounding, the ends of the work by forgetting to lessen the pressure. Stay on top of the work as you plane.

Planing should be done diagonally from corner to corner. For large surfaces use the largest plane available to ensure a flat surface and speedier work. At various stages, test the flatness of the surface in various positions with a try square or a steel square. The edge should lie flat at all points. High spots should be marked with chalk or pencil and planed away.

For finishing, plane lightly with the grain, using a very thin chip adjustment of the blade. Proceed carefully to get a smooth, square edge, testing frequently for straightness by sighting its length and for squareness with the try square.

Planing the working face smooth and flat is easy, and making the edge square is no more difficult. It requires nothing more than a little practice. If your hands are skillful enough to hold the plane square to the working face, you will go through the operation rapidly.

Besides having your cutter sharp and set to take a fairly fine shaving, and holding the tool as square as you can while you work, there is really little to think about when planing a larger surface except that at the beginning of any stroke, you put a little more downward pressure on the knob of the plane than on the handle. In the middle of the stroke the pressure is equal. At the end of the stroke you apply pressure with your right hand on the handle and practically no pressure on the knob. (These directions are for a right-handed user.) Thus you make a cut of approximately the same thickness from the beginning to the end and ensure the straightness of the edge to the very ends.

Planing an end is more difficult. A block plane should be used with the blade adjusted for a thin or medium cut. Scrape off any foreign matter such as glue or paint, using an old plane or chisel. The work must first be fastened securely, usually in a vise. Begin at the outside of the board and plane toward the center, then reverse the board and work from the opposite side.

Planing a narrow edge presents the problem of an irregular cut caused by tilting of the plane. Clamp a strip of scrap wood in the vise alongside the work to provide a base sufficiently wide to keep the plane in position.

If the wood has an irregular grain, it may be necessary to plane one end of the board in one direction, and the other end in the opposite direction. On a fairly rough job like a work bench, this won't bother you.

The first cutting on a long surface really requires a jack plane, which is ordinarily 14 inches long. Its long bottom surface, called the sole, rides over the low places and enables you to take off the high places, preserving the general plane of the surface.

Finishing is usually done with a smoothing plane, which has a shorter sole. For many craftsmen who putter around the house the junior jack plane, which is 11½ inches long, serves both purposes adequately.

A small block plane about 6 inches long is the proper tool for cutting across the end grain and smoothing up the ends of any piece of wood. The cutter of a block plane is set at a low angle and consequently cuts the end grain easily. The first time you try to use one you may split off a quarter or half inch of wood at the end of your stroke, spoiling the piece on which you are working. This can happen because working across the grain in this fashion, even with a small block plane, is not far different from actually splitting the piece of wood when you cut over to the far corner.

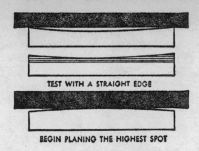

TEST WITH A STRAIGHT EDGE

BEGIN PLANING THE HIGHEST SPOT

THEN PLANE PARALLEL TO DESIRED SHAPE
GRADUALLY LENGTHENING THE STROKE

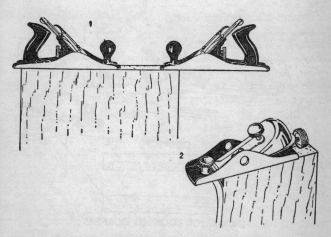

1. *Avoid breaking corners on end grain by planing from the corner to the middle.*
2. *Do not plane from the middle to the corner.*

Methods of planing ends without breaking corners:
1. Corner cut off relieves pressure on last fibers.
2. Hold tight against work in the vise.

CORRECT

INCORRECT ROUNDED CORNERS

1. Down pressure on the handle at the end of the stroke.
2. Pressure on both knob and handle.
3. Down pressure on knob at start to keep plane straight.

To start planing, take an easy but firm position directly in back of the work.

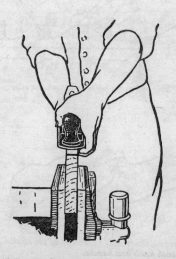

Hold the plane square with the work face of the wood.

At the end of the stroke the weight of the body should be carried easily on the left foot.

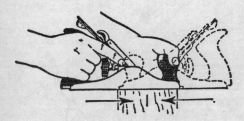

Plane end grain halfway from each edge.

If the plane is pushed all the way, the corners will break.

*To cut a smooth straight edge, the plane is pushed with the grain—that
is, in the uphill direction of the fibers.*
*To keep the plane straight, press down on the knob at the beginning of
the stroke, and on the handle at the end of the stroke.*
*Avoid dropping the plane as shown by the broken lines. That rounds the
corners.*

*To obtain a smooth surface, plane with the grain. If the grain is torn
or rough after the first stroke, reverse the work.*
*If the grain is cross or curly, sharpen the plane iron carefully; set the
plane iron cap as near the cutting edge as possible; and adjust the
plane iron to take a very thin, even shaving.*

*It is easier to plane a long edge straight with a long plane than with a
short one. A long plane bridges the low parts and does not cut them until the high spots are removed.*

The best procedure is to clamp the wood on the edge of the board that will be at the end of your block plane stroke; or better, plane from the edges to the middle, not making a through stroke. Sometimes it is necessary to turn the wood in the vise several times rather than to approach the side of the board away from you. Always saw as close as you dare to your mark, leaving only minimum finishing to be done at the end with the block plane.

Using Spokeshaves and Scrapers

Most spokeshaves have adjusting nuts that set the depth of blade, but some have thumbscrews or ordinary screws that loosen the blade to permit manual adjustment. A slight tap on the blade will help adjust it.

Of course, always cut with the grain, pushing away from you.

A smaller plane that looks like a spokeshave is the cabinet scraper, used to prepare surfaces for sanding. For small areas the blade should protrude only a hair's width. This is useful for clearing up small ridges left by a plane, or for removing paint.

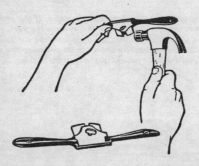

To set a spokeshave without adjusting nuts, gently tap the end of the blade to make it project the thickness of a hair. To adjust the blade laterally, to take an even shaving, tap it on the side that projects too much to draw it in. Tighten the thumb screw.

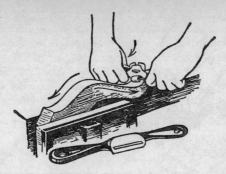

The convex-bottom spokeshave is designed to cut concave curved edges having small sweeps.

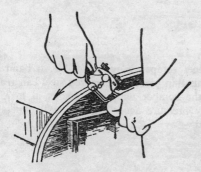

The spokeshave is also used to chamfer and to round edges.

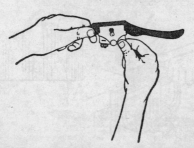

To set a Stanley No. 151M spokeshave, hold the spokeshave with the bottom in line with the eye. Turn the adjusting nuts until the cutting edge projects for an even shaving and about the thickness of a hair. Test for depth of cut.

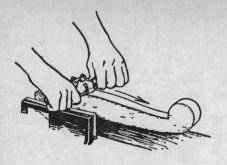

The spokeshave is usually pushed. The flat-bottom spokeshave is used on convex and concave edges where the curves have a long sweep. Care must be exercised to cut with the grain of the wood.

When a cabinet scraper is not available, a hand scraper can be used. This thin piece of tempered steel can reach into corners. Hold the scraper with both hands at a 75-degree angle and apply pressure according to the thickness of the shaving required.

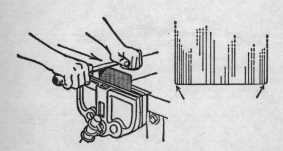

To sharpen the hand scraper: File the edges square and straight by drawfiling with a smooth mill file. Round the corners slightly, as shown above.

Whet the edge, holding the blade square to the surface of the oilstone. Some prefer to hold the scraper square to the edge of the oilstone.

Remove the burr by whetting the scraper flat on the oil stone. The edges should be very smooth and sharp.

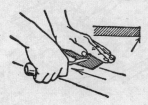

Draw the edge with three or four firm strokes of the burnisher held flat on the scraper.

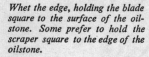

5A 5B 5C

Turn the edge with a few strokes of the burnisher. The scraper can be held in any of the three ways shown above. Draw the burnisher toward you the full length of the blade, with a sliding stroke.

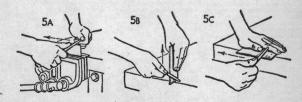

To turn the edges out, the burnisher is held at 90° to the face of the blade for the first stroke. For each of the following strokes, tilt the burnisher slightly until at the last stroke it is held at about 85° to the face of the blade. A drop of oil on the burnisher helps.

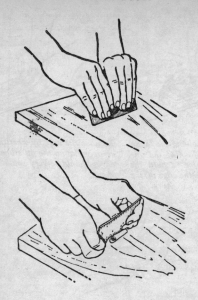

The hand scraper can be either pushed or pulled as the grain of the wood demands or whichever is more convenient.

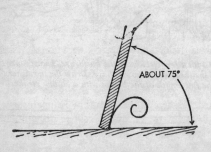

ABOUT 75°

The hand scraper is held firmly between the thumb and fingers at an angle of about 75° and sprung to a slight curve, by pressure of the thumbs.
Dust, instead of a shaving, indicates a dull scraper.

*The hand scraper is used for the final smoothing before sandpapering.
It removes the slight ridges left by the plane. It is also used to smooth
surfaces that are difficult to plane because of curly or irregular grain.*

Using Wood Chisels

Wood chisels are used for removing chips or sections of wood. A chisel consists of a steel blade with a single-bevel cutting edge; a plastic or wooden handle is fitted over the tang of the blade. Sizes are designated by the width of the cutting edge.

For light cuts in softwood, the chisel can be operated by hand pressure. For hardwood, however, a soft-face hammer is used to force the chisel into the wood. The chisel is held in one hand, bevel edge down against the wood, and the end of the handle is struck lightly with the hammer, which is held in the other hand. When finished work is required, the chisel is used with the beveled edge of the blade turned away from the finished surface.

Skillful use of the chisel requires studied practice. In general, the chisel is held and guided by the left hand and powered with the right hand. The angle at which the chisel is held depends upon the wood and the work to be done. For most work, one corner precedes the other as the chisel is moved forward. Always make sure that your chisel is sharp before you begin to work. A dull chisel is difficult to guide and dangerous to use.

In chiseling, work with the grain from the edge toward the thicker end; otherwise the board may split along the grain.

To make a concave corner, hold the beveled side against the work, pressing down and inward.

To clean a corner in a notch, tilt the handle away from you, and move the chisel toward you, using the chisel like a knife while holding the wood with the left hand.

The chisel should not be used to cut metal, and care must be taken that no foreign substance such as nails damages the blade. The chisel should be oiled to prevent rust.

In cutting with a chisel be very careful, especially when finishing, to make the shavings thin and to cut with the grain of the wood so the surface will be left smooth and bright.

Hold the chisel, when possible, at a slight angle to the cut, instead of square across. This gives a paring or sliding cut that is easier to make, and one that leaves the work smoother both on the end grain and with the grain.

A chisel is frequently used for roughing, but in cutting curves on ends, corners, and edges, both convex and concave, it is better to remove as much waste as possible with a saw.

The two principal chisel cuts are vertical and horizontal paring. Always chisel from the line toward the waste wood, and start in such a way that, if the wood should split, the split will be in the waste wood and not in the good wood.

A coping saw may be used for curves in thin wood, a compass saw or a keyhole saw for curves in thick wood, and a backsaw or crosscut saw for straight, oblique cuts. A chisel should then be used to finish the work.

A chisel can be used to cut a chamfer, a stopped chamfer, or a rabbet, but with a spokeshave or bullnose rabbet plane the work may be easily and decidedly better done. Only the ends need be cut with a chisel.

For straight and convex cuts the chisel must be held with the flat side on the work and the bevel up. The left hand holds the chisel; the right hand guides it, applies the power down on the wood, and acts as a brake. On occasion an exception may be made to this method. When cutting a long groove or a dado in wide wood, the chisel may cut in too deeply. It should then be turned so the bevel is down; this will allow clearance for the handle.

Gouges, of course, are also chisels, the most important difference being that they are rounded, with a curved cutting edge.

They are classed as firmer and paring gouges and furnished with either a flat, medium, or regular sweep from ⅛ to 2 inches wide.

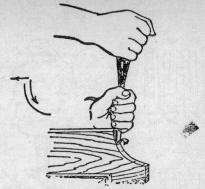

A concave curve may be cut by pressing down on the chisel and at the same time drawing back on the handle. Observe the grain.

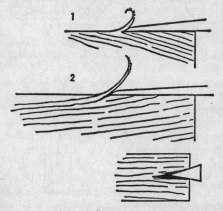

1. *Cutting with the grain, the fibers are severed, leaving the wood smooth.*
2. *Cutting against the grain leaves the wood rough. The chisel acts like a wedge, cutting and forcing the fibers apart in advance of the cutting edge. The cut cannot be controlled.*

The chisel cuts more easily and smoothly when slightly slanted in the direction of the cut. This is because the edge is minutely serrated, or saw-toothed, and because turning has the effect of decreasing the cutting angle of the bevel.

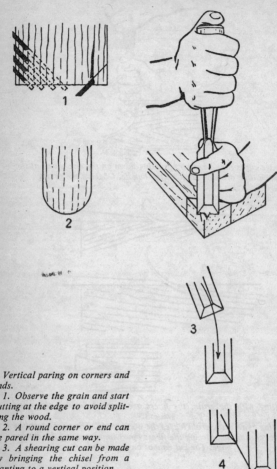

Vertical paring on corners and ends.

1. Observe the grain and start cutting at the edge to avoid splitting the wood.

2. A round corner or end can be pared in the same way.

3. A shearing cut can be made by bringing the chisel from a slanting to a vertical position.

4. The chisel can also be slid to one side as it is pressed down.

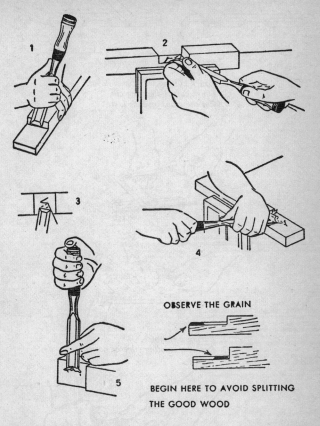

OBSERVE THE GRAIN

BEGIN HERE TO AVOID SPLITTING
THE GOOD WOOD

1. *To pare a shoulder or to clean a corner, the chisel can be held vertically, then tipped so as to secure a shearing cut when the chisel is drawn toward the workman.*

2. *Flat or horizontal paring.*

3. *Take a shearing cut where possible. In close places the chisel can be moved this way.*

4. *Cut half from each side.*

5. *Vertical paring across the grain.*

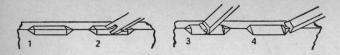

To chisel a stopped chamfer.
1. Layout.
2. Rough cutting with bevel down.
3. Finish cut. A shearing cut.
4. Cut the stops or ends last.

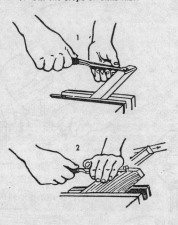

1. Paring a chamfer.
2. Paring a slanting edge or corner.

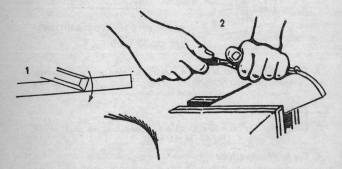

1. A convex curve may be cut in this way.
2. Hold the chisel at all points tangent to the curve to avoid digging in the side. Hold the chisel sideways to secure a shearing cut.

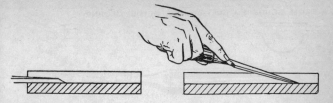

When cutting a dado or a rabbet, the chisel is sometimes held bevel down. This gives clearance for handle and fingers.

Firmer gouges are made with the bevel ground either on the inside or on the outside and with a tang or socket handle. They are used for cutting hollows and grooves.

Paring gouges are inside-ground—that is, the bevel is on the inside—and they have the tang handle. They may be had with offset handles.

Paring gouges are used to cut surfaces or ends needed to match in irregular forms, as, for instance, moldings. Pattern-makers use these gouges to finish shaping core boxes and for similar work.

The woodcarver's tools and gouges differ from the ordinary tools in that the sides, instead of being parallel, taper toward the shoulder and are beveled on both sides. In ordinary practice gouges come with eleven different sweeps or curves, ranging from those that are almost flat to those of a deep U-shape.

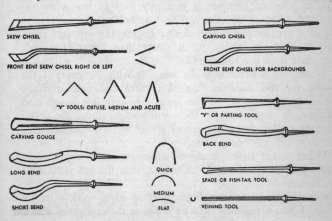

SKEW CHISEL

FRONT BENT SKEW CHISEL RIGHT OR LEFT

"V" TOOLS: OBTUSE, MEDIUM AND ACUTE

CARVING GOUGE

LONG BEND

SHORT BEND

QUICK

MEDIUM

FLAT

CARVING CHISEL

FRONT BENT CHISEL FOR BACKGROUNDS

"V" OR PARTING TOOL

BACK BEND

SPADE OR FISH-TAIL TOOL

VEINING TOOL

A FIRMER GOUGE IS A CURVED CHISEL OUTSIDE GROUND

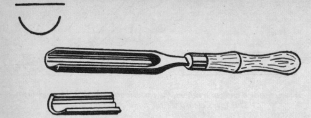

INSIDE GROUND   PARING GOUGES ARE INSIDE GROUND GOUGES
                            OF FLAT MIDDLE AND REGULAR SWEEPS

The small, deep, U-shaped gouges are called veiners. The larger ones with quick turns are called fluters. Those with slight curves are called flats.

There are three V-shaped tools—acute, medium, and obtuse—called V or paring tools.

The chisels are square or oblique on the ends and are known as firmers and skew firmers. Skew firmers with bent shanks may be had for either right or left hand.

Using the Soft-Face Hammer

The soft-face hammer is a handy tool to use when restrained force is necessary. For wood-chiseling, tapping in wooden pegs or joints, and similar chores, the soft-face hammer is ideal. Its plastic tip is softer than metal and other materials used for hammers.

Never use a hammer while working with the grain of the wood, for this deprives you of control and may split the wood. In working across the grain, however, use a soft-face hammer to give power to the cutting edge, tilting the chisel to right or left. Some carpenters prefer to tilt the chisel after the first cut has been made.

When a cut to be made is wider than the chisel edge, allow part of the chisel to be held against the cut portion to act as a guide.

For chamfering or making a beveled edge, work with the grain. When a chamfer is to be made at the end grain, move the chisel sideways across the corner, making sliding horizontal cuts.

A circular cut is made by taking small bites at a tangent, and moving the chisel sideways across the wood. When the rough cut is completed, the finished curve is completed with file and sandpaper.

When cutting across the grain, especially when the wood is in a vise, create a brake for the blade with thumb and forefinger pressing down on the blade. It is usually wise to cut from both sides toward the center to avoid chipping the outside edge.

Using Surform Tools, Files and Rasps

Every carpenter uses a Surform file or woodworker's file on wood and a regular file for work on his tools. But filing woodwork is usually not considered good practice. The Surform tool or file is used to enlarge round holes and also to finish curved work that has been sawed near to the line. To the craftsman this is permissible only when the work is exceedingly difficult to reach with a chisel or a spokeshave.

When working with the Surform tool or file, hold it at the level of your elbow. The handle should be grasped in the right hand against the fleshy part of the palm, with the thumb extending on top. The front end of the tool should be held with thumb and first two fingers of the left hand, with the thumb on top. These tools are made to cut in only one direction, so that pressure should be placed only on the forward stroke.

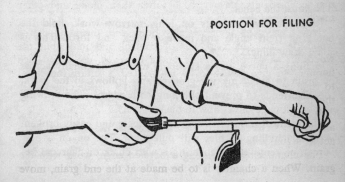

POSITION FOR FILING

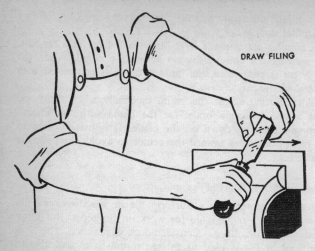

DRAW FILING

Every file should be worked with a handle, except when a file is used for jointing a saw. Many accidents occur when a file without a handle meets resistance and the tang pierces the operator's skin. Handles are available in metal and wood and are usually removed when the file is not in use. To attach a small handle, insert the file with the handle on the bench striking the point until the fit is firm. Be careful not to strike too hard, or the handle will split. To remove the handle, place the ferrule at the edge of the bench so that the handle is above the bench and the file is free; then tap the file against the bench.

To make finishing cuts on long, narrow work, hold the tool at a right angle and move it back and forth. This is called draw filing.

In filing a curve, use a sweeping motion diagonally across the grain to avoid making grooves and hollows in the work. This also tends to prevent chipping both edges. (The drawing on the next page shows how to file a curve.)

The teeth of a Surform tool are delicate and easily broken. Careless handling of files will dull them. The oil on a new file can be removed by covering it with chalk or charcoal before using.

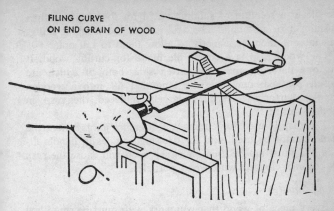

FILING CURVE
ON END GRAIN OF WOOD

Files will last much longer if they are cleaned with a file card or brush every time they are used. This does not sharpen the file but will restore its usefulness.

A file used on metal will soon become dull because of the accumulation of filings. These can be removed by dipping

TEMPERED STEEL WIRE FILE CARD FOR CLEANING FILES

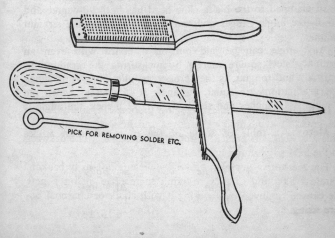

PICK FOR REMOVING SOLDER ETC.

the file in a solution of sulphuric acid for five minutes, then washing it in ammonia. The acid eats at the clogging filings and loosens them sufficiently to allow them to fall out.

The wood rasp is a coarse file made for cutting wood. It has one flat side and one convex side, both of which are closely toothed; one end is a tang that fits into a wooden handle. Surform tools have largely replaced the rasp in modern usage.

The rasp is used for cutting and dressing joints where the plane cannot be used, and for dressing handles in handle fitting. Oil must not be used on a rasp, as it will cause the rasp to become clogged with wood particles.

Using Squares

Every piece of wood that you work with must be smoothed flat and have its corners and edges squared—unless, of course, it is designed for another shape.

The exact right angle is probably the one elementary dimension you will have to use most. To help you get it right, three types of tools are useful. These are the steel square, the try square, and the mitre square.

The steel square is completely flat. The try square has a raised wood or metal handle that serves as a right-angle fence, and the mitre square has a handle with a 45-degree angle gauge. An instrument that combines the best features of these is the combination square, which has an adjustable head clamped to the blade. The head has both 90-degree and 45-degree angle gauges and can be moved along the straight edge.

Any angle can be laid out on a board with even an ordinary steel square merely by measuring the graduations on body and tongue, as they cross a parallel line. Thus, when the graduations are equal, the angle is 45 degrees; when the tongue is 12 inches and the body 3 7/32 inches, the angle is 75 degrees.

Here is a table of some of the more common angles required.

Angle	Tongue	Body
30°	12 in.	20⅞ in.
45°	12	12
60°	12	6 15/16

Angle	Tongue	Body
70°	12	4⅜
75°	12	3 7/32
80°	12	2⅛

The steel square, or framing square, is the speedy calculator of the amateur carpenter. Most models of this measuring tool have many calculations on them and a fine graduation of measurements. Shaped in a right angle (one side is the tongue; the other is the body), the square usually carries graduations on both sides, one in sixteenths of an inch and the other in tenths, twelfths, sixteenths, and twentieths.

In using the square, the long body side is held in the left hand and the shorter tongue in the right hand. The most common sizes are 24 by 16 inches and 12 by 8 inches. The face of the square is the side that carries the manufacturer's name; or when the blade is held in the left hand, the tongue in the right, and the heel points away from the body, the face is the side that is up. The reverse side is called the back.

In using the square, the blade should be held along the edge of the work with the tongue across the face. The face of the wood should be smooth and free from dust or dirt. The line is drawn along the tongue.

On the square are marked scales and tables. The scales are inches and graduations of the inch and are found on all edges of the square. On the back of the tongue, in the corner of the square, is a hundredth scale for the inch. An octagon scale may be seen along the center of the face of the tongue. There are three tables: the Essex board measure table, the brace table, and the rafter table.

The Essex board measure table appears on the back of the blade and is used to find quickly the number of board feet in a piece of lumber. It is a simple table to use, and once its few essentials are understood, it saves the carpenter a great deal of time in estimating lumber requirements for a particular job.

To find the number of board feet in a piece of lumber, its three dimensions must be known—width, thickness, and length. Two of these dimensions are taken care of simultaneously by the inch markings on the outer edge of the blade. These figures represent the width in inches of a board

1 inch thick. The third dimension of the wood is found in the vertical column of figures under the inch mark 12 (12 is the base number of the table). The figures under the number 12 represent lengths in feet. All other figures in the table represent totals of board feet.

To find the number of board feet in a piece of wood, find its length in the column under 12 and guide laterally along this line until the figure under the width of the board is reached. This figure is the number of board feet, in feet and inches, of a piece of wood 1 inch thick. To find the result for wood of other thicknesses, simply multiply the first result by the thickness of the piece. In the answer table, the figures to the left of the vertical lines represent feet, the figures to the right inches.

For example: How many board feet of lumber in a piece of wood 8 inches wide, 3 inches thick, and 13 feet long?

1. Find the length, 13 feet, under the inch figure 12.
2. Move along the line to the left until directly under the figure 8, which represents the width of the piece.
3. Read the figure in the table: 8/8, or 8 8/12 (8 2/3) feet. This figure is for a board 1 inch thick.
4. Multiply 8 2/3 by the thickness of our board, 3:

$$8 \ 2/3 \ x \ 3 =$$
$$26/3 \ x \ 3 = 26 \ board \ feet.$$

The try square is composed of a steel blade set at right angles into a head (beam) of wood or iron. The blade is graduated into inches and fractions of an inch. It is used for several purposes:

1. To serve as a guide for the pencil in marking lines at right angles to an edge or surface.
2. To test an edge or end to determine whether it is square with the adjoining surface or edge.
3. To test the surface or edge to determine whether it is the same thickness throughout its length.

The bevel square, or T-bevel, is composed of a steel blade 6 to 12 inches long with a 45-degree bevel point at one end. The other end is fitted into a slotted wooden or metal beam and is held in place by means of a thumbscrew. The blade has a long slot in the beam end to allow ample working movement and can be set at any desired angle. It can be used for transferring angles from one piece of wood to another, and it can be used in places where other types of squares cannot.

Before you use the try square, check the edge of the stock with your eye by sighting along the edge. This is done by holding the stock level just below the eye, and training the vision along the length. Bumps and irregularities then become quite visible.

Although most boards you buy are assumed to be square, this is not always the case. Assuring yourself that the stock you use is truly square is a first step in any project. Start by making sure that all your boards have smooth surfaces and that the edges are parallel and at true right angles. Then testing a board proceeds with the try square.

Plane one broad surface smooth and straight. Test it crosswise, lengthwise, and from corner to corner. Mark the work face X.

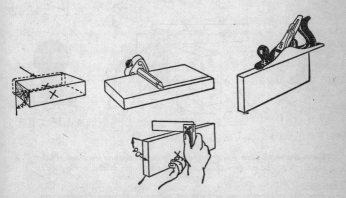

Plane one edge smooth, straight and square to the work face. Test it from the work face. Mark the work edge X.

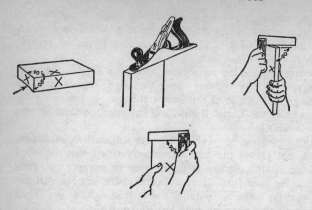

Plane one end smooth and square. Test it from the work face and work edge. Mark the work end X.

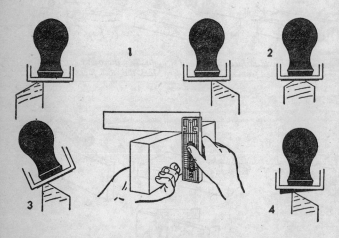

From the work face gauge a line for thickness around the stock. Plane the stock to the gauge line. Test the second face as the work face is tested.

From the work edge gauge a line for width on both faces. Plane smooth, straight, and square to the gauge line. Test the second edge from the work face.

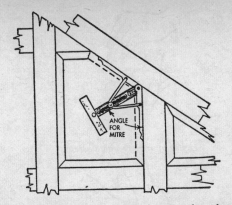

The Stanley angle divider is a double bevel. It is used to take off and divide angles for the mitre cut in one operation. The handle is graduated on the back for laying off 4-, 5-, 6-, 8- and 10-sided work.

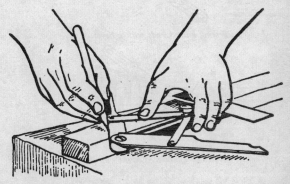

Laying off a mitre with a Stanley angle divider. The square blade may be used for a try square.

Duplicating lines drawn at the same angle as in laying off dovetails for a drawer.

Laying off a mitre with a bevel.

Testing mitred ends with a bevel.

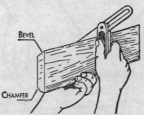

BEVEL

CHAMFER

Testing beveled or chamfered edges with the bevel.

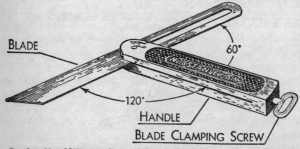

BLADE

60°

120°

HANDLE

BLADE CLAMPING SCREW

Stanley No. 18TB Bevel. Used for marking and checking off mitre and other angle cuts.

Squaring a board is a basic operation. It is done simply in stages: (1) Smooth the best surface and make sure it is flat. (2) Smooth and square a working edge. (3) Smooth and square a working end. (4) Measure, mark, and cut to the required length and width and thickness. (5) Plane edges and ends smooth and square. (6) Test with a try square.

If you do not begin with a finished board, use a plane to create the first finished surface. Mark this with an X for identification. Hold the try square handle along this finished surface and the four corners to see what adjustments must be made. Slide the try square along each of the edges to test their accuracy. Then finish the back side to the proper thickness.

Using the Brace and Bit

For the job of boring holes we have that marvelous piece of machinery known as the brace and bit.

In boring holes in wood, after a few turns, the bit feeds into the wood without pressure. To drive screws, the pressure must be maintained. To work in corners or other close places where a full turn of the crank is impossible, a ratchet mechanism is provided to ratchet the bit either to the right (to drive) or to the left (to withdraw) by rotating the cam ring.

Holes are often bored at the wrong angle because the woodworker just doesn't know how simple it is to bore them perpendicular to the pierced surface. The only problems involved in boring a hole are to get it straight and not to break through the wood at the bottom of the hole.

To bore straight you have only to sight on the piece of wood twice more after your hole is fairly well started in the fashion shown on page 89. (The same applies when boring horizontally.) One sight shows you whether or not you are holding the bit straight in one plane; the other sight shows you the same thing in the other plane.

If you have any doubts, it is wise to use a try square to make certain the bit is at a right angle to the surface of the wood. For horizontal borings, cup the brace in the left hand, supported by the stomach. This settled, you have nothing to do except to turn the handle and give a reasonable amount of pressure on the head of the brace. The tool does the work. You can bore just as fast as you wish, knowing that for the

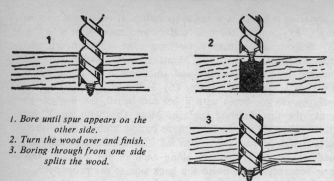

1. *Bore until spur appears on the other side.*
2. *Turn the wood over and finish.*
3. *Boring through from one side splits the wood.*

ordinary hole nothing can go wrong, provided you are doing it carefully. That is, until you get near the bottom of the hole.

A problem arises in boring through a board when the bit comes through the far side of the board. To avoid splintering, reverse the bit when the tip of the bit appears. Toward the end, turn the brace slowly, watching or feeling for the point of the bit—and as soon as it comes through, stop. Then you bore through from the other side. The result is a clean hole where you want it. Another way to prevent splitting on the reverse side is to clamp a piece of waste wood over the exit area of the piece that is being worked.

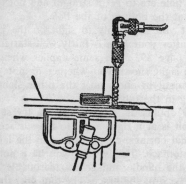

Test with a try square or learn to judge by eye.

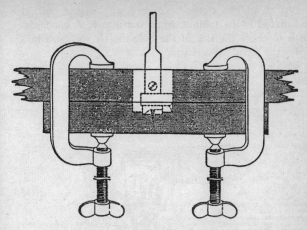

How to use expansive bit without causing rough edge.

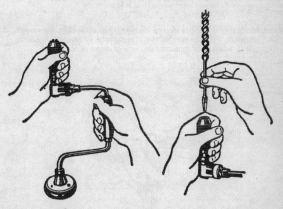

To place the bit in the chuck, grasp the chuck shell and turn the handle to the left until the jaws are wide open. Insert the bit shank in the square socket at the bottom of the chuck and turn the handle to the right until the bit is held firmly in the jaws.

Before a hole is bored, make sure the wood is free from nails, spikes, metal, and dirt. These materials, no matter how small they may be, can damage the auger bit. Once the points or spurs are broken or the lips rolled, the bit is of no value. Bits should be cleaned, covered with a thin coat of oil, and placed in the toolbox when not in use. A good suggestion is to check the size of the hole the bit will bare in a piece of scrap wood beforehand.

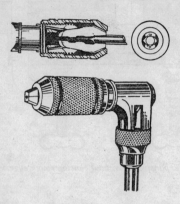

Bit brace chucks of the above design without a square socket are operated in like manner. The corners of the taper shank of the bit should be carefully seated and centered in the v grooves of the jaws.

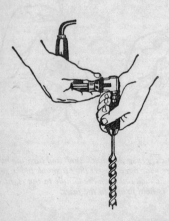

To operate the ratchet turn the cam ring. Turning the cam ring to the right will allow the bit to turn right and give ratchet action when the handle is turned left. Turn the cam ring left to reverse the action.
The ratchet brace is indispensable when boring a hole in a corner or where some object prevents making a full turn with the handle.

If a hole is to be enlarged, some difficulty will be encountered in centering the bit. Filling the hole with plastic wood or a wooden plug will solve this problem.

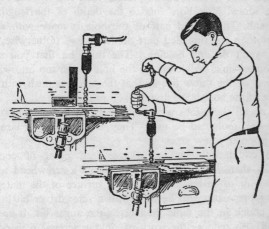

To bore a vertical hole, hold the brace and bit perpendicular to the surface of the work. Test by sight. Compare the direction of the bit to the nearest straight edge or to sides of the vise. A try square can be held near the bit.

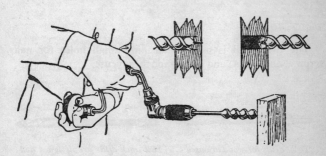

To bore a horizontal hole, hold the head of the brace cupped in the left hand against the stomach and with the thumb and forefinger around the quill. To bore through without splintering the second face, stop when the screw point is through and finish from the second face. When boring through with an expansive bit, it is best to clamp a piece of wood to the second face and bore straight through.

Countersinking Screws

Whenever a flathead screw is to be set in and countersunk, you really need three different bits to do a proper job. The first tool is a bit slightly larger than the smooth shank of the screw. You bore this to the depth of the length of the shank. The second part of the hole is made with a bit smaller than the threaded part of the screw. (Otherwise, the screw won't do any holding.) The third bit that you need is a countersink, which widens the hole at the top into which the head of the screw fits, so that the screw is flush with the surface of the board. See drawings on page 96.

To do all these jobs accurately and fast in one operation, screw sink tools can be used. They are available in sizes to mate popular screw sizes.

The countersink bit has a rose-head point of conical flutes, a shank, and a tang. This permits a screwhead to be set flush or to be lowered below the surface of the material.

Your brace can also be used with a screwdriver bit in the brace chuck in the same manner as the auger bit. It speeds up and also reduces the work of sinking screws in wood or metal. The correct bit size is determined by the size of the screw. Care must be exercised in selecting size; a bit of improper size may be damaged by, or may damage, the screw.

The Twist Drill

The twist drill is used for drilling small holes for nails, screws, and bolts, and will stand heavy use.

Twist drills for wood are used to make holes for screws, nails, or bolts. They are sized by 32ds of an inch and range from No. 2 (1/16 inch) up.

Bit stock drills are designed and tempered to make holes in metal, but can also be used in wood, especially in repair work where contact with nails or metal is possible. They are sized by 32ds of an inch and range from No. 2 (1/16 inch) up.

FOR BIT BRACE   **FOR HAND DRILL**

Countersink bits are used to widen screw holes so that the heads of flat-head screws may be flush with, or slightly below, the surface of the work.

To place the drill in the chuck, open it only slightly more than the diameter of the drill. This helps to center it. Insert the drill. Tighten the chuck by pushing forward on the crank with the right hand, while holding the chuck shell tight with the left thumb and forefinger.

To remove the drill, hold the chuck shell tight with the left thumb and forefinger, and turn the crank backward, with the right hand, as shown by the arrow.

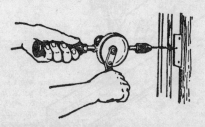

Hold the drill straight. Do not wobble while turning; it makes the hole oversize and is likely to break the drill.

It is sometimes desirable to hold the drill by the side handle and press the body against the frame handle like a breast drill.

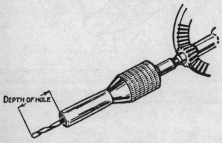

To drill holes of uniform depth, make a depth gauge. Cut a piece of wood or dowel the right length, so the drill will project the desired depth. When the piece of wood is drilled, slip it over the drill.

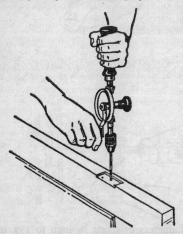

Hold the drill steady in the direction desired and exert an even pressure. Turn the crank at a constant speed and not too fast.

After it is used, the drill should always be replaced in the toolbox to keep it from being damaged. To prevent rust, it should be kept cleaned and well oiled.

The Auger Bit

The auger bit is used for all ordinary boring in wood. It has a steel shaft about 8 inches long and is composed of six characteristic parts: the feed screw, spurs, cutting edge, twist or flutes, tang, and shank. The feed screw is at the end of the bit and feeds the bit into the wood. The spurs are vertical cutters that cut the side of the hole. The cutting edges are horizontal cutters that chip out the wood in the hole.

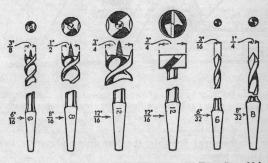

Auger Bits, 16ths of an inch   Fostner Bits, 16ths.   Twist Bits, 32ds of an inch.

Bits are marked for size by a single number. The numerator of the fraction stands for the diameter of the bit. Auger and Fostner bits are marked by 16ths of an inch. No. 8 stands for 8/16 or ½ inch. Twist Bits for wood are usually marked in the same way, by 32ds of an inch. No. 8 stands for 8/32 or ¼ inch.

Bits are sized in sixteenths of an inch. A No. 11 bit will bore a hole 11/16 inch in diameter. The size is indicated on the shank, or tang. The size of holes bored ranges from 1/4 inch to 2 inches in diameter.

The expansive bit is a drill with an adjustable cutter. One expansive bit takes the place of several large bits. It is issued with two interchangeable cutting blades, one of which cuts holes with diameters of from ⅞ inch to 1½ inches, the other, holes 1½ to 3 inches in diameter. The expansive bit

The diamond point is used for machine boring with power feed.

The single thread feed screw is best for fast cutting in green or gummy wood.

The standard double thread feed screw is best for general work with seasoned wood. It is preferred for cabinet and pattern making.

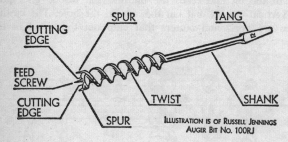

ILLUSTRATION IS OF RUSSELL JENNINGS
AUGER BIT NO. 100RJ

Auger bits are sized by 16ths of an inch, measuring the diameter. Bits vary in length from 7 to 10 inches. Dowel bits are short auger bits about 5 inches long.

has no twist; except for this, the remaining parts are similar to the auger bit.

To set the expansive bit, a screwdriver is used to loosen the setscrew and the cutter is adjusted to the desired setting, reading the diameter of the hole from the scale on the blade; then tighten the screw. By moving the cutter 1/32 inch, the diameter of the hole is changed 1/16 inch. It is a good rule to test the setting by boring a hole in a piece of waste wood.

The expansive bit takes the place of many large bits. The cutter may be adjusted for holes of various sizes. Moving the cutter adjusting screw one complete turn enlarges or reduces the hole 1/8". One half turn 1/16". Test the size on a piece of waste wood. For boring through, clamp a piece of waste wood on the back of the work to prevent splitting.

The Screwdriver

A screwdriver looks like a very simple tool. Perhaps that is why so many people have never bothered to master its correct use. First, you should always select a screwdriver of a length and tip fitted to the screw. Screwdrivers are specified by length of blade. The tip should be straight and nearly parallel-sided. It should also fit the screw slot and be not wider than the screwhead. A tip that is too wide will scar the wood around the screwhead. If the blade is too thin you may twist and break the tip, or if the tip is too narrow, the screwdriver will destroy the slot. A driver that is not held in line with the screw will slip out of the slot and mar both the screw and the work. And if the screwdriver tip is rounded or beveled, it will rise out of the slot, spoiling the screwhead. If the tip is damaged, you can regrind or file it to make it straight.

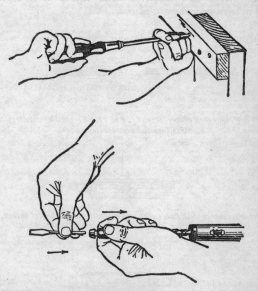

To insert the screwdriver bit into the chuck with the spiral spindle extended, place the ratchet shifter on the center position. Pull the chuck sleeve down. Insert the bit. Turn the bit until you feel it is seated. Release the chuck sleeve.

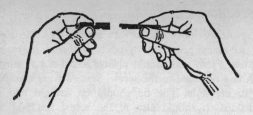

With the drill points and chuck adaptor the spiral ratchet screw-driver becomes an automatic push drill. A drill point is inserted into the chuck adaptor. Turn the drill point until you feel it is seated. The two assembled pieces are then placed in the chuck in the same manner as a screwdriver bit.

The Spiral Ratchet

When you have many screws to drive or draw in a hurry, a spiral ratchet screwdriver is most useful. It is especially helpful in tight or awkward places.

      Drill Point   *Countersink*

There are eight drill points, sizes 1/16 to 11/64 inch. The countersink also fits into the screwdriver chuck.

To drive screws or drill holes with quick return spiral ratchet action, set the ratchet shifter on the position nearest to the chuck.

To use as a long rigid screwdriver, without spiral or ratchet action, set the ratchet shifter on the center position.

To draw screws with quick return spiral ratchet action, set the ratchet shifter on the position nearest the handle.

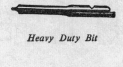

Heavy Duty Bit

Phillips Screw Driver Bit

Always use the longest screwdriver convenient for the work. More power can be applied with a long screwdriver than with a short one, usually because the longer screwdriver has a larger diameter handle. Hold the handle firmly in the palm of the right hand with the thumb and forefinger grasping the handle near the ferrule. With the left hand (if you are right-handed) steady the tip and keep it pressing into the slot while renewing the grip on the handle for a new turn.

If no hole is bored for the threaded part of the screw, the wood is often split or the screw is twisted off. If a screw turns too hard, back it out and enlarge the hole. A little soap on the threads of the screw also makes it easier to drive.

There is a regular procedure that is best used to fasten two pieces of wood together with screws: (1) Locate the positions of the screw holes. (2) Bore the first hole in the first piece of wood slightly larger than the diameter of the body under the screwhead, as in the illustration. (3) Bore the second hole slightly smaller than the threaded part of the screw. Bore as deep as half the length of the threaded part. (4) Countersink the first holes to match the diameter of the heads of the screws. (5) Drive the screws tightly in place with the screwdriver.

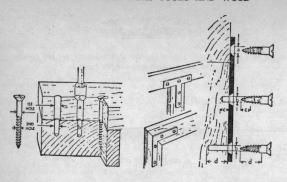

To fasten hinges or other hardware in place with screws, follow this step-by-step procedure: (1) Locate the position of the piece of hardware on the work. (2) Recess the work to receive the hardware, if this is necessary. (3) Locate positions of screws. (4) Select the screws that will easily pass through the holes in the hardware, as in the illustration. (5) Bore the pilot holes (second hole) slightly smaller than the diameter of the threaded part of the screws. (6) Drive the screws tightly in place.

If the wood is soft (pine, for example), bore as deep as half the length of the threaded part of the screw. If the wood is hard (oak, for example) or the screw soft (for example, brass), bore three-fourths of the depth. If the screw is large, the hole must be nearly as deep as the screw. Holes for small screws are usually made with an automatic push drill or a hand drill. For a description of various screws, see pages 195 and 196.

Using the Grinder and the Oilstone

The grinder—whether powered by hand or by a motor—is used to grind the edge of a plane iron, a chisel, or any other cutting edge. An aluminum oxide wheel is desirable for most tool-sharpening operations. Speeds range from 1,500 to 3,300 r.p.m. Slower speeds give protection against overheating the metal edge, but the wheel must be able to cut while it rotates slowly.

Although the grinding wheel is essentially a tool sharpening instrument, it is also useful for shaping and smoothing small objects. On both hand-powered and electric-powered grinders, attachments may be affixed which will polish to any finish desired. Circular shaped wire brushes are useful for removing spots from metal, taking off rust, and for rough polishing. Buffing attachments for final polishing are also available. Especially on power tools these attachments save a great deal of muscle power.

When grinding small metal or wood parts, it is best to clamp the part to a handscrew, similar to the ones used by cabinet makers. This eliminates the risk of bruised or burnt fingers which sometimes get too close to the grinding wheel.

When you have a great deal of grinding to be done, or when you make a habit of keeping the blades of your plane at top sharpness, it may be wise to construct a slide rest. A base board 2 inches by 6 inches x 6 inches is pieced midway through the edges with a bolt or iron bar approximately ½ inch in diameter, so that the board can swing freely. The iron bar is used as an axle and mounted on raised brackets like a miniature see-saw. On the top of the base board, a ¼ inch bolt with a wing nut is attached to hold the plane blade while the board is moved to provide the proper grinding angles.

Oilstone and wet grinders are particularly suitable because they can operate at greater speed with less heat hazards.

When sharpening a tool, make sure the edge is made square with the shaft of the tool. Hold the blade with the bevel resting lightly on the face of the wheel. Do not grind the straight side of the tool or it will be made useless. The wheel should be moving toward the user. It is best to stop frequently to allow the metal to cool. Dip the edge in cold water, but restore the edge to the same position when you begin grinding again. Keep the left forefinger on the tool rest as a guide while cutting and when you replace the edge. When you resume, sharpening is completed by whetting on an oilstone. Oilstones vary in size. The rectangular oilstones measure from 1 to 2¼ inches in width and from 3 to 8 inches in length.

Oilstones should, of course, be used with oil. The oil tends to clean the pores of the stone, providing a better cutting surface. It also acts as a lubricating medium. If the stone becomes too oily, it may be boiled in clear water for a thorough cleansing.

When the cutting edge is nicked.

When the bevel has been worn down by much whetting.

When the bevel has been rounded by careless whetting.

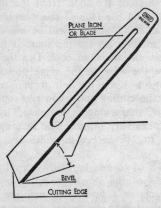

To get the right grinding angle about 25° to 30° make the bevel a little longer than twice the thickness of the plane iron.

Avoid a bevel too short and thick. It will not enter the wood easily.

Avoid a bevel too long and thin. It is weak and will nick easily.

The oilstone is made in three finishes—fine, medium, and coarse. Often each side of the stone is of different coarseness. The finer the surface of the stone used, the finer is the edge finally achieved. Most oilstones are packed in a wooden box to protect the stone from chipping and to keep it clean.

When you use a stone, anchor it firmly on a hard base. Before placing an edge to the stone, clean it thoroughly and apply a thin film of oil. Whet only the beveled side of the tool edge. While the right hand powers the tool, use the left hand as a guide, applying an even, moderate pressure—less on the back stroke than on the forward stroke. A figure 8 motion tends to wear the stone more evenly. Apply enough pressure to make the stone cut. The tool to be sharpened must be free from all spurs or sharp corners, for these will certainly gouge the stone.

If the tool is sharpened too much on one side, a wire edge may be formed—a cutting edge so thin that it would not have the required strength to do a job. This should be removed by running the stone lightly against the cutting edge. To avoid creating a wire edge, reverse the tool occasionally while it is being sharpened.

Use the coarse side of the stone first for 10 or 12 strokes; then use the finer side. The flat side of the tool may receive a few strokes here until the edge becomes almost an invisible line. When an edge of satisfactory fineness has been ob-

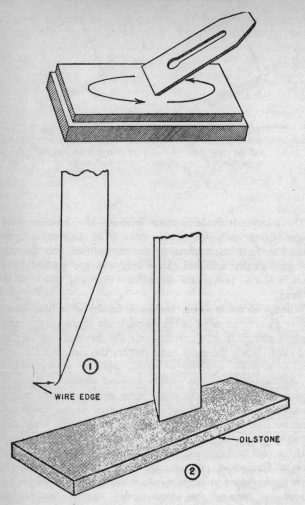

WIRE EDGE

① ②

OILSTONE

tained, remove the scrap and the oil from the stone and store it in the proper place.

For a final sharpening, the edge can be honed on a lily stone or a leather strop attached to a board. A flat piece of aluminum can also be used for this purpose. Honing motions are made away from the cutting edge, in contrast with the whetting action described. Test the final sharpness against a sheet of paper.

After several uses, an oilstone should be thoroughly cleaned with a rag and linseed oil thinned with kerosene.

The Carpenter's Level

A carpenter's level is usually made of wood, aluminum, or magnesium, and is rectangular in shape, from 9 to 24 inches in length. It may have one or more true surfaces with a glass vial in the center of each surface. The glass vial in the center of a horizontal surface and parallel with it is used in leveling; a glass vial in the end of a level, perpendicular to the true surface, is used to check the plumb or vertical trueness.

To make certain that the level is properly adjusted, place it on any surface and note the position of the bubble in the vial. Reverse the level end-for-end. The bubble should be in the same relative position as it was in the first instance. If it is not, the level is out of adjustment and should not be used until proper adjustments are made. Usually adjusting screws, which hold the vial in place, can be tightened to provide a correction of the reading. A similar testing and adjusting process should be used for checking the plumb.

To check whether a surface is level or plumb place the level on the surface to be leveled or plumbed, holding the level still with the hand. If the position of the bubble is not in the center of the vial, the surface is not level or plumb, the bubble will move toward the higher side.

The level is a delicate instrument, easily damaged, and great care must be taken so that it is not abused. It must be kept in a toolbox and protected from the danger of being broken by the other tools in the box.

Some spirit levels incorporate two or more glass vials so that measuring may be done from two directions at the same time—one or two horizontal vials and the vertical vial for "plumbness." Some instruments have vials in pairs as a check against each other, and as a margin of safety against breakage. As with all tools, the accuracy of the level depends on its material and workmanship. Wood levels may sometimes warp. Aluminum and magnesium levels are more accurate. A variation of the carpenter's level in usage is a "line level"

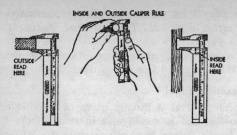

INSIDE AND OUTSIDE CALIPER RULE

OUTSIDE READ HERE

INSIDE READ HERE

The inside and outside caliper rule is useful for many small measurements.

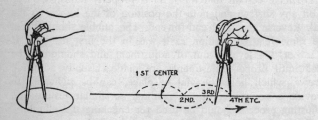

1 ST CENTER

2 ND.

3 RD

4TH ETC.

Dividers are used for scribing circles or an arc.

Also for combinations of circles and arcs.

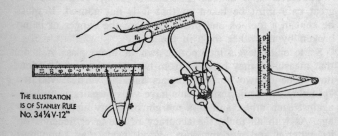

THE ILLUSTRATION IS OF STANLEY RULE No. 34¼ V-12"

To set dividers hold both points on the measuring lines of the rule.

To set calipers hold one leg on end of rule and other on measuring line.

that can be hooked onto a line between two points and check for level accuracy.

Using Wing Dividers and Similar Tools

To make a circle or any curve or arc, any of several types of adjustable compasses may be used. Wing dividers are used principally for measuring off equal distances. They have solid metal legs, one of which can be removed and a pencil substituted. When a board has to be shaped to fit against an irregular surface, the pin leg is run along the surface, while the pencil makes a parallel mark on the board.

Plumb Bob

The plumb bob is a tool made of metal (iron, brass, or lead), with one end pointed, the other with a fixture to which a line or string can be attached. When it is in place, it is used to indicate a point perpendicular to a point above.

The Extension Stick

For inside measurements, a carpenter's measuring stick is used. This consists of two overlapping rules held together by brass clamps which serve as a guide. The rules are made in lengths from 2 feet to 12 feet. A thumbscrew permits the rules to be extended and fastened at the correct length, then the stick can be removed and the measurement read. Zig-zag rules and coilable rules also have this feature for short measurements.

Trammel Points

Trammel points are used for marking and checking a piece of work, especially when a compass is too small for the measurements. These small metal pins are clamped and adjusted to a piece of wood. If a pencil line is required, a pencil can be clamped next to one of the points.

Where the job involves distances too large for even trammel points, a layout mark of white cotton mason's line can be used. Lines may be coated with chalk so that, when they are laid on the floor and snapped, a chalk line indicates the borders.

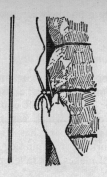

Dividers may be used to scribe a line to match an irregular surface, masonry, or woodwork.

TRAMMEL POINTS

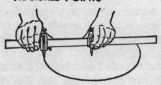

On a stick, these are used to make circles too large for dividers.

SCRATCH AWL

The chalk line is used for long straight lines. Be sure to snap the line taut.

Clamps

Clamps are used to hold glued pieces of wood together while the glue dries. The use of various types of clamps is explained in the section on gluing.

The Matter of Safety

The misuse of hand tools is the cause of many injuries in the home, some of them quite serious.

Most accidents occur for quite simple reasons:

(1) Failure to use the right tool for the job. (2) Failure to use the tool properly. (3) Failure to keep tools in a safe condition. (4) Failure to keep tools in a safe place when they are not in use.

The National Safety Council makes several suggestions that help to lessen tool injuries in the home. When you are not using them, keep tools in tool cabinets or in a tool rack on the wall where they are easily accessible. If you have to handle or sort tools to select the right one, you may cause injuries as well as damage to the tools. Using a dull or damaged tool often results in an injury. Always keep tools in good condition. Wood handles should be firm and smooth to eliminate the possibility of injury by slivers. The handles should be made of straight-grained materials such as hickory, ash, or maple. Handles should be securely fastened to the heads of tools, such as hammers, mallets, and sledges, to keep the head from flying off the handle when a blow is struck with the tool. Blades of cutting tools should be kept sharp and have the proper angle, because sharp tools are safer and more efficient than dull ones. Dull tools may slip, stick, or slide and cause injuries to the user and damage to the material being worked.

Chisels, punches, and similar tools with mushroomed heads are unsafe to use because when struck a blow a piece of the

mushroom may break off, fly, and injure the worker or some-
one nearby. You can make mushroomed tools safe by grinding off the excess wood. The handle of a wood chisel should
be strong and substantial. Because it is necessary to use both
hands on the handle of a wood chisel to do a good job, the
work should be securely braced or clamped. When a mallet is
used for striking the end of the handle of a wood chisel, it
is good practice to use a chisel with a plastic, leather, or
metal band around the end of the handle so that the handle
does not slip or spread.

Accidents occur with the use of a file when there is no
handle on the tang end. The file slips and the sharp point of
the tang pierces the hand of the user.

Driving or pulling nails is an operation you will often
have to do. A claw (carpenter's) hammer is best for this
purpose. The hammer should be in good condition and the
head securely and squarely fastened to the handle by wedges,
or other effective means. Keep your eyes on the subject being
hammered and give attention to striking an accurate blow;
otherwise you may strike and smash a finger or thumb. The
face of the hammer and the handle must be clean and free
from grease, dirt, and the like; otherwise, the hammer
may slip in the effort to strike a blow. Don't strike the faces
of two hammers together, both being hard may cause a chip
to fly off the hammer.

There is little danger in using hand planes if the blades
are kept in good condition and they are properly used. The
chief hazard is a dull blade, which may jam and stick. When
using a plane, raise the plane slightly on the back stroke
to protect the blade from dulling.

Axes and hatchets should be kept sharp, and the handles
should be of good material well secured to the tool head.
When using an ax or hatchet, be careful that there is no
obstruction in the line of swing, and see that no one is
standing close enough to be hit by flying chips. The eyes
should be kept focused on the object to be hit, and the handle
of the tool should be as nearly horizontal as possible when
the blade strikes the object.

Sharp tools often cause accidents when left lying about
where they can be stepped on or struck accidentally. Extra
care must always be taken after using these tools to make
sure that they are placed where they will not be cause for

injury. Leather cases should be used for carrying double-edge axes. Where this is not possible, the tool should be carried with the cutting head forward, the handle gripped directly behind the head. Single-edge axes should be carried on the shoulder, the ax head in back of and close to the shoulder, with the blade turned out away from the carrier.

It is important to select the correct size and type of knife for each job—a small knife for carving woods. Sharp knives of all kinds are safer than dull ones; they do not require as much pressure to do their work, and therefore do not slip as easily as dull ones when being used. In making a cut, always cut away from yourself; otherwise if the knife slips, a finger or some other part of the body may be injured. Sharp knives should be washed separately, not handled along with other utensils. Each knife should be dried separately, holding the sharp edge away from the hand using the towel.

A wrench, rather than pliers, should be used to loosen or tighten nuts, because pliers can slip off. Pliers and wrenches, like screwdrivers, should not be used as substitutes for hammers, etc.

Screwdrivers are the cause of accidents when misused or when the user lacks knowledge or skill in using them. These tools should have smooth, firm handles, and the blades should be kept in good condition, because the screwdriver becomes useless and dangerous if the blade is broken. Always use a screwdriver with a blade that fits the screw to be turned. The blade of the screwdriver should be seated squarely against the bottom of the screw slot. Never hold the work in one hand and the screwdriver in the other, because the screwdriver may slip from the screw slot and cut the hand holding the work. Never use screwdrivers as substitutes for chisels or hammers or for purposes other than to turn screws.

The vise should be solidly mounted directly over the leg of the workbench on a two-inch plank. It is important that the vise be heavy enough for the work that is to be done. The solid jaw of the vise should extend at least one-half inch beyond the edge of the plank. The vise should be bolted onto the plank rather than be fastened with wood screws. Before opening the vise, be sure to have a firm hold on the object in the vise so that the object will not fall or fly off when the grip of the vise is released.

A Final Word

It is impossible to economize on tools and produce work that will give you the satisfaction to which the woodworker is entitled. It is far better to work with one plane, one saw, one chisel, and a few accessories, all of them good, honest steel, properly sharpened, than it is to have a cellar full of inadequate devices. A good hammer and a good free swing will drive a nail home straight and true. A tap with the nail set and the job is done, and done to stay. A few strokes with a plane, properly held, and your edge is square, smooth, and true. You have something from which to work. But without that good tool you have nothing. You cannot produce even the simplest bathroom shelf properly.

Whether you are sawing a thin board that requires no effort, or a large piece of timber, a good tool is essential. Properly treated, carefully kept sharp, a saw or a chisel, a plane or a brace and bit, will last a lifetime. It will always do good work.

Now with proper patience and care, there is no carpentry chore around the house you cannot undertake with the greatest confidence in the world.

Cut with the grain. Mark sharply and accurately with the point of a knife and a marking gauge. Keep your tools sharp. Do a little bit at a time. Nothing should be too much for you.

CHAPTER FOUR

From Plan to Product

Just as in most things you do that involve several steps, your first task in a woodworking project—if you want to avoid much waste of time—is to create a plan.

Never start to work until you have an exact note of shapes and dimensions and method of working. Even if you are merely making a simple shelf, you should put on paper a rough drawing of what you are going to make before you turn the first shaving. If you are "eye-minded," you will have no difficulty in drawing a little picture of the project and marking on it the measurements to fit the space for which you are designing it. If you are not "eye-minded," you can accomplish much the same result by listing the various pieces of wood in the project, with the dimensions you wish them to have when they are done.

Obviously, whatever you make must have a certain width and a certain length. It must have something to hold it in place: metal shelf brackets or wooden brackets that you make yourself. Your shelf must be a little wider than the brackets. There must be screws or nails to fasten the shelf to the bracket and to fasten the bracket to the wall. The brackets must take a certain position. They must go into solid wood, for they will not hold well in plaster. Tap the wall and locate the solid wood beams and the hollow places behind the plaster.

Settle all your problems of design in advance. You may add decorations to your shelf after it is ready to put up, such as chamfered corners, but changes in its basic design may result in a poor job and a great deal of extra work if they are made after the shelf is started.

The professional carpenter has a blueprint to guide him. It is the complete diagrammatic sketch, with dimensions, and when properly made, it contains all the information needed in his work.

The blueprint used by carpenters is a reproduction of a working drawing transferred from the original to a sensitized sheet of paper by means of exposure to light, and developed by being washed in plain water. The dark lines or objects in the original are white on the blueprint and the blank spaces are blue. Usually you will make your own plan for a home project, but often you will want to buy one or use one from a magazine.

A plan or blueprint is in a sense a picture of the structure to be built. This picture is made up of views—the front or side view, the top view, and the end view. These views are made up of the lines that are visible when the structure is viewed from the various positions. A front view consists of those lines that can be clearly seen if the observer views the structure from the front. The plan shows clearly all of the essential dimensions of the structure, and indicates the surface from which they are taken.

A professional uses several types of lines in a blueprint. "Working lines" represent the edges of surfaces and are somewhat heavier than the other lines on the drawing. These

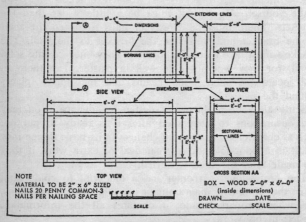

Blueprint of wood box.

lines may be straight or curved, depending upon the shape and view of the object.

Dotted lines are the same as working lines, except that the surface edge represented by a dotted line is hidden from sight when the object is viewed from the side shown.

Dimension lines show the size of any structure, or a part of it. These lines are light lines drawn between two working lines to show the distances between two points. To indicate the place where the measurement begins and ends, each end of the dimension line has an arrowhead, the point just touching the line where the measurement starts or stops. Somewhere in the length of a dimension line are placed numerals that give the exact distance between the arrow points. In some cases, where the distance is too small to use a dimension line between the working lines, the dimension lines are placed on the outside with the dimension shown at the end of one of the lines.

Extension lines are used where the dimension lines cannot readily be placed on the view; the working lines are lengthened or extended so that the dimension line may be drawn. The end of an extension line never touches the working line from which it extends.

Section lines are made in the form of a shaded area of a drawing, a series of parallel lines drawn close together at an angle to the working lines of the view. These lines represent what would be seen if that part of the view covered by such lines were cut through and a portion removed.

All plans have marginal data of various kinds. These include such items as the title or name of the object or structure represented, the scale, construction data. These are the "legend" which gives the plan a setting and explains the terms used.

Scale is the relative size of the pictured object compared with the actual size of the finished product. The length of the working lines in the plan has a definite and accurate proportion to the length of the line of the work itself. Thus, a full-scale drawing means that the lines on the blueprint represent the actual length of the object drawn. The scale $\frac{1}{4}'' = 1'$ means that $\frac{1}{4}$ inch in the drawing equals 1 foot in the actual structure. Although many plans note specific dimensions, some plans are made to scale and require that you measure on your own and compute the final dimensions.

To be able to read a plan is often as essential as to be able to read printed matter. The first step in reading a blueprint is to read the title and learn what is to be made. The title should give you a mental picture of the object and make clear what the lines represent.

The next step is to read the lettered data or legend at the lower edge of the paper. These notes give the type and size of certain materials and other pertinent data concerning the structure.

The scale is next considered. This is found in most cases at the bottom of the print, in the right-hand corner.

When the title, scale, and lettered data are thoroughly understood, study the views.

After the views have been mastered, the dimensions should be studied to obtain the size of the building and its different parts. These dimensions are placed on the dimension lines and are shown clearly.

Detail drawings are studied next to obtain the special information needed to frame certain parts of the project. Here the sections may be drawn to a larger scale in order to give a clearer detail of the section.

On some plans, special notes give information about the method of doing certain things.

After you have made a plan or studied the plan submitted, your next step is to make a list of materials—and perhaps tools—which you will need. This list includes details of the quantity, size, and purpose of all the things you will use—lumber, hardware, nails, sashes, doors, paint, and fixtures. Bills of materials are usually made out by the draftsman who makes the blueprint. At first glance, all this detail appears complicated and difficult to obtain. But such a table is built up easily from a study of the blueprint. Note carefully the steps in the process.

First the names of the various parts in the project are listed. Their dimensions are taken from the drawing and the quantity of each piece is determined. Finally all pieces of similar size are listed together and an estimate is made of such items as nails and screws.

Any project, large or small, should have a series of working steps specifically noted and checked so that operations follow with a minimum of waste motion and a minimum of redoing.

There is, to be sure, much more to be said about tools and working with wood, but at this point you will be itching to make something, not just read about it.

Let's start with a simple pilot project. You start, of course, with a sketch or blueprint. When all your pieces are cut to size, you check A:

1. *Dimensions.* Use rule, try square, or steel square. Check thickness over entire length.
2. *Shape and squareness.* Use try square and steel square.
3. *Joints.* Check by fitting the joints together individually. Try especially joints where more than two pieces come together.
4. *Position.* Check areas that are finished for inside and outside positions.
5. *Fit.* Make an actual mock-up, fitting each piece into its proper place. If necessary, clamp or tack some parts together.
6. Identify pieces as to position, especially if several pieces of stock are similarly shaped. Number joints in pairs— 1*a*, 1*b*, etc.
7. Locate hardware so that nails or screws that are not decorative are placed where they are least visible or can be conveniently countersunk.
8. Select hardware, including nails and screws, as to type, size, and shape.
9. Select and prepare glue and joints (not more than three pairs) to be set in the first operation.
10. Remove surplus glue and allow piece to dry. Then re-examine for glue droppings and joint firmness.
11. Recheck inside and outside angles and moving parts (drawers, doors, etc.).
12. Check all surfaces for dents, grooves, blemishes, and proper smoothness.

A working drawing, the first time you see one, looks like the scratching of a hen in wet sand. The easiest way to learn how to take anything off a working drawing is to sit down and make one, then to go on and build the article that you have designed.

Suppose, as an experiment, you were to make a little bookrack to hold this volume on your bench, as well as a catalogue of tools with the various tables of screw sizes, metric system, weights and measures, board measure, weights, etc. The simplest design is by far the most appropriate.

This bookrack has only seven pieces when it is done.

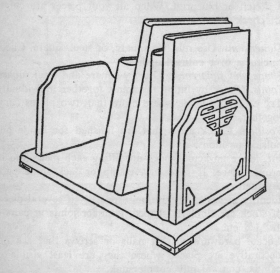

It will be easy to balance this design because a bookrack has two ends and a flat plate upon which the books stand. It balances automatically because the weight is evenly distributed throughout. It would also be a good idea to put feet on the bottom plate so it will stand up above your bench surface. Then you can put your fingers under the edge if you want to lift and move the whole thing.

How wide should you make it? The answer is easy. The average book is about 5 inches wide when it is closed. Therefore, if you make the plate 6 inches wide, it will accommodate almost any books you want to keep there. You won't want many books on your bench, so if your rack is 12 inches in overall length, that should be plenty. Since the bookrack base is to be 12 inches long, making it just half as wide puts it in splendid proportion, the proportion of 12 to 6—that is, 2 to 1. For some reason the human eye enjoys simple proportions—those that can be reduced to the relationship of 1 to 2, 1 to 3, 2 to 3, 3 to 4, and a few others.

It is very easy to decide the design of your bottom plate then. Make it 6 by 12 inches. Draw a rectangle on a piece of paper with these dimensions, as in the drawing.

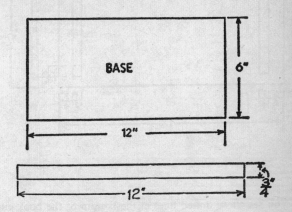

Remember the sizes in which wood comes from the lumber dealer—the 1-inch thickness, when dressed, is 13/16 inch. Allow a little for planing smooth, and we have ¾ inch, which will be convenient and plenty strong enough. Therefore, you have at once the side view of this bottom board. It looks like this:

The book ends themselves should be added to the base. They will be high enough if they extend 5 inches above the base. They need not be as thick as the base, so we will plan to plane them down to ½ inch thick.

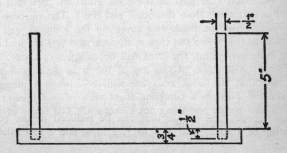

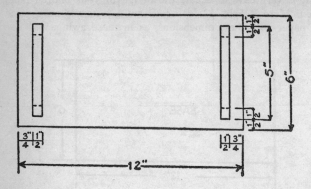

You see those dotted lines at the bottom of the book ends? They show the kind of joint between the book ends and the base. It is easy to make. It is easy to draw. It will be strong enough to hold your books.

The reason the lines are dotted is that you cannot see the joint when the bookrack is done, but on the drawing dotted lines should show that both these joints are there.

On the top view are the two book ends. Remember that when you look down on the bookrack from straight above, the book ends will become merely lines on top of the drawing, as on page 121.

Again you notice some dotted lines. They show the hidden joint between the book ends and the base. They also show that the tenon (the part of the book end that goes into the base) is narrower than the book end itself. The purpose of this is to have the book end cover up the joint as well as possible so that when the rack is all done and you are looking at it from any point, the joint will be completely concealed.

From the diagram at the top of the next page, you will see also that the book ends are square—always a pleasing proportion. Next is a complete front view of our bookrack.

Did you notice one thing not mentioned? The edges of the board are rounded. This is one of those fancy touches that one always uses one's own judgment about. Rounded edges

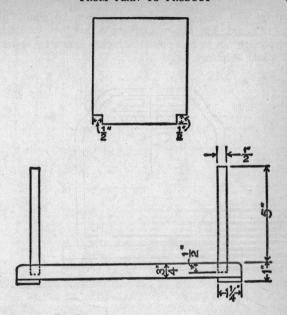

can be made by first chamfering with a plane, then rounding with sandpaper, or else with a little cornering tool, shown here, that is finger-shaped.

Edge rounded with cornering tool used only with the grain.

If you prefer a chamfer, draw that on your sketch.

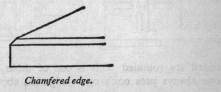

Chamfered edge.

Perhaps you have added feet. They can be plain little blocks of wood. The important thing is that they should be broad enough not to be tippy; 1¼ inches square by ¼ inch thick would be plenty.

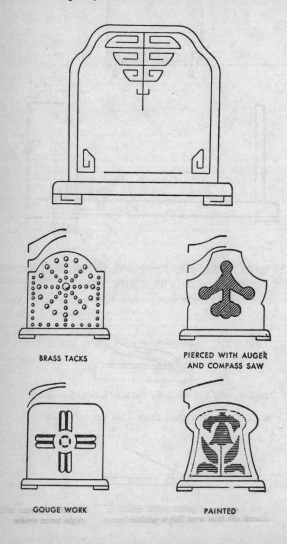

BRASS TACKS

PIERCED WITH AUGER
AND COMPASS SAW

GOUGE WORK

PAINTED

Now what can be done to decorate the ends? It would be fun to take a little saw and a chisel and arch the top. Several designs illustrated on page 120 show how a skilled workman might do it. You do not put these on your working drawing. You make a separate sketch.

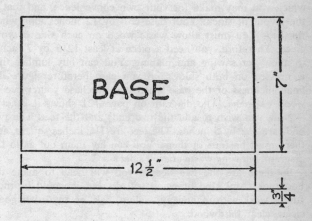

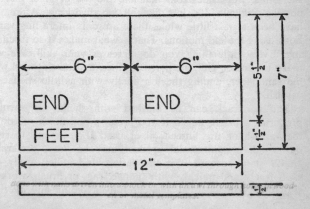

Having drawn this plan yourself, it is perfectly obvious that you can now work from the plan to the wood. In other words, you can now take it from the working drawing, and you can do a better job than you could if you had taken it from your imagination.

There is one more part of a working drawing, however, which you may make for your own convenience, and that is the layout of stock. Your base is 6 by 12 inches long when finished. You must allow waste wood on each side of your piece. Therefore, you need a piece at least 12½ by 7 inches to allow for sawing and planing. You can buy lumber that is dressed on both sides, and you can therefore figure the final thickness of the base when you purchase your piece of wood (¾ inch). The diagram on page 121 shows it exactly.

Now you wish to add the two ends and the feet. The two ends are 5½ by 5 inches. The feet are 1¼ inches square, and there must be four of them. You can lay them out as in the diagram, allowing waste at each side:

So there are the two boards you will need to make the bookrack. Any kind of wood will do, but it would be most fun to work with mahogany, walnut, oak, or any other good, clean, clear hardwood.

You are now ready to translate your diagram into wood. There it is all waiting for you. It must be planed, square, and to size—each and every piece, one piece at a time.

You are going to want to drive some brads through the feet into the base plate to hold them on. You must make the joints. But aside from that and the use of glue, there is nothing difficult. It's just like all woodworking. After you have been at it a little while, there are only interesting variations using the old motions. That is what makes it so fascinating. Every little thing you do increases your skill. We will make the joints, glue the parts together, and take a hand with the sandpaper, ending the job finally with a little shellac or varnish.

The bookrack can be finished with shellac or varnish, procuring a bright finish. If you prefer a dull finish rub down the varnish or use linseed oil or wax. If you want to stain the wood, a commercial product may be used, preferably an oil stain because it is the easiest to handle. Apply the stain freely and quickly with sponge, rag, or brush, working with the grain as usual and carefully avoiding any overlap.

As the color begins to dry, with a soft rag rub off any surplus stain not absorbed by the wood. This prevents the grain from becoming obscure or clouded. Cover the surface well, but do not apply the stain too lavishly.

Shellac is easily applied with a brush, and if either shellac or varnish is used, it should be rubbed down when thoroughly dry with very fine sandpaper before a second coat is put on. After a coat of shellac has been applied to seal the pores of the wood, ordinary floor wax can be used to produce a soft, dull finish.

And now, with the bookrack either mentally or actually completed, you have gone through much more of your apprenticeship than you may realize. If you have not merely read and have actually gone ahead with the work described, you have certainly learned the rudiments of reading a working drawing, and you have thought through every step of making an article that you had in mind.

CHAPTER FIVE

Finishing up the Project

When you have finished the end pieces and the plate, you are ready to lay out the joint. There is a problem, the mortise itself (the hole or slot the tenon fits into).

Holes should be bored for this mortise. This must be done accurately and carefully. In laying out joints, make the measurements with great accuracy and mark the joints with a knife line or a hard pencil well sharpened. Accurate work does not result from thick guidelines.

The first step in making this mortise is to bore a row of holes with an auger bit. These must be bored to a uniform depth. Some woodworkers regulate the depth of the holes by counting the turns of the bit brace, because the screw of an auger bit will pull the bit into the wood at a constant rate if it is held firmly against the wood. This method, however, is not very accurate. A simple contrivance is to bore a hole through a block of scrap wood, then saw the block to the proper length so that the bit protrudes only enough to bore the right distance through the hole. The most convenient method is to use a bit gauge, which automatically controls the depth of the hole.

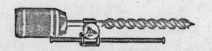

Auger bit with bit gauge.

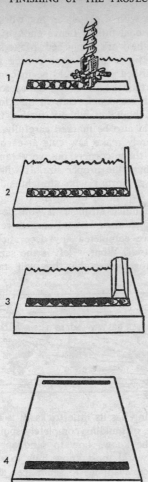

1. Remove waste wood with auger bit.

2. Cut ends with chisel and mallet.

3. Cut sides to line with the chisel.

4. Clean corners and bottom of mortise with chisel.

In cutting joints with a chisel, do not work exactly up to the lines until the final fitting. Leave enough edge to permit a perfect fit after the work is finished. Make sure which side of the line is the waste side before cutting the wood. The surfaces in the finished joint should be in contact with each other throughout their entire areas, so as to make strong, sightly joints. With reasonable care in marking, boring, and cutting, the joints should fit without further trimming.

The tenon should also be marked carefully. It is very easy to make. You merely make saw cuts at each lower corner. A chisel will dig these corners out very rapidly, and it is simple to make them the proper size. It will be a little bit difficult to make a mortise with straight sides and square corners. It is just a question of patient paring with a chisel. The joint will be much stronger if you do this carefully than if you let the sides or bottom corners remain rough.

You should have completed any decoration of the ends of the bookrack itself. What is left is the sandpapering and putting the parts together so that they will stay put.

SANDPAPER THIS WAY---NOT AS SHOWN BELOW

Even sandpapering has its little tricks. It is not uncommon to find a fine piece of molding completely spoiled by a workman who thinks he knows how to sandpaper—who thinks everybody in the world must know how to sandpaper. The same general principle applies to sandpaper as to any other cutting tool. It is easy to sandpaper with the grain. It is not only difficult but almost disastrous to the final finish if you sandpaper across the grain, because this will tear and roughen the surface fibers. If you are going to stain the piece, the entire job can be spoiled by sanding across the grain; the torn fibers of the wood will absorb more of the staining fluid than the rest of the wood, causing dark, unsightly spots and lines.

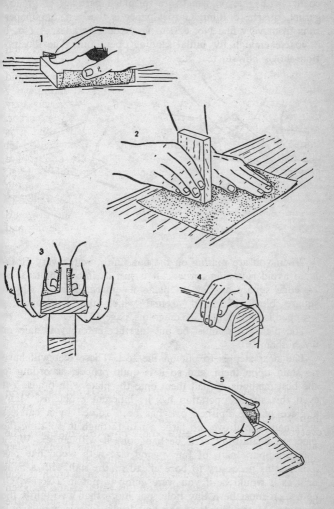

1. To sand a surface.
2. To sand the end of a small block.
3. Using a block to keep corners sharp.
4. To sand a rounded edge.
5. To sand a curved surface.

The best sandpaper is made of tough prepared paper coated with glue on which are sprinkled particles of graded garnet, quartz, or flint. Garnet paper is the best. Sandpaper runs from very fine No. 6/0 to very coarse grades. A No. 1 is coarse enough for initial sanding operations. The illustration shows how to tear it.

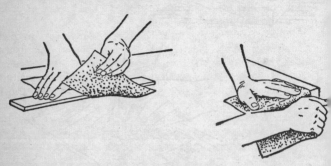

How to tear sandpaper.

When you are putting on the fine finish, watch very closely to avoid rounding corners. It is just as important to sand an edge square as it is to plane it square. That is why a square block of wood around which the sandpaper is wrapped is important. (See diagrams, page 127.)

The pieces now must be put together before you stain or finish them.

The next step is to put on the feet. These feet will have no stain upon them, and so it is quite proper, according to the best methods, to nail them onto the plate with brads. Yet even this simple operation has its inherent problems. Many a piece of fine finished oak has been ruined by a careless workman who drove too large a nail through it, splitting the piece as beautifully as if he had done it with an ax. When using ordinary nails of fairly good size with wood like oak it is just as necessary to bore ahead of the nail with a hand drill as it would be if you were going to put in a screw. Of course, it must be a tiny hole, not more than two-thirds the diameter of the shank of the nail itself. In this case a hole will ensure that you do not split the feet.

Even those little brads should be put in carefully and in the right place, not too near the edges and not driven in straight. They should be slanted (or "toed"). They then act as cleats or dovetails and will hold beautifully.

It is equally important that the feet be placed squarely on each corner so that they form an integral part of the finished design. (See the drawing on page 121.)

A much better job of putting on the feet will result if you not only nail them but also glue them. The gluing, of course, must be done before the nailing.

Glue is one of the cabinetmaker's secrets for producing good work. Good glue is so strong that, when properly used, it is frequently much stronger than the wood itself. Ordinary liquid glue is very convenient because it is always ready for use. Many professional cabinetmakers prefer glue that has to be "cooked." Recently new casein and resin dry-powder glues have been made that can easily be prepared with cold water. They are most satisfactory and easy to use. Put a thorough thin coating of glue on the joints, then firmly fasten these joints together with good clamps. Before it sets, wipe off any glue that shows and give the joint plenty of time to dry. (If you want to use hot glue, full information will be found in Chapter 8.) After the glue has hardened (twenty-four hours should be allowed), it is very important to go over the work again to remove any surplus exposed glue and to finish with fine sandpaper.

When gluing is done, you have only staining and polishing to do—one of those little jobs that, with reasonable care, you can accomplish very quickly with a good deal of fun. It is a modern idea to finish wood as naturally as possible. You have undoubtedly noticed that some furniture is advertised as having a "natural wood finish." This does not mean, however, that you can leave the wood as it is when you finish sandpapering.

A well-executed piece of woodwork displaying the natural color and sheen of the wood, with its smoothly finished surfaces and tightly fitted joints, has a distinction and charm peculiarly its own. To the eye of a good workman, however, an article is not finished until something has been done to preserve the beauty of the wood. The fine color of a freshly cut piece of wood soon fades as the action of light, settling dust, and dirt from handling gradually mar the natural beauty. Then too, the absorption of moisture and subsequent drying out are detrimental to the wood and to the joints.

Bare wood, when washed, soon takes on a grayish, parched look and the grain becomes rough and splintery. Many woods do not fully show their beautiful color and grain until they have undergone a process of finishing.

There may be many colors in one piece of work because of the natural variations in the wood or the use of different kinds of wood for the several parts. In such cases, it may be desirable to equalize the different colors. Decide beforehand some arrangement for the colors that will make a pleasing distribution.

Finishing a piece of wood serves two purposes—its preservation and the enhancement of its beauty. All work should carry out both of these ideas, but unfortunately in many cases preservation is favored to the exclusion of beauty. See Chapter 17 for details on finishing techniques.

CHAPTER SIX

Choosing the Wood

For your first project there was no problem about the wood you wanted to use: a clear piece of easily worked lumber prefinished on both sides. But as you grow more sophisticated in the projects you undertake, you will want to use more knowledge in selecting lumber.

The wood you select will make a great deal of difference in both the difficulty of the work and the appearance of the finished project. It is also the biggest single cost factor.

Whatever wood you buy, make certain that it is well seasoned and dried. Unseasoned wood will warp, shrink, check, and generally lessen the worth of the finished product. Make sure that the cut is straight and there are no knots—unless you want to have them. For some purposes, as finishing a basement, knotty pine is considered attractive; but for others, the possibility of a knothole can be catastrophic.

The selection of wood involves several factors, all of which will affect its cost. First decide what kind of wood you want from the types available from your lumber dealer. The hardwoods are more difficult to work, tend to be more expensive, but generally result in a better-looking and sturdier finished product. Among these woods are ash, birch, black walnut, chestnut, mahogany, maple, oak, and yellow pine. The softwoods are easier to work and easier to finish, and are usually used for more informal purposes. Among these are basswood, cedar, cypress, poplar, redwood, white pine, and white spruce.

All of us know that the fibers in a tree vary in thickness and fullness. Fibers are elongated tree cells that run vertically, tapering upward as the tree narrows. They are held together by a resin called lignin. In softwood trees the fibers may be ⅛ inch in length; in hardwood trees they are as little as 1/24 inch. The diameters of fibers are about 1/100 inch. Surrounding the fibers are bands of cells called wood rays, or medullary rays, which form the pattern of rings from the center of the tree. The thickness of the cell walls varies in woods and is largely responsible for the difference in weight and strength of the lumber the tree provides. In general, woods are classified commercially as:

Hard	and	Soft
alder		cedar
ash		cypress
aspen		Douglas fir
basswood		fir
beech		hemlock
birch		juniper
buckeye		larch
butternut		pine
cherry		redwood
cottonwood		spruce
elm		tamarack
hackberry		yew
hickory		
locust		
magnolia		
maple		
oak		
sycamore		
walnut		
willow		
yellow poplar		

However, there is no real measure of hardness that divides these groups. In fact, the most general classification puts coniferous (evergreen) trees into the softwood class and deciduous trees (those with seasonal leaves) into the hardwood. The fir is a hard softwood and basswood is a soft hardwood.

Another way of classifying wood depends on its closeness to the bark. The outer layers, and newer growth, are called sapwood; the inner layers, or older portions, are called heartwood. The strength of both types from the same tree are equal; but sapwood is more porous and can absorb chemicals better, and heartwood resists outdoor decay better. This may be important if untreated wood is to be used for outdoor work.

The rings of a tree indicate its annual growth, and also the growth in each season. In general, trees that grow rapidly (and thus have wide rings) produce timber that is not as strong as a tree that grows slowly. The fast-growing tree produces a coarse grain, the slow-growing tree a close or fine grain. These refer to the cross-section grain of the tree, of course. The grain made by the vertical fibers is referred to as the straight grain—the one that is most usually worked in carpentry.

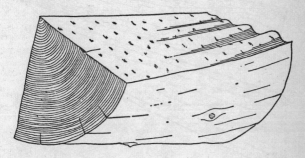

Spiral grain of varying or fluctuating slope indicated by split radial surface.

Coarse-grained woods that produce a rough-textured surface include oak, walnut, and chestnut. Fine-grained woods that make a compact, smooth surface include maple, birch, and pine.

Most lumber used at home presents a flat-grain surface. For burl design effects, a cross grain can be used. A further distinction in the way wood is cut is reflected in the grain pattern. When the timber is sawed so that the annual rings form an angle of 45 degrees or more with the wide faces of the board, the term *quarter-sawed* is applied to hardwoods, and *vertical* or *edge grain* to softwoods. When the angle is less than 45 degrees, the term *plain-sawed* is applied to hardwoods and *flat grain* to softwoods.

Lumber contains considerable water when it is cut. As it dries, it shrinks and warps in proportion to the moisture lost. In the process of seasoning the lumber, the surface of green woods dries more quickly than the inside of the wood, and tends to shrink more in the direction of the rings (the width

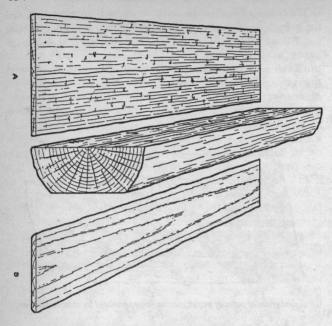

A, quarter-sawed and B, plain-sawed boards as cut from a log.

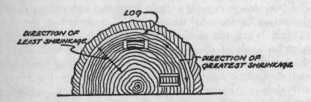

The shrinkage of wood from end to end is negligible, but in cross section it shrinks approximately one-half as much at right angles to the annual rings as it does parallel to them. Edge or vertical grain flooring, if not properly seasoned when installed, will shrink approximately only one-half the amount of similar unseasoned flat-grain flooring. The above illustration shows in an exaggerated manner the results of seasoning in different parts of a log.

and thickness of most boards). It is best to buy seasoned lumber from which most of the moisture has been evaporated; and when raw lumber is used, allowance should be made for this type of shrinkage.

Just as no two trees are exactly alike, no two pieces of lumber are exactly alike. Lumber has two types of impairment: defects, which impair strength or usefulness; and blemishes, which impair appearance. Among the blemishes are pockets of bark; a crack in the length, called a check; a split, called a shake; a twisting of the fibers, called a cross grain; fungi or decay; holes; knots; pitch pockets; spongy tissue, called pith; cup-shaped breaks caused by the wind, called wind shakes; edge defects, called wanes; and, of course, warping.

All these factors enter into the grade of lumber. For most purposes, however, the following grades of lumber will be used by the home carpenter.

Firsts and Seconds, or 1 and 2 Clear: Highest quality, almost free of blemishes, used for fine cabinetwork.

C grade: Has some pin knots and minor imperfections. Often one side has no blemishes.

D grade: This is the lowest grade suitable for finishing. It is a good all-round wood for a workshop, for natural-finish shelves, or built-in furniture.

No. 1: A good general-purpose wood. It may have sound, smooth knots up to about 2 inches, but takes paint well.

No. 2: An all-round utility grade. It is used for flooring or knotty paneling, has other blemishes, including larger knots, sometimes loose.

No. 3: Occasionally has knotholes, a limited amount of pitch, and season checking. It is used for rough jobs (shelves for garage or workshop).

No. 4: The lowest board grade you are likely to use. It is used for temporary structures.

No. 5: The poorest quality. It has many imperfections, is used for crating, etc.

The next step is to select the size. Some are standard. Special sizes may not be available or may be very costly.

Buying Lumber

For ordinary lumber, prices are figured by the board foot. A board foot is the amount of lumber in a piece 1 inch thick,

Standard widths and thicknesses of rough and surfaced yard lumber

Lumber described as nominal—		Actual dimensions when surfaced shall not be less than—	Actual dimensions when rough dry* shall not be less than—
	Inches	*Inches*	*Inches*
	1	25/32	29/32
	1-1/4	1-1/16	1-5/32
	1-1/2	1-5/16	1-13/32
	1-3/4	1-7/16	1-9/16
Thickness...................	2	1-5/8	1-3/4
	2-1/2	2-1/8	2-1/4
	3	2-5/8	2-3/4
	4	3-5/8	3-3/4
	3	2-5/8	2-3/4
	4	3-1/2	3-5/8
	5	4-1/2	4-5/8
	6	5-1/2	5-5/8
	7	6-1/2	6-5/8
Width of finish...............	8	7-1/4	7-3/8
	9	8-1/4	8-3/8
	10	9-1/4	9-3/8
	11	10-1/4	10-3/8
	12	11-1/4	11-3/8
	3	2-5/8	2-3/4
	4	3-5/8	3-3/4
	5	4-5/8	4-3/4
	6	5-5/8	5-3/4
Width of boards and dimension.................	7	6-5/8	6-3/4
	8	7-1/2	7-5/8
	9	8-1/2	8-5/8
	10	9-1/2	9-5/8
	11	10-1/2	10-5/8
	12	11-1/2	11-5/8

*In a shipment of rough dry lumber 20 per cent may be not more than 1/32 inch under the thicknesses shown.

1 foot wide, and 1 foot long. A piece 1 inch by 6 inches by 6 feet will contain 3 board feet. But lumber only ½ inch thick is charged as if a full inch because the board had to be milled down. Because drying and milling reduce the thickness of lumber, 1-inch lumber is really 25/32 inch thick. From 2 to 6 inches, the actual dimension is ⅜ inch less than the expressed dimension. (A 2-by-6-inch is really 1⅝ inches thick and 5⅝ inches wide.) Boards 8 inches wide and wider lose ½ inch.

Some lumber, such as shingles and laths, comes in bunches.

Kindling wood is usually sold by the bushel or by the truck-load. Molding, poles, and railings are sold by the running foot. Windows and doors are ready-made and are priced according to size and type. Plywood and wallboard are sold by square foot or panel.

When ordering three boards of first-quality white oak, 1 inch thick, 6 inches wide, and 12 feet long, smooth on both sides and on both edges, you ask for 3-1x6-12-Fas-Wh. OakS4S. "Fas" means firsts and seconds, the top grade in hardwood. The "S4S" means surfaced on all four sides. Lumberyards usually have a power saw that can bevel edges of heavy lumber and rip to specified width when stock sizes won't fit and to exact lengths. Request this if your job calls for a large amount of cutting.

After the requirements have been determined, it is relatively easy to check the properties of the different woods to see whether these requirements would be met.

Modified Woods

Modified woods are now an important material for home carpenters.

Plywood is made of thin plies or veneers glued together with the grains at right angles. In three-ply plywood there is a center core with two "faces" of veneer. Five-ply panels have a core, two inner plies called crossbands, and a veneer surface. Plywood provides equal strength in width and length of the panel and greater resistance to splitting and moisture changes. Another marked advantage is the extra width that is available.

Laminated wood and paper-faced plywood are built up of wood, or layers of wood and plastic, or wood and paper held together with resins treated under pressure. These provide interesting patterns and stain-resistant finishes useful for sink tops and highly decorative work. Some of the resin-impregnated finishes resemble fine veneers, inlays, and interesting designs in a variety of colors.

Wood-fiber boards and plaster boards are widely used for insulation, ceilings, and interior walls. Some are flexible, others semi-rigid.

Fiberboards are stiff panels made of waste materials—cork, sawdust, paper, straw, corn stalks, and the like. Made like paper in a water suspension, they are available in all

BROAD CLASSIFICATION OF WOODS ACCORDING TO CHARACTERISTICS AND PROPERTIES

A, among the woods relatively high in the particular respect listed;
B, among the woods intermediate in the particular respect listed;
C, among the woods relatively low in the particular respect listed.

Kind of wood	Hardness	Weight, dry	Freedom from shrinkage	Freedom from warping	Ease of working	Paint holding	Nail holding	Decay resistance of heartwood	Proportion of heartwood	Amount of figure	Freedom from odor and taste (dry)	Bending strength	Stiffness	Strength as a post	Toughness	Number of knots	Size of knots	Number of pitch defects	Size of pitch defects	Number of other defects	Size of other defects	Farm or Home	Commercial
Ash: White	A	A	B	B	C		A	C	C	A	A	A	A	A	A	C	B	None		B	B	Handles, implements	Handles, vehicle parts, Fixtures, furniture parts
Basswood	C	C	C	B	A		C	C	C	C	A	C	B	C	C	C	B	None		C	C	Woodenware	Woodenware, flooring,
Beech	A	A	C	C	C		A	C	B	B	C	A	A	B	A	B	B	None		A	A	Woodenware, containers	Woodenware, flooring, furniture
Birch, yellow	A	A	B	B	C		A	C	C	B	A	A	A	B	A	C	A	None		B	B	Millwork, furniture	Millwork, furniture
Cedar: Western red	C	C	A	A	A	A	C	A	A	B	C	C	C	A	C	A	A	None		C	C	Shingles, siding, posts, and poles	Poles, shingles, siding
Eastern red	A	B	A	A	C		B	A	B	B	B	B	C	A	B	C	C	None		C	C	Posts	Chests, pencils
Cherry	B	B	B	C	B		B	B	B	C	B	B	B	B	B	A	C	None		C	C	Furniture	Electrotype blocks
Chestnut	C	C	B	B	A		C	A	B	B	B	C	C	C	C	C	B	None		A	B	Poles, posts, trim	Caskets, poles, core stock
Cottonwood	C	C	C	C	A		C	C	C	C	B	C	C	C	B	C	B	None		C	C	Wagon boxes, containers	Boxes, cases, and furniture parts
Cypress, southern	B	B	B	B	A	A	B	A	B	A	A	B	C	B	B	C	B	None		B	B	Silos, tanks, construction	Greenhouses, tanks, construction
Douglas fir	A	A	B	B	C	C	B	B	A	C	A	A	A	A	A	B	B	B	B	B	B	Construction	Construction
Elm: Soft	C	B	C	B	C	B	A	B	B	B	A	A	C	B	A	B	B	None		A	A	Cheese boxes	Containers
Rock	A	A	C	C	C	B	B	B	B	B	A	A	B	B	B	B	C	None		B	A	Implements	Cooperage
Fir: Balsam	C	C	B	B	B	B	C	C	C	B	A	C	C	B	C	A	B	None		B	B	Light construction	Pulpwood
White	C	C	B	B	B	B	C	C	B	B	A	C	B	C	B	B	C	None		B	A	Light construction	Light construction, pulpwood
Gum, red	B	B	C	C	A	C	B	B	B	B	B	B	B	B	B	C	B	None		C	C	Fruit and vegetable boxes	Furniture, millwork, containers

Hackberry	Furniture.	Automobile bodies.
Hemlock: Eastern	Construction.	Construction.
Western	Construction.	Construction.
Hickory: True	Handles, Implements.	Implements, handles, sporting goods.
Pecan	Wagon and buggy parts.	Furniture, automobile bodies.
Larch, western	Construction.	Construction.
Locust: Black	Fence posts.	Insulator pins.
Honey	Implements, flooring.	Flooring, furniture, machine parts.
Maple: Hard		Furniture.
Soft	Fuel.	Furniture.
Oak: Red	Implement parts, construction.	Furniture, flooring.
White	Implement parts, posts, construction.	Cooperage, furniture, flooring.
Pine: Ponderosa	Millwork, light construction	Millwork, construction, boxes.
Southern yellow	Construction.	Construction.
Northern white	Millwork, siding.	Millwork, containers.
Western white	Millwork, siding.	Millwork, containers.
Sugar pine	Millwork.	Patterns, millwork.
Poplar, yellow	Millwork.	Millwork, furniture.
Redwood	Silos, tanks, construction.	Tanks, construction.
Spruce: Eastern	Construction.	Pulpwood, musical instruments.
Sitka	Ladders, construction.	Airplanes, construction.
Engelmann	Construction.	Construction.
Sycamore	Baskets and boxes.	Boxes and crates, millwork.
Tupelo	Fruit and vegetable boxes.	Factory flooring, boxes and crates.
Walnut	Furniture.	Furniture, millwork.

[1] Exclusive of the all-heartwood grades that are available in special order in birch, cedar, cypress, Douglas fir, red gum, southern yellow pine, redwood, and walnut.

[2] Conflicting opinion and absence of adequate test data preclude a definite rating; the authors recommend against relying on high decay resistance when this wood is used untreated.

thicknesses from 1/16 inch to ½ inch. Highly compressed, they are strong and rigid and can be made weather-resistant.

Some plastics made of wood or wood products are used as substitutes for hardwood mixed with synthetic resins. They are widely used for tool handles, toys, machine parts and the like.

CHAPTER SEVEN

About Putting Pieces Together

Most amateurs never expect to get much beyond using a plane, a saw, a screwdriver, and a hammer with reasonable skill. But if in the shop you will follow the various processes that have been described on previous pages, you will undoubtedly find that you can do much better than you supposed, and that if you put your mind to it, you can become a craftsman merely by following the methods professionals have learned through the years.

Already you have stepped beyond the ordinary householder by working with tools in a consciously proper way. Now you are going to enter into the department of joinery. The moment you have put two pieces together—jointed two members—you have stepped into this department, although of course, in its proper meaning *joinery* refers to the inside work of constructing and installing the fittings of a house. Essentially, when you have learned to make the joinings described here, you will have passed a milestone in your capacity for fine carpentry.

All connections between pieces of timber are classified either as splices or joints. Splices are connections between two pieces of wood that extend end to end in the same line; they are widely used in heavy construction. Joints are connections between two pieces of timber that come together at an angle; they are used in making any work of real craftsmanship.

Joints are classified into a number of types, the most common of which are square or butt joint, plain, oblique, and mitre joints. Each of these is used for a specific job. The home carpenter should be familiar with each type and know when and where to use each to secure best results.

Splices

A splice is designed to connect two or more pieces of stock in such a way that the joining will be as strong as a single piece of wood of equivalent size would be. Since the splice that is efficient for compression is usually worthless for tension or bending, each splice must be made to meet the requirements for which it is to be used. The home carpenter should know about each type of splice and be able to make and apply each properly.

Splices for compression are designed either to support weight or to exert pressure. There are several types of splice for compression; the fished splice and the halved splice are the most common. Compression splices will stand compression only.

The fished splice is made when two pieces of stock are squared at their ends and butted together. Two short pieces called fishplates, or scabs, are fastened one on each side of the splice. These short pieces serve to keep the splice straight and prevent buckling. The term "fishplates" usually refers to metal plates used for splicing. These plates are best fastened with bolts or screws. Wooden plates, commonly called scabs, can be fastened with bolts, nails, or ring connectors. For best results, the nails are staggered and driven at an angle away from the splice. Too many nails or nails that are too large weaken the splice.

The halved splice is better for direct compression, and when combined with fishplates or scabs can be used where some tension is required. This splice is made by notching each piece halfway to any desired length, and placing the two halved sections together. A splice can be fastened either by nailing or bolting only the halved sections together, or by adding fishplates or scabs. The latter method of fastening is recommended and should be used when the material is available.

There are several types of tension splices. Of these, the most common and simplest is the square splice. These splices are made to resist tension and are used in trusses, braces, and joints, where the material available is too short.

The square splice is a modification of the compression halved splice, but it has an extra notch to keep it from slipping. More time is required to make this joining, but if properly made, it is very efficient. When the splice is fastened by a fishplate or scab with bolts or nails, its strength is greatly increased.

Sometimes a piece of stock subjected to a bending stress must be spliced. When a horizontal piece of stock supports a weight, the upper part is under compression and this has

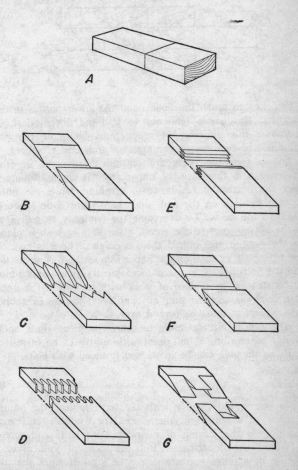

End-to-end-grain joints: A, End butt; B, plain scarf; C, serrated scarf; D, finger; E, Onsrud; F, hooked scarf; G, double-slope scarf.

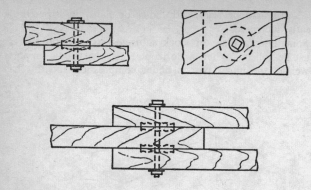

a tendency to crush the fibers, and the lower part is in tension and this has a tendency to pull the fibers apart. To overcome this difficulty, a splice must be made that will combine the features of compression and tension splices.

To do this, the parts are scarfed together as in other splices, but in this case the upper piece is cut off square to offer the maximum resistance to crushing, while the under piece is beveled on the end, since here there is no tendency to crush the stock. To overcome the tendency to pull apart at the bottom part of the wood, a fishplate or scab is placed on the bottom and bolted there securely. There is no need for a fishplate or scab on the upper side as there is no tension and the bolts hold it in place. Occasionally such a splice must be constructed in a piece of stock with tension in the upper part, such as overhanging or cantilever beams. In such a case the splice must be turned over.

Where it is not desirable to scarf the pieces in a splice subject to tension, a butt joint with fishplates or extra-long scabs on the side can be made and fastened with bolts.

Joints

No one would dignify with the term *joinery* the nailing together of a couple of members. Nor would a craftsman regard even the joining of members with bolts and screws as within the department. But the moment you make a mortise or a mitre you are doing the kind of work that the joiner regards as peculiarly his. The cabinetmaker, into whose

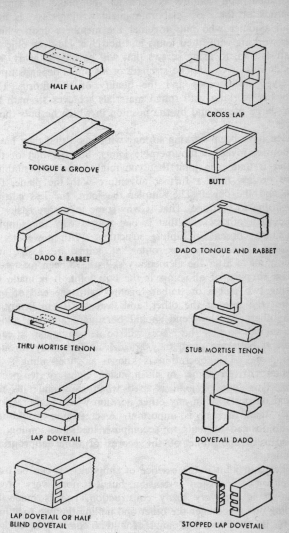

HALF LAP

CROSS LAP

TONGUE & GROOVE

BUTT

DADO & RABBET

DADO TONGUE AND RABBET

THRU MORTISE TENON

STUB MORTISE TENON

LAP DOVETAIL

DOVETAIL DADO

LAP DOVETAIL OR HALF
BLIND DOVETAIL

STOPPED LAP DOVETAIL

department you venture as soon as you make the simple bookrack or the most elaborate inlaid writing desk, is first of all a joiner who puts together the members upon which he is working with fitted joints and hot glue. He even objects, as an artisan, to using screws that will be hidden away. He uses dowels of wood. The strength of his joints depends upon the type he chooses and the quality of the fitting. The carpenter working with rough materials achieves strength by using large pieces and by the position in which he puts those pieces.

Men have been working so long with wood that they have, of course, invented innumerable joints. But the fact of the matter is that each joint that you might attempt is nothing more or less than a further adventure with the plane, the saw, and the chisel. The simpler the joint, the less cutting and fitting to be done. That is why some joints are easier to make than others, and that is one reason why the simpler joints are chosen for simple structures. With power tools, however, particularly the router, all joints are easily and quickly made after the elementary skills have been mastered.

The simplest of all joints is the butt joint. It is made by placing two pieces of timber together with the end of one against the side of the other, and fastening them firmly to each other. The butt end should be square and the joined side smooth so that the pieces will be perpendicular to each other. If nails are used, they are driven diagonally through both pieces. This operation is known as "toe-nailing"; the nails are driven home, or flush, using eight- or ten-penny nails. This type of joint is used when caps and sills are placed on posts, or in any other position where compression, rather than tension, is important. A craftsman would use dowels instead of nails to accomplish the same joining, or would rely upon one of the scores of other appropriate techniques.

The plain joint is the essence of simplicity. It can be used for either compression or tension, but it is not a very strong joint. It is for very hasty construction, and is made by lapping one piece over the other and nailing the two together. There is no prescribed angle for this connection, and it requires no square ends or straight edges. When 2-by-4's are joined in this way, about 5 ten- or sixteen-penny nails are sufficient; too many nails will weaken it.

An oblique joint is made when two pieces of stock do not meet at right angles. Bracing is a typical application for this joint. One piece is cut at an angle to fit the other and

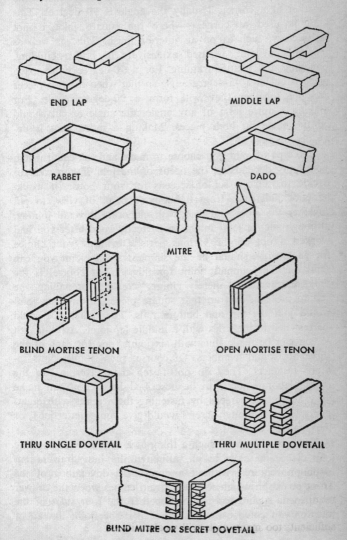

END LAP

MIDDLE LAP

RABBET

DADO

MITRE

BLIND MORTISE TENON

OPEN MORTISE TENON

THRU SINGLE DOVETAIL

THRU MULTIPLE DOVETAIL

BLIND MITRE OR SECRET DOVETAIL

they are nailed securely. The joint depends entirely upon the size of timber used. Here too, avoid using too many nails.

A mitre is a joint between two pieces of timber that come together at a corner. Usually the angle is 90 degrees. This joint is used at corners where the square joint is not satisfactory, such as on an interior finish. This, as well as the oblique joint, is used extensively in bridge building, paneling, and picture framing. For a 90-degree mitre, each piece is cut at a 45-degree angle so that when the two pieces are put together they will form a 90-degree angle. For making a mitre joint of any angle, the angle of cut should be the same on both pieces. Making a mitre joint is described on page 159.

The type of joint you choose to make and the detail which you apply depends on the needs of the job. If you were to decide to make a set of screens for your house, it would be poor judgment, from the joiner's point of view, to put together the stiles and rails with elaborate dovetail joining, although such a joint might be perfectly good after you had worked it out on the various parts. Obviously your choice for such work should be the simplest strong joint you can think of. The simplest joint for this job, of course, is the butt joint made by merely gluing, screwing, or nailing one square piece against another square piece. An end lap joint would join the top and bottom rails. The center rail could be fastened to the stiles with a middle lap joint. A full-length screen can be made thus with six joints, one for each of the three horizontal members. Of course, such simple joints require fasteners. They do not fasten themselves, as do the more elaborate joints to be described here. You can make very acceptable screens by fastening these joints with eight-penny nails (although screws would give you a better job), or they can be doweled.

You can also make such a thing as a drawer without using any elaborate joints at all, although the best drawer construction requires, without a doubt, the dovetailing of the front board on which so much strain comes when the drawer is opened. Again, for putting together the four sides of the drawer you could use a plain nailed rabbet joint instead of the elaborate dovetail.

The moment, however, you want to make a drawer that is a real drawer, you are faced with the necessity of making a dovetail corner. You can use dowel pins to hold the two ends of the drawer to the front board—and that will give you a workmanlike joint. It will be quite strong and much easier to make than the dovetail. It requires only the usual careful fitting of this simple joint and the insertion of three or four dowel pins. Glue, of course, should also be used in putting this joint together.

As a matter of fact the dowel-pin method, which is much stronger than nailing and much more acceptable in all furniture than either nailing or screwing, is perfectly easy.

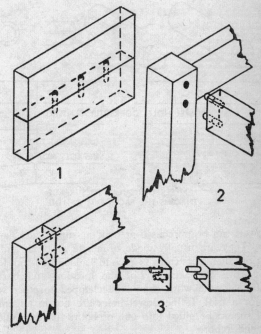

1. *Dowels used to strengthen long jointed edges.*
2. *As a substitute for mortises and tenons in the legs and rails of chairs and tables.*
3. *To join stiles and rails in frames and where ends are squarely butted together.*

Dowels are round wooden pegs cut a trifle shorter than the sum of the depth of each of the two holes into which they are set. Each of the dowel pins is slightly chamfered with a knife or dowel sharpener to prevent binding when they are forced into place. Usually there is also a little V-groove cut in a dowel pin with a knife or saw the entire length of the peg to permit the escape of excessive glue and imprisoned air when the dowel is driven in. Such a little groove prevents splitting the piece upon which you are working.

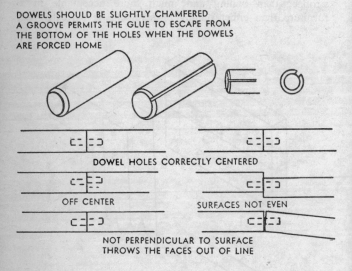

DOWELS SHOULD BE SLIGHTLY CHAMFERED
A GROOVE PERMITS THE GLUE TO ESCAPE FROM
THE BOTTOM OF THE HOLES WHEN THE DOWELS
ARE FORCED HOME

DOWEL HOLES CORRECTLY CENTERED

OFF CENTER   SURFACES NOT EVEN

NOT PERPENDICULAR TO SURFACE
THROWS THE FACES OUT OF LINE

Dowels can be purchased at building-supply and hardware stores. They are usually made of maple or birch and come in various diameters from ¼ inch to ¾ inch in 3-foot lengths.

To prove the accuracy of the location and boring of dowel holes, the work should be clamped together without glue for a trial. If the dowel holes are not in alignment, a dowel should be glued into one or both; you then cut it off flush and rebore.

To make a dowel butt joint (illustration page 151) proceed as follows: gauge a line along the middle of the end of one piece parallel to the face, and a little way down each edge so that it may be located when covered up.

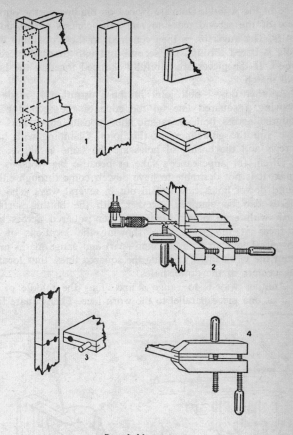

Doweled butt joints.

1. Pieces marked so that they can be clamped together and dowel holes
   correctly centered, bored in both at one time.
2. Boring dowel holes.
3. Holes bored ready to glue.
4. Method of clamping together while boring.

Then gauge a line parallel to the edge on both faces of
the second piece. A hand screw is clamped to the first piece
with the side of the screw even with the marked end of the
wood. This in turn is clamped to the second piece, with the
ends of the line on the first piece matching the line on one

face of the second. Dots are placed on the line on the outside face of the second piece to mark the centers of the dowel holes. The auger bit is then centered on these dots and each hole is bored through the second and into the first piece of wood. If the pieces are carefully clamped together the holes will match.

Another dowel butt joint in the illustration is made by drawing a squared line on the edge of the second piece, squared across both faces and the opposite edge. This will give you the guidelines for this joint. Clamping with hand screws and the boring of holes are the same as above.

Often, for appearance's sake or because the wood is too thick, it is not desirable to have dowels come through either. Blind dowel holes can be laid out in several ways. The two pieces can be clamped together with the butting surfaces flush with each other. Lines are then squared across both surfaces at the same time, showing the locations of the dowels. They can then be taken apart and gauge marks made from the work faces, crossing the squared lines, thus locating the centers of the dowel holes.

Another way is to gauge a line along the middle of the end of one piece parallel to the work face. Then square lines

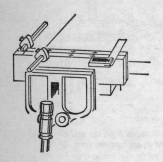

Centers for dowel holes can be marked by placing two pieces of wood together, edges even, work face out. Square lines across both pieces the required distance from the ends. Set the gauge in order to locate the crossing lines, showing the distance of the holes from the edges.

For accuracy in locating the bit, the center of boring holes should be carefully sunk with the point of a scratch awl.

across the end, square to the work face, the correct distance from the work edge. Where these lines cross are the centers for the dowel holes. A line is squared or gauged on the second piece to correspond to the center line gauged on the end of the first piece. The arris (corner) of the piece is matched to this line with the first piece held the correct distance from the end. The location of the squared lines is then transferred to the line on the second piece with an awl, knife, or sharp pencil, as shown on this page.

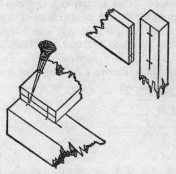

Centers for dowel holes can be located by marking them on end of the rail with gauge and square, then on the legs, gauging the distance from the edge with the rail held in place and matching this line. The centers are marked off on the line on the leg. The awl makes a good hole for centering a bit.

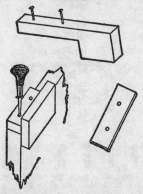

Where many dowel holes are to be marked, similarly spaced, it can be done with nails driven into a block or with an awl through holes in wooden or metal templates.

If many pieces are to be marked alike, it will save time and result in more accurate work if a wood or metal template (a pattern) or marker is made.

After setting out the centers for the holes, they should be carefully bored with an auger bit, square to the surface of the wood. A bit gauge can be used to regulate the depth of the holes.

There is a tool, the doweling jig, designed especially for this work. (Recommended: Stanley No. 59.) It enables the user to bore dowel holes in the edge or end of work with ease and accuracy. It will take material up to 3 inches thick. It is an excellent bit guide for mortising.

The pieces are clamped together and lines squared across the edges, or ends, as the case may be. The instructions with the illustrations show clearly how this tool is operated.

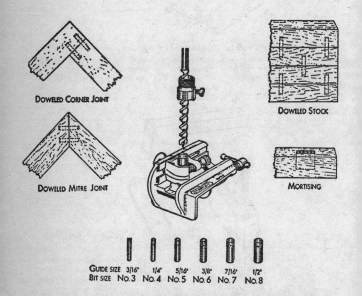

DOWELED CORNER JOINT

DOWELED MITRE JOINT

DOWELED STOCK

MORTISING

GUIDE SIZE	3/16"	1/4"	5/16"	3/8"	7/16"	1/2"
BIT SIZE	No. 3	No. 4	No. 5	No. 6	No. 7	No. 8

Stanley Doweling Jig No. 59

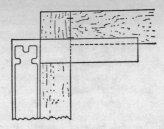

1. Indicate on face side a center line for any number of dowels desired.

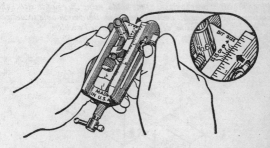

2. Select a suitable size dowel for your wood and the same size guide. Secure the bevel end up, in slide with bottom of guide practically flush with under side of the guide.

3. Adjust the slide, aligning the index line for the guide selected at the proper graduation to bring the center of the hole the distance desired from the face side of the wood. An index line is given on the slide for each guide or bit size. Example: For a ⅜-inch guide, adjust the slide to bring the index line No. 6 to the desired graduation mark. If the dowel is to be in the middle of a 1-inch piece of wood, adjust the slide to the ½-inch graduation mark and fasten securely with thumbscrew.

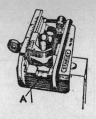

4. *Place the jig on one of the pieces of stock with the fence next to the face side of the wood, and bring the center line A in alignment with the mark on the wood, illustrated in No. 1. Clamp the jig securely.*

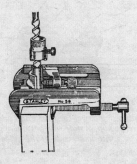

5. *Place the bit of proper size into the guide, using care not to strike the cutting edges of the bit against the guide. Bore each hole to desired depth, using depth gauge clamped on bit.*

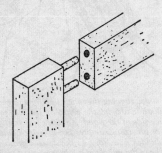

6. *Place dowels in hole and complete the joint.*

The cylinder locates the hole the correct distance from the face and guides the bit perpendicularly to the surface. The bit gauge furnished with the jig regulates the depth of the holes.

The Mitre Joint

Another joint that you might have used in making screens is one of the very commonest that there is. You use it on door frames, always on picture frames, and even on pieces of furniture.

Mitre joints are butt joints with the angle at the corner shared equally between the two pieces. The right-angle mitre is cut at an angle of 45 degrees—that is, half a right angle.

A 45-degree mitre can be laid out by squaring a line across the face of the wood, then measuring along one edge to a point equal to the width of the wood, and connecting this point with the other end of the squared line.

Mitre joints are usually sawed in a mitre box. A homemade box is illustrated.

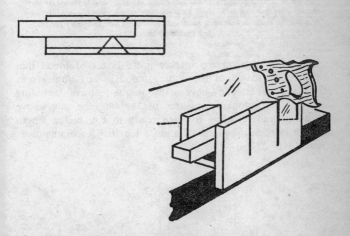

A homemade mitre box.

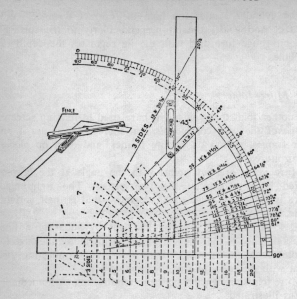

Set the bevel for these angles with the steel square. A fence of two strips of wood, shown above, will help to obtain a proper setting.
The bevel can also be set by a protractor, shown at the left, or by a line drawn at a desired angle to the edge of a piece of wood, shown at the right. The line can be laid off by a protractor, by measurement, or by geometric construction. The blade can extend on one side only for testing inside corners.

There are also on the market mitre boxes of metal that are accurate machines for cutting wood at any angle from 30 to 90 degrees. They have many unique features, including catches with automatic releases for holding the saw above the work, and releasing it when ready to cut, and a length stop for duplicating pieces of a given length. (Recommended: Stanley No. 2246.)

The quadrant is graduated in degrees and is numbered for cutting figures of 3, 4, 5, 6, 8, and 12 sides. The illustration below shows a large complete mitre box. There are also available smaller boxes that are less expensive.

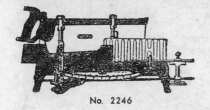

No. 2246

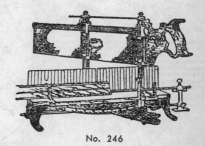

No. 246

Two types of mitre boxes

Mitre joints are usually nailed, or nailed and glued. When nailed and glued, a picture-frame vise or some other special clamp is usually used. The joints may be strengthened with dowels, tongues, or slip feathers.

Doweled mitre joints are doweled in the same way as butt joints.

In tongued mitre joints, each piece is grooved and a tongue, or spline, is glued in, the larger gluing surface giving greater strength and preventing the pieces from warping.

A slip-feather, or splined, mitre joint has a groove cut part way through it with a saw, into which is glued a thin piece of wood. The excess wood is then trimmed.

There are many varieties of notched and halved joints. The most important and most frequently used are the middle half-lap joint, the end half-lap joint, and the half-lap joint with a rabbet.

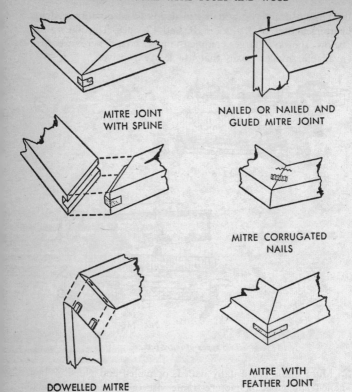

MITRE JOINT
WITH SPLINE

NAILED OR NAILED AND
GLUED MITRE JOINT

MITRE CORRUGATED
NAILS

DOWELLED MITRE

MITRE WITH
FEATHER JOINT

The middle half-lap is laid out by superimposing each piece upon the other to mark the width of each cut.

The pieces may also be clamped together and the lines for the width of the cut squared across both work edges as far apart as the wood is wide. This is sometimes done by measuring from a center point half the width of the wood on each side of the point. The pieces are then taken apart and the square lines continued across the work faces and down the other edge. The depth of each cut is equal to one-half of the thickness of the pieces and is gauged from the work face of both pieces. One piece is cut above the depth line, and the other piece is cut below it. The sides or shoulders are then sawed on the waste wood outside of the line. The waste wood is removed to the gauge line by paring, if necessary.

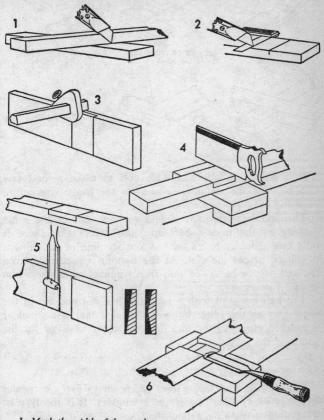

1. *Mark the width of the notches.*

2. *Square with shoulder lines on face and edge.*

3. *Gauge the depth of the notches.*

4. *Saw the shoulders.*

5. *Chisel to the gauge line on each side. To avoid breaking the grain, slant the chisel slightly outward.*

6. *Then finish to a uniform depth.*

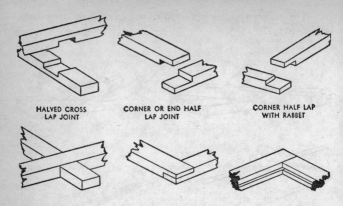

HALVED CROSS
LAP JOINT

CORNER OR END HALF
LAP JOINT

CORNER HALF LAP
WITH RABBET

It is an aid in chiseling wide cuts to make several saw cuts between the shoulders almost to the gauge line before chiseling out the waste wood.

The end half-lap joint is laid out and cut in the same manner as the middle half-lap joint, except that there is only one shoulder to be cut, so that the line of the bottom is gauged across the end. As the bottom is accessible from the end, it can be sawed out, then trimmed to line with the chisel, if necessary.

The half-lap joint with a rabbet is laid out and cut in the same way as the other lap joints, except that one shoulder is marked closer to the end than the other to allow for the width of the rabbet.

Mortise and Tenon Joints

The mortise and tenon joint is known to every carpenter who has ever looked closely at a hammer. It is the type of joint used in making a bookshelf.

In cutting out a mortise, the waste wood is generally removed by boring a row of holes with an auger bit and trimming the cheeks straight and smooth to the line with a chisel. In order to accomplish this, keep the chisel perpendicular to the face of the wood.

The illustration shows where the try square is used for marking guidelines for the tenon, ends of mortises, grooves, gains, and the squaring of an end.

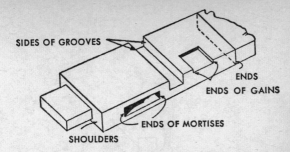

SIDES OF GROOVES

ENDS

ENDS OF GAINS

ENDS OF MORTISES

SHOULDERS

THE TRY SQUARE IS USED TO MARK GUIDE LINES SQUARE TO EDGE
OR FACE

Mortises can be beaten out with the chisel alone. This is done by driving the chisel, held squarely, with a mallet or hammer, starting in the center and working to each end. The back of the chisel faces the ends. The tenon should be tried in the mortise, and any part that binds noted and corrected. Glue can be spread evenly on all abutting surfaces and the work clamped together.

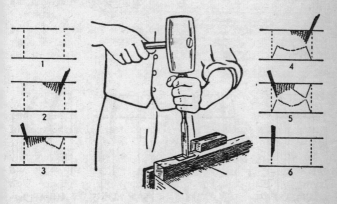

Beating out a mortise.

1. *Start in the center.*
2. *Pry out the first chips.*
3. *Cut each way to end. Bevel to mortise.*
4. *Chisel out chips and repeat on opposite side.*
5. *Chisel out chips until through.*
6. *Finish by truing ends.*

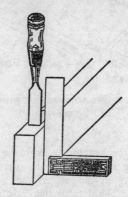

Test for perpendicularity.

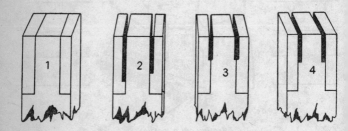

1. *Tenon marked out.*
2. *Correct: Saw on waste side of line—tenon left full size.*
3 and 4. *Incorrect: Sawed on line or inside of line—making tenon too small.*

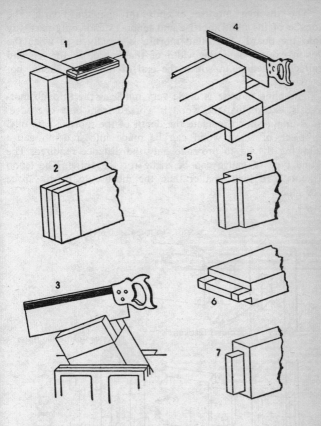

1. *Square lines for shoulder, marking length of tenon.*

2. *Set the mortise gauge and use the same setting between spurs to mark both tenon and mortise for thickness of tenon and width of mortise. If the marking gauge is used, be sure to draw both lines from the work face.*

3. *Saw cheeks.*

4. *Saw shoulders.*

5. *If necessary finish with a chisel.*

6. *Mark shoulders on the edges.*

7. *Saw shoulders on the edges and finish with a chisel.*

The through mortise extends through the board. The tongue of the blind mortise and tenon extends only part way into the board. The blind mortise is usually used when the tenon extends into the width of the board, as for leg and rail construction, in which the end of the tenon should not be visible.

The blind mortise is made very much as the through mortise is, except that the wood is worked from only one edge. It is important to regulate the depth of the mortise carefully. A piece of scrap wood can be made into a depth gauge allowing the bit to protrude only the distance required. The same type of gauge can be made for the chisel. The tenon is cut 1/16 inch smaller than the mortise to permit space for glue.

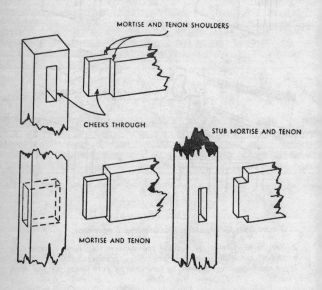

MORTISE AND TENON SHOULDERS

CHEEKS THROUGH

STUB MORTISE AND TENON

MORTISE AND TENON

The haunched mortise and tenon is used in the corners of panel doors. The rails and stiles have grooves to hold the panel. This joint has a short tongue from the top cheek of the tenon to the edge of the wood to fill the part of the groove between the mortise and the end that otherwise would be left open.

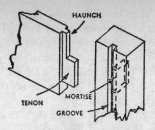

The cheeks parallel to the faces and their shoulders are marked and cut in the usual manner. The length of the haunch is then measured and squared as long as the groove is deep. The cheeks parallel to the edges are gauged and the work sawed to the lines. The mortise is laid out and cut as usual, except that the mortise is at the bottom of the groove that is to hold the panel.

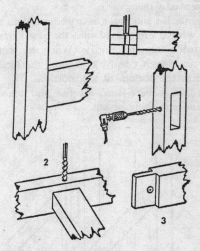

Bored and pinned mortise and tenon.

1. *Bore hole through the member containing the mortise.*

2. *Insert tenon in mortise and mark center of hole with bit.*

3. *Bore hole a little closer to the shoulder so that pin, when driven, will draw up the shoulders tightly.*

In a pinned mortise and tenon joint, a hole is bored through the sides of the mortise and through the tenon, and a dowel or pin is inserted, somewhat like a bolt. The mortise and tenon is laid out and cut as usual, and a hole is bored through the sides of the mortise with an auger bit. The tenon is then inserted and the center of the holes in the sides of the mortise marked on it. The hole in the tenon is then bored slightly closer to the shoulder. This is done so that when the joint is closed and the pin is driven into the offset hole, the shoulders are drawn up tightly and held securely. Strength is imparted to the joint independent of the glue.

Wedged mortise and tenon joints are laid out and cut the same way as other mortise and tenon joints, except that the mortise is given a flare on the side away from the tenon shoulder. When the joint is glued, wedges with glue are driven between the tenon and the end cheeks of the mortise. Sometimes two saw kerfs are made in the tenon and the glued wedges driven into them.

A foxtail mortise and tenon is a wedged blind mortise and tenon. The wedges are started into the saw kerfs before inserting the tenon into the mortise. When the joint is closed, the wedges are driven deeply, expanding the tenon by being pressed against the bottom of the mortise.

The tenon of a bare-faced mortise and tenon has only one cheek and one shoulder cut.

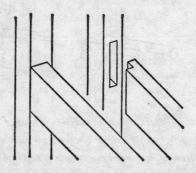

Bare-faced tenon.

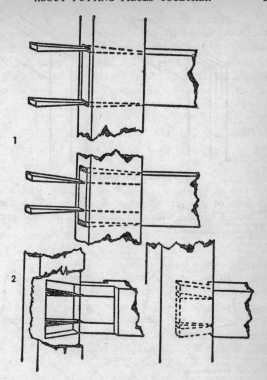

1. *Wedged mortise and tenon joints.*

2. *Fox-tailed mortise and tenon.*

The open mortise and tenon, or slip, joint is used on corners. It is like a through mortise and tenon with one end of the mortise removed. The only difference lies in marking and cutting the mortise. The gauge lines for the mortise are extended across the end. The mortise cheeks are sawed in the same way as the cheeks of the tenon, the saw being placed in the waste portion of the wood. The waste wood is finally removed by boring a hole near the inner end of the mortise and trimming with a chisel, or by beating waste out with a mallet and chisel.

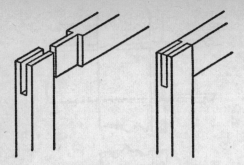

Open mortise and tenon or slip joint.

A lock or pin joint consists of a series of open mortises and tenons in line with one another. It is used principally in box construction.

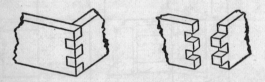

Dovetail Joints

Dovetail joints are difficult to make, but are often worth the effort since they have great strength because of the flared sides of the pins and the dovetails. The projections at the end of the member on which one can see the flare pattern are called pins, and the spaces between them sockets or mortises. The projections on the piece where the flare is seen on the face are called dovetails, and the spaces between them the sockets or mortises.

The ideal tool for making a dovetail joint is the router, but it is possible to make these joints with hand tools alone. Power tools make dovetailing a comparatively simple task.

The angle of the dovetails should not be too great or the joint will be weak because of the short gain at the corners. The angle can be laid out by squaring a line from the edge of a board measuring 5, 6, 7, 8, or 9 inches along it from the edge, then measuring 1 inch from the line along the edge and connecting the points. The angle selected can be transferred to the work with a T-bevel or a template made of wood or brass.

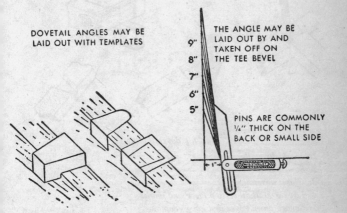

DOVETAIL ANGLES MAY BE LAID OUT WITH TEMPLATES

THE ANGLE MAY BE LAID OUT BY AND TAKEN OFF ON THE TEE BEVEL

9"
8"
7"
6"
5"

PINS ARE COMMONLY ¼" THICK ON THE BACK OR SMALL SIDE

The strongest dovetails are those in which the pins and the dovetails are the same size, although for appearance's sake the dovetails are usually made larger, but not greater than four times the width of the pins.

While the thickness of the pin and the width of the dovetails may vary according to the size and nature of the work, it is good practice to make the pin or its corresponding socket on the dovetail piece about ¼ inch thick on its narrow side. Mark the lines with great care. Use a well-sharpened knife in laying out this joint.

There are several kinds of dovetail joints.

The half-lap dovetail is made by laying the dovetail members out as for an end half-lap joint. The angle of the dovetail is then marked. The shoulder is sawed and the sides are pared with a chisel. The dovetail is then placed on the second member and the shape marked with a knife or very sharp hard pencil. These lines are squared down the edges, and the depth of the notch is gauged. The sides are sawed and the waste wood chiseled to the bottom line, as in a middle half-lap joint.

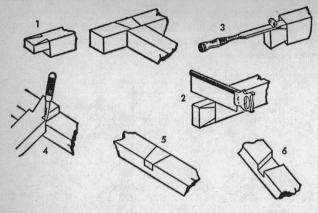

Half-lap dovetail joint

1. *Mark dovetail.*
2. *Saw shoulders.*
3. *Chisel dovetail.*
4. *Lay dovetail on second piece and mark.*
5. *Square down edges and gauge depth.*
6. *Cut the socket in the same way as a half-lap notch.*

A single dovetail can be made in the form of two half pins and a whole dovetail, or as a whole pin fitting into a socket between two half dovetails. The thickness of each piece of wood is measured on the other piece from the end, to locate the shoulder lines. In the first form, the half pins are laid out and cut first. The sides are sawed with a backsaw or a dovetail saw and the waste to the shoulder line removed with a chisel. This piece is then held on the other member in order to mark the shape of the dovetail. These marks are squared across the end, and the angles reproduced on the other side. The sides and shoulders are then sawed. In the second form, the socket between the two half dovetails is first marked and cut. The pin is then laid out from it and cut.

A through multiple dovetail joint is a series of single dovetails.

The dovetail dado combines half the dovetail and the dado to make a strong but more complicated joint. Only on fine furniture and cabinetwork is use made of this. A dado groove

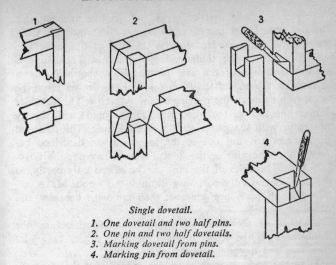

Single dovetail.
1. *One dovetail and two half pins.*
2. *One pin and two half dovetails.*
3. *Marking dovetail from pins.*
4. *Marking pin from dovetail.*

is cut into half the thickness of the receiving piece, with one side shaped into half a dovetail. In cutting the housed piece, first cut it as a square dado at the widest distance; then mark the cutback flare on both edges and cut with hacksaw and chisel. The fit must be especially tight for this joint.

Another type of blind or hidden joint used on highly crafted furniture is a combination of the end lap and the multiple dovetail, called the stopped lap dovetail. Here the dovetail and pin are not cut all the way through, and the sockets are not quite at the end. Thus the sockets are covered when the joint is finished. The dovetail and sockets must match exactly. When properly made, the joint is almost undetectable.

Lap dovetail, or half-blind dovetail, is an adaptation of stopped lap dovetail and through dovetail; it is slightly less difficult to make and leaves the dovetail visible at one end. The dovetail is cut as in an ordinary multiple through dovetail, but the housing piece with the sockets is cut through only partially, leaving the pins and the dovetails concealed at the top. Lap dovetails are used for jointing the sides of a drawer with the front.

This joint, illustrated on page 145, is like the multiple dovetail except that the dovetails do not come through. Only the ends of the pins are seen on the side of the joint. The sides of drawers are thinner than the fronts. The gauge is set the thickness of the side piece, and a shoulder line is marked on the end of the front piece of the drawer from the work face to mark the overlap of the dovetails. The shoulder line on the face of the front piece can be made with the try square or with the gauge with a single setting. The pins and the sockets are laid out in the same way as described before, either the pins or the dovetails first. Lay out the dovetails first. The sides of the pins can be sawed only partly, as the cuts extend only part way through the wood. Make certain that all parts are squared; then cut with backsaw and chisel.

Another of the more difficult joints, and therefore one rarely used, is the secret dovetail, or blind mitre. This joint combines the dovetail and the mitre.

Here the ends of each piece are mitred, but the dovetails and the pins are squared so that they extend beyond the 45-degree angle. After each piece is made true, the cuts are marked on the ends, the required portions removed, and the housing properly mitred at both edges.

Whether the pins or the sockets should be laid out first is the choice of the woodworker. In any event, the shoulder lines are squared first, the distance being determined by the thickness of the corresponding pieces. To lay out the pins, the width of the wood is divided into as many equal parts as there are pins, counting the two outer half pins as one. Sometimes half the thickness of a pin is laid off first from each edge on the shoulder line, and the intervening space then divided equally. This gives extra strength to the outer half pin. Half the narrow thickness of the pin, usually ⅛ inch, is now marked on each side of each point, and also from each edge. On these points, lines are squared to the end. The angles are then marked with the T-bevel or a template, and the lines squared down the other side to the shoulder line. The waste wood is marked to avoid mistakes. The sides are sawed and the waste wood removed with a chisel. The pins are held over the other piece, matching the shoulder line. The dovetails and sockets are then laid out. The waste wood is marked and the sockets are sawed and chiseled.

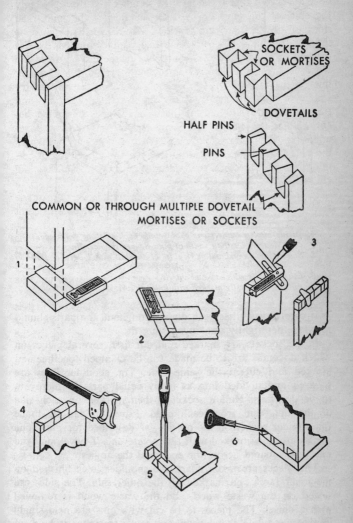

SOCKETS OR MORTISES

DOVETAILS

HALF PINS

PINS

COMMON OR THROUGH MULTIPLE DOVETAIL
MORTISES OR SOCKETS

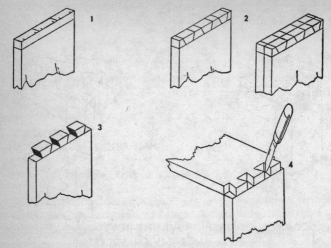

1. *Divide into as many parts as dovetails each side and from edges. Measure one-half width of pins. Square shoulder lines.*
2. *Square line on end and mark sides of dovetail with T-bevel or template.*
3. *Cut dovetails with saw and chisel.*
4. *Pins may be easily marked with knife or awl.*

If careful work has been done throughout, the parts should slip together tightly, making a snug fit.

If the sockets are marked and cut first, several pieces on which dovetails are to be made can be clamped together and marked and cut at the same time. The shoulder lines are squared and divided into as many equal parts as there are to be dovetails. Half a socket is then marked on each side of the dots and from each edge. Provision can be made for a wider socket on the outside, as described for pins. The angles are now marked with a template or a T-bevel, and the lines are squared across the ends and the angles.

The pieces are taken apart, the shoulder lines finished on the inner faces and marked on the other side. The sides are sawed on the waste wood, and the waste wood is removed with a chisel. The pieces to be cut with pins are held singly in the vise while the dovetail-and-socket member is held on the end of each, on which the shape of the pins is scribed. The lines are continued down each face to the shoulder lines with a try square. The sides are now sawed and the waste wood between the pins removed with a chisel.

Rabbet Joints

A rabbet is a recess cut out of an edge of a piece of wood. The bottom is parallel to the face, and the side is parallel to the end or edge, thereby forming a re-entrant square corner for another piece of wood.

A rabbet joint is a square edge or end fitting into a rabbet, two rabbeted edges fitting into each other, or two adjoining rabbets with a spline fitting into them. It is used for cabinets, shelves, drawers, and wherever the end grain of wood is to be concealed.

There are several types of rabbets—the corner, which has a square edge, a groove cut into the end of one board into which another board fits. The groove should be parallel with the end of the board to make a correct fit regardless of the thickness of the two pieces.

A rabbet on the end of a piece of wood is laid out by squaring a line for the side or shoulder across the face and down the edges. This should be as far from the end as the joining piece is thick. Depth from the work face is then gauged, and lines marked on the two edges and on the end. Waste can be cut out with a backsaw, or the shoulder can be sawed and the bottom cut with a chisel. A rabbet plane will also do this work. A spur is provided for cutting across the grain of the wood. A power router, of course, simplifies the operation.

A rabbet on the edge can be cut with a fillister, plane, or a rabbet—or with a router, of course. The depth gauge and the fence regulate the depth and the width of the cut. Wide and deep rabbets can be cut by plowing grooves, one from the face and one from the edge. The thin strip that remains can then be cut out with a chisel.

A rabbet that fits into the length of a board is known as a shiplap. This is quite similar to a half lap with both sides of equal thickness. Stock boards of this type usually have the ends cut in rabbet joints as well.

Sometimes the rabbets are cut into both sides and a spline, or fillet, is used to hold the two pieces together.

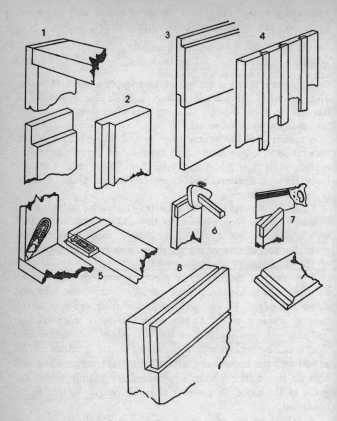

Rabbet joints.

1. *Rabbet on end.*

2. *Rabbet on edge.*

3. *Shiplap.*

4. *Rabbet and fillet or spline.*

5. *Mark thickness of one member and square line for shoulder.*

6. *Gauge depth of rabbet.*

7. *Saw on waste-wood side of lines and finish with a chisel.*

8. *A wide or deep rabbet may be cut by plowing two grooves.*

The Dado

A dado is the groove cut across the grain of a piece of wood into which a second piece is fitted. It is used for drawers and shelves, and is known as a housed joint when the entire end of a second piece fits in the dado. Another form of this joint is the stopped or grained dado, in which the dado does not extend entirely across the face of the work.

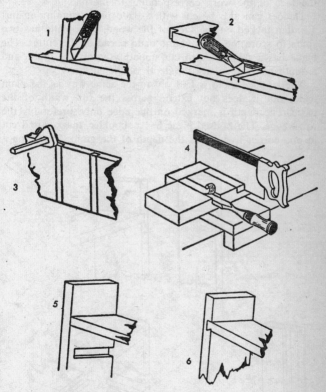

1. *Mark width of dado.*
2. *Square lines on face and edges for shoulders.*
3. *Gauge depth of dado.*
4. *Saw on waste-wood side of shoulder lines. Chisel out waste wood to gauge lines and uniform depth.*
5. *Stopped dado or gain.*   6. *Dovetail dado.*

Besides these there are the shoulder-housed, or dado and rabbet, and the dovetailed dado described above.

To lay out a plain dado, the piece to be housed in is set on the piece in which the dado is to be cut, and the width of the dado is marked. Lines are then squared across the face of the work through these points and down both edges. The depth of the dado is then marked with a gauge. The sides can be sawed with or without the aid of a batten tacked on the face of the work corresponding to the line.

Dadoes can also be cut with a dado plane running against a batten tacked on the face of the wood. This plane has two spurs to score the sides of the dado ahead of the cutter. The blade has a skew edge to cut smoothly across the grain, and a depth gauge regulates the depth of the cut.

The stopped dado is laid out in the same way as the plain dado, but it does not extend across the full width of the piece. The depth is marked on one edge only, preferably the work edge. The housed piece has a shoulder, marked and cut in one corner as long as the depth of the grain. In cutting a

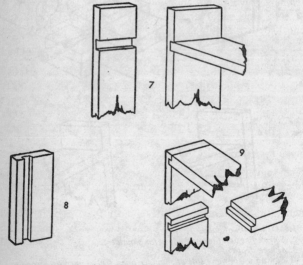

7. Housed joint.   8. Groove.
9. Shoulder-housed, or rabbet and dado, joint.

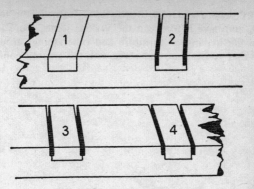

1. *Groove or dado marked out.*
2. *Correct—Sawed on waste side between lines.*
3 and 4. *Incorrect—Groove made too large.*

stopped dado, a small part at the inner end is cut with a chisel to regulate the depth and to help in sawing the sides with the backsaw. The bottom is removed with a chisel or router. Sawing and chiseling can be done alternately, a little at a time, in order to avoid cutting the inner part too deep. The depth can be tested with a rule or with a nail driven into a stick.

The end dado (or dado and rabbet, or box corner, or shoulder-housed dado) is often used for box corners. Similar to a dado, this joint uses only a portion of the end piece (a rabbet edge) for the joint. A dado and rabbet joint is made in the same manner as a plain dado, except that a rabbet is first laid out and cut on the end of the housed piece.

Tongue and Groove

The tongue and groove, or matched joint, or matched lumber, is used for flooring, partitions, doors, table tops, etc. This consists of a grooved end of one board and a matching raised tongue on the end of the other. The two boards must be of the same thickness. Special tongue and groove planes cut these edges, but for most purposes, standard stock sold in lumber yards suffices.

Now you have a good picture of most of the common joints, and instructions how to make them. If you can make a board square and true, if you have learned how to use a chisel, and have before you the various joints, there is nothing in the making of furniture and other things around the house that you cannot undertake with the greatest confidence.

CHAPTER EIGHT

Holding the Pieces Together

No matter how good a joint you cut, that alone will not be enough to hold two pieces of wood together. Although some joints are self-locking, all edges require a binding agent—glue, nails, screws, or some other device—to hold the two pieces together.

Gluing

By far the best, and probably the most difficult, work in joining is done by gluing. Anyone can complete an ordinary gluing job without much thought or pain; but a proper, lasting joint, stronger than even the wood itself, is possible only if, first, the proper glue is selected and, second, the glue is correctly applied.

The efficiency of a glued joint is determined by (1) kind of wood, (2) its moisture content, (3) type of joint, (4) precision with which contact surfaces match, (5) type of glue and the method of its preparation, handling, and application, (6) degree and duration of pressure used while setting, (7) method of conditioning glued joints, and (8) service conditions.

In general, heavy woods are harder to glue than light woods; hardwoods are harder to glue than softwoods; and heartwoods are harder to glue than sapwoods.

All eight types of glue widely used are commercially available. Of these, the first six are particularly useful for the home carpenter: (1) liquid glue, (2) casein glue, (3) blood-albumen glue, (4) synthetic resin glue, (5) cellulose cement, (6) rubber compounds, (7) vegetable glue, and (8) animal glue. There are many prepared glues on the market that are easy to use, but the hobbyist will want to know about some of the glues used by professionals.

The most satisfactory glue for the home craftsman is the plastic-resin type. It comes in powder form to be mixed with water as needed. This glue is waterproof, does not stain, and is easily handled.

Liquid glues come ready to use, and are usually quick-drying.

Casein glue, made from cow's milk, comes in powder form.

Classification of various hardwood and softwood species according to gluing properties

HARDWOODS

Group 1	Group 2	Group 3	Group 4
(Glue very easily with different glues under wide range of gluing conditions)	(Glue well with different glues under a moderately wide range of gluing conditions)	(Glue satisfactorily under well-controlled gluing conditions)	(Require very close control of gluing conditions, or special treatment to obtain best results)
Aspen	Alder, red	Ash, white[2]	Beech, American
Chestnut, American	Basswood[1]	Cherry, black[1,2]	Birch, sweet and yellow[2]
Cottonwood	Butternut[1,2]	Dogwood[2]	Hickory[2]
Willow, black	Elm:	Maple, soft[1,2]	Maple, hard
Yellow poplar	American[2]	Oak:	Osage orange
	Rock[1,2]	Red[2]	Persimmon
	Hackberry	White	
	Magnolia[1,2]	Pecan	
	Mahogany[2]	Sycamore[1,2]	
	Sweetgum[1]	Tupelo:	
		Black[1]	
		Water[1,2]	
		Walnut, black	

SOFTWOODS

Bald cypress	Cedar, eastern red[2]	Cedar, Alaska[2]
Cedar, western red[3]	Douglas fir	
Fir, white	Hemlock, western[3]	
Larch, western	Pine:	
Redwood	Eastern white[3]	
Spruce, Sitka	Southern yellow[1]	
	Ponderosa	

[1] Species is more subject to starved joints, particularly with animal glue, than the classification would otherwise indicate.

[2] Glued more easily with resin glues than with nonresin glues.

[3] Glued more easily with nonresin glues than with resin glues.

It becomes effective when mixed with water and allowed to stand for a short time. When dried, it is water-resistant.

Animal glues, made largely from hides, come in twenty-one different qualities. None of them, however, is water-resistant.

Blood-albumen glues, soluble in a special solution, are not generally available for home use.

Vegetable and resin glues are soluble in various solutions; they also are not generally satisfactory for home use.

Animal glue is used hot. Fish and vegetable glues are usually liquid glues used cold. A hot glue can be made into a slow-setting cold liquid glue by adding either nitric, hydrochloric, or oxalic acid to it. (These acids are active and require great caution in their use.)

Casein glue and resin glues are available as cold-water glues, resin glues being waterproof and therefore excellent for all marine work. There are also many commercial liquid glues that can be used for minor quick repairs. Shellac, while not a glue, is very useful for sticking paper, rubber, felt, glass, and the like to wood.

Cold glue comes in liquid form and is worked at room temperatures. Usually made from processed waste parts of fish, it has the big advantage of being always ready. Cold glue, however, is not as strong and sets more slowly than hot glue. This, of course, has the advantage of permitting mistakes to be corrected.

Cold glue should be applied in stages. Each piece should first receive a thin coat of glue that is allowed to sink into the grain and dry almost completely. Apply a thin second coat to both surfaces. Allow the second coat to dry until it feels "tacky"; then bind the two surfaces together, removing excess glue as the clamp is tightened. Avoid too tight a bind, for this will squeeze out too much of the glue. Most cold glues require at least twenty-four hours to harden.

Hot glue can be desirable if you have a big job to do. It is sold in sheets, flakes, powders, and strips and must be heated before it is suitable for use. Usually made of animal wastes—bones, skin, and muscles—it must first be liquefied by double-boiler process, placing the glue can into a pot of boiling water. Special electric gluepots with thermostat controls are best for this purpose. For the home workshop, a one-pint pot is sufficient. The glue should be stirred as it is heated, and must be kept hot while binding is taking place. Working with hot glue requires even more precision than working with cold glue. Work in an area with a temperature of 60 to 95 degrees Fahrenheit for good results. Then assemble approximately the right amount of glue for your purpose, overestimating slightly. Place the dry glue in the pot with enough water to cover and set the thermostat at 130 degrees Fahrenheit. Stir with a clean paddle as the glue melts until it reaches the consistency of ordinary paint.

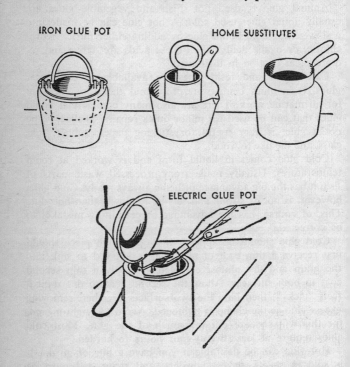

IRON GLUE POT

HOME SUBSTITUTES

ELECTRIC GLUE POT

Almost any kind of brush can be used for spreading glue —of either bristle, wire, or shredded rattan. It is well to keep a small wooden paddle in the gluepot for stirring, and for wiping the brush on, instead of using the edge of the pot. The paddle can be used for spreading the glue, particularly for working into holes and crevices.

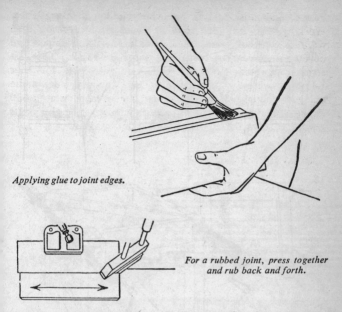

Applying glue to joint edges.

For a rubbed joint, press together and rub back and forth.

Work quickly, because if the glue chills before the work is finished, it will not hold. Afterwards, draw the joints tight with clamps. Test the corners with a try square and adjust the clamps until the corners are true. As hot glue hardens as it cools, each joint must be clamped quickly and squarely within seconds. Allow twenty-four hours for drying.

Wherever possible, gluing work should be divided into small units. This will help in getting clamps on quickly and in making joints true. It is very difficult to glue the four sides and legs of a small table in place in one operation and have all sides true and the joints drawn in place before the glue chills.

Common practice is to divide the work into three operations. Glue one end or side, two legs, and the intervening rail and stretcher. Then glue the opposite end or side in the same way. When the glue is hard, remove the clamps, spread glue on the joints, insert the rails and stretchers, and join the two ends, tightly clamped and true.

Long-edged joints present special problems, particularly if the edges are to be matched for figure and grain. For this

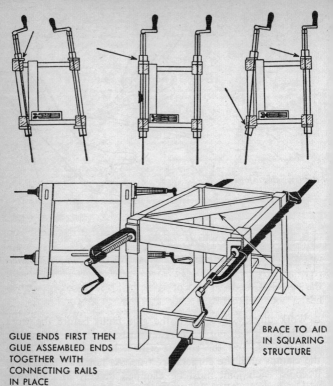

GLUE ENDS FIRST THEN
GLUE ASSEMBLED ENDS
TOGETHER WITH
CONNECTING RAILS
IN PLACE

BRACE TO AID
IN SQUARING
STRUCTURE

kind of work, careful preparation is all important. Not only should the pieces be matched as closely as possible, but the edges must be perfectly squared so that no crack is visible when the edges are joined.

When glued, long-edged joints are put together by being either rubbed or squeezed together by clamps. Before rubbing, the edges should be carefully planed with a jointer plane and the two pieces of wood matched for figure and grain. When the two edges match throughout their length and no cracks show on either side, the glue can be spread. With a hand screw or a piece of wood clamped on as a guide, press down on the upper board and rub it back and forth until the glue begins to set. This will be the signal to stop rubbing, and the work can be carefully laid away to dry.

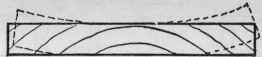

1. SOLID BOARD, SHRINKAGE TENDENCY INDICATED BY DOTTED LINES

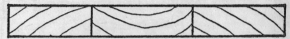

2. GLUED-UP CONSTRUCTION BALANCED STRESSES

To prevent shrinkage shown in 1, rip board into thirds, invert center section, and reglue.

In joining boards edge to edge, it is wise to match grain wherever possible, and to use only either heartwood or sapwood throughout to provide uniformity. If there are only a few pieces to select from, the bolder patterns should be in the center. Glued sections of work will adhere best if joined heartwood to heartwood and sapwood to sapwood.

Squeezed joints are usually left very slightly open in the center. This slight crack will be closed by the clamps. The greater pressure on the ends will counteract the tendency of long-edged joints to open on the end.

As no stain will penetrate a film of glue, it is important that all excess glue be removed before finishing work begins. Hot water, sandpaper, or a scraper can be used. Watch particularly for spots where a finger or a clamp may have carried some of the adhesive. A black spot that cannot otherwise be removed can be bleached out with a solution of half a cup of oxalic acid crystals in a quart of hot water. Note that this solution is poisonous. When bleaching, cover the entire area, for bleached wood will show lighter in color. If an entire piece is to be bleached, however, use a commercially prepared solution. This work must be done with extreme caution.

Clamps

Many types of clamps are manufactured, each designed for a different gluing problem. Basic large clamps are not too difficult to make. For making table tops and other large edge-glued pieces, a simple U-shaped device, a series of

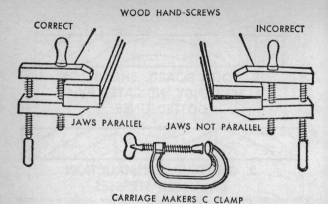

WOOD HAND-SCREWS

CORRECT   INCORRECT

JAWS PARALLEL   JAWS NOT PARALLEL

CARRIAGE MAKERS C CLAMP

fences, or a cross-tacking piece can be used. Cleats are inserted between the two preset edges to ensure a tight fit. A pivotal device with two swinging fences attached by pivoting pegs or bolts can also serve as a clamp.

Commercially made clamps serve each gluing problem.

1. Carriage maker's clamps are most widely used. Each consists of a C-shaped base with an adjustable bolt through one end.

2. Wood screw clamps are made of two heavy baseboards connected by parallel bolts. These must be maintained parallel to each other to be effective.

3. The bar clamp has a wide mouth and closes very much like a small vise.

4. The band clamp, used for circular work, encloses the work and is held tight by hand screws.

5. The column clamp encloses circular work with a chain tightened at one end. A rope tourniquet can be substituted.

6. The web clamp, made of heavy-duty webbed tape with a steel fastener which has a ratchet action, is placed around the objects to be held. Staples, or dogs, are used as temporary fasteners to hold pieces together while glue dries.

Types of Glued Joints

With most species of wood, straight, plain joints between side-grain surfaces can be made substantially as strong as the wood itself. The tongue and groove joint and joints of other shapes have the theoretical advantage of larger gluing sur-

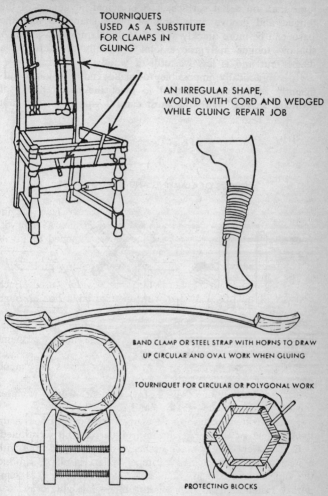

TOURNIQUETS
USED AS A SUBSTITUTE
FOR CLAMPS IN
GLUING

AN IRREGULAR SHAPE,
WOUND WITH CORD AND WEDGED
WHILE GLUING REPAIR JOB

BAND CLAMP OR STEEL STRAP WITH HORNS TO DRAW
UP CIRCULAR AND OVAL WORK WHEN GLUING

TOURNIQUET FOR CIRCULAR OR POLYGONAL WORK

PROTECTING BLOCKS

faces than straight joints, but in practice they do not give greater strength with most woods. The theoretical advantage is often lost, wholly or partly, because shaped joints are more difficult to cut than straight, plain joints to obtain a perfect fit of the parts. Because of poor contact, effective holding area and strength may actually be less in a shaped joint than on a flat surface. The principal advantage of the tongue and groove and joints of other shapes is that the parts can be more quickly aligned in the clamps or a press. A shallow tongue and groove joint is usually as useful as a deeper cut and is less wasteful of wood.

It is practically impossible to make end-butt joints sufficiently strong or permanent to meet the requirements of ordinary service. With the most careful gluing possible, not

METHODS OF CLAMPING AND GLUING MITRES

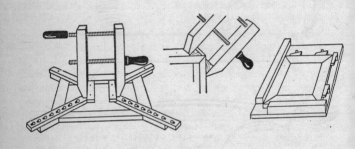

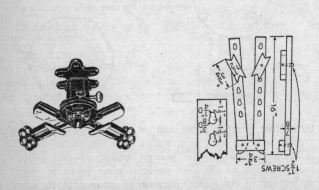

Stanley Mitre Vise No. 400

more than 25 per cent of the tensile strength of the wood parallel with the grain can be obtained in butt joints. In order to approximate the tensile strength of various kinds of wood, a scarf, serrated, or other form of joint that approaches a side-grain surface must be used. The plain scarf joint is perhaps the easiest to glue and entails fewer difficulties in making than the many-angle forms.

Doweled mitre joints are doweled in the same way as butt joints.

In tongued mitre joints, each piece is grooved, and a tongue or spline is glued in, giving greater strength through the larger gluing surface. This also helps prevent the pieces from warping.

A slip-feather mitre joint has a groove cut part way through it with a saw, into which is glued a thin piece of wood. The excess wood is then trimmed.

End-to-Side-Grain Surfaces

End-to-side-grain joints are also difficult to glue properly and, further, are subject in use to severe stresses because of unequal changes in the two pieces of wood as the moisture content of each changes. It is therefore necessary to use irregular shapes of joints, dowels, tenons, or other devices to reinforce such a joint in order to bring the side grain into contact with side grain, or to secure larger gluing surfaces. All end-to-side-grain joints should be carefully protected from changes in moisture content.

Conditioning

When boards are glued edge to edge, the wood at the joint absorbs water from the glue and swells. If the glued assembly is coated before this excess moisture is dried out or distributed, more wood is removed along the swollen joints than elsewhere. Later, when the joints dry and shrink, permanent depressions are formed that may be very conspicuous in a finished panel.

When pieces of lumber are glued edge to edge or face to face, the glue moisture need not be dried out but simply allowed to distribute itself uniformly throughout the wood.

In plywood, veneered panels, and other joinings made by gluing together thin layers of wood, it is best to condition the panels to average service moisture content by allowing

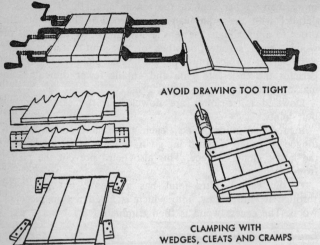

AVOID DRAWING TOO TIGHT

CLAMPING WITH
WEDGES, CLEATS AND CRAMPS

them to remain in the area for several days, at least. In cold-gluing operations, it is often necessary to dry out at least part of the moisture added in gluing. However, drying glued wood to too low a moisture content increases warping, and creates checking. After hot-press operations, the panels will often be very dry, and it may be desirable to recondition them under circumstances that will cause them to regain moisture.

Durability

The durability of glued joints depends upon the type of glue, the conditions under which it is used, the gluing technique, and the design of the joints. Moisture conditions are particularly important not only because of the effect of moisture on the glue itself but because of the effect of moisture content on the internal stresses on the glued joint. The behavior of a joint in use also depends on the design of the joint, the thickness of the plies, and the density and shrinkage characteristics of the wood used.

Generally joints made with any of the commonly used woodworking glues will remain strong indefinitely if the moisture content of the wood does not exceed 15 per cent and the temperature remains within the range of human comfort.

Screws and Bolts

More lasting and stronger than nails, screws have several advantages for the home carpenter. Especially if the work must be disassembled for repair, cleaning, or packing, ability to open the joint can be essential.

To use screws rather than nails is more expensive in both time and money, but is often necessary to meet requirements for good results. The main advantages of screws are that (1) they provide more holding power, (2) they can be easily tightened to draw parts being fastened securely together, (3) they are neater in appearance when properly driven, and (4) they may be withdrawn without damaging the material. The common wood screw is usually made of unhardened steel, stainless steel, aluminum, or brass. The steel may be bright-finished or blued, or zinc-, cadmium-, or chrome-plated.

Wood screws are threaded from a gimlet point for approximately two-thirds of the length of the screw and have a head slotted for driving with an inserted driver. Screws vary in length from ¼ inch to 6 inches. Screws up to 1 inch long increase in size by eighths of an inch; screws 1 to 3 inches long increase in size by quarters of an inch, and screws 3 to 6 inches long increase by half inches.

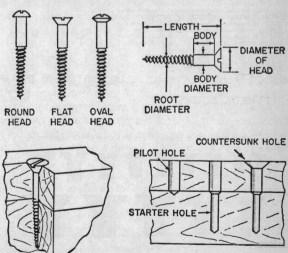

ROUND HEAD   FLAT HEAD   OVAL HEAD

LENGTH
BODY
DIAMETER OF HEAD
BODY DIAMETER
ROOT DIAMETER

COUNTERSUNK HOLE
PILOT HOLE
STARTER HOLE

Screws also vary in diameter as well as length of shaft. Each length is made in a number of shaft sizes specified by an arbitrary number that represents no special measurement but indicates relative differences in diameter. Complete specifications for a screw includes type, material, finish, length, and screw size number. The last indicates the wire gauge of the body, drill or bit size for the body hole, and drill or bit size for the starter hold. The adjoining table shows size, length, gauge, and applicable drill and auger-bit sizes for screws, and gives lengths and diameters of lag screws.

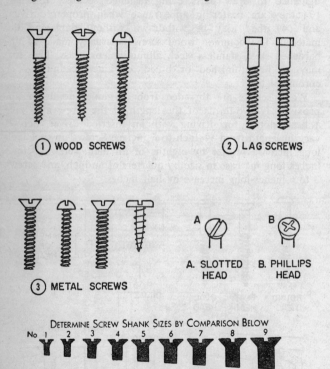

① WOOD SCREWS   ② LAG SCREWS

③ METAL SCREWS

A. SLOTTED HEAD   B. PHILLIPS HEAD

DETERMINE SCREW SHANK SIZES BY COMPARISON BELOW

No 1 2 3 4 5 6 7 8 9
    10   12   14   16   18

SIZES OF BITS OR DRILLS TO BORE HOLES FOR WOOD SCREWS

NUMBER OF SCREW	1	2	3	4	5	6	7	8	9	10	12	14	16	18
BODY DIAMETER OF SCREW	.073	.086	.099	.112	.125	.138	.151	.164	.177	.190	.216	.242	.268	.294
FIRST HOLE — TWIST DRILL SIZE	5/64" −	3/32" −	3/32" +	7/64" +	1/8"	9/64" −	5/32" −	11/64" −	11/64" +	3/16" +	7/32" −	15/64" +	17/64" +	19/64" −
FIRST HOLE — AUGER BIT NUMBER							3	3	3	3	4	4	5	5
SECOND HOLE — TWIST DRILL SIZE		1/16"	1/16"	5/64"	5/64"	3/32"	7/64"	7/64"	1/8"	1/8"	9/64"	5/32"	3/16"	13/64"
SECOND HOLE — AUGER BIT NUMBER											3	3	3	4

Exact sizes cannot be given for the holes for wood screws. The above are approximately right for average needs. Variations in hard and soft wood, moisture content, and snug or loose fits, if desired, should be considered. Number and letter sizes of drills are available, if more exact sizes are wanted. A trial fit in scrap wood is practical.

The selection of the best shape for the screw to use depends on the purpose it must serve. Some common shapes and sizes are as follows.

Flat head. The most popular, this screw can be countersunk, that is, screwed in till the head is flat with the surface of the stock, or slightly below the surface.

Oval head. Although this type can be countersunk, and usually is sunk to the rim, it usually protrudes slightly.

Round head. The head of this screw protrudes entirely and is somewhat decorative.

Fillister head. The head is shaped like three checkers on top of each other so that it may be easily countersunk.

Bung head. The small head, not much wider than the shank, is easily countersunk.

Binding head. This has slightly tapered sides and a rounded top.

Lentil head. The head is shaped like a small M & M candy.

Headless. The slot is recessed in the shank.

Truss head, or stove head. The head is wide and thin.

Pan head. The head is shaped like an upside-down frying pan, narrower on the top, flat on top and bottom.

Drive. A steel, spiral knurl (a raised twirl) is hardened so that the screw can drive into soft metal.

Dovel. A wood screw with threads on both ends.

Winged. The head is wing-shaped (like a bolt) so that it can be turned by hand.

Hanger bolt. A wood screw on one end, a machine bolt on the other.

Screws vary in diameter, length, and thread. The diameter is expressed in gauge numbers ranging from 0 (equal to 1/16 inch) to 20 (equal to 29/64 inch). Lengths are specified in inches and fractions of an inch.

Common lengths are ¼, ⅜, ½, ⅝, ¾, ⅞, and 1 inch, and 1¼, 1½, 1¾, 2, 2¼, 2½, 2¾, 3, 4, 4¼, 5, and 6 inches.

Each screw has a smooth portion between the head and the threads called the shank.

The screw slots most widely known are the straight slot and the Phillips cross slot. The Freason cross slot is similar to the Phillips, and the Pozzi drive has even more grooves, to permit maximum drive. Several other cross slots are also

Screw sizes and dimensions

Size numbers

Length (inches)	0	1	2	3	4	5	6	7	8	9	10	11	12	13	14	15	17	18	20	22	23	24	25	28	30
¼	×	×	×	×	×	×																			
⅜	×	×	×	×	×	×	×	×																	
½		×	×	×	×	×	×	×	×	×															
⅝		×	×	×	×	×	×	×	×	×	×	×													
¾			×	×	×	×	×	×	×	×	×	×	×												
⅞			×	×	×	×	×	×	×	×	×	×	×	×	×										
1				×	×	×	×	×	×	×	×	×	×	×	×	×	×								
1¼					×	×	×	×	×	×	×	×	×	×	×	×	×	×							
1½					×	×	×	×	×	×	×	×	×	×	×	×	×	×	×						
1¾						×	×	×	×	×	×	×	×	×	×	×	×	×	×						
2						×	×	×	×	×	×	×	×	×	×	×	×	×	×	×	×	×			
2¼							×	×	×	×	×	×	×	×	×	×	×	×	×	×	×	×			
2½							×	×	×	×	×	×	×	×	×	×	×	×	×	×	×	×			
2¾									×	×	×	×	×	×	×	×	×	×	×	×	×	×			
3									×	×	×	×	×	×	×	×	×	×	×	×	×	×	×		
3½										×	×	×	×		×	×	×	×	×	×	×	×	×		
4												×	×		×	×	×	×	×	×	×	×	×	×	×
4½													×		×	×				×	×	×	×	×	×
5																				×	×	×	×	×	×
6																					×	×	×	×	×

Gauge and Diameter

Size number	0	1	2	3	4	5	6	7	8	9	10	11	12	13	14	15	17	18	20	22	24	25	28	30
Steel wire gauge	17	15	14	13	12	11	10	9	8	7	6½	6	5	4½	4	3	2½	2	1	0½	0			
Diameter (inches)	0.054	0.072	0.080	0.091	0.105	0.120	0.135	0.148	0.162	0.177	0.184	0.192	0.207	0.216	0.225	0.243	0.25	0.262	0.283	0.306	0.331	0.362	0.333	

made. Each type of slot requires a different type of screw-driver, if the slot is not to be damaged. The bolt head has a special rosette head to prevent tampering.

Locks in the thread are created in some patented bolts and some screws. Nylock has a resilient nylon insert in its threaded section which wedges the screw tightly against the opposite threads. The Thredlock Screw has a bulge on one thread which resists removal. The Springtite has a coiled spring-lock washer. The Spin-Lok has locking teeth under the head that act like a ratchet. The Sems Screw has a lock-ing washer unit. Saf-lok has one or more ringed expansion in-serts which stay in place even if the screw is removed.

Some very large screws made without slots are known as lag bolts or lag screws, and are turned with a wrench. Stock sizes range from 1 inch to 16 inches long and from ¼ to 1 inch in diameter.

For heavy construction, bolts offer more strength than screws. These are made in stock sizes from ¾ inch to 20 inches long and from 3/16 to ¾ inch in diameter. Those with round heads are known as carriage bolts; those with square heads are called machine bolts.

Recent improvements in screw design include screws with grooves in the ends of the thread to hold metal against wood, and other fine details.

To start a screw, carpenters make an entering or pilot hole with an awl or drill. Avoid tapping the screw with a hammer, for this may split the wood and destroy the head of the screw. Unless the screw is properly started, it may enter at an angle or force the screwdriver to slip off the groove and mar the wood.

When metal hardware—a hinge, a bolt, a catch, or a pull —is to be attached to wood, first locate the position of the screws by placing the hardware in the desired position and marking the entering point. Select the screw proper in gauge and length. Carefully drill a hole smaller than the gauge of the screw, one-half the screw length on softwood, slightly deeper on hardwood. For small screws, the pilot hole can be made with an awl or, if that is not available, with a nail. In making wood joints, follow the same procedure in locating screw locations.

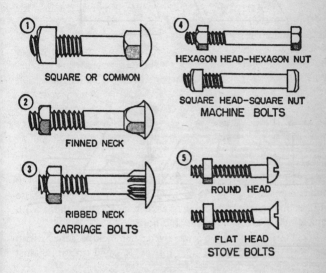

SQUARE OR COMMON

FINNED NECK

RIBBED NECK
CARRIAGE BOLTS

HEXAGON HEAD—HEXAGON NUT

SQUARE HEAD—SQUARE NUT
MACHINE BOLTS

ROUND HEAD

FLAT HEAD
STOVE BOLTS

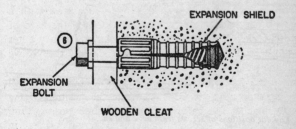

EXPANSION SHIELD

EXPANSION BOLT

WOODEN CLEAT

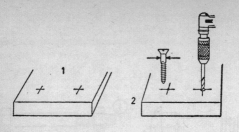

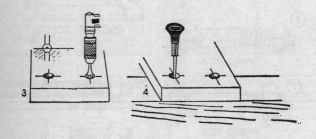

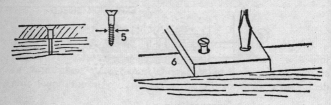

1. *Lay out positions of screws from edge and end.*

2. *Bore holes equal in diameter to thickness of screw shank.*

3. *Countersink the holes to the diameter of the screw head.*

4. *Mark location of holes on under piece.*

5. *Bore smaller holes for threaded part of screw.*

6. *Drive screws home.*

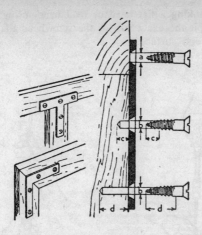

To fasten hinges or other hardware in place with screws:

1. *Locate the position of the piece of hardware on the work.*
2. *Recess the work to receive the hardware, if it is necessary.*
3. *Locate the positions of the screws.*
4. *Select screws that will easily pass through the holes in the hardware, as at a.*
5. *Bore the pilot holes (second hole) slightly smaller than the diameter of the threaded part of the screws, as at b.*
6. *Drive the screws tightly in place.*

If the wood is soft, bore as deep as half the length of the threaded part of the screw, as at c. If the wood is hard (oak), the screw soft (brass), or if the screw is large, the hole must be nearly as deep as the screw, as at d. Holes for small screws are usually made with brad awls.

The next step depends on the nature of the wood to be joined. If both pieces are softwood, or the bottom piece is softwood, make a hole approximately as wide and as deep as the shank of the screw. Then bore an additional area

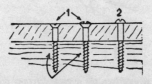

1. *Countersink for flat and oval heads.*
2. *Do not countersink for round heads.*

for countersinking a flat head or oval head, using a special countersink bit the exact size of the screwhead that is to go below the wood surface.

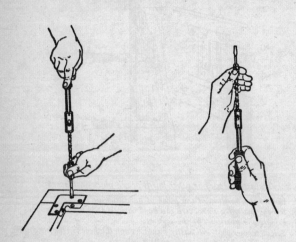

The "Yankee" spiral ratchet screwdriver is most useful for the rapid driving or drawing of screws, or for use in awkward places. It is especially practical in repetitive production work in industry. It can be steadied by holding the revolving chuck sleeve with the fingers of the left hand.

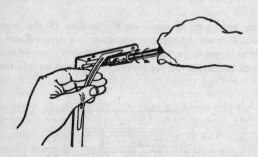

With a ratchet screwdriver, the screw is driven or drawn by turning the hand right and left. The left hand is free to hold the work after the screw is started.

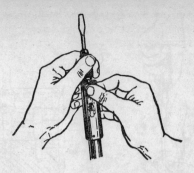

To use as a ratchet screwdriver, draw the spindle in, then turn the locking ring to the left to lock it. Vary the shifter position to change the ratchet action. To release the spiral spindle safely, hold it by the chuck while turning the locking ring to the right so that the spindle will not fly out.

If both pieces of stock, or the bottom piece, are hardwood, bore a hole through the top piece slightly narrower than the screw, and continue a hole of smaller diameter in the second piece. Always drill for one screw at a time.

In using a power drill, a special device, the Screw-Mate, makes it easy to drill a pilot hole, shank clearance, and a head countersink in a single operation. These are made for numerous screw sizes and are available in sets (recommended: Stanley No. 1525) of five or more. (The use of the Screw-Mate is discussed in the section on power tools.)

When nails or screws are to be stored in boxes or cans, a sample should be Scotch-taped on the outside for identification. Many home carpenters use small glass jars so that the contents are always visible. One widely used device is to tack the screw covers onto the bottom of an overhead board or the bottom of an eye-level shelf; the jars can then be unscrewed and opened in a simple motion, and the whole stock is visible at a glance.

When you replace a screw you may find that it fits loosely and fails to provide the rigidity the job requires. If the fit is good, you can get additional grip by dipping the screw in glue or paint. However, if the hole is too large, inserting a wooden match or a toothpick can be helpful. Tight screws can be loosened slightly by soaking them in a few drops of peroxide.

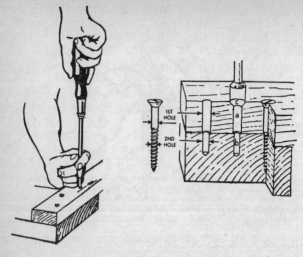

Use the longest screwdriver convenient for the work. More power can be applied to a long screwdriver than a short one, with less danger of its slipping out of the slot.

Hold the handle firmly in the palm of the right hand with the thumb and forefinger grasping the handle near the ferrule. With the left hand, steady the tip and keep it pressed into the slot while renewing the grip on the handle for a new turn.

If no hole is bored for the threaded part of the screw the wood is often split or the screw is twisted off. If a screw turns too hard, back it out and enlarge the hole.

A little soap on the threads of the screw makes it easier to drive.

Fasteners

In addition to nails and screws, glue and dowels, certain specialized devices are used for holding pieces of wood together. These include anchors, bolts, builders' hardware, metal wood connectors, and wood joints.

Special fasteners have been devised for many special purposes. A hand rail bolt has threads on both ends. Rings and plates are metal washers with special grooves or cuts that hold to the wood and prevent slipping. Mending plates are screwed to two connected pieces to provide a rigid support. Similarly, angle irons, T-irons, and corner-angled (L-shaped) irons provide reinforcement for various types of corners.

The clamp nail, available from ¼ inch to 6 inches long, is a newer type of joining device. It has two flanges that fit into sawed grooves in each end of a joint, and are held with a drop of glue.

Toothed rings are corrugated and toothed, and are made from 16-gauge plate low-carbon steel. They are used between two timber frames for comparatively light construction and are embedded into the contact faces of the joint members by means of pressure.

Special hardware is used for fastening into plaster, concrete, and masonry. One group of items is inserted into a hole bored into the base. Into this an anchor or plug (usually of lead) is inserted to receive a screw. Among these are the rawl pins, the star driving anchor, the Johnsen and Ackerman anchor, the lead shield, and the expansion iron shield.

A second group is designed to hold onto an anchor by expanding. Among these is the togglebolt, which is inserted flat into the hole and expands, butterfly-fashion, when tightened, and the molly expansion anchor. A third group includes a variety of clips, ties, and tapped inserts.

Awls are used to make holes for small screws and nails. To avoid splitting the wood, start the awl with its edge across the grain, turning it back and forth slightly as you press down. Do not let the edge come parallel with the grain.

Bit stock drills are designed and tempered to make holes in metal, but may also be used in wood, especially in repair work in which contact with nails or metal is possible. They are sized by 32ds of an inch and range from No. 2 = 1/16 inch and larger.

*Twist bits for wood are used to make holes for screws, nails, or bolts.
They are sized by 32ds of an inch and range from No. 2 = 1/16 inch and
larger.*

*Countersink bits are used to widen screw holes so that the heads of flat
head screws may be flush with, or slightly below, the surface of the work.*

*Fostner bits are used to bore holes part way through where the auger
bit screw or spur would go through the work, also on end grain, thin
wood, or near an end where an auger bit would split the work. To center
or start a Fostner bit, scribe a circle the size of the hole with dividers
and press the rim of the fostner bit into it. Fostner bits are sized by 16ths
of an inch from No. 4 = ¼ inch and larger.*

Nails

Through the years the nail has had a long evolution from
the first blunt, square-cut piece of iron. The old-fashioned cut
nail had a rectangular cross section and a taper from a flat
head to a blunt point. You may remember it as the horseshoe nail. It is still made, but now it is carefully designed.

Today there are many other types of nails, each made to do
a particular job better than the others.

The wire nail has a circular cross section, without a taper.
This is generally used for indoor projects, and it is available
in many sizes and shapes, with and without heads.

The common flathead nail is used for most rough work. In
general, the head of the nail you select depends on the
hardness of the wood and the chance of the head's working
through. Large flatheads are best for soft materials: Fiberglas,
top Masonite, shingles, and the like. The finishing nail has a
small head and is used for more purposes than any other.

The box nail is thin and can also be used for rough work.

Size, type, and use of nails*

Size	Length (inches)	Diameter (inches)	Remarks	Where used
2d	1	0.072	Small head.....	Finish work, shop work.
2d	1	.072	Large flat head.	Small timber, wood shingles, lathes.
3d	1¼	.08	Small head.....	Finish work, shop work.
3d	1¼	.08	Large flat head.	Small timber, wood shingles, lathes.
4d	1½	.098	Small head.....	Finish work, shop work.
4d	1½	.098	Large flat head.	Small timber, lathes, shop work.
5d	1¾	.098	Small head.....	Finish work, shop work.
5d	1¾	.098	Large flat head.	Small timber, lathes, shop work.
6d	2	.113	Small head.....	Finish work, casing, stops, etc., shop work.
6d	2	.113	Large flat head.	Small timber, siding, sheathing, etc., shop work.
7d	2¼	.113	Small head.....	Casing, base, ceiling stops, etc.
7d	2¼	.113	Large flat head.	Sheathing, siding, subflooring, light framing.
8d	2½	.131	Small head.....	Casing, base, ceiling, wainscot, etc., shop work.
8d	2½	.131	Large flat head.	Sheathing, siding, subflooring, light framing, shop work.
8d	1¼	.131	Extra-large flat head.	Roll roofing, composition shingles.
8d	1½	.131	Extra-large flat head.	Roll roofing, composition shingles.
9d	2¾	.131	Small head.....	Casing, base, ceiling, etc.
9d	2¾	.131	Large flat head.	Sheathing, siding, subflooring, light framing.
10d	3	.148	Small head.....	Casing, base, ceiling, etc., shop work.
10d	3	.148	Large flat head.	Sheathing, siding, subflooring, framing, shop work.
12d	3¼	.148	Large flat head.	Sheathing, subflooring, framing.
16d	3½	.162	Large flat head.	Framing, bridges, etc.
20d	4	.192	Large flat head.	Framing, bridges, etc.
30d	4½	.207	Large flat head.	Heavy framing, bridges, etc.
40d	5	.225	Large flat head.	Heavy framing, bridges, etc.
50d	5½	.244	Large flat head.	Extra-heavy framing, bridges, etc.
60d	6¼	.262	Large flat head.	Extra-heavy framing, bridges, etc.

*This chart applies to wire nails, although it can be used to determine the length of cut nails.

The brad has almost no head at all and is used for work that is to have a good finish. Usually the heads are countersunk below the surface of the stock.

Nails with decorative heads are also used for fine work and upholstery, where the head becomes part of the decoration. These heads may be oval-shaped, or they may have a decorative design.

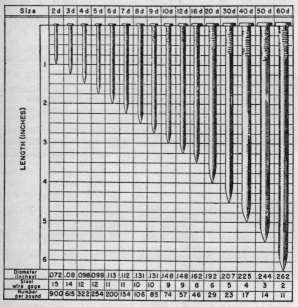

Size	2 d	3 d	4 d	5 d	6 d	7 d	8 d	9 d	10 d	12 d	16 d	20 d	30 d	40 d	50 d	60 d
Diameter (inches)	.072	.08	.098	.098	.113	.112	.131	.131	.148	.148	.162	.192	.207	.225	.244	.262
Steel wire gage	15	14	12	12	11	11	10	10	9	9	8	6	5	4	3	2
Number per pound	900	615	322	254	200	154	106	85	74	57	46	29	23	17	14	11

Nail sizes.

A double- or duplex-headed nail has two heads, one over the other. These are used for work that must be disassembled later. The extra head remains above the stock and can be grasped by the clutches of a claw when the nail is to be removed.

Special nails are made for all purposes. Masonry nails are specially hardened. Nails for riveting are annealed or softened. Specially hardened aluminum is used for rust-proof outdoor nails. A nail with a slotted head is designed to be removed with a screwdriver. Boatbuilders use a copper clout nail for outdoor jobs. A lead-capped nail is leakproof when used on metal roofing. A dowel pin has a roughened edge to hold it in joints.

In addition to variations in their heads, nails vary at their points. In general, the duller the point, the less is the danger of splitting the wood. In fact, where the danger is great, the end of the nail may be clipped with a pair of pliers or otherwise blunted. Blunt points appear on cut nails (some floor nails and shingle nails). These tend to prevent wood from splitting because they cut their way through wood fibers. However, blunt-pointed nails do not hold as well as sharp nails.

A duck-bill point is used on clinching nails to lessen the danger of breaking. As the name indicates, the point is shaped like a duck's bill, with one edge not tapered at all.

Diamond points come to a sharp point quickly.

Long diamond points taper to a sharp angular point with a diamond cross section in a distance equal to about three diameters. They are used for parquet flooring, hinges, plaster boards, and the like. Easier than most nails to drive, they also have great holding power.

The needle-point nail has a similar taper, but it has a circular cross section to the end. These are cheaper to make from wire and are used on all small brads. The needle point holds best in softwoods but offers more danger of splitting than a diamond point.

A chisel point, virtually a two-sided point, is used on boat spikes and for paneling.

Another difference in nails occurs in the shank. The holding power of a nail varies directly with the amount of area in contact with the wood. Therefore, some nails are designed to have a maximum outside area. A square shank has more area than a round one. Some shanks have grooves and spirals, and even barbs, to give them more holding power. Other nail shanks are etched or coated. Etching triples the holding power of nails in soft or hard woods. Cement-coated nails will hold from 75 to 100 per cent stronger in softwoods than will uncoated nails.

Among the other special nails in use are resin-coated, copper-plated, brass-plated, tin-coated, cadmium-plated, nickel-plated, chromium-plated, galvanized, blue, acid-etched, painted, and japanned.

The size of a nail is measured on a penny system. This was originally based on the number of nails of that size in one pound. In time, this came to be mispronounced till it became "penny." A ten-penny nail weighed 10 pounds (or pennies) per thousand nails. The English penny is abbreviated *d*. So the ten-penny nail is now written 10d. Expressed in length, the 2d nail is 1-inch, the 3d nail is 1¼-inch. Smaller nails and nails more than 6 inches long are written ½-inch or 6½-inch.

1 -inch = 2d	3¼-inch = 12d
1¼-inch = 3d	3½-inch = 16d
1½-inch = 4d	4 -inch = 20d
1¾-inch = 5d	4½-inch = 30d
2 -inch = 6d	5 -inch = 40d
2¼-inch = 7d	5½-inch = 50d
2½-inch = 8d	6 -inch = 60d
2¾-inch = 9d	
3 -inch = 10d	

Nailing is considered the least sophisticated joining and generally is used for work in which apearance is not too important, for rough work, for temporary jobs, and for quick fastening.

A big danger in nailing is splitting the stock. Hardwoods, especially, resist nailing, and even some softwoods like Douglas fir, white cedar, and eastern hemlock will split easily. You can reduce this danger by using a blunt nail, or by boring a pilot hole with an awl or a small blunt nail, or by dipping the nail in wax, grease, or a heavy oil.

For holding small brads or tacks that are too small for the fingers to grip without their being in the way, use heavy paper, cardboard, or a drinking straw. Slip the nail through the paper and hold the paper.

By far the strongest—but most unattractive—kind of nailing is clinch nailing. A long nail is passed through both boards and the protruding end bent over and hammered below the surface. This type of joining is used where strength is important and appearances are inconsequential.

For especially strong joining, anchor nailing is recommended—driving the nails through both pieces of stock at opposite angles. Where the position of the boards makes it

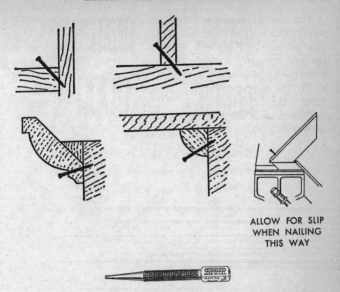

ALLOW FOR SLIP
WHEN NAILING
THIS WAY

*Use the nail set to finish driving nails in corners and on moldings, etc.,
where the hammer might disfigure the wood.*

impossible to drive a nail in straight, "toe-nailing" can be
used. Here the nails are driven at an angle less than a right
angle to the base.

Steel Corrugated Fasteners

One type of nail is purposely not straight. It is a piece of
corrugated steel with one edge sharpened. When two flat
pieces are to be joined at the same level—particularly mitre
joints—these "wiggle" nails will do a creditable strengthening
job on joints that are glued or have other additional support.
They are available in depths of ¼, ½, or 1 inch, and they
can have as few as two or as many as seven corrugations.

The wiggle nail is made with plain edges for hardwood
and saw edges for softwood. Manufacturers of furniture and
boxes use enormous quantities of them. They are inexpensive
and will quickly and easily do a job that would otherwise
require expert work. They are made in two styles: one with
the ridges running parallel, the other with the ridges running

Corrugated fasteners.

1. *Divergent corrugations with plain edge.*

2. *Divergent corrugations with saw edge.*

3. *Parallel corrugations with plain edge.*

4. *Parallel corrugations with saw edge.*

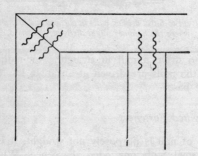

Circular corrugated fastener when more than two edges are to be joined.

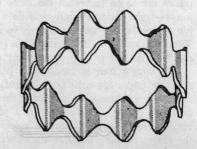

at a slight angle to one another. The second type has a tendency to compress the material because the ridges and grooves are closer at the top than at the bottom.

Almost anything you choose to make will require some metal parts besides the nails, screws, and fasteners. Wherever there is a moving part, you will need a hinge and a knob or a pull. Select the proper hardware while you are planning your project, for often the type of hinge will affect the depth of the grooves in working and the overall appearance of your work.

Both Leaves Half-Swage

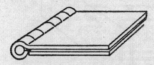

● *Hinge leaves "swaged" to reduce the space between them when closed. (The swaging operation slightly increases the width of the hinge.)*

*One Leaf Half-Swaged,
One Leaf Flat*

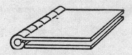

*One Leaf Full-Swaged,
One Leaf Flat*

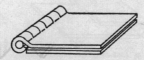

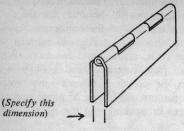

Both Leaves Boosted

(*Specify this dimension*) →

● *Barrel "boosted" to increase space between the leaves.*

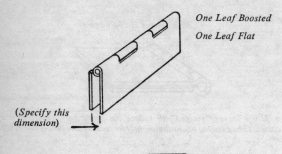

One Leaf Boosted
One Leaf Flat

(*Specify this dimension*) →

● *Offset for profile and travel of reverse leaves.*

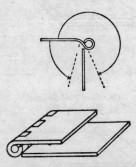

● *Leaves of unequal width.*

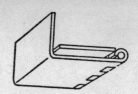

● *One or both leaves bent or offset.*

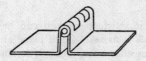

● *Special hole locations, slots, or welding projections.*

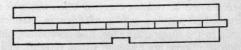

● *Special cut-offs or notches.*

DOORS LARGER THAN 5 FT. SHOULD HAVE THREE BUTT HINGES, ONE FOR EACH 2½ FT. OF HEIGHT	
SIZE AND TYPE OF DOOR	SIZE OF BUTT HINGE
¾", ⅞" CUPBOARD DOORS UP T O24" WIDE	2½"
⅞" TO 1⅛" SCREEN DOORS UP TO 36" WIDE	3"
1⅛" TO 1⅜" DOORS UP TO 32" WIDE	3½"
1⅛" TO 1⅜ DOORS OVER 32" TO 37"	4"
1 9/16", 1¾", 1⅞" DOORS UP TO 32" WIDE	4½"
1 9/16", 1¾", 1⅞" DOORS OVER 32" TO 37"	5"
1 9/16", 1¾", 1⅞" DOORS OVER 37" TO 43"	5" EX. HEAVY
1 9/16", 1¾", 1⅞" DOORS OVER 43" TO 50"	6" EX. HEAVY
2", 2¼", 2½" DOORS UP TO 43" WIDE	5" EX. HEAVY
2", 2¼", 2½" DOORS OVER 43" TO 50"	6" EX. HEAVY

CHAPTER NINE

Sharpening the Tools

One of the biggest satisfactions you can have when you get interested in tools is to take a dull blade and put a good sharp edge on it—an edge sharp enough to shave a hair off the back of your hand.

The small piece of natural stone which every carpenter of the eighteenth century carried with him for putting an edge on his tools, as well as the large mill-cut circular stone that was turned with a handle or a foot treadle, has gone out of style because we have learned to make stones that serve our purposes better. The little bench stone, driven by a hand crank, which some carpenters carry, is often made of natural emery crushed to varying grades of fineness. Artificial materials made in the electric furnace, like corundum, alundum, and carbide of silicon, are crushed, sifted, molded, and baked to form stones of every size, shape, and degree of fineness needed.

For the amateur the common oilstone with a rough surface on one side and a fine surface on the other is all that is necessary. If, in the course of time, you find that the edges and bevels of your tools are worn down badly, it may be necessary to have them professionally ground so that you can start all over again, unless you wish to buy or borrow a revolving stone with which to do your own grinding.

The grinding of edged tools is best accomplished on a wet sandstone grindstone, because there is then no danger of burning or drawing the temper from the steel. If a dry emery stone is used, the tool should be dipped frequently in water to keep it cool.

An improved slow-speed electric grinder with a special wheel and an excellent control mechanism is now available. This grinder is highly satisfactory, although it uses a dry wheel.

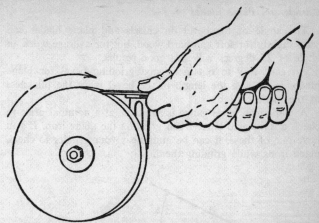

Grinding straightens the edge and restores the bevel preparatory to sharpening by whetting on the oilstone. The grindstone should turn toward the plane iron. Use the guide; it assures a flat, even bevel. Bear on the wheel lightly and dip the plane iron frequently in water to prevent burning or softening the steel.

In grinding, the bevel of the tool is placed against the surface of the revolving stone, and either held by hand or clamped in an adjustable guiding device. It is lightly pressed against the wheel, which revolves toward the tool.

The tool should be shifted from side to side evenly across the wheel.

Move the plane iron from side to side to grind all parts of the bevel and to keep the wheel true. The edge should be straight and almost at right angles to the sides of the plane iron.

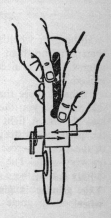

Chisels and Plane Blades

The angle of the bevel on chisels and plane blades can vary slightly for soft and hard wood, but for average work an angle of 25 degrees will give good results.

An easy way to obtain a good grinding bevel for plane blades is to have the length of the bevel twice the thickness of the blade.

A plane-iron bevel gauge is available at a nominal price to check a 25-degree bevel when grinding the plane iron. If you have one of these, it can be hung near your grinder to check plane irons while grinding them.

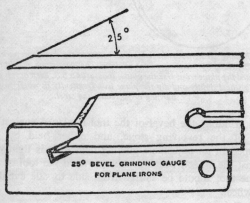

Plane iron bevel gauge.

Honing or whetting your edge tools is done much oftener than grinding them. Edge tools should be ground only when a new bevel is necessary or when the edge of the tool is nicked.

Perhaps, more than words, the diagrams on page 222 and 223 will tell you the do's and don't's of honing plane cutters and chisels. A light oil should be used on the stone to float the particles of steel and prevent them from filling the pores of the stone. Kerosene or kerosene and light motor oil mixed do very well. The important fact about chisels and plane cutters is that there are two different angles of the blade. One is the grinding angle, the other the whetting angle. It is only the whetting angle that you will ordinarily attack with an oilstone. In whetting, place the bevel down on the stone with the back edge of bevel slightly raised.

Your sharpening problem is to keep the hand absolutely steady, moving parallel to the stone back and forth to ensure the use of the entire surface of the stone and avoid wearing hollows in it. If the surface of this oilstone is not a comparatively perfect plane, you can't do much with it. You must have the blade approximately square when you are through with the process. When you have cut this bevel on the oilstone at the proper angle of approximately 30 degrees, you will find that there is a wire edge on the back of the blade which must be removed. A stroke or two on the oilstone with the back of the blade held perfectly flat on top of the stone will take this off. A refinement can be given to the edge by stropping the edge a few times on leather or canvas.

There is one excellent way to determine whether or not you have really made a sharp edge, and that, strange to say, is by looking at it. A blade that is dull reflects light. A blade that is sharp does not reflect light. Hold your newly sharpened tool where light will shine on it; if there are no white spots, you can know without touching the edge that it is in good condition for even a trying piece of work.

As soon as you are through, the stone should be wiped dry.

Gouges

Grinding and whetting gouges is, of course, more difficult than sharpening chisels because the work must be done on a curve, but the principle is precisely the same as in the sharpening of a chisel.

The gouge with the outside bevel is ground as illustrated on page 223, but it is necessary to have a cone-shaped or round-edged wheel for grinding the gouge with an inside bevel.

The illustrations show how to whet the gouge with the outside bevel and the method employed for gouges with the inside bevel. A slip stone with a round edge is used to remove the wire edge of the gouge with an outside bevel and for whetting the gouge with an inside bevel. The slip stone is held in the hand, taking care to keep the cutting arc true. It is easy to remove the wire edge of the gouge with the inside bevel because the unbeveled side can be held flat to the stone,

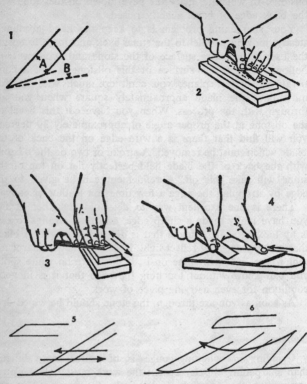

1. Grinding A angle, from 25 to 30 degrees. Whetting B angle 30 to 35 degrees.

2. Whet the plane iron on the oilstone to produce the really sharp cutting edge. Hold the plane iron in the right hand, with the left hand helping. Place the bevel on the stone with the back edge slightly raised. Move the plane iron back and forth.

3. Remove the wire or feather edge by taking a few strokes with the flat side of the plane iron held flat on the stone. Avoid the slightest bevel on this side. If a nick or a shiny edge of bluntness can be seen, repeat both processes of whetting.

4. Finish with a few strokes on a leather strop to produce a keen edge.

5. Keep the bevel constant by keeping the hands moving parallel to the stone. Avoid rocking.

6. Edge too blunt to cut well.

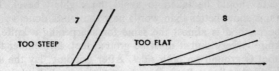

7   8

TOO STEEP   TOO FLAT

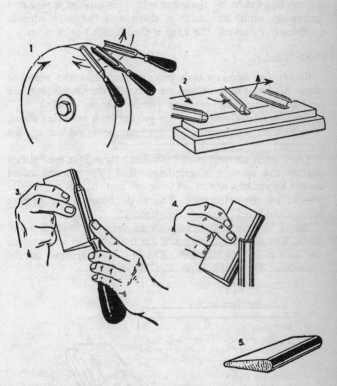

1. Grind the gouge as if it were a chisel, but turn from side to side to keep the shape and to grind all parts to the edge.
2. Turn the gouge from side to side as it is pushed forward on the oilstone to whet the edge.
3. Rub the inside edge of an outside-ground gouge very lightly to remove wire edge.
4. Sharpen the bevel edge of an inside-ground gouge with a round-edge oilstone slip.
5. Round-edged oilstone slip.

but care should be taken to avoid the slightest bevel. The diagrams show better than words how the job is done.

The method is almost the same for sharpening a knife. If the knife is very dull it must be ground first. Remember that this tool is ground on both sides. After grinding, lay the side of the blade almost flat on a whetstone and rub it back and forth—that is, both against the blade and with the blade. Repeat this action on the other side. This process is repeated frequently until the blade is sharp and the wire edge is completely removed. The edge is then finished on a strop.

Other Blades

Blades for iron spokeshaves are sharpened the same as plane blades. Draw knives are ground like chisels but are held in the hand and whetted with an oilstone or slip.

Axes, hatchets, and adzes are ground on a revolving stone, then held in the hand while a whetstone is rubbed against the edge.

Twist drills are reground by holding them in a special rest against the side of a grinding wheel. The cutting edges should be straight and equal in length and the lips sufficiently ground to give clearance. The angle between the cutting edges should be 59 degrees. See page 225.

Auger bits are sharpened with an auger-bit file and a slip stone. The spurs are sharpened on the inside so as to retain the correct outside diameter. The lips are sharpened on the upper side. The diagrams on page 225 show this.

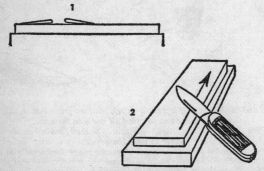

1. *Raise the back of the knife blade very slightly while whetting.*
2. *Rub back and forth on stone; reverse and whet the other side.*

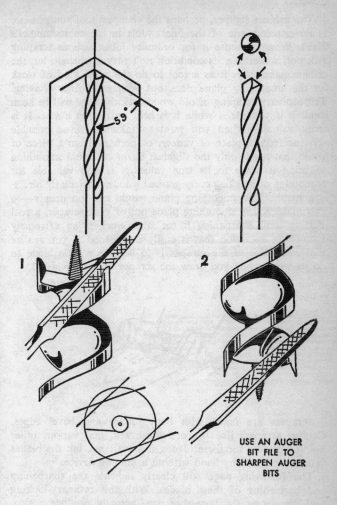

1. *File the spurs on the inside to avoid reducing the diameter of the bit.*

2. *File the cutting edge on the side toward the shank to avoid losing clearance on the bottom.*

Remove the burr with an oilstone slip.

Scrapers

The cabinet scraper, perhaps the cheapest tool you possess, is nevertheless one of the finest tools in the cabinetmaker's chest. When you use it for ordinary jobs, such as scraping paint off something, its condition isn't very important; but the cabinetmaker uses it as a tool to do the same kind of work as the smoothing plane does but with even finer shaving. For ordinary scraping of old woodwork the edge will be keen enough if you file it while it is held upright in a vise. It is most valuable when you want to take the finest possible shaving from a piece of veneer, or perhaps from a piece of wood that needs only the slightest bit more actual smoothing to bring it down to its true value. It is also valuable for smoothing or finishing curly grained woods, particularly bird's-eye maple. The smoothing plane would cut too deeply—so you make a tiny smoothing plane out of your scraper, a real cutting tool. Sharpening it for such work is an extremely interesting operation that is easily understood if you realize that each edge of the scraper is to become a little blade to do its work while you draw the scraper across the wood.

Scrapers are made with both square and bevel edges. Cabinet scrapers like the one illustrated, and various other holding devices for these blades, are available, but the blades can also be used by hand without a holding device.

The following page will clearly indicate the sharpening and burnishing of these blades. With this ordinary-looking tool, known as the burnisher, you actually produce a fine, keen-cutting wire edge. This wire edge is capable of doing a smooth scraping job without any tendency to tear or rough the wood even on curly hardwoods.

If you have ever seen a professional floor scraper operate,

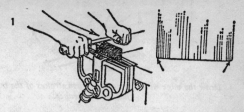

1. *File the edges square and straight by draw-filing with a smooth mill file. Round the corners slightly.*

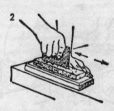

2. *Whet the edge, holding the blade square to the surface of the oilstone. Some prefer to hold the scraper square to the edge of the oilstone.*

3. *Remove the burr by whetting the scraper flat on the oilstone. The edges should be very smooth and sharp.*

4. Draw the edge with three or four firm strokes of the burnisher held flat on the scraper.

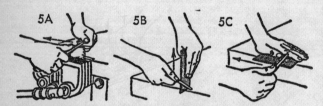

Turn the edge with a few strokes of the burnisher. The scraper can be held in any of the three ways shown above. Draw the burnisher toward you the full length of the blade with a sliding stroke.

To turn the edges out, the burnisher is held at 90 degrees to the face of the blade for the first stroke. For each of the following strokes, tilt the burnisher slightly until at the last stroke it is held at about 85 degrees to the face of the blade. A drop of oil on the burnisher helps.

HOW TO SHARPEN A BEVEL EDGE SCRAPER

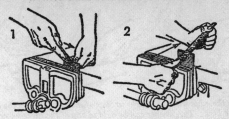

1. *Remove the old burr with a smooth mill file held flat against the face or flat side of the blade.*
2. *File or grind a bevel of about 45 degrees. Push the file forward and to the side with one sliding motion.*

3. *Whet the bevel side of the blade on the oilstone.*
4. *Whet the face side of the blade to remove the wire edge.*

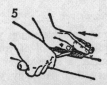

5. *Draw the edge with a few firm strokes on the face side of the blade. Hold the burnisher flat on the face side of the blade.*

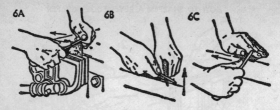

Turn the edge with a few firm strokes of the burnisher on the bevel side of the blade. The scraper can be held in any of the three ways shown above. Draw the burnisher toward you the full length of the blade with a sliding stroke. Some prefer to stroke both ways from the middle toward the ends. A drop of oil on the burnisher helps.

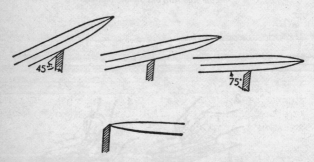

The first stroke should be made with the burnisher held at an angle a little greater than the bevel. Increase the angle until, at the last stroke, the burnisher is held at about 75 degrees to the face of the blade. If the edge should be turned too far over, it can be raised by drawing the point of the burnisher along the edge, under the burr.

you were probably astonished at the beautiful fine shavings he could take off with his scrapers. Perhaps you also learned by watching him work that the edges can be renewed several times with the burnisher.

Shaping the Screwdriver

One of the most valuable things you will learn about tools is to use a grindstone on all of your screwdrivers. Properly speaking, of course, a screwdriver isn't sharpened at all—it should be very dull. Actually you can find more grief with a screwdriver that is improperly formed than with any other tool. If you look at the poor shapes shown in the diagrams you will see pictures of tools that act like grass-hoppers. Such a tool can jump out of a screw, cut into the piece of fine-finished wood you are working with—in fact, drive you utterly mad. With a good screwdriver, properly shaped, you can easily drive home a screw that fits it without much hazard of its slipping out of the slot and damaging your work.

Poor shapes will slip out of slots and damage screws and work.

Screwdrivers are ground on an emery wheel or grindstone to obtain their correct shape. The edge should be made straight across the end and the faces near the ends parallel or almost parallel to each other. This is necessary to keep the screwdriver from slipping.

Filing a Saw

Filing a saw is really a job for an expert. There have been men who thought they knew how, but they have ended up by ruining a saw. That is why it is not recommended that you tackle the job yourself. Nevertheless, it is a mighty fine thing to know how to do it. You may discover some day when you are in a hurry that the saw you need to use has been used by your wife as a cleaver on a beef bone. The facts about filing the saw (with diagrams) are therefore included in this chapter. One word of warning, however: start your first saw-filing experiment on an old saw, not on your finely geared-up 22-inch crosscut. In saw filing practice counts.

The saw should first be placed in a saw clamp and the points evened with a flat file or a handsaw jointer.

Then set the teeth by bending each alternate tooth to the right or to the left so as to secure clearance for the blade when cutting. Set every other tooth on one side first, then those on the other side.

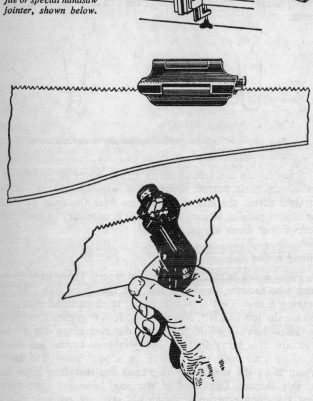

Hold the saw in a saw clamp for the first step in sharpening. Joint or even the points with a file or special handsaw jointer, shown below.

The second step is to set or lightly bend out every other tooth to secure clearance for blade when cutting.

The best way is to use the tool made for this work, a saw set. (See illustration on page 233.) The shape of the body and handle of this tool enables the user to operate it with ease. The saw is held firmly against the gauge while the tooth is being set. The saw teeth are in plain view, and that enables the user to adjust the tool quickly to the tooth to be set. The average set for a saw would require that the anvil be so adjusted that the lower line of the bevel is placed about one-third the height of the tooth from the point. It should never be lower than half the height of the tooth, as that might cause the blade to spring or crack and is liable to break out a tooth.

Another method of setting the teeth of a saw is with a hammer and a special anvil, giving each tooth a sharp blow. This method, however, requires much skill.

The set of a saw varies according to the work; soft, wet wood requires more set than dry hardwoods.

The saw is next readied for sharpening by filing the teeth with a three-sided blunt or taper file.

The workman takes his position at the left of the clamp and at the point of the saw.

For crosscut saws, the file is held at an angle of 45 degrees and is allowed to drop into the gullet between the first and second tooth. This position of the file determines the location for each succeeding stroke. Each alternate tooth is filed, working from the point to the handle, filing against the front edges of the teeth. The saw is then turned around and the workman changes his position to the right side of the clamp. The remaining teeth are then filed in the same way.

After all the teeth have been filed, the saw is laid flat on the bench. A file or an oilstone is gently slipped over the sides of the teeth to correct any slight differences in the set, and also to remove any wire edge.

Saw Set.

Let the file settle into the gullet to find its proper position in order to keep the teeth the same shape as when new.

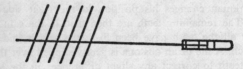

Begin at the point, turn the file to an angle of 65 degrees toward the handle and file every other tooth.

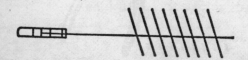

Reverse the saw and file the intervening teeth the same as before.

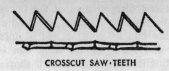

CROSSCUT SAW · TEETH

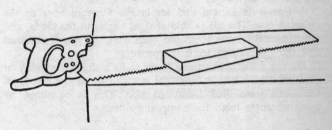

The sides of the teeth should be very lightly dressed with a file or oil-stone after filing to even the set and to remove any burr or wire edge from filing.

TO FILE A RIPSAW

PREPARE BY JOINTING AND SETTING THE TEETH
AS FOR A CROSSCUT SAW

FILE EVERY OTHER TOOTH FROM POINT TO HANDLE AT RIGHT ANGLES TO THE LENGTH OF THE BLADE

REVERSE THE SAW AND FILE THE INTERVENING TEETH

HOLD THE FILE STRAIGHT ACROSS

SIDE-DRESS RIPSAW THE SAME AS
IN SHARPENING A CROSSCUT SAW

RIPSAW TEETH

Some expert saw filers claim that the saw should be filed from the handle toward the point, contending that the file can more readily find its position in the gullet and that the original angle and shape of the teeth can be more easily retained. Working in this way, the file is sharpening the front edge of the tooth—that is, set away from the operator—and is cutting as it moves away from the edge. This has a tendency to produce a wire edge. By the other method, the file cuts as it moves toward the edge of the tooth, bringing it up keen and clean. This holds true when grinding a chisel or knife, less wire edge being made when the stone revolves toward the tool edge.

A ripsaw is jointed and set in the same manner as the crosscut saw. The file is held at right angles to the blade, and when each alternate tooth has been filed, the saw is reversed and the intervening teeth sharpened.

During a file stroke there is apt to be a slight inequality of pressure which would cause the saw to run off the line if all the teeth were filed from one side. This is equalized by filing alternate teeth from opposite sides.

CHAPTER TEN

Some Fancy Touches

Beveling, Chamfering, Beading

In carpentry there is almost an axiom that reads: "A finished piece of wood abhors a sharp edge." Sharp edges break off, and that will make the whole piece unsightly. Sharp edges cut and jab when a passer-by gets too close. Sharp edges are formal and stiff. They lose their color as stain is worn off or as enamel chips. Sharp edges are just a problem. Whatever edge you make, the final sanding should round off the arrises—the joining portions—so that they are rounded to the same arc as the lead in a pencil.

In addition, there are ways of finishing an edge to give it distinction.

The bevel edge is an angled edge. It can be made by cutting the stock at an angle, or by planing. Bevels are also used in making mitred corners for frames, columns, box joints, and the like.

The bevel can be 45 degrees (a true mitre), or it can be any other angle. To make a bevel, mark the proper angle with a line at both ends of a piece to be ripped, using a mitre square, a combination square, or a bevel. The bevel has a slotted blade that can be pivoted to any desired angle. If the angle is specified in degrees, you can set it by using the square or by using a protractor.

Sometimes carpentry specifications are given in terms of "rise and ruin." In these terms, two sides of the angle are specified—as 2 and 3 inches or 4½ and 5 inches. To mark such an angle, measure one side, say, 1½ inches down the edge, and the other side, say, 3 inches along the top of the stock. Connect the two points at the ends of the stock to get the angle.

A bevel is ripped simply by holding the saw at the angle marked. If you find this difficult to do free-hand, you can make a sample block to guide the saw, much like a jig.

Or you can mark both top and sides of the stock and follow the markings.

Planing a beveled edge is a bit more difficult. Holding your fingers under the plane, supported by the stock, will generally serve as a guide for the plane. Here, too, making a sample block or jig with the proper angle may be helpful. The jig can be clamped to the side of the plane. Whichever method you use, remember to test the angle from time to time to make sure you are not going astray.

Crosscut bevels are similarly marked and cut after the end has been carefully squared. Bevels all around should be made ends first, then edges.

Curved edges are beveled with a compass saw tilted outward. It is best to mark the stock at least with the top dimension. A convex curve is made by first making a bevel, then gouging the curve.

A chamfer is a bevel that extends over only part of the edge (◢ compared with ◢). To make a chamfer, mark the dimensions on the inside of the cut, using a pencil, not a knife cut. Plane with the grain until the pencil marks have been cut away. Check the straightness and the angle of the chamfer with a T-bevel.

An end chamfer is cut from two directions at a 45-degree angle, working from edge to center. Take care not to cut the grain at the corners. End chamfers must be made with compass saw, knife, or plane. Where a board is to be chamfered all around, edge chamfers are better cut first, for this leaves less of the more difficult end chamfer to be cut.

Chamfers must be marked on both top and side with a pencil. It is not wise to use a gauge, as is usually recommended for marking, because the gauge may leave a visible scratch. Most workmen prefer to make a chamfer by first cutting with a chisel, then finishing with a plane. A stop chamfer, which does not extend to the ends of a board, is cut from both ends toward the center with a chisel. Where size permits, a plane or spokeshave can be used.

Special care is required in sanding a bevel or a chamfer so that the angle is not distorted.

A nosing is a round edge on the stock. Lay out the arc of the nosing with a compass or scriber; then with a block plane make small, taut cuts to the rough arc and finish with a file and fine sandpaper.

Do not confuse the bevel with a taper, which is a narrowing of the length or width of a board, as in making a flower box, a column narrower at the top, or a similar table leg or lamp. Column work is common in many kinds of projects. If the work is to be stained, mitred corners are essential. With a power saw these can be joined by a spline or tongue glued into grooves in each of the side pieces. These splines must be placed close to the heel of the cut. Cut these grooves with the mitred face down to avoid difficulty. For thin woods a single saw kerf is usually wide enough for a spline. Attractive columns can be made with 5-, 6-, 7-, or 8-sided columns.

Routing

In the same way most of the special shapes you will wish to give particular pieces in a bookcase, a kitchen cabinet, or the panels of a door can be produced with the ordinary tools of your kit but are much easier and much quicker to produce by the use of that remarkable tool known as the router. (See Chapter 15.) This device, used by the cabinetmaker for much of his work, enables him to produce flutes, beads, reeds, rounded corners, and other finishing touches of almost every type. It is really astonishing how much of the work of cabinetmaking can be done with such a power tool.

Moldings

The easiest "fancy touch" you can put onto your work is a molding. With power tools you can create your own designs or make any of a hundred different versions.

Of course, you can buy moldings ready-made at the lumber-yard, and they are sold commercially in a score of different patterns. Some moldings are sold already finished in popular stains or varnishes.

Moldings are the essence of frames, but they are also used to put a finished edge on a plywood top, a tray, or any grained edge. They can be used to increase the size of a form or to hide a seam or a blemish. Or on a large area, they can be used to create the effect of a small panel, perhaps matching the shape of a window or a door, or in an octagonal or diamond shape. As a finish on the crown of a cabinet or

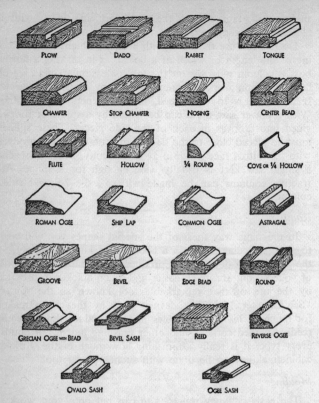

PLOW DADO RABBET TONGUE

CHAMFER STOP CHAMFER NOSING CENTER BEAD

FLUTE HOLLOW ¼ ROUND COVE OR ¼ HOLLOW

ROMAN OGEE SHIP LAP COMMON OGEE ASTRAGAL

GROOVE BEVEL EDGE BEAD ROUND

GRECIAN OGEE WITH BEAD BEVEL SASH REED REVERSE OGEE

OVALO SASH OGEE SASH

clock or column, or on the base, moldings serve a major decorative purpose. To support these on thin woods, backing cleats can first be screwed to the base piece, then the molding fastened to the cleats with screws from the inside. Moldings are also used for holding in place such things as windows and screen doors, and for panel moldings on drawer fronts, doors, and the like. However you use them, it is wise to put some sealer or paint on the area below the molding to prevent warping or decay.

Among the more popular moldings are the quarter-round, half-round, flat-edge, fluted, beaded, and grooved styles. Adaptations are made for baseboards, casings, coves, picture frames, cabinetwork, paneling, and battens.

Panels and frames should be mitred (see p. 157) and can be joined with splines, dowels, glue, screws, corrugated fasteners, or nails. Where mitres are glued, the end grain must first be sized with a thin coat of glue. This coat should dry and be scraped smooth before the final coat of glue is applied. Mitring is also necessary for moldings used for edgings. For this type of edge, moldings should be cut into four pieces, slightly oversize, with enough stock left to allow for mitred corners. The moldings should first be tacked into place and any irregularities trimmed with a block plane. A rabbet, mortise and tenon, or other concealed joint is suggested. If a power tool is used for cutting, a wooden spring should be clamped to the ripfence to hold the molding against the dado blades. A stick should be used to push the molding against the fence into the blade.

Moldings often have a hard grain and tend to deflect a brad. This can be minimized by drilling a small hole, using a brad with head removed (or a good steel needle cut off above the eye) as a bit. Another safeguard is cutting off the point of the nail before driving it into the wood.

Carving

When it comes to actual carving, there is no machine that will do it for you. There is no substitute for steadiness of hand and eye and long practice. Probably more tools have been designed for wood carving than for any other mechanical operation. Each of the tools is, of course, a kind of chisel, and the fundamental requirement of wood carving is to be able to use a chisel skillfully and successfully.

Various chisels are made in eighteen sizes, ranging from 1/32 to 1 inch, with straight, long-bend, or short-bend shanks. Veiners are made as small as 1/64 inch. The other tools are made in six sizes between 1 inch and 2 inches. Most of the small sizes are either spade- or fishtail-shaped, and that enhances their usefulness in modeling. Greater clearance is given just in back of the cutting edge.

To carve a design in low relief, sketch or trace an outline of it on the wood. Go over the outline with a small gouge or a paring tool, and cut on the background side of the line. When doing this, observe the direction of the grain on the raised part. Set down the outline with a chisel or gouge that conforms with the curve of the design, using a mallet or a

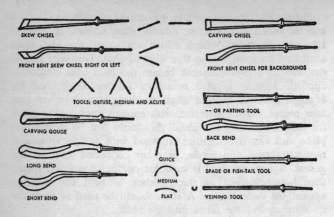

SKEW CHISEL

CARVING CHISEL

FRONT BENT SKEW CHISEL RIGHT OR LEFT

FRONT BENT CHISEL FOR BACKGROUNDS

TOOLS: OBTUSE, MEDIUM AND ACUTE

-- OR PARTING TOOL

CARVING GOUGE

BACK BEND

LONG BEND

QUICK

SPADE OR FISH-TAIL TOOL

MEDIUM

SHORT BEND

FLAT   VEINING TOOL

soft-faced hammer for tapping. Cut down the background with a flat gouge. Model the surface of the design so as to have an even degree of finish. Complete the modeling by putting in details and veining. Clean up the edges and the background. Stamp the background if a stamped texture is desired. Try to avoid undercutting the outline, or having the edges too sharp or the background too smooth.

Many beautiful yet simple designs on panels, bookracks, cabinets, or chests can easily be made by merely outlining with a small gouge or veiner. The effect may be improved by cutting or stamping down the background, and still further by slightly modeling the raised parts. The gouge lends itself to the forming of beautiful units and borders by simply combining gouge cuts. The skew chisel and the carving knife are particularly adapted to the type of notching called chip carving. Chip carving is effective if not overdone and may be as simple or ornate as the taste of the carver dictates.

Wood carving is the kind of thing that men spend a lifetime doing and is, of course, one of the great arts. There has been a great deal written on the subject, and anyone who wishes to go into it deeply should by all means go to the public library and find what books he can. He will indeed be amply repaid for his interest.

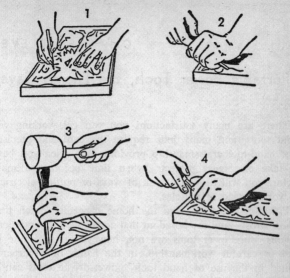

1. *Trace design on wood or draw it geometrically if its character permits.*
2. *Outline with a gouge or veiner. Be sure to cut outline on background side of line.*
3. *Set down outline with a mallet and gouges of suitable sweeps, to fit the curves of the design.*
4. *Cut out background with a flat gouge. Model surface add detail, clean up corners.*

CHAPTER ELEVEN

Portable Power Tools, the Energy Savers

There are many satisfactions you can get working with hand tools, and many jobs require the care and precision that hand-tool craftsmanship provides. But when you begin to take on bigger projects, when time becomes a major factor, you will begin to think of ways of putting electricity to work instead of muscles.

Power-driven tools save the home carpenter much time, labor, effort—and the boredom that comes from doing a long, tedious job. Power tools are not, however, a substitute for skill or careful workmanship. In the hands of a carpenter skilled in the use of hand tools, power-driven tools can do the job more quickly and perhaps more smoothly, but in the hands of a careless or ill-trained carpenter, these tools can ruin a job and waste materials. Most power-driven tools are available as electric-driven tools or air-operated tools. For the air-powered tools the power unit is the mobile air compressor. There are numerous other power-driven tools, gasoline-, electric-, steam-, and recently battery-operated, but the number of such tools that the home carpenter will find accessible is small.

The home carpenter will use electric-powered tools, usually of the type that can be plugged into an ordinary 110- or 115-volt outlet.

Each power tool is designed to do one type of work. But because each tool has a motor, and manufacturers continually seek to make each tool more versatile, many power tools can do many things they were not originally designed to do.

Although almost any other power tool with a motor can be adapted into a makeshift device to do the work of most other power tools, the most efficient work is done with a tool made for the particular purpose. For this reason, it is important first to select a good basic power tool, one that will do as many of the jobs you want done as quickly as possible.

In general, the jobs a power tool can do efficiently are:

drilling	grinding
sawing	polishing
joining	routing
planing	screwdriving
sanding	nut-running
shaping	hammering and impacting

When you select a power tool, make sure just what it can and cannot do. A good power tool is expensive. Of course, if you cannot afford any power tool except an inexpensive one, you must settle for a minimum. But a power tool is a long-term purchase—an instrument you will use for many years. You will get longer and better use from it if it is well made and sturdily built.

In most cases a portable power tool will do all the jobs as well as a table model. If budget is a factor in making your choice, it is better to select a good portable tool than a cheap bench model. You may well find that one or two portable tools will do as well for you as a large bench tool costing many times as much. In fact, two portable electric tools—the drill and the saw—can be the foundation for a whole home workshop.

The Motor

The series-wound universal type of motor is used in portable power tools for several reasons. It is light in weight for its power output, and therefore easy to handle. It operates on either A.C. or D.C., 60 cycles or less, at either 115 or 230 volts. Voltage is stamped on the nameplate of the unit. Look at the nameplate to make sure that a particular motor will operate on the current you are using. Some motors are designed for only alternating current (A.C.).

Overloading causes overheating, and overloading of long duration will cause motor failure. Temporary overloads, of short duration, are permissible. So when you must overload the tool, operate it intermittently, with off periods, or periods of light loads, to allow the motor to cool off. The quality of the motor and the brand name of the manufacturer are your best assurance of a satisfactory life span for your equipment.

General instructions for operating the motor include the following rules. Turn off the motor when you're not using it. Never insert anything in the vent holes in the motor housing. Keep the vent holes free from sawdust, dirt, and the like. Disconnect the plug from the outlet when changing sandpaper, drill bit, blade, and the like. (You might brush against the switch accidentally.)

Grounding

Many power tools are equipped, for your protection, with a three-wire cord and a three-pronged grounding type of plug. The longest prong of the plug is connected by a green wire to the metal frame of the tool. Grounding-type plugs should be used in approved grounding-type receptacles. The extension cords you use with the tool should be of the three-wire type, in order to ensure the continuity of the grounding wire. If you are in doubt whether your tool is properly grounded, consult a licensed electrician.

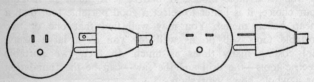

Grounding Type of Receptacle and Plug For use on 125 Volts Maximum

Grounding Type of Receptacle and Plug for use on 150 to 250 Volts

For your protection most power tools are equipped with a three wire cord and one of the above approved grounding type plugs in accordance with the National Electric Code. A green grounding conductor in the cord is connected to the metal frame of the tool and to the longest blade of the grounding type plug. The tool should be used in combination with an approved grounding type receptacle as indicated in the above sketch. If in doubt as to whether the receptacle is the correct one or is properly grounded, consult a licensed electrician.

Lubrication

Many portable power tools have permanently lubricated and sealed ball bearings, which never need lubrication for the life of the bearings. Some, on the other hand, have grease plugs that need to be repacked with grease periodically. On power tools, it is necessary to lubricate the moving parts from time to time.

Extension cords should be of the three-wire type with approved connector caps to insure continuity of the tool grounding wire. Also, the wire should be of the correct gauge to maintain adequate voltage at the tool.

Brushes

The brushes are a critical part of motor construction. They must make continuous contact with the spinning armature with a minimum of friction and wear, and they must offer little or no resistance to the flow of electricity. Spring-loaded carbon brushes, with stranded copper "pigtails," accomplish this. Brushes that do not have "pigtails" have direct contact with the commutator. The little spring holds the brush against the armature as the brush gradually wears down. Carbon conducts electricity and is slippery enough to present little friction. The stranded copper "pigtails" conduct electricity and are flexible.

Brushes should be inspected occasionally, and replaced when necessary. Motor failure is often attributable to worn-down brushes. Follow the manufacturer's instructions in inspecting and replacing the brushes. If you don't use the tool much, you will probably never need to replace the brushes. If you use the tool a good deal, however, you must replace the brushes when necessary to keep the tool operating.

CHAPTER TWELVE

The Portable Drill

If you are starting a home workshop, or if you are adding power tools to a hand-tool shop you already have, which power tools should you buy first? Because of its simplicity and versatility, in woodworking and its many all-around uses, the portable drill is your best choice as the first power tool. It is best to buy it as part of a kit with several accessories, selecting additional accessories as you find them useful. Even a basic kit will make it easy for you to do drilling, sanding, buffing, grinding, wire-brushing, polishing, and eventually many additional carpentry chores easily and skillfully. Additional accessories will help you to drive screws, countersink and counterbore for screws, or mount the portable drill as a drill press.

Selecting Your Drill

Most drills are made with a pistol type of handle. This has a trigger switch in the handle. Some models, however, pat-

Trigger Switch Drill

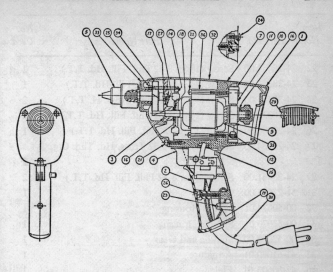

Anatomy of the Portable Drill

Item No.	Part No.	Part Name	No. Used
1	01-32126.04	Motor Housing Cover	1
2	29-29831.00	Switch Handle Cover	1
3	16-27709.00	Gear Cover	1
4	21-28875.00	Switch	1
5	23-22768.00	Chuck	1
7	28-10419.00	Data Plate	1
9	55-29613.00	Carbon Brush	2
10	56-28086.00	Brush Holder	2
11	56-28323.00	Brushholder Cap	2
12	27-29029.00	Carbon Brush Spring	2
14	22-28055.00	Baffle	1
15	32-30595.05	Insulation Tubing	1
16	32-23506.00	Armature Thrust Washer	2
17	24-23380.00	Thrust Washer	3
18	32-23552.00	Washer	2
19	24-22907.00	Lock Washer	Max. 1
21	24-28342.00	Screw (¾ x 8-32 Phil. Fill. Hd. T.T.)	1

Item No.	Part No.	Part Name	No. Used
22	24-28464.00	Screw (1¾ x 8-32 Phil. Fill. Hd. T.T.)	2
23	24-28341.00	Screw (⅜ x 8-32 Phil. Fill. Hd. T.T.)	1
24	24-28465.00	Screw (½ x 8-32 Phil. Truss. H. T.T.)	2
25	24-28339.00	Screw (1½ x 8-32 Phil. Fill. Hd. T.T.)	2
26	24-29406.00	Screw (1 x 8-32 Phil. Fill. Hd. T.T.)	1
27	24-27734.00	Screw (7/16 x 8-32 Truss. Hd. Thd. Ctg. Type 23)	2
29	24-28461.00	Screw (⅝ x 8-32 Phil. Fill. Hd. T.T.)	2
31	51-27695.00	Cord	1
32	00-50674.01	Motor Housing	1
33	00-52070.01	Spindle Housing	1
34	00-52035.00	Spindle and Gear	1
35	41-61020.01	Armature	1
36	42-60603.01	Field	1
	23-24862.00	Chuck Key (Not Shown)	1

terned on those designed for industry, have a hammer type of grip with the switch in the handle and an additional control handle on top.

The size of the drill is determined by the largest width or diameter of shank that can be held by the chuck. This may be a ¼-inch (thus a ¼-inch drill), a ½-inch, up to a 1-inch drill. Most popular chuck sizes are ¼, ⅜, and ½-inch. Most attachments are designed for the ¼-inch size.

A small, compact drill is preferred because it permits work in tight corners and narrow areas. In working between floor joists and building studding, the space available is less than 16 inches, and in drilling inside drawers or behind pipes even less space may be available. Some good drills are only 5¾ inches from chuck to the end of housing and only 3⅜ inches wide. Other models have removable handles for this kind of tight work.

The power capacity of drills is by either horsepower, amperes, or revolutions per minute, all of which reflect the size of the motor, and not the power delivered to the drill bit. Horsepower can mislead you, however. High amperage and high horsepower are of no use in doing a job for which they are not required. In addition, they tend to add cost to the operation, and may burn out faster. A drill for household use will be effective with ⅛ to ¼ horsepower for most needs, with 1,750 r.p.m.

Drill Speed

The speed necessary for a drill depends on the size of the bit and the material being worked. Most tools for home use operate in the speed range around 500 r.p.m. for ½-inch drills and between 1,600 and 2,800 r.p.m. for ¼-inch drills. Attachments on ¼-inch drills should be operated at 1,500 to 2,500 r.p.m. Depending on the load, drill size, and material, speed will drop from 30 to 50 per cent.

In drilling into heavy lumber or timbers, it is sometimes necessary to back out of work from an uncomfortable position. The better larger capacity drills made primarily for professionals have a reverse-action feature. The motor is reversible, or "neutral"-wound. This makes removal of the drill easier. A safety button prevents an accidental reverse action.

The slower the rate of revolution, the more "twist" or torque it creates. High-speed models drill quickly and cleanly through wood but do not have sufficient power to be used successfully on harder materials. Slower-speed models have sufficient power to drill into masonry. For heavy-duty work on wood, larger-type drills are preferred. In drilling heavy beams, a ½-inch or larger drill will do the job much more effectively than a smaller model. Models of intermediate speed can be used in either wood or masonry—with the proper bit, of course. If you plan to use the drill only for wood 2 inches thick or less, or for sheet metal, select a high-speed model; if you have occasion to drill harder materials, you can buy an intermediate-speed model and save the cost of buying two drills, a high-speed and a low-speed.

Because the speed requirement of each job is different, some drills are equipped to operate at two different speeds.

Reversible drill is handy for tight working conditions

A special device is geared to reduce speed to your requirement.

The chuck of a drill holds the working tool—the bit, screwdriver, grinder shank, and the like. Inexpensive chucks are tightened with a twist of the head. After some use, the head may be so tight that a wrench or pliers is necessary to loosen it. Better tools have a gear type of chuck, some of which are operated by a key. This minimizes the chore of changing bits and other tools.

The best type of chuck for home use is the geared chuck, which is tightened by means of a chuck key. Economy type

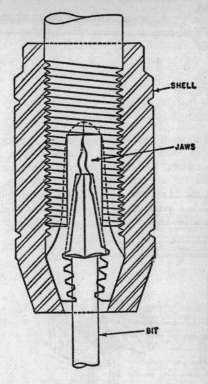

Drill Chuck

of drills, utilizing hand-tightened chucks, and hex-key chucks, are adequate for straight drilling, but are often not dependable for such heavy loads as wire-brushing the rust off a porch swing. The chuck key provides the extra tightening power that holds up during heavy jobs as well as straight drilling.

A right-angle drive attachment that can be used with some models permits the drill to work at a 90-degree angle from the shaft and simplifies the job of working in tight corners.

Bits

There are many types and sizes of bits for drills. The common twist drill is useful for most household purposes because

Power Bore Bit

it can cut through both wood and metal. The power bore bits are made in ⅜-inch, ½-inch, ⅝-inch, ¾-inch, ⅞-inch, and 1-inch diameters. The tip on each of these is a sharp point that makes for extreme accuracy in centering. A precision spur cuts the fibers and adds stability to the full-circle cuts. Somewhat less popular are auger-type bits similar to those used with a bit and brace. Because they have a point at the

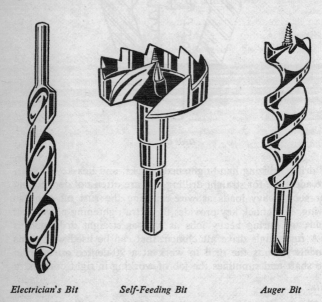

Electrician's Bit   *Self-Feeding Bit*   *Auger Bit*

Auger Bits

tip, these can be centered more accurately at a point indicated with an awl mark. Auger bits for power drills are made in the larger diameters—usually 1⅛, 1¼, and 1½ inches. These bits have a spur to outline the hole by severing fibers. The cutters then remove the stock without tearing.

The electrician's bit is heat-treated to withstand severe use in boring both soft and hard woods. It is made with a ¾-inch diameter to permit standard cables to be passed through obstructions, and it has a tapered head so that preliminary marking and cutting can be avoided.

The self-feed bit is for drilling in even larger diameters—from 1¾ inches to 2 9/16 inches. This cuts large holes with a minimum of power in either hard or soft wood. It looks like a bit with a ripsaw edge but can cut on an angle, overlap, or cut on close centers.

Flat bits are useful for extending the diameter of a hole larger than the capacity of the standard bits. Even with a ¼-inch shank the flat bit will make a rough boring up to 1 inch, whereas ordinary twist bits are not available for more than ¾ inch. The flat bit must be used with great care to avoid overheating the motor or splintering the wood.

Several sets of bits are widely available.

The Twist drill set includes several small sizes, 1/16 through ¼ inch. A ¼-inch drill will accept all sizes of twist drills up to and including ¼ inch, but not larger, because the shank of a twist drill usually has the same diameter as the rest of the bit.

Power bit sets are available in sizes from ¼ through 1 inch, usually in a vinyl plastic holder that keeps them from knocking against one another's edges. These cut a clean hole efficiently through wood, with much less friction than a twist drill of the same bore, and consequently less binding of the bit, burning of the wood, or stalling of the motor.

However, because of their shape, working them is not as easy in drilling a straight hole as with a twist drill. For this purpose the flat-bottomed boring bit is a good substitute.

Just as important as its basic use for drilling is the extra utility and versatility of a power drill. With a score of attachments it can do almost any woodworking jobs, although not always as efficiently as a special tool designed for the purpose.

Hole Saw. Available is a hole saw that cuts out a disc

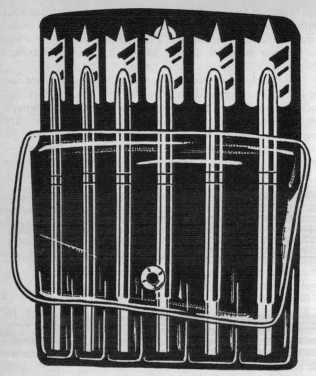

Spade Type Power Bits

instead of merely boring a hole. This device comes with a whole nest of blades ranging from ½ inch to 2½ inches in diameter. A pilot bit, or mandrel, holds the saw in place. The saw requires a light pressure.

Screwdriver. Did you ever try to drive ten or twenty or more screws into hardwood with a hand screwdriver? Even if you had drilled properly beforehand, you probably had difficulty unclenching your fist after that experience. A screwdriver attachment for your drill removes the exertion and tension. You will find it almost indispensable if you are making a cabinet or other piece of complicated furniture. Screwdriver blades that fit any type of screw head or slot are sold commercially, and are easily interchangeable.

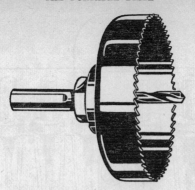

Hole Saw with Pilot Bit

Several attachments to aid screwdriving are made. These can drill a hole for the thread and the shank and the countersink hole. Stop adjustments regulate the depth of the holes so that small wooden plugs can be used in the countersink to hide the head or the screw. (Screwmate.®)

Screwdriver bits are standard equipment for drills, but these require a screwdriver attachment. Just as the hand tools come in various lengths and shapes, the screwdriver bits offer a wide choice in length, tip, and design.

Disc Sander. Two types of sanders may be used with the drill—a flexible rubber disc, which usually comes in the standard accessory kit, and a ball-jointed rigid disc. (Swirla-way.) The flexible rubber disc is best for curved surfaces, such as automobile bodies or furniture legs, but cannot be held flat against the work surface because it tends to "walk away." The ball-jointed disc sander is best for use on flat surfaces because it can be held flat against the work and will not gouge it. All grades of sandpaper, as well as a lamb's wool or cotton polishing bonnet, are used with both types of disc sander. The disc sander is useful for removing paint, shaping and smoothing irregular surfaces.

The rubber backing minimizes gouging, but it requires some skill to feather off the finish so that there are no offsets. A fine sandpaper should be used to remove cross scratches. Where a large surface is to be sanded, it is wise to construct a sliding base on which the motor can be locked at a slight

angle. The drill is moved forward slowly with the raised edge in front.

The same type of device can be used for smaller areas where a regular finish is important. Often it is better to hold the small pieces against the mounted sand disc to get greater evenness.

A ball-jointed, self-leveling sanding attachment will avoid the danger of gouging. The device (Swirlaway) finds the angle of the surface by itself and therefore does not require pressure. A polishing bonnet can be placed over the base for buffing or polishing in the same way.

Drum Sander. This is a special tool that you will use for smoothing curved edges such as those on valances for windows. Rougher steel-forming tools are available for shaping curved edges in sheet rock.

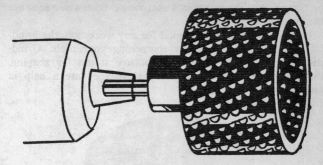

"Surform" Drum

"Surform" Drum. The rasp-type teeth of the Surform can be put to work with a drum device that will cut wood easily. This is especially useful for shaping and heavy cutting in awkward places.

Wire Brush. For the otherwise tedious job of removing paint or rust from metal, the wire brush is usually included in the drill kit. Since side pressure is applied to the arbor when wire-brushing, be sure that the chuck is well tightened. A small wire brush can be used to apply decorative brushings to aluminum or copper.

Wire brushes are used for cleaning tools, pans, and wood on which the paint is peeling. They help remove grime, rust,

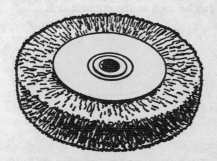

Wire Brush

or tarnish, and do many jobs that would otherwise require a brush and muscle.

Grinding Wheel. An essential for any workshop, the grinding wheel is most used for sharpening your tools. Grindstones or grinding wheels are abrasive stones for shaping, smoothing, or sharpening. In a garage they are a help in fender-repair work.

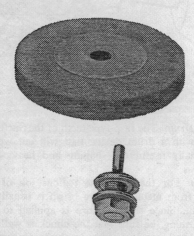

Grinding Wheel and Arbor

The drill should first be mounted on your bench, and a tool rest should be provided to hold the tool against the wheel. Most drills are capable of being mounted in a stand. Abrasive wheels come in many sizes and shapes for special uses, and can be used in the portable drill.

Rubber Disc forms Base for Sanding and Buffing

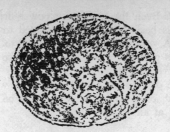

Polishing Glove

Polishing Glove Is Placed Over Rubber Base in Portable Drill

Buffing Wheel. Buffing wheels, made of layers of cloth, are used for waxing or polishing. Sizes range from 3 to 6 inches in diameter.

Stirrer. This is simply a specially bent rod that speeds up the job of stirring and mixing paint. It is included in most portable-drill kits.

Stirrer

Drill Stand. Even the work of a power drill press can be done with this basic tool if it is clamped to a bench stand or mounted. A yoke should be constructed to hold the motor firmly. This is placed on two ½-inch rods so that the depth of borings can be regulated. On some models a collar can be locked on the drill to act as a barrier. The whole apparatus can be hinged, or a hinged table top can be constructed to permit boring at an angle.

This type of drill stand is used for wire brushing, buffing, etc. Other types of drill stands can be made for special uses so that the drill performs specific jobs with a minimum of effort.

Using the Portable Drill

When boring into any material, the drill bit has a tendency to "walk away" from the mark you start it on. To avoid this, center-punch the location in the work before you start to drill. First locate the work area with a ruler and intersecting lines or dots where you want to drill. Next punch these marks with a center punch or an awl to provide a seat for the drill point and to keep it from traveling away from the mark when you apply pressure. Drill from a dead start: do not turn the motor on until the drill is in position. If the drill is too heavy for accurate guiding, provide a guide by drilling the proper size of hole in a waste block of wood, then clamping the drilled block into proper position. This is almost always necessary if the hole is to be drilled at an angle.

The underside or breakout side of a hole almost always splinters unless special precaution is taken. One safety device is the backing block—a waste piece of wood clamped to the underside. Some drills (Stanley All-purpose 80797, ½-inch) have a neoprene cushion to prevent damage to the top surface at the breakout, when the housing may hit the surface of the wood.

When you drill, align the drill bit and the axis of the drill in the direction you want the hole to go and apply pressure only along this line, with no sidewise or bending pressure. Changing the direction of your pressure can snap small drills or distort the dimension of the hole. The amount of pressure you apply to the drill should be enough to keep the tool cutting but not so much that it overloads or stalls the motor. If you do not apply enough pressure, you may merely be polishing the bottom of the hole, as well as wearing down the point of the drill.

Experience in drilling and some experimentation will "give you a feel" of what is the proper pressure for various materials and drill bits. The harder materials and larger-size holes will naturally require more pressure. Heavy-duty drills have an extra handle with which you can get both hands on the drill. On smaller models you can place both hands on the drill itself for applying extra pressure.

Small pieces of wood or metal that are to be drilled should be clamped or held in a vise, because the twisting force of the drill, especially when it breaks through, is considerable. Here it is particularly important to back up pieces you are drilling with pieces of scrap lumber. This will prevent damaging your workbench and will also minimize splintering when the drill breaks through. On a difficult job, especially on hardwood or metal, drilling a hole of smaller bore first, a pilot bore, will often make drilling easier and more accurate because the larger drill bit will have less stock to remove and will go through easier because the center of a twist drill does not actually cut.

For easier drilling in metal or hardwood, put a few drops of oil or kerosene on the drill bit. For soft metals, use paraffin on the drill.

It is easy to mislay the geared key that is essential to the operation of your drill, but not if you tape or wire it right to the electric cord of your drill about a foot away from the tool.

When you think of the ordinary use of a drill, you expect to use it for drilling holes for screws, bolts, or attachments. But boring can be used effectively for decoration too. Many decorative effects can be achieved by clamping two boards together either horizontally or vertically and drilling from

Drilling dowel holes

the point where they meet. Different-size bits used at a variety of depths at various distances can give many interesting effects.

For doweling, special care should be taken to hold the drill at a right angle and in the right position. The best way to position dowels is to clamp the two boards in a vise and mark both ends at the same time with an awl.

Doweling guides are available to help control the size and direction of borings, but you can make your own guide by drilling proper holes of various dowel sizes in a piece of scrap lumber or on a metal spool of used-up adhesive tape.

Dowel holes should be drilled slightly larger than the diameter of the dowels, to allow space for the glue. A depth gauge should be used to make sure the dowels will fit even when some of the space is filled by the glue. If many dowels are to be used, a cardboard gauge or a jig should be made to make sure the holes are properly spaced. For long edgewise joinings, dowels should be 6 to 12 inches apart and the entire edge should be glued.

CHAPTER THIRTEEN

Power Saws

The Portable Power Saw

The portable power saw is so much a muscle-and-time saver that it rates a high place in the home workshop.

The portable electric saw is designed to substitute electrical power for muscle power. In general, it saves 50 to 90 per cent in time for most operations, and a proportionate amount of energy. But most important, by taking some of the drudgery out of your work, it makes home carpentry more interesting and satisfying. Your own effort is limited to lifting and guiding the saw along the markings.

Cutting where the saw must be taken to the work, or cutting lumber down to a size which your other saws can handle are the chief functions that this saw performs better than any other. The portable saw will be found in the shop that already has a table saw.

There are a great variety of saws manufactured but the 7-inch is the right one for the home workshop. (Recommended: Stanley 80277.) By using special blades, you can cut other materials besides wood—Fiberglas, corrugated sheet metal, slate, and others.

Regardless of your accuracy with a handsaw, the power saw will provide a more accurate cut after you have adjusted your own skills and learned to use the built-in guides and other guides that can be purchased or improvised. These will help achieve true and even cuts.

Saws are classified by the size of the blade they carry. A blade 6 inches in diameter is considered a small saw, one 10 inches in diameter a large saw. A 6½- or 7-inch saw will cut 2⅛ inches vertically. At 45 degrees, it will cut 2 inches. Thus, the cut is sufficient for cutting a 2-by-4.

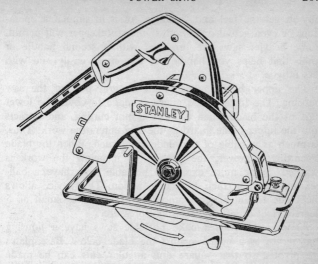

Using the Portable Saw

Depth of cut is regulated by an adjustable base that supports the saw on the work and is held in place by a convenient tightening device, such as a winged nut. A notch in the forward edge of the base enables you to saw a straight line without using a guide. Just follow a penciled cut line "free hand," keeping the line in the notch. The base also tilts laterally, providing the means of accurately controlling the bevel angle of your cut. Here again, a convenient tightening device, such as a wing nut, holds the base at the cutting angle you select, and the angle is indicated in degrees on a scale. Also on the saw is usually a ripping guide that enables you to make a straight cut a measured distance from the edge of a piece of material. The guide is removable when not in use.

The saw is turned on and off by a trigger type of switch located in the pistol-grip handle. This arrangement is an efficient way to grip the saw, work with it, and control it with minimum fatigue. The weight of the saw makes a big difference, of course, in how quickly you tire while using it. For this reason, do not choose a saw with too heavy construction or one that is not well balanced. Such a tool will be too fatiguing to use. Heft it in the store before you buy it, get the feel and "balance" of it in simulated operation, or even actual operation, if the storekeeper will permit. Some heavier saws are provided with a second handle or knob that helps you handle the saw more easily and with less fatigue.

The upper blade guard is an integral part of the saw housing. The lower blade guard is made to cover the lower part of the blade when the saw is not cutting, and retracts into the upper blade guard as the saw enters the work. Thus, as much as possible of the blade is guarded. When the blade is cutting, however, the portion of it below the work is exposed. Some more expensive portable saws have a ball-bearing guard in their telescopic action. This device allows the blade to enter a cut smoothly at angles as small as 5 degrees right or left, at very slight pressure.

Almost all standard-make portable saws have a housing that serves as a guard against the blade below. Base plates are pivoted so that square and angular cuts can be made easily. Provision for regulating the depth of the cut is also standard on most machines. Another feature to look for is the "motor-saver" drive (Stanley Pat.) which allows the blade to slip to relieve mechanical shock if it hits a nail or other strong obstruction. This safeguards the motor.

When using the saw, there are a number of do's and don't's to remember to ensure safe operation and minimize fatigue. (1) Make sure the work is held sufficiently secure to prevent shifting position or flying off during the cut. If you cannot hold it firmly with one hand, clamp it to your workbench or in your vise. (2) The blade should not be touching anything when the saw is turned on. (3) Do not stand directly behind the saw when operating it. Stand off to one side and keep your other hand well out of the line of cut. (4) Don't hold the board with a finger underneath the board. (5) Do not be careless when you reach the end of the cut. Remember, the lower blade guard will not return until the blade is clear of the material. (6) Do not support the saw on the work that is to be cut off. If you do, the saw will not be supported at the end of the cut. Position the work, the saw, and yourself so that the saw is supported by the work during and after the cut.

When a machine is used out of doors, it is particularly important that the circuit be grounded. All modern saws (except those marked "Double Insulation") have a special cord for grounding.

The instructions that come with the saw will tell you how to set the blade for 45-degree bevel cuts and other special work.

Special blades for the portable saw are made for cross-cutting and ripping, but unless a great deal of one type of work is to be done, the combination blade will serve the home carpenter best. Deep hardened-steel blades or carbide-tipped blades are available for difficult rough cutting. These last up to twenty times as long as ordinary blades and are useful if a great deal of work is to be done on plywood or hardwood.

Power Saw blades

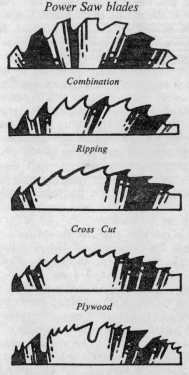

Combination

Ripping

Cross Cut

Plywood

Mitre

Special blades are also made for cutting hardboard, wall-board, and various kinds of metal. Abrasive blades are also made for cutting slate and marble.

To make a cut with your saw, set the correct depth of cut by means of the adjustable base and tighten the wing nut. For safety's sake, the less blade you have projecting underneath the work, the better. Then turn on the switch, rest the base on the piece to be cut, and apply the saw to the piece. To make an accurately dimensioned cut, first pencil a line where you want the cut to be. When following a penciled line, keep the line in the notch of the shoe. A little practice will enable you to keep the saw cutting along the line.

Remember that the saw blade has width and that if you keep the line in the middle of the blade, you will be removing a fraction of an inch too much material. It is better to keep the "inside" edge of the blade cutting along the line, which will still be there when you finish your cut. Then the dimension you mark off will be the dimension of the finished piece. The saw revolves at such a high speed and the blade is so efficient that the cut will be clean and smooth, with no sawtooth marks or open-grained edges. Some sanding may be necessary to get perfectly smooth edges of furniture quality, but for construction jobs the saw-cut edge will be smooth enough without further work. Sharpening the blade from time to time helps get smooth, clean edges and helps it cut easier and faster, reducing fatigue. Just loosen the nut holding the blade on the spindle and remove the blade for sharpening. Make sure the saw is disconnected when you remove the blades.

To make a crosscut, the saw should be turned on and allowed to run for a few seconds before cutting. Place the saw at the edge of the stock, making sure that the guide is on the line of cut. Press and guide the saw firmly at a moderately slow pace. If you exert too much pressure, the cutting will be slowed. A stalled blade should be pulled back slowly and allowed to turn for a moment before you proceed.

Care must be taken not to rest the weight of the machine on a piece of lumber that is to be in the finished project unless the board is properly supported. If sawhorses are used, this support is usually sufficient, but clamping the boards is more certain to provide a firm base.

For ripping, measure the distance from the inner face of the board to the far side of the blade tooth and set the gauge. Slide the gauge along the straight edge of the board. This is more accurate than following a guide line. If the board is too wide to use the finished edge, tack or clamp a straight-edged fence to the stock to serve as a guide.

For long cuts, cutting is faster and cleaner if a guide is used. Some portable saws come equipped with guides that can be adjusted to grip the edge of the stock. However, making a T guide is quite simple. Some cutoff guides are sold commercially and some are equipped with protractors. A simple ripping job can be done with the use of a guide board clamped along a line marked on the stock. This is especially useful if thin pieces are to be cut off.

Ripping Guide

The ripping guide enables you to cut off a measured amount without marking the material. Just extend the guide to the desired mark in inches and let the T-shaped guide travel right along the edge of the material, or against a straight edge clamped to the material. For easy crosscutting without marking a line, use a crosscutting guide. When cutting along a line or with a guide and the blade starts to run off the intended cut line, don't try to force it back into line, but back it up, then go ahead again carefully.

Different types of wood vary greatly in density and, hence, in the resistance they offer the saw. Moreover, the same piece of wood may vary in density because of knots, burls, and the like. Oak, maple, and other hardwoods will be a lot harder to saw than spruce, pine, and other softwoods. The denser the material, the more pressure you will need to apply, and the more slowly the blade will cut. Apply as much pressure as you need up to the point where the saw begins to labor—that is, to run at low speed. At this point, reduce the feed pressure until normal running speed is resumed. Using this technique, you can get through knotty 2-by-4's, or an even larger piece of material, oak or maple flooring, or denser material without difficulty. For pieces thicker than 2 inches, you will have to mark the piece on both sides and make two cuts, first on one side, then on the other side. If you have marked correctly, the edges should be level.

While a table saw will leave some splinters on the bottom side of a cut because it cuts "down," a portable saw will leave some splinters on the top side of a cut because it cuts "up"—just the opposite. If the piece you are sawing has a good side, therefore, keep this side down when sawing with a portable saw.

Angle and compound angle cuts are easy with your portable saw, but take a little more care because, if the cut is a little off on either angle, the parts won't fit together properly.

When it is necessary to cut across the horses, place 2-by-2- or 1-by-2-inch blocks under the stock.

Special Cuts

To make a bevel cut, loosen the wing nut at the tilt quadrant and on the adjustable protractor set the angle as you wish to have it. Then make sure to tighten the nut to keep the blade in place. Proceed as you would in ordinary crosscutting, following the marked guideline. If there is no guide on your machine, you can make one with three strips of wood and a carriage bolt.

Dadoes and lapped joints are made by making a series

of kerfs about ⅛ inch apart. The wood that remains standing can be hammered and chiseled out without difficulty.

To make a dado or a groove, merely set the blade to the required depth and make two parallel cuts. The groove can then be cleared with a chisel or by making additional cuts between the two edges. If the groove to be cut is too shallow for the depth gauge, clamp a piece of hardwood over the face and saw through it. As in all cuts, a guide fence clamped to one side of the saw makes for a more accurate cutting. The same fence can be used for the second side of the dado by adding a strip the width of the dado (but allow for the width of the kerf). Some model saws have grooving cutters.

Adjust the shoe for the depth of cut you want; mark the two sides of the dado with pencil and make the two outlining cuts with the blade just inside the line on either side. For greater accuracy, clamp a guide strip on the work for one cut, then reclamp it for the other cut. Any stock remaining between the outlining cuts can be removed by making careful free-hand cuts, as many as necessary, or by reclamping the guide strip for each pass with your saw.

For rabbet cuts, which are L-shaped cuts, use the same procedure as for dado cuts. This will be easier than trying to cut in from the edge of the piece. If, however, you have a large rabbet to cut and it is easier to cut in from the edge, then use guide blocks clamped to the edge of the piece to help support the saw.

Rabbet cuts can best be made by cutting first from the edge of the stock, then from the face of the stock. This provides maximum support for the saw. Stock 1 inch thick will not support the saw at the beginning and end of the cut, so an additional waste piece must be attached to either the stock or the edge of the workbench. If the strip is added to the bench, room for a guide strip can also be provided.

To cut notches, make two parallel cuts to the desired length and knock away the material between them. If the notch is wide, make a number of cuts. If the bottom of the notch has to be square, hold the board on its side in a vise and make the cuts by passing the saw over it, holding the saw level by hand. Many boards can be notched in this way at the same time. Where appearance is not important, intersecting cuts are made by overcutting slightly with the saw.

When no overcutting is permitted, cut up to the intersection but not beyond, then complete the cut with a handsaw.

Notching cuts take special planning because the saw must be supported for both cuts. The cuts should be made with the largest possible blade so that the cleaning cut is kept shallow. Where one cannot overcut, the sawing must be finished by hand.

You can make plunge cuts or inside cuts with your portable saw—that is, internal cutouts in a panel—without having to cut in from the edge of the panel. Mark the cutout on the panel in pencil, then rest the front edge of the shoe on the panel with the blade raised above the panel. Align the blade with the cut line and turn on the tool. Lower the blade carefully so that it starts to cut. Continue to lower the blade carefully until the base is resting on the work. Then cut the length of the line as usual. Remember that the portable saw never cuts squarely up and down. On intersecting cuts like this, you will either have to overcut or, when appearance is important, complete the cut with a handsaw. Turning the tool off before removing it from the plunge cut will keep the edge you have cut from being damaged by the blade.

Where several pieces are to be sawed to the same size or shape, a premade setup will save time in marking and guiding. Guides can be so clamped that the board falls into position for cutting. Sometimes it is fastest to cut two or more pieces at the same time.

When it is necessary to make inside cuts, as an opening for a door grille or an insert in a counter top, draw back the guard and lower the rotating blade using the forward end as a rest. Allow enough space so that the cut will not pass the end mark. Narrow holes can be finished with a saber saw, a compass saw, a jig saw, or a chisel and file.

Where the saw cannot be adjusted to shallow cuts, a smaller blade can be used, or an extra piece of waste wood should be clamped or screwed into place to provide the extra height needed.

Butt joints are the easiest to make, especially with an electric saw. To make certain the two ends match exactly at the point, clamp the two pieces of stock together and cut through both pieces simultaneously.

The portable saw is adaptable for a variety of other home carpentry jobs. Even a stucco wall can be cut if an abrasive disc is substituted for the saw blade. Be sure to wear protective goggles for this job.

The portable saw is easily converted to a bench saw by the acquisition of a table. With a proper mounting, the entire tool can be placed under the table. Brackets are then installed so that the blade can be tilted to any angle desired, and so that cuts of any width are possible.

A sanding drum is a simple accessory useful for smoothing. It is a spool of sandpaper on a shank and can be inserted into the motor to create a rotary sander.

The Sabre Saw

The sabre saw is invaluable because of its ability to make cuts no other saw can make so easily, and earns a place in the home workshop for this reason. Its prime asset is versatility. It is actually a portable jig saw and will do almost everything that any other saw will do. Also, it is powerful enough, and uses such a variety of blades, that it can make cuts that a circular saw cannot make.

As a circular saw has several different blades for different types of cuts and materials, the sabre saw also has a great variety of useful and different blades, for cutting wood or metal, for cutting flush to a surface horizontally or vertically, for cutting curves, for heavy cutting. Blades with more teeth per inch will cut smoother, and those having fewer teeth per inch—that is, bigger teeth—will cut faster. If the teeth are too big, however, they may not cut at all in hard materials. The reciprocating action of this tool causes vibration that does not make for as smooth edges as are possible with other types of saws. The blades cut on the upstroke; hence the good side of your work, if any, should be down, in order to preserve that side. If you are going to shellac the piece anyway, shellac it before you saw it; this will hold the wood fibers together and minimize splintering. A length of transparent tape over the cut line will also make for a smoother edge.

A unique advantage that some sabre saws have (Stanley) is the way they can cut flush, right up to, or within a fraction of an inch along a surface. This feature can be used, for example, in cutting a hole in a wall without cutting the

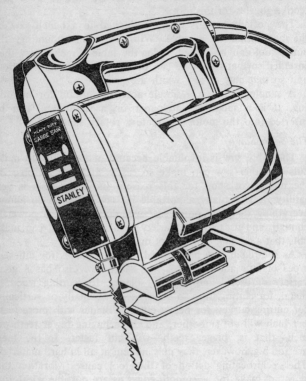

Tilting Base Sabre Saw

studs. Another advantage is the way the sabre saw can make plunge cuts. This is useful, for example, in making cutouts for switches in walls, for fixtures in ceilings, and the like. To make a plunge cut, tilt the tool forward, resting the forward edge of the shoe on the material. Align the blade with the cut line, switch on the tool, and lower the blade into the material.

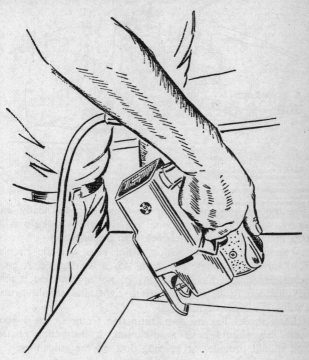

Plunge Cutting

For a square hole, make four insertions with the blade. For a round hole, you can make just one insertion and continue the cut around. Do not try to cut tight corners with a wide blade. Never force the tool; that will just result in breaking a blade. Where necessary, you can back the blade up and make another cut to get around a tight corner. A ripping guide used with the sabre saw enables you to make long, straight, accurate cuts. You can also follow a guide strip clamped to the work, as you do with a circular saw.

Cutting Conduit

The tool is very handy for notching 2-by-4's neatly and easily, without having to chisel out the stock. Make parallel cuts first, then remove the stock with a plunge cut.

The saw is available with a tilting base, like the circular saw, for making angle cuts from 45 to 90 degrees. A good sabre saw should have versatility of position so that it may be tilted on its base from left to right, and should permit cutting at a right angle.

Each model has its own distinctive features, but a good sabre saw should have a minimum of distracting chatter and should provide for keeping dust off the guidelines.

CHAPTER FOURTEEN

Portable Power Sanders

The sander is much more than a simple smoothing tool. It also serves as a shaper if a piece of wood is held against it. Although some other power tools, especially the power drill, can be used as sanders, the electric sander is designed to do its specific job more effectively than any other.

There are three types of sanders.

1. The belt sander has an endless belt like a tractor tread. The belt is kept centered on its track by a tracking mechanism and can be removed and replaced easily. It serves best for big jobs like paneling.

2. The orbital or reciprocating sander has a rectangular platform (platen), which holds the sandpaper and moves it back and forth. It is best for finishing, especially for small pieces—furniture and the like.

3. The disc sander spins on a shank like a phonograph record. It serves for all purposes, especially rough-shaping, but tends to create grooves. The disc sander is a standard attachment for portable drills. (See Chapter 12.)

Although belt sanders can do an excellent finishing job, where two sanders are available the belt sander is used for rough-sanding and the orbital sander for finishing.

The Orbital Sander

Sanding a perfectly smooth finish on your woodworking project is not the time-consuming, tedious, laborious job it once was, thanks to great improvements not only in sanding machines but in abrasive paper.

The abrasive papers of today are substantially improved: particles are sharper, the glue is stronger, the backing is stronger, and where desired, the paper is waterproof. Consider three things when selecting an abrasive paper for a job.

279

Orbital Sander

First, is it open-coat or closed-coat? Closed-coat sand-paper has the abrasive particles very close together. This produces the smoothest surface because you have many more abrasive "teeth" doing the cutting, just as a saw blade with many teeth cuts smoother than one with fewer teeth. Open-coat sandpaper has the abrasive particles spaced farther apart, with not so many abrasive "teeth" and, hence, does not do as smooth a job: But this paper will clog as quickly as the closed-coat paper. This is an advantage, particularly in rough-sanding and removing old paint, varnish, and other finishes.

Second, what type and quality of abrasive do you need for a job? Flint paper, the cheapest type of sandpaper, is very common. It can be used on jobs that clog the paper quickly, such as rough-sanding and paint and varnish removal. Garnet paper is very good for woodworking. It is more expensive than flint paper, but lasts much longer; therefore, it is cheaper to use in the long run. Aluminum oxide paper has tougher and sharper abrasive particles than garnet paper and is excellent to use on wood or metal. It is especially good to use on a power sander. Silicon carbide paper is the toughest of all the abrasive papers. It is especially good in the finer grits for sanding undercoats and smoothing finishes between applications.

Third, what grit should you use for a certain job? There are various systems of designating the coarseness of the grit. One system runs from a designation 2½ for rough, to 1 for medium, to 3/0 for smooth. Another system calls rough 40, medium 70, and fine 100. For woodworkers, the first system is the most common. Purchase an assortment of sandpaper for your shop and keep a supply of the different grits on hand; then you won't have to run out for a little piece of sandpaper when you need it. What is a fine grit for one material may be too rough for another. A sandpaper that is fine for softwood might be too rough to use on metal, while a medium sandpaper for metal would probably clog quickly if you used it on softwood.

Using the Orbital Sander

The sanding pad makes tiny orbital movements in all directions, so that you don't have to move the tool with the grain. You can move it any way in order to cover every bit of the surface. Start with as coarse paper as is necessary and do the entire surface with it. Then go over the entire surface with medium paper, and finish up with fine paper. If your lumber is quite smooth to begin with, perhaps you can skip using the medium and coarse papers, and use just the fine paper.

The abrasive paper has to be firmly secured in the clamps —that is, tight—in order to cut properly. Otherwise the action of the sanding pad is not transmitted to the cutting particles and nothing happens. You also have to apply enough pressure to keep the sandpaper cutting, but not so much that the work is scratched. Check occasionally for buildup of wood dust on the abrasive paper. You can make your paper go further between replacements if you scrape off the spots where wood dust has accumulated.

Before the final sanding with fine sandpaper, go over the wood with a damp sponge, and let it dry. This raises the grain of the wood. When you sand it once more with the fine sandpaper, the result will be as smooth as glass!

Because of its fast motion, the orbital sander can be moved in any direction without leaving grain marks.

The rectangular sanding paper used is usually just a third of the standard 8½- by 11-inch sheet. Inasmuch as the coarsest stock used is an abrasive that would be considered medium or fine for a belt sander, the terminology here is different: 60 grit (½) is coarse, 100 grit (2/0) medium, and 150 grit (4/0) fine.

The Belt Sander

Belt sanders vary in size from 2 by 21 inches to 4½ by 26 inches. The bigger the machine, the faster it finishes the work, but of course, the more it weighs. A large machine may weigh 25 pounds. Recommended sizes are 3 by 21 inches (Stanley H493), 3 by 24 inches (Stanley H31), and 4 by 24 inches (Stanley H494). Most belts have an arrow on the back of the belt to indicate the direction in which it should be run.

In some machines (Stanley) there is a protective carbide insert that prevents the belt from wearing through the housing. This cuts maintenance costs.

The type of work to be done determines which belt you should use. (See chart.) However, the size of the machine may limit your choice. A light machine cannot support a belt with a grit coarser than No. 2.

The toughest and longest-lasting belts are coated with aluminum oxide.

A safe stock of belts should include medium grits ½ and 1, fine grits 2/0, and coarse grits 1½ or 2.

Your skill with the belt sander comes only with use. Your touch must be adjusted to give you an even-pressured stroke. Otherwise your work will show ripples and gouges.

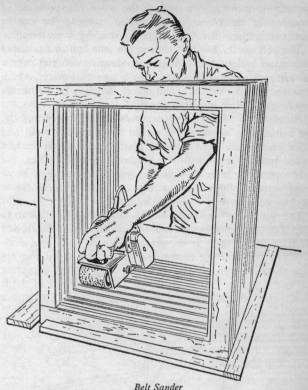

Belt Sander

The sanding stroke is a simple straight, short, back-and-forth motion, with each stroke overlapping the one before.

After the switch has been turned on, push the sander forward in a gliding stroke, with the heel touching the surface first, then the rest of the belt. After the first stroke, the motions come naturally. It is important to work systematically to avoid resanding the same area.

Special care must be taken that squared corners are not given a rounded edge. The belt may extend slightly beyond the edge for the finish, but pressure should be very light at this point.

Some models can be turned on their back (Stanley H31) and used as a sort of table sander for holding small objects against the moving belt. Where the work has a degree of precision or the object to be sanded is lighter or smaller than the machine itself, this type of sanding is preferred.

The belt sander has two rollers, one idle and one powered that move a cloth belt coated with abrasive material over a flat pressure plate. It is powered by a universal motor, which operates on A.C. or D.C. The on-off switch is in the handle as a trigger switch or sliding switch.

Because the abrasive belt removes material very quickly, the belt sander is just the thing for removing old paint and other finishes and, unlike paint remover, leaves the surface clean, smooth, and dry. When removing old finishes, use only open-coat belts to avoid clogging. Make short backward strokes. Start each stroke in a new area. Some machines can be used to sand sideways.

The weight of the tool and your arms is sufficient to keep it cutting, so that no additional pressure need be applied when operating on a level surface. In fact, additional pressure will just slow the motor and the cutting speed. Always keep the sander in motion. Allowing it to rest in one place will make gouges. Guide the sander back and forth in short, overlapping strokes with the grain of the wood. To remove

Belt sander with dust collecting attachment

material faster, allow the sander to point diagonally to the grain and move the tool with the grain. To get a smooth finish, point the sander in the direction of the grain and move it with the grain.

Abrasives

All the principles pertaining to abrasives outlined for the orbital sander apply equally to the belt sander. Only the means of applying the abrasive to the work is different. You work from coarse through progressively finer grits until the desired smoothness is reached. Use only quality cloth-backed belts. Belts are easily changed. Push on the forward roller to release the tension on the belt. Slip off the old belt, and slip on the new. Release the forward roller to put tension on the belt. When necessary, adjust the tracking screw, which keeps the belt aligned on the two drums.

The belt sander can be used, with coarse paper, as a power plane. You can cut doors to size, trim molding, and cut other objects to size just as you would with a power plane. When sanding millwork, doors, and the like, be careful not to sand across the grain. The belt sander can also be used to sand such small areas as taped joints on sheet-rock walls, plaster patches, and glued joints. Use fine paper and extra care when working on plywood and veneered panels. There is the danger of cutting right through the veneer and ruining the panel.

Walls are sanded at an angle so that the right edge of the machine can be kept in view.

When you work on large areas that have grain running in different directions, sand each area separately. On a door, first sand the rails, then the stiles.

Wet sanding, using waterproof paper with water or oil as a lubricant, can be done effectively with the orbital sander. This can be dangerous, however, because water carries electricity and special care must be taken for protection from the electric source.

Meshed sandpaper allows the dust to fall through, thus avoiding clogging.

When holding the wood to be sanded, it is best to use the upper portion of the disc. If the sanding is done with the grain there should be very few scratches. Avoid applying too much pressure, as this burns the wood and destroys the paper.

A new type of polishing belt (Stanbrite, Stanley TM) is excellent for ultra-fine finishes and makes possible results unthinkable with ordinary sandpaper. Made of an unwoven nylon mesh impregnated with an abrasive, the belt produces a finer finish than any that can be obtained with ordinary sandpaper, because the finish of the abrasive is so much finer. The material is oil- and water-resistant and can thus be used under conditions that would destroy ordinary papers. The mesh has openings that practically eliminate clogging. Large openings between the fibers permit the waste to fall through so that waste from the material being finished cannot build up. This, too, keeps the machine cooler and increases the life of the belt. These abrasives are suitable for working on all types of materials—wood, metals, Fiberglas, plastics, marble, and the like. The durability of the nylon provides insurance against belt damage in this intensive kind of work.

Aluminum oxide abrasives are best for power sanding on wood and metal. They are available in open and closed coat. Use open-coat belts for roughing soft pine, for removing old finishes, and for sanding nonferrous metals—aluminum, copper, and others. The closed coat is for use on hardwoods, steel, and plastics, where they can do more cutting than the open coat and not get clogged as easily by those materials. For work on marble, stone, glass, slate blackboards, and ceramics, silicon carbide abrasives are best. As no grain is present in these materials, a sweeping, overlapping rotary motion can be used.

The life of the motor in your sander, as in all your power tools, depends in part on proper ventilation. Check the ventilating holes in the motor housing occasionally to be sure that they are not clogged with sawdust. It is also a good idea to follow the other maintenance procedures recommended by the manufacturer. Cleaning and lubricating your sander according to instructions supplied with it will permit many years of trouble-free operation.

If the jobs that come along in which you could use this sander are few and far between, then rent one when you do need one. However, whether you rent or buy, for heavy duty sanding nothing can beat the belt sander, the work horse of the power sanders. In the days when craftsmen finished their projects by hand, they were often left with little but perceptible dents and scratches, which could be excused because of the labor involved. Today, with the belt sander and modern abrasives, there is no reason for not getting a mirror-like finish. You can take the same pride in a beautiful hand-rubbed finish that craftsmen used to take—without the quantities of elbow grease that that finish used to require.

CHAPTER FIFTEEN

The Router

The router is probably the most versatile of all the portable shop tools, for it both cuts and shapes. It can do most of the jobs any power tool can do and it also can do the work of a lathe, a shaper, and other highly sophisticated factory equipment.

The essential parts of the router are much the same as for other portable tools—a motor (which here is usually more powerful than in other power tools), a chuck to hold the cutting tool, and a base.

Basically, the router is designed to cut into the surface of the stock, routing out areas, making all types of joints, shaping edges, cutting grooves, mortising, or doing any cutting job that has to be done. The router can do 90 per cent of all woodworking jobs.

The router depends on a sharp, precision-shaped cutting bit and a high rotation speed—18,000 to 27,000 r.p.m., compared with 5,000 r.p.m. for a fast drill. In this way, the router leaves a smooth edge that requires no sanding.

The router cuts into a piece of wood at the depth and in the shape required. If you are going to make an inlay, trace the design on the wood, set the depth, and cut out the shape required. Whether you need a channel for a window, a guide for a drawer, grooves or dadoes for shelving, hinge cuts, grooves for weather stripping, or merely decorative cutouts, the router does the job simply and efficiently.

But the router can cut in many other ways. It is ideal for making decorative edges and for trimming veneers. Whether it is a rounded-over edge, a cove cut for a drop-leaf table, or a beaded edging for a table top or shelf, the job is done quickly and easily. Once its use has been learned, it is no more difficult to operate than the more common tools and is substantially more rewarding in the things it can do.

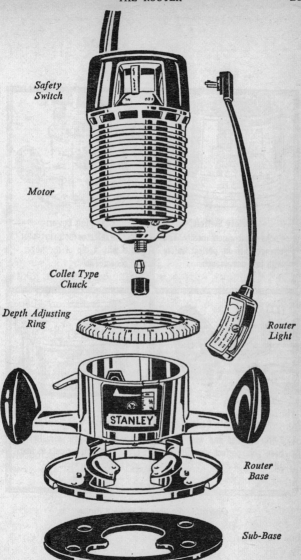

Safety Switch

Motor

Collet Type Chuck

Depth Adjusting Ring

Router Light

Router Base

Sub-Base

STANLEY

Anatomy of Stanley H264 Router

Safety Switch:
Locks shaft automatically. You change bits in perfect safety with just one wrench.

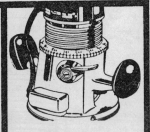

Clamping Lever:
Holds or releases motor in router base with a flip of the finger. So convenient.

Comfortable Control:
3-grip handles and wide open base give perfect visibility on all cuts.

Precision Accuracy:
Micrometer depth adjustment quickly sets bit for cuts as fine as 4/1000 of an inch.

Operating features of Stanley Router

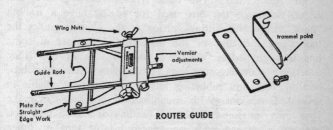

ROUTER GUIDE

Router bits are available in a great many shapes and sizes for specific woodworking or metal jobs. Unless you have a particular job for your router, a router bit kit containing the most popular bit sizes and shapes is the most practical buy.

Basically, the router consists of an enclosed universal motor and a base with two handles. In some models, the handles are on either side of the base and the on-off switch is on the motor. The router bit is held in the chuck in the lower end of the motor unit and is wrench-tightened. It is important always to use a wrench to tighten the chuck. Cutting depth is regulated by raising or lowering the motor unit in relation to the base. This is done by rotating a collar on the base. The actual depth that is to be cut is indicated on the side of the base. The collar is marked off in fractions of an inch so that depth can be adjusted with great precision. Identical cuts can be made by adjusting the collar to the same mark. A clamping lever holds the base at the depth desired.

Some models have a push-button shaft lock that simplifies and speeds changing bits. A few models (Stanley) have a light fixture that gives greater visibility in guiding the router.

Bits

The router makes two basic types of cuts: grooves and edges. Some of the bits used for edging have a smooth "pilot" below the cutting portion of the bit that guides the tool along the edge of the material. The names of some bits that cut edges will give you an idea of how they function: rounding-over bits, chamfering bits, cove bits, beading bits, and rabbeting bits. Each type is available in several dimensions. With rounding-over bits you can make your own stairsteps. With the beading and cove bits, you can put a shaped edge on veneered table tops or other furniture parts. Thus these router bits can increase the quality of your workmanship in a thousand ways.

The grooving bits are for cutting grooves of different depths, widths, and shapes. The width, of course, is usually determined by the diameter of the bit, but some models have a special guide that extends the cutting width of a ¼-inch or ½-inch bit to ¾ inch or 11/16 inch. The depth is regulated by adjusting the router motor in the base. The V-grooving bits cut a V-shaped groove. The core box bits cut a groove semicircular in cross section. Veining bits cut a nar-

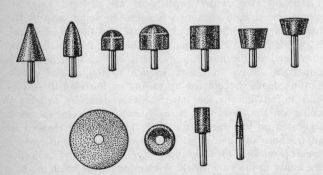

Grinding Wheels for sharpening Router Bits

row, shallow groove with a rounded bottom. The straight bits cut square-bottom grooves, and are used most frequently, particularly for wood inlaying. Hinge-mortising bits cut a wide swath for insetting door hinges. Dovetail bits cut a groove that is wider at the bottom, for making dovetail joints.

Manufacturers also provide bits in tungsten carbide, the hardest metal in existence, as well as high-speed steel. The carbide bits keep their cutting edge twenty-five times longer than high-speed steel and are necessary for cutting Fiberglas or hard plastic laminates. Commonly used bits are available in kits as well as individually.

Router Bits

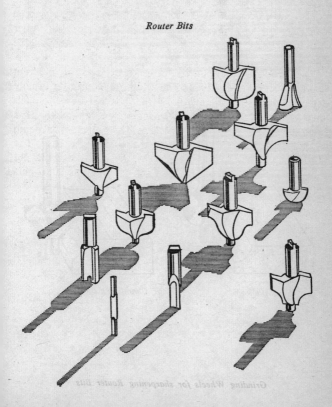

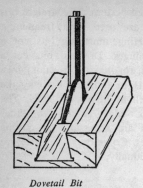

Dovetail Bit

Spiral Bit Right Hand

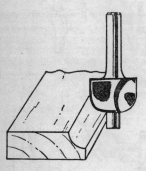

Cove Bit

Chamfering Bit

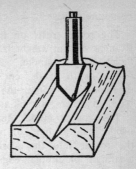

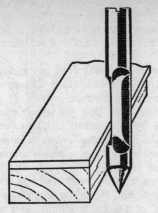

Combination Panel Bit,
Carbide Tipped

"V" Grooving Bit

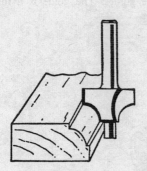

Beading Bit

Straight Bit

Special Router Bits Make Molding Edges

Using the Router

The router rests on the work and requires little lifting. Routers vary in weight from 3¼ to 9 pounds but are, nevertheless, easy to handle.

The depth of the cut is regulated differently on various machines. On some, the motor is rotated in a channeled base. In others, a rack-and-pinion mechanism is used.

The router guide attachment fits into the base when needed and is held in place by two screws. As you feed the router into the work, the attachment guides it along a straight or circular edge, or the length of a radius around a stationary point, or around an angle. The guide attachment, which is sufficient for most of the work that you will do, is capable of precise adjustment. A vernier thumbscrew precisely adjusts the distance of the bit from the edge of the work. Circular grooves can be routed with a radius up to the length of the guide rod by attaching a trammel point to one of the guide rods and swinging the router around it as a center. A needle on the trammel point holds it in the wood.

Two other types of devices also are used in guiding the router—templates and template guides. The guide is a thin

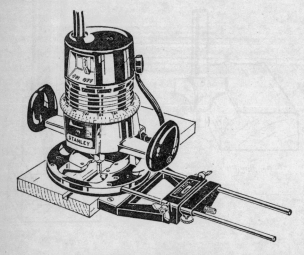

Portable router (Stanley H 264)

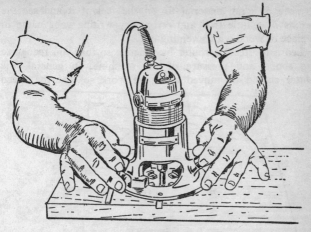

Cutting a dado

metal sleeve through which a bit is inserted. These are used to follow the outlines of a template.

The template can be made of plywood, hardwood, or metal, to form an outline of the groove to be cut. Templates for routing dovetail joints and hinge-butt mortises are two examples of manufacturers' guides. They enable you to perform these operations quickly and easily and are worth the cost if you have much of this type of work to do. You can reproduce any design by tracing it onto ¼-inch plywood or hard board and cutting a template. The router then follows this template and cuts the design into the wood, exactly reproducing the design. You can easily improvise straight-edge guides for your router by clamping pieces of lumber to your work, provided they have straight, smooth edges.

To make a template, first draw the shape on paper, then sketch it slightly larger or smaller, depending on the kind of template, to allow for the thickness of the ring. Transfer the design to ¼-inch plywood by making the outline in soft pencil, turning the paper over, and rubbing with a fingernail. Then with the bit set at 1/16 inch below the template, move the router around the inside of the design.

In free-hand routing, without the use of any guide, success depends upon your skill and artistry. Practice first on a piece of scrap material to get the feel of it and see the results of a little trial and error. Try writing your name in a piece of wood with a veining bit.

Learn to "feel" a router by practice so that you recognize the sound and pressure of the machine. In general, the router should be moved along its work so that the speed

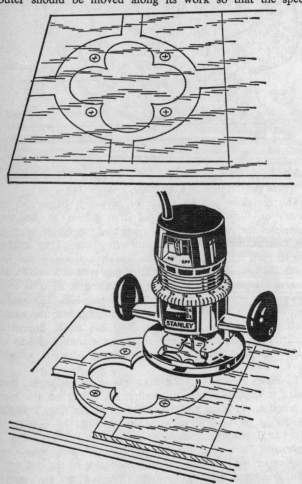

Template Routing

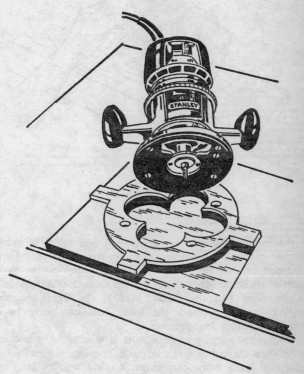

Template Routing

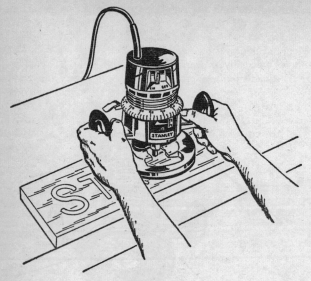

Sign Making

of the motor is slowed no more than one third. Working too fast overloads the motor; working too slowly may burn the wood or spoil the cutter. Always keep the cutting tools sharp to make the work easier for the tool. On those models with a light (Stanley H264, H267), the light becomes brighter as you increase the load. This can serve as a warning to reduce feed pressure.

To prevent gouging at corners it is wise to have a close fit between the cutter and the guide opening, especially for rabbeting. Some home carpenters attach a wooden strip up to 1 inch thick to the guide when using the straight guide, allowing the cutter to make a recess as the bit is lowered. Splintering is avoided by attaching scrap wood to the edge.

One of the most useful functions of the router is in the making of wood joints, which it does better than any other tool. The dovetail joint is very difficult to cut by hand, but with the router, a dovetail bit, and dovetail fixture it can be cut quickly and easily. The dovetail is a very useful joint, and a little study and practice is worth while. As a matter of fact, tool demonstrators do the task blindfolded. When properly done, the parts fit snugly; the joint requires no glue and is very strong. It is used extensively in making furniture, especially drawers.

The dado joint, a groove cut with or across the grain of a piece of wood, is much used for installing shelves in furniture, such as bookcases, cabinets, and desks. If you have a bit the same size as the thickness of the shelving, you can cut the dado to the exact size in one pass with the

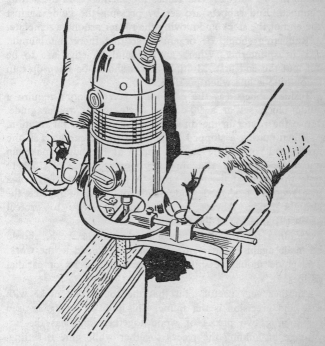

Cutting a mortise

router. Otherwise, you can make several passes to cut it to the required width. Use the router guide to get the desired distance from the edge. Make sure, of course, that the edge from which you guide is straight and smooth. For the grooves into which drawer bottoms are to be placed, use a ¼-inch spiral bit and cut a groove about ¼ inch away from the bottom of each of the sides of the drawer. Then you can slide the drawer bottom into these grooves from the back, after the drawer is put together. The router is the only power tool that can cut a "blind dado"—that is, a dado that doesn't extend to the edges of the piece and therefore doesn't show from either side.

For rabbeting, a special cutter is used and the bit is lowered to the depth required. (Large rabbets should be made in two stages.) The guides are then set and the setting clamped. End rabbets are set by pressing the guide against the end of the stock and moving the router around a template.

Rabbeting should be organized so that there is minimum risk of splintering. Where an end and an edge are to be cut, cut the end first. Multiple pieces should be lined up into a continuous line when possible.

Inside rabbets (as the edge of a screen door) require a guide block set at a 90-degree angle to the router guide. Move the router in the direction opposite to the bit rotation.

When cutting a stopped rabbet, the router can start at the inside end; or, if the start is made at the edge, make an automatic block by attaching a proper-size piece of stock to hold the guide at the right point. A rabbet on the edge of a disc requires a shaped guide made of wood to replace the straight guide. Always be sure to use strips to protect against splintering at the edges.

Guiding for dadoing, especially for angle work, should be made against a strip of waste stock clamped to the work. The guide should be shifted for each of a series of parallel dadoes.

Another very useful joint that the router can make with ease and precision is the spline. This joint is strong, is used for joining two pieces of wood together, and has the advantage of holding the pieces together while glue is setting. As you will remember, the spline consists of a groove in both pieces and a spline, usually a narrow piece of ¼-inch plywood, that fits into both grooves and holds the pieces together with the aid of wood glue. For splining mitre joints, as in picture frames and window screens, the router can make a "blind dado" on the end of each piece. When

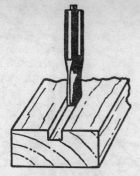

Straight Bit, Single Flute

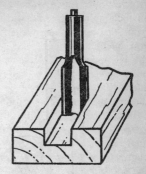

Straight Bit, Two Flutes

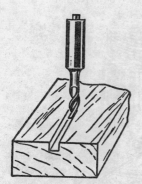

Shear Cut Bit, Right Hand

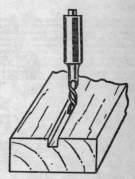

Shear Cut Bit, Left Hand

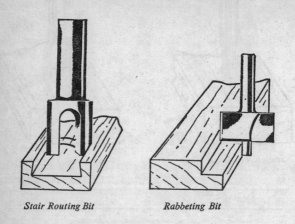

Stair Routing Bit   *Rabbeting Bit*

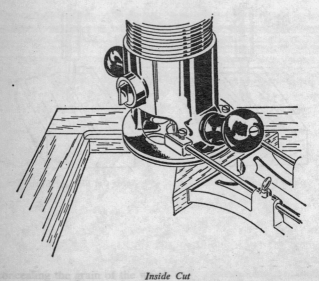

Inside Cut

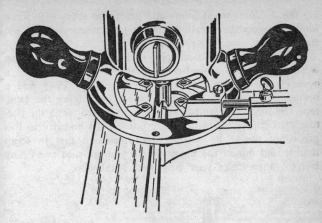

Rabbet Cut

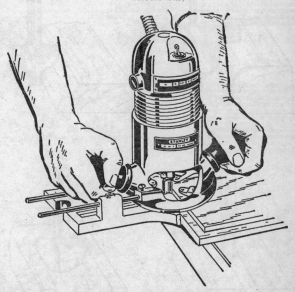

The Router makes rabbeting an easy process

dadoing on the edge or the end of a piece, it is usually necessary to clamp other pieces on either side of the work to help support the router and prevent it from tilting. Studying the different wood joints and practicing them with scrap lumber is good preparation for the time when you will use them in a woodworking project.

A special type of wood joint that the router makes easy work of is the drop-leaf-table joint. For this, you need a cove bit for edging the drop leaf (see page 294) and a rounding-over bit of the same radius for edging the table top. The hinge barrel fits into a groove routed along the bottom of the table top with a core box bit. As an error in this procedure would be costly, make the joint first in scrap lumber and mount the hinge. When you are sure everything is right, then make your cuts in the table top.

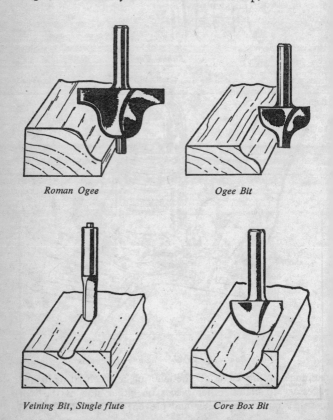

Roman Ogee   *Ogee Bit*

Veining Bit, Single flute   *Core Box Bit*

The mortise and tenon joint, laborious and difficult to cut by hand, is easy to cut with a router. The mortise is marked and is cut just as the groove on an edge. Squaring the cut usually requires a chisel. The tenon is cut in the same way as a rabbet, working from the shoulder to provide support. If a number of mortise and tenon joints are to be made, a jig setup will be a big timesaver.

It is important that the mortise be located in the center of the piece of wood so that the sides of the piece will make a flush surface when fitted together. If making a number of joints of this type, cut all the tenons at the same time, thereby assuring that they will be of uniform size. The mortises will have round corners and the tenons will have square corners. So either square up the corners of the mortises with a sharp chisel, or round the corners of the tenons with a file or chisel. There is a certain procedure for making this joint, which, once learned, will result in proficiency. Detailed instructions for making this and other wood joints will probably be included with the router when it is bought.

Decorative designs can be routed out and left hollow, or raised bas-relief can be made by routing out the surrounding

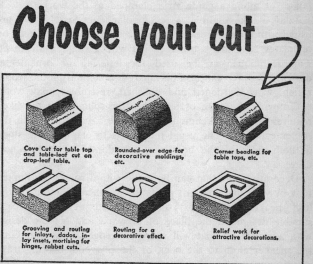

Choose your cut

Cove Cut for table top and table-leaf cut on drop-leaf table.

Rounded-over edge for decorative moldings, etc.

Corner beading for table tops, etc.

Grooving and routing for inlays, dados, inlay insets, mortising for hinges, rabbet cuts.

Routing for a decorative effect.

Relief work for attractive decorations.

area. By selecting the proper bit, the bottom of any groove you make can be shaped into a rounded, V-shape, or rectangular form, or it can be narrow and shallow for ornamentation. Thin grooving is called veining.

Wood inlaying, formerly the specialty of professional cabinetmakers, is brought within the province of the hobbyist by the router. Wood inlaying produces truly beautiful results that can be works of art. A separate field of skill in itself, it utilizes the router fully. Inlaid wood strips, circles, ovals, and other patterns are available at fancy wood dealers. You just make your design, mark it, rout a groove, circle, or oval for them in your project, glue them in place and, voilà, a master's touch. The thickness of veneer and inlays is 1/28 inch. The groove or area you rout should be slightly less deep in order to leave some veneer or inlay that can be sanded down. This is easier than sanding the entire area of the piece down to the level of the inlay. Here again, if the size of your bit is the same size as the inlaid strip, you can rout the groove in one pass with your router. Otherwise, you can make several passes with a smaller-size bit, guiding along the edge of the piece with your router guide, or along a guide strip clamped to the work.

Inlay work requires a rectangular cut. Spot inlays are usually mortised free-hand or from outlines marked on templates. The inlays are then cut with a shape knife to fit. This technique can be used for lettering or ornamental designs. Grooves can also be filled with colored plastic wood, which, when hardened and polished, resembles inlay work.

Grooving the edge of a board (for splines and the like) requires a special technique to provide a base on which the router can slide. The usual method is to clamp waste stock to both sides of the board to provide the extra thickness necessary.

Decorative cuts that can be made with a router are limited only by your imagination: perhaps a speaker grille for a large hi-fi speaker, cut from ¼-inch veneered plywood. Trace a suitable design on the piece of plywood and cut the design with a router bit that will shape the edge of the cut. Glue the speaker cloth to the back of the plywood. Serving trays can be routed from a piece of 1-inch solid mahogany, walnut,

Router inlaying

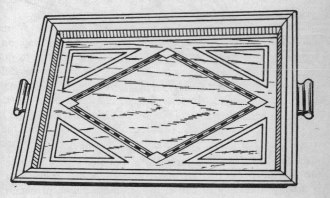

Finished project with inlay strips

oak, or other hardwood. If you haven't a wide enough piece, glue two or more pieces together to get the desired width. Many glues available today make joints stronger than the wood itself.

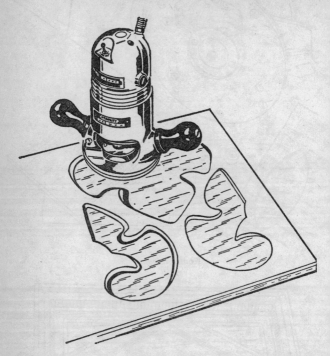

Making a Template

A fancy and handy cheese tray is made by routing out a place in a wooden serving tray for a round or square ceramic tile to cut cheese on. To make wooden dishes or trays, it is usually necessary to cut in two or more passes to obtain the necessary depth. The area to be cut is first marked out, then cut free-hand in the rough on the first pass. Decorative ceramic tiles are available at pottery and ceramic supply centers. Center the tile on the tray, mark with a pencil, set the depth of the bit so that the tile will be flush, and rout out the area. Then glue the tile in place.

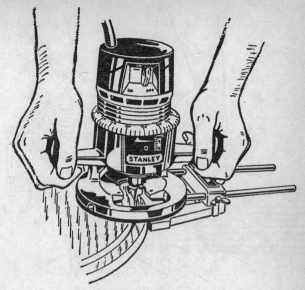

Using the circular guide

Drawer fronts, table legs, and table tops are amenable to decoration with a router, using a veining bit.

The router manufacturer offers many bits, cutters that make possible decorative molded edges. This work is not difficult, especially if a guiding ledge of ⅛ inch or so is left uncut. Many router bits have projecting from the bit a 3/16-inch pilot tip that can be held against this uncut portion and follow the contours of the edge. Circles can be cut precisely by using a trammel point with the router guide.

When shaping covers the entire edge, a template must be tacked to the underside, and the bit is guided to follow the outline. If the bit has no pilot tip, a template must be attached to the surface of the stock.

Like other motorized tools, the router can be implemented with a basic assortment of bits and accessories that will expand its usefulness.

In addition, conversion kits available with some routers adapt them for use as planes or shapers.

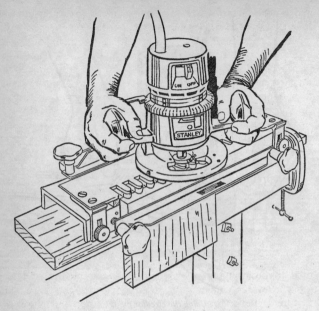

Making a dovetail joint

The Router Used as a Bench Shaper

Because of its high-velocity motor (18,000 to 27,000 r.p.m.), the router is designed by some manufacturers to be convertible for use as a bench shaper. The advantages of using the router in this manner rather than as a portable tool, for cutting moldings and other shapes, is apparent when you consider the awkwardness of clamping small-size pieces of wood to a bench and attempting to move the router over them. A shaper plate, which converts your router into a bench router, is first installed in a bench. When you plan to use your router to cut moldings, unscrew the router from its base and mount the router motor on the shaper plate underneath the bench. This permits tilting the motor 45 to 90 degrees. The shaper cutter extends through a hole in the bench top. Work is fed into the cutter by pushing it along the shaper fence, which extends across the bench top on either side of the cutter. By using different shaper cutters and by tilting the router motor to various angles, an almost infinite variety of shapes can be produced.

The shaper cutter is of high-speed steel with three shaped blades spaced 120 degrees apart around it in one integral piece. Some shaper cutter blades are carbide-tipped for much greater resistance to wear. As with other cutting tools, it is important to keep a sharp edge on the shaper cutters. A silicon carbide hone, especially shaped for router bits and shaper cutters, is available and is very useful for honing router bits and shaper cutters to keep them at peak cutting efficiency. It can be used on either high-speed steel or carbide-tipped tools.

One or more shaper cutters fit on the shaper arbor and are secured by means of a nut. This nut should be wrench-tightened. It turns counter to the rotation of the shaper arbor in order to prevent its being loosened by shocks and vibration. The shaper arbor, like the router bits, is held in the chuck of the router, which also should be wrench-tightened. Spacing collars of various thicknesses can be used to position the shaper cutter, or cutters of the shaper arbor. Several shaper arbors are provided by the manufacturers, those for use with shaper cutters having 5/16-inch or ¼-inch arbor holes, for use in 5/16-inch or ¼-inch chucks, the length of which permits the use of spacing collars.

Many types of shaper cutters are provided, each type available in a wide range of dimensions. They find great usefulness in the quantity production of moldings by home builders, as well as in woodworking projects by the homeowner and craftsman.

Straight face cutters. The cutting edge is straight across on this one. It will cut a chamfer if tilted to an angle.

Convex cutters. Convex cutters cut a concave surface on the piece. They can be used to cut fluting in the surface of a piece, or to make a concave angle on the corner of a piece.

Surface bead cutters. These cut a bead into the surface or on the edge of a piece. Not used for joinery work but to add decorative touches to moldings.

Concave cutters. Concave cutters cut a convex surface on the piece—in other words, round off corners.

Operating the Table Shaper

When shaping a piece either against the fence or against a collar, the piece must be held flat against the table and against the fence or collar. A spring hold-down can be used to keep your fingers out of harm's way.

When the shaper is used as a jointer, the outfeed half of the fence supports the piece after it has been shaped. It should be adjusted so that it is out of line with the infeed half of the fence by a distance equal to the width of stock you wish to remove. In other words, to make a cut ¼ inch deep, move the outfeed portion of the shaper fence back ¼ inch. With shaper blades that do not remove the entire edge of the piece, the two sections of fence are in line with each other.

The fence is used only to shape straight edges. Curved and circular edges are shaped against a collar. The collar, on the shaper arbor, rides along the edge of the work and controls the depth of cut. A fulcrum pin can be used to position the work more exactly. Collars are available in various diameters.

Always feed the work on your shaper against the rotation of the cutter, and with the grain of the wood. When a cut

Shaper cutters in position

across the end of a piece must be made, cut that first, then make the finishing cut with the grain of the wood. The easiest way to make a small-size molding is to shape the edge of a larger-size board, then rip off the molding with a saw. This can be repeated for as many moldings as you wish and is easier for quantity production of moldings as well as just one.

Shaper plate mounted in bench top

Special guides, or jigs, for shaping curved and circular pieces can be cut from plywood and clamped to the table. More positive control of the piece to be shaped can be gained if the jig has the same radius as the piece, though this need not be so. The jig can have a larger radius than the piece; it is especially important in this case to clamp the jig carefully to the table to obtain the correct depth of cut. A V-shaped jig will accommodate circular pieces of many sizes.

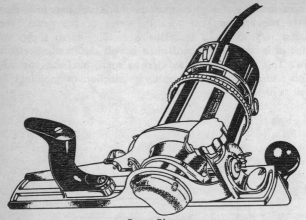

Power Plane

The Power Plane

The power-plane attachment (Stanley) is another useful accessory to your basic router unit. The same motor that powers the shaper and router also powers the plane attachment. You may buy one as part of the router kit, or later as the need arises. The power-plane attachment is a precision tool capable of exact control of the depth of cut. While its principal use is in sizing doors, screens, and the like for installation, it can be used to good advantage anywhere a hand plane can be used. Unlike some other tools that are sometimes used to trim doors, the power plane leaves smooth, clean, even edges.

The power-plane cutter makes a cut up to $2\frac{1}{16}$ inches wide. Made of high-speed steel, it requires occasional sharpening. Also available, but more expensive, are carbide-tipped cutters, which require sharpening very infrequently. Whichever type of cutter you choose, be sure it is sharp at all times, as a dull cutter overloads the motor, causing overheating and producing work of lower quality. The straight flute-plane cutter can be sharpened by hand on an oilstone, but the spiral flute-plane cutter requires a special attachment for sharpening. The spiral flute cutter is placed in a movable holder on the grinding attachment, and a cup-grinding wheel is placed in the chuck of the router motor unit, also mounted on the attachment. Moving the cutter slowly back and forth a few times against the grinding wheel sharpens it. Straight flute cutters can also be sharpened on the plane cutter grinder attachment.

Operating the power plane is simply a matter of setting the depth of cut and passing the plane over the work. The door, screen, or piece of wood being planed should be held in a vise, clamped to the edge of a bench, or otherwise firmly held. The depth of cut that can be made in one pass is about 3/32 inch on some models, up to 3/16 inch on the larger models. First, make careful measurements of the piece, where it is to fit, and determine how much material has to be removed. Check the smoothness and straightness of all the edges. If a smoothing cut is desired, make that first, then check the dimensions again. Make as many passes as necessary with the plane to reach the desired dimension, checking frequently so as not to remove too much. The greater the depth of the cut, the slower you must feed the tool into the work. Feed pressure should be enough to keep the tool cutting but not so much as to slow it down excessively. Keep chips off the work, as they can mar the surface as the tool passes over them.

The L-shaped base or fence of the plane should be pressed snugly against the work when planing, assuring that the edge will be cut square. For bevel cuts, loosen the setscrew on the base, set the base at the desired bevel, and tighten the setscrew.

Veneer Trimmer

Another very useful accessory for your router, the veneer trimmer is designed for the specific purpose of trimming hard plastic laminates, like formica, on counter tops and other veneered surfaces. It is available as a separate tool or as a kit that converts your present router into a veneer trimmer.

The veneer-trimmer kit fits some but not all models of conventional routers. If you are interested in adding the veneer-trimmer kit to your collection of router accessories, first check to see if it will fit your present router. In addition to the veneer-trimmer attachment, separate veneer trimmers are also available.

A feature that distinguishes the complete veneer-trimmer unit from a standard router is its shape. This shape, plus a wall guide bracket, enables the veneer trimmer (Stanley) to be guided along an irregular wall while simultaneously scribing and trimming the back edge of a counter or other surface.

The base for the kit is circular in shape, while the base for the veneer-trimmer unit is square.

The veneer-trimming kit consists of a special base, a precision adjustable trim guide, and a carbide veneer-trim bit. Also available for use with the veneer trimmer are carbide bevel cutters of several different bevels, combination carbide straight and bevel trim bits, carbide flush trim cutters, solid carbide trim saws, veneer-trimmer arbor for saws, and carbide slotting cutter. The special base is attached to the router by means of four screws, and is easily interchangeable with the conventional router sub-base. The precision adjustable trim guide has two thumbscrews, one to adjust the distance of the trim cutter from the edge of the work, and the other to lock the setting of the first thumbscrew.

When constructing counter tops of decorative plastic laminates, leave a slight excess of the laminate material when cutting it to size. When gluing this to the wood backing, be sure some of the excess overhangs each edge. Then trim this flush with your veneer trimmer.

The base of the veneer-trimmer unit tilts 45 degrees in either direction to permit bevel trimming with a straight bit. Carbide cutters cut plastics, even formica, easily without getting dull quickly. The depth of the cut on the veneer-trimmer unit is controlled by two thumbscrews. One raises or lowers the base in parallel channels, and the other locks the adjustment of the first. This procedure can be used to position the cutting portion of the bit, cutter, or saw at the level of the surface to be trimmed. If you are using a standard router with the veneer-trimmer attachment, set the depth of cut in the usual manner prescribed for that router.

CHAPTER SIXTEEN

The Matter of Safety

In the design of portable tools, safety is a prime consideration. But care and common sense are still necessary in using them.

All kinds of machines, whether motor driven or not, present hazards when not properly guarded and properly handled. Too great care cannot be exercised when purchasing mechanical equipment to assure that all possible protection against accidents has been provided. Machines that have gears should have them so enclosed or protected that fingers and clothing cannot be caught in the gears.

All tools should be kept well lubricated. They should never be cleaned or oiled while running. When operating any machine with moving parts, wear a snugly fitting short-sleeved shirt or jacket with no loose or torn parts, and thus avoid the possibility of being severely injured because your clothing has caught on a moving part. Neckties offer a similar hazard, as do rings and wrist watches. All stationary power tools should be securely mounted on suitable benches, stands, or the floor.

While the machine is running, chips and sawdust should never be brushed off a saw, a jointer, a shaper, or other woodworking machine by hand. Use a suitable brush for this purpose, preferably after the machine has stopped.

Young children should never be permitted to operate any machine, especially a power-driven one, unless they have been trained in its use or they are operating the machine under the direction of a person skilled in safe operation. Young children should not have access to such machines, because they do not realize the dangerous possibilities involved in trying to operate them.

Circular saws are usually provided with guards that should be kept in place while the machine is in use. If the guard is of the type that forms a unit with the splitter, it may become necessary to remove it when the saw is used for grooving or for another special operation, but it should be replaced before the saw is again used for normal purposes. The saw blade should be kept sharp, with the teeth properly set, because more pressure against the work is required if the saw is dull. This increases the danger of the operation.

A motor-operated grinding wheel for sharpening tools and doing other work presents special hazards for the unwary. Learn about the safe speed of the wheel, the proper method of mounting it, and how to keep it when not in use so that it will be protected against dampness and damage that might be caused by dropped tools or other falling objects.

Severe personal injuries or property damage can result if a grinding wheel bursts. Even a tiny, lightweight piece of a small wheel might easily cause the loss of sight if a person's unprotected eye were struck by it.

Mounting a grinding wheel, regardless of its size, is important. Use properly recessed flanges; place washers of compressible material (blotting paper or rubber-gasket material) between the flanges and the sides of the wheel and avoid drawing up the flanges too tightly. Before a wheel is mounted, it should be examined carefully for cracks and other defects, and tapped lightly with a screwdriver handle or a wooden mallet. This test should be used when the wheel is dry and free from sawdust or other material in which it has been packed; otherwise it will not give a clear ringing tone, even if it has no cracks or flaws.

When the grinding wheel is in use, avoid striking with tools or other objects, because even slight blows are likely to crack or break the wheel. The safe speed of a grinding wheel (revolutions per minute) varies with diameter and type of the wheel and the kind of machine or stand on which it is mounted. A label affixed to the wheel by the manufacturer will indicate the safe speed.

When not in use, grinding wheels should not be placed in (dry) toolboxes or drawers where objects are likely to be dropped on them.

Sometimes wheel breakages and injuries occur because work has become wedged between the tool rest and the wheel. Such accidents can be largely prevented if the tool rest is constructed substantially and is securely clamped in position with not more than ⅛-inch space between tool rest and the wheel.

When operating a grinding wheel, wear a pair of safety goggles, which will prevent particles of metal and abrasives from entering the eyes.

Breaking of a tool while it is being used is a common cause of injury. Insecurely or improperly placed tools often work loose, and cause trouble in other ways. They can dig into the work, and unless it is stopped immediately, the tool is likely to break or be forced out of the tool post; or the work can be thrown out of the chuck. To prevent such accidents (*a*) select a tool that is suited to the job; (*b*) make sure it is in good condition; (*c*) set it properly in the tool post; (*d*) secure it and the work firmly; (*e*) see that the tool is not set for an excessively deep cut or too rapid feed. When filing revolving work, the file should be held in the left hand (for a right-handed person), especially when near the lathe dog, or chuck. Also see that the file is equipped with a handle and that you are standing in such a position that if the file is forced upward, it will go past your body instead of against it.

Secure shaper cutters firmly on the spindles, because they revolve at high speed and might cause injuries if they work loose and fly off. Cutters should be kept sharp and in balance. A guard should be provided that will keep the operator's hands away from the cutting edges of the blades.

CHAPTER SEVENTEEN

The Finishing Process

There are so many ways of finishing a piece of wood that it often seems after you get through making something, oiling, varnishing, or whatever, that you will wish you had another just like it so that you could try a different kind of finish to see how it would look. A list of the various common ways to preserve wood must include stain, paint, enamel, French polish, varnish, wax polish, oil polish, and lacquers.

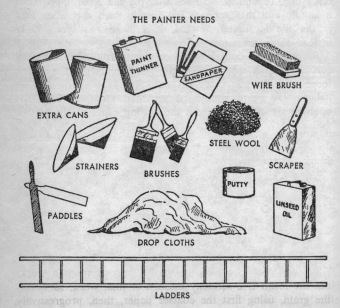

THE PAINTER NEEDS

EXTRA CANS

PAINT THINNER

SANDPAPER

WIRE BRUSH

STRAINERS

BRUSHES

STEEL WOOL

SCRAPER

PADDLES

PUTTY

LINSEED OIL

DROP CLOTHS

LADDERS

WHICH PAINTBRUSH TO USE

Ceilings	large flat
Floors	large varnish
Furniture (wicker)	½-inch flat, spray gun
Furniture (wood)	½-inch flat
Pipes	oval
Radiators	flat
Moldings	small varnish, sash tool
Trim, narrow edges	varnish, sash tool
Walls	4-inch, spray gun
Windows	small varnish, sash tool
Large areas	flat wall brushes 3–5 inches, wide or oval brushes

Nowadays paint and varnish manufacturers make a great variety of ready-to-use materials that are far better than even the most skilled home workman could possibly hope to produce from basic raw materials. Complete directions, of course, are always furnished with prepared paints, varnishes, and stains, but not all the rules of good work are given. Before you paint anything, unless you are an old hand at it, it is wise to read the suggestions that follow.

Sanding

Sandpaper is your first finishing tool. Without it, no job is really complete and even a good piece of work can look shoddy. The smoothness of a finish depends on the fineness of the final sandpaper used.

Sandpaper is coated with an abrasive that cuts the surface. Garnet abrasives are best for hand-sanding operations although "flint" sandpaper is cheaper. For a professional job, aluminum oxide grits are best. A stock of garnet papers should include:

1/0 or 60 grit
1/0 or 80 grit
2/0 or 100 grit
4/0 or 150 grit
6/0 or 220 grit

Sandpaper can be used across the grain for rough work, but the result is a scratchy finish. For final work, sand with the grain, using first the coarser paper, then, progressively, the finer ones. Holding the sandpaper is a nuisance unless you wrap it around a block of wood or make a special sanding block of felt, cork, or rubber, cutting a slot in both sides of a square and inserting the two edges of the sandpaper. A good size is 1¼ by 3 by 5 inches. An energy saver is a sponge-rubber face. Another good holder for sandpaper is a cube of upholsterer's foam rubber. The hole is ideal for that extra finger and provides an added element of control. Sometimes it is more convenient to move the stock and tack the sandpaper onto the bench.

Sanding jobs tend to become boring and can take much of the steam out of your creativity. Small portable electric sanding machines take the drudgery out of this chore and turn out better work much more quickly. Machines can do 90 per cent of the job, leaving only a small amount of touch-up for hand sanding.

It is most important that the final sanding be done with the grain, avoiding circular or cross motions. Deviation from straight sanding causes scratches, scoring, surface blemishes, ripples, and tear-outs that spoil the appearance of the surface. Sometimes these are not visible on unfinished wood, but running your finger over the surface will make the imperfections apparent.

Immediately after sanding, sandpaper dust should be brushed or scrubbed off with a dry, hard brush. A hand brush is suitable for small work and a floor brush for larger projects.

Sharp edges present a problem to the discriminating workman. From the beginning of work to the end of its use, a sharp edge requires special frustrating care against damage and wear. Smoothing the edges (arrises) just a trifle round to the diameter of a pencil lead saves a great deal of trouble and adds to the durability of the work. When moldings are attached, they may have to be sandpaper-molded to fit, but the job is worth the extra effort.

Finishing

Although the intrinsic workmanship in a project will largely determine its value and usefulness, the biggest factor in its appearance will be the finish you give it. So many materials and techniques are available to provide distinction and a professional look that this last step in your workmanship deserves a great deal of planning and care in execution.

Your finishing workshop should be selected with special qualities in mind. It should be ample in space, with plenty of light (daylight, if possible), in an area that can be kept free of dust, with provision for ventilation, with a room temperature of 63–73 degrees Fahrenheit, and a good distance from any open flame.

If you are to do any extensive work you should have a rack for equipment. A basic stock will include—

Sandpaper, steel wool, pumice, rottenstone
Paints, enamels, varnishes, shellacs
Turpentine (for thinning paint)
Brush cleaner
Cleaning rags, cheesecloth
Brushes
Polishing rubbers
Plastic wood or putty, or both
Linseed oil
Empty coffee cans (never work from a brimful can of paint if you can avoid it)
Mixing paddles
Dusting brush (for use before painting)
Sponge
Brush-cleaner fluids
Alcohol (used for cleaning and for French polishing)
Wax

Because each type of finish has a different solvent, it is best to use each brush for only one type of finish. Mark the handles of your brushes to indicate that they have been used for stain, paint, enamel, varnish, or shellac.

Before you use a brush, it is wise to clean it thoroughly with a shakeout of dust, a bath in turpentine, and a further shakeout of dirt after it has dried.

The best brushes are made of long hog bristles, tough and springy, with center bristles slightly longer than those on the outside, tapering smoothly to a straight, narrow edge. Good brushes are also made of nylon bristles. Cheaper brushes are made of horsehair.

The type of work determines the best brush to be used. Never use for paint a brush that has been used for varnish-

SASH TOOL

7/8" OVAL PAINT BRUSH

3" FLAT PAINT BRUSH

4" FLAT PAINT BRUSH

1" FLAT VARNISH BRUSH

1-7/8" OVAL VARNISH BRUSH

2-1/2" FLAT VARNISH BRUSH

1-1/2" FLAT VARNISH BRUSH

ing, because such switching tends to create a cloudy film on the new paint surface.

Storing Brushes

It usually pays to have good brushes and to take care of them. Brushes should be cleaned, suspended in a thinning liquid (linseed oil or turpentine for paint, turpentine for varnish brushes, denatured alcohol for shellac brushes, lacquer thinner for lacquer and gilt paint brushes). Thorough cleaning after each use can be achieved by washing with yellow kitchen soap. Brushes that contain old, dried paint should first be soaked in turpentine or commercial paint-brush cleaners. Brushes that have been cleaned and dried can be wrapped in paper and stored flat.

Commercial closed containers of solvents called brush conditioners are available. (Similar containers are easily made.)

Rollers

For walls and ceilings, rollers can be substituted for brushes. They are easier for the amateur to handle, take on more paint at a time than a brush, and cover more than twice the area per stroke. They eliminate dripping. A pleasing texture results from this method.

To use a roller, pour paint in a shallow pan, prop the pan so that paint covers two-thirds of bottom, roll in roller, wipe off the excess on the dry third of the pan. Start 3 feet from the ceiling, work up, then down. Do three strips, then apply roller horizontally. Use a small brush to reach corners and edges.

Spraying

Machine spraying saves time, is easy to do, but must be done correctly. Practice before you begin to work to get the proper distance and technique and to avoid unequal paint distribution. The gun should be held at a right angle to the surface, 6 to 10 inches away, and should be moved parallel to the surface. Spraying at an angle or with disproportionate time in one area will give unequal distribution of paint. Regulate the thickness of the coat by adjusting the speed of paint flow and trigger action. Always keep the spray clean.

Here is a summary of some of the ways to finish your work.

About an Old Finish

A first step for any finishing project is to *remove the old finish*. Three processes can be used.

Scraping-sanding is the most common. If the old finish is dry and brittle, a sharp scraper can be used on hardwood. Be careful, of course, to avoid digs and gouges in the wood surface. Grinding off the corners of your scraper will help. It may be necessary to sharpen the scraper every few minutes while it is in use. For this purpose use a burnishing tool and file. An electric scraper now available heats and softens the paint as it scrapes.

Blowtorch burning is also used, especially over large areas (floors or sides of buildings). Handle the torch carefully so as to avoid fire. Never use the blowtorch on furniture. Take care to avoid burning paint too deeply and thus scorching the wood. It is best to soften the top layer, then repeat the operation until the wood surface appears.

Chemical removers are best for the inexperienced worker, but these sometimes raise the grain of the wood. After the chemical has dried, sand down the wood. Trisodium phosphate is probably the safest chemical remover you can use. Make up a saturated solution in a pail of hot water, then

brush or "mop" it onto the surface. Commercial paint removers, often made with trisodium phosphate, are used in
the same way. After the solution has soaked the time specified in the instructions, neutralize it with denatured alcohol,
which will not raise the grain. Repeat the application, then
scrub with a stiff brush while the solvent is at work. Use a
scraper as is necessary and scrub after half an hour; then
repeat if necessary, and sand. Old paint on hardware can be
loosened by soaking in ammonia 60 to 90 minutes.

If an old finish is in good condition, has not scaled or
cracked, it may not be necessary to remove it at all. All that
is necessary then is to apply an undercoat. Sand the old
finish to a smooth feel and dust the surface. Begin with a
coarse abrasive (pumice, rottenstone, or sandpaper) if the
wood is rough; then use finer abrasives for smoothing off
and polishing. If sandpaper is used, wrap it around a block
of wood; if steel wool is used, hold the wool with crushed
paper, cloth, or rubber gloves.

Undercoating, Sealing

Undercoating is designed to form a base for a final paint
finish, to prevent or reduce the soaking-in of the final coat.
It seals the pores of, or sizes, the wood. The sealer minimizes the absorption of ingredients of the paint or varnish,
which otherwise would be left on the surface unevenly. It
holds oil stains down and protects water stains from dis-
coloration. The sealer should always be thinned so that it
does not leave a shine. If shellac is used as a sealer, it should
be thinned with 5 parts denatured alcohol added to an equal
part of shellac mixing lacquer. Allow this to dry and smooth
with 6/0 split-garnet paper. Under enamels, use varnish, not
shellac, as a sealer. Shellac tends to make chipping easier
because of poor adhesion.

For applying sealers, use a light bristle brush; the usual
varnish brush is a bit too stiff for this purpose. Bristles
should have split-tip hairs to help spread the thin liquid. A
1½-inch and a 3- or 4-inch brush will be most useful. After
the wood dries, sandpaper the sealer coats with unblemished
6/0 garnet finishing paper. Be especially careful not to sand
the edges white.

Filler

Fillers are inert stones, dissolved in pure linseed oil, which are applied after the sealer. A paste filler will do for open-grain woods, but a liquid filler is necessary for close-grained hardwood. Each type of wood has different filler requirements. The table presents a summary of suggested filler for various kinds of wood.

Wood	Hardness	Grain	Filler
Apple	Hard	Close	None
Ash	Hard	Close	None
Basswood	Soft	Close	Liquid
Baywood	Hard	Open	Paste
Beech	Hard	Close	Liquid
Birch	Hard	Close	Liquid
Black Walnut	Hard	Open	Paste
Butternut	Hard	Open	Paste
Cedar	Soft	Close	Liquid
Cherry	Hard	Close	None
Cypress	Soft	Close	Liquid
Douglas Fir	Soft	Close	Liquid
Elm	Hard	Close	None
Hemlock	Soft	Close	Liquid
Larch	Soft	Close	Liquid
Mahogany	Hard	Open	Paste
Maple	Hard	Close	None
Oak	Hard	Open	Paste
Pine (South Yellow Ga.)	Hard	Close	Liquid
Sugar Pine	Soft	Close	Liquid
Walnut	Hard	Open	Paste
Western Yellow Pine	Soft	Close	Liquid
White Fir	Soft	Close	Liquid
White Pine	Soft	Close	Liquid

After the filler has soaked in for a few minutes, wipe across the grain with a rough cloth. Allow the stock to dry for 20 to 30 minutes and sand lightly.

Wallboard may be filled with commercial wall sealer or

wall size. Allow this to dry, then sandpaper. Floor cracks less than 1/16 inch wide should be filled with wood filler or plastic wood. (This shrinks as it dries, so repeat the process if necessary.) Large holes should be filled by shaping matching wood, gluing it in, and filling the edges with plastic wood or putty. Furniture cracks should be filled with shellac stick or liquid. After it is applied, the filler should be inspected for particles or cloudiness. These areas can be wiped with a rag soaked in a mixture of 2 parts gasoline and 1 part turpentine. Crevices, joints, and moldings can be cleaned with a sharpened stick (a dowel is fine) used as a pick.

For a filler under varnish, use the same varnish reduced by an equal amount of turpentine. This will penetrate the sealer. Allow 24 hours for drying. Shellac has the ability to serve as both filler and finish because it creates a cap over the pores of the wood.

Whatever system of undercoating you use, keep it uniform throughout the same project.

Painting

The big job of painting is to hide blemishes. Paint covers nails and screws, cracks, knots, grain, and sometimes poor workmanship. Painting has other purposes too, of course. It preserves the wood, adds color, and creates character for the work.

Paints are readily available in many colors, types, and for many special purposes. If you must be an artist and won't use standard colors, you can select pigments, mix them to the exact shade you want, and create a personalized color.

Preparing Paint

Even ready-mixed paints must be well shaken or stirred with a stick before using, as pigments tend to settle. It is best to remove the top liquid first and put it back as you mix. Then pour the paint back and forth to ensure a smooth flow. Paint should have the consistency of heavy sweet cream when ready for use.

Powder or paste paints should be dumped into a can and mixed with lukewarm water until proper consistency is achieved. Oil paint in paste form is thinned with mineral spirits.

Paints can be made thin enough by adding the proper thinner—water for water paints, casein or calcimine, turpentine or benzine, or lacquer thinner for oil and other paints. Remove lumps by straining the paint through a wire strainer or cheesecloth.

Mixing Paints

When you mix paint, make certain to mix enough for the whole job. When it is dry, check the color under a light in which it will be seen. Keep the color slightly lighter than the effect you want.

It is best to use a can only half filled with paint. Inasmuch as new cans come filled to the brim, pour one-third

THIS IS CARELESS
WILL DRIP PAINT

STICK OR WIRE FOR A REST
IS NEAT AND CLEAN

FLAP THE BRUSH AGAINST
THE INSIDE OF THE CAN LIKE THIS

NOT LIKE THIS

of the can—or less, if you will be using less—into another broad-based can. Coffee cans are good for this purpose.

Dip the brush so that only half the length of the bristles is covered. Then remove excess paint by pressing against the side of the can. Professionals put a wire or stick across the paint can for wiping the brush. (Pressing against the brim tends to spill some of the paint over the sides.) A paper plate glued to the bottom of the paint can will help keep your working area clean.

Here are the steps in getting a good painting job:

1. Clear the working area of unessentials, and gather all the things you will need.

2. Prepare the surface. Sand down irregularities and blemishes. Fill holes with plastic wood. (If plastic wood is not available, use putty after the priming coat has been laid on.) For a good finish, repeat sanding with No. 0 or No. 00 paper. Brush off all dust before continuing.

Old wood should be reduced to a surface free of peelings, cracks, and varnishes. Old paint can be removed by sanding, or with chemicals plus sanding, and a thorough washing with laundry soap or kitchen detergent. Make sure the wood is thoroughly dry before painting.

3. In painting, first remove loose bristles from your brush by ruffling or brushing over the palm of your hand.

4. Hold the brush handle between thumb and forefinger, as a pencil is held, supporting the wide part of the handle with the fingers. For relief, hold the brush as you would a tennis racket. Stroke wood first with the grain, then across grain, and finally with the grain, at a 90-degree angle.

5. Cover all blemishes and knots with shellac to prevent "bleeding." Bleeding occurs when paint oils dissolve turpentine, pitch, or sap in the wood.

6. Prime the wood with a coat of thin paint to fill in the pores. The prime coat can be a special base paint of white or a neutral color, or it can be a thinned version of the finish paint you plan to use. Apply the first coat firmly with a brush; do not merely "flow" the paint. The brush marks can show after this coat, but will be covered by the second, heavier coat that follows. Allow the prime coat to dry for at least 24 hours.

7. Paint can be applied over stain if water stain or non-

grain-raising stain has been used. Otherwise, the surface should first be shellacked (one or two coats) or be treated with aluminum paint.

8. Paint a second coat, using firm strokes with the grain. Check the paint periodically for consistency. Allow 48 hours for drying.

9. If necessary, paint a third coat. Allow 72 hours for drying.

Painting Order

The order in which you paint sometimes puzzles a beginning finisher, especially with a chair or a bench. In general, the best policy is to begin with the areas that are least seen—bottom parts, legs, and the like. For the final coat it is best to start high and work down.

On panels, the molding should be brushed first, then top to center and bottom to center. After the main panel, brush the top and bottom rails and legs. The rails are brushed right to center, then left to center. Never work an area from corners to the center.

On chair or table legs, paint around with the turnings, holding the brush close to the ferrule.

Some Helpful Hints

Here are tips on painting outdoors after you have put a new rail on the porch stairs, or put a new piece of siding on the outside of a house, or perhaps even tackled a bigger job.

1. A white blotter will give you a good idea of the color of a paint when it is dry.

2. Do not paint in very cold or frosty weather.

3. Do not paint wet or moist surfaces, or dirty and greasy surfaces.

4. Shellac any knots in the wood to prevent pitch or sap from coming through the paint.

5. Do not paint over blistered, loose, cracked, or peeling paint. Remove these imperfections.

6. Do not apply second or third coats until previous ones are dry.

7. Putty all holes after the first or priming coat.

8. Do not use cheap paint oils—use pure linseed oils.

9. Do not use old worn-out brushes and expect a good job.

10. Brush the paint in. Do not flow it on.

11. Do not prime with ocher or cheap paint.

12. Several thin coats are better than one thick coat.

13. Any paint can be made insect repellent by adding a few teaspoonsful of citronella, D.D.T., or oil of wintergreen to each gallon.

14. When you store paint, it is a good idea to indicate on the outside label the color and how much is left in the can.

15. To eliminate lumps in paint, cut a piece of screening to the diameter of the paint can. After you have stirred the paint, insert the circle of screening and allow it to settle. Any lumps will settle below the screen, keeping the top portion clear.

16. Paint odor can be minimized by adding a teaspoon of vanilla to each gallon of paint.

17. For painting a ceiling, a long-handled roller, made by attaching a broom handle, will save much bending and ladder moving.

18. Steps that are in current use should be painted alternate steps at a time. When one set dries, paint the other set. Thus an entrance need never be blocked.

In painting walls, of course, it is usually necessary to size the plaster or surface upon which you are going to paint. A plaster wall will have a considerable amount of absorptive capacity for any liquid. Obviously if this wall could be coated with an impervious film and the absorption of the paint lessened, the net result might be a saving in expense and an even color on the surface when it dries. If part of an area —hardware or decoration—is to be left unpainted, you can mask the area or cover it with vaseline. After painting, any droppings can be removed easily.

Enameling

Enameling is more difficult than painting, but the results are worth a great deal of effort because a hard, durable coating which nothing else will produce is possible with enamel. Enamel has the additional advantage of being washable.

All enamels require undercoats to ensure the proper foundation before the finish coat or coats are applied. These undercoats dry with a flat finish. The use of an undercoat is necessary because the enamel is partly transparent, for it is made with the best light-colored varnish to assure proper gloss and flow.

To enamel a surface—

1. Prepare the surface as you would for painting. Clean painted surfaces require little preparation, but stained surfaces should be treated as new surfaces.

2. Apply one or more coats of enamel undercoat (available in white) or flat paint, using a brush ordinarily used for paint. Allow this to dry for 24 hours. White enamel retains its color better if grayed by the addition of 1 teaspoonful of black enamel to a gallon. Enamel paint can be slow and sticky, particularly in cold weather. Place the can in a pot of hot water and you will have a smoother solution that goes on more easily.

3. Check for blemishes. Resand with No. 00 paper.

4. Apply any necessary additional undercoats and allow to dry. Resand as necessary.

5. Apply a coat of enamel, using flow-on strokes of the brush to avoid brush marks. Enamel paints are "self-leveling" and should require no rebrushing if paint is applied properly. Allow the enamel to dry for 48 hours unless a special quick-drying paint is used. Resand the surface with No. 00 paper.

6. Apply second and third coats following the same process. Allow 72 hours for drying. If enamel is to be applied over enamel, a little cornstarch added to the second coat will give a better bind.

7. For a dull finish, rub with a paste made of pumice and linseed oil, using straight strokes with the grain. Remove excess with a wet rag and brush.

8. Save a small amount of the paint of any mixed color for later touch-ups. A Q-tip or a swab of cotton on a toothpick makes a handy touch-up brush that can be discarded after it has been used.

Staining

Staining is the finishing process used to preserve the appearance and beauty of the grain while preserving the wood and creating a natural color. Stain penetrates the fibers of wood, but it hides no blemishes—and very few errors of workmanship. In most cases, staining is only the first of a series of finishing processes.

Stains are dissolved in five different kinds of base: water, spirit (turpentine), chemical, oil, and varnish.

Water stains are water-soluble dyes. In some instances they have a tendency to fade, but care in selection can prevent trouble. Chemical stains may have no pigment of themselves, but have a chemical reaction with the wood that produces color. For instance, ammonia is used to give wood the appearance of age, and to open the grain. Some stains penetrate more deeply and color more evenly when the wood has first been treated with ammonia. This ammonia treating, called "fuming," is done by exposing the work to ammonia fumes in an air-tight box or room. Another example is bichromate of potash, which produces an old appearance on mahogany, chestnut, and walnut. The immediate effect is a yellow color, but in time the action of the daylight and oiling changes it to brown.

Water and chemical stains on application have the effect of raising the grain of the wood, and therefore require sanding lightly before any further part of the finishing process is undertaken. To hold this raising of the grain to a minimum, give the wood an application of water with a sponge or brush. This, as it dries, raises the grain, which can then be sanded. Then an application of the stain, after drying, may require only a very slight further sanding.

Spirit stains are dyes dissolved in alcohol or naphtha.

Oil stains are an appropriate oil solution of oil-soluble materials, and the subsequent suspension of pigments in these vehicles. They are best for new wood, and work easily. All natural wood shades are commercially available.

Varnish stains are very similar to oil stains. They are also varnishes either containing oil-soluble colors or merely with pigments suspended in them, and they are used mainly to save money by combining staining and varnishing. Varnish stains are preferred for old wood that has been previously stained so that the pores are sealed.

The method that probably produces the best results in wood finishing is that in which water or chemical stains are employed. They produce good colors that are sufficiently transparent so that the natural grain and beauty of the wood are apparent. Stains containing insoluble pigments are very apt to produce a cloudy or muddy effect, thereby partially concealing the grain of the wood.

In staining wood with water, spirit, and oil stains, apply the stain freely and quickly with a sponge, rags, or a brush, working with the grain. Work in such a manner as to avoid overlapping edges of strokes. Considerable care must be exercised in applying water stains; the work must be done quickly and evenly.

Except when using varnish or chemical stains, as the color begins to dry, rub off with a soft rag any surplus stain not absorbed by the wood. This will prevent the grain from becoming obscured or clouded. This applies especially to oil stains and to a combined stain and filler. Cover the surface well, but do not apply the stain too lavishly.

To Stain—

1. Prepare the surface: sand out blemishes, fill holes, wash out stains, and prepare a uniform surface, sanding finally with No. 00 paper. Remember that stain is transparent, and that everything visible before you begin will be visible when you finish.

2. Sand old surfaces until the gloss is removed. If necessary remove the old paint surface by sanding or with chemicals. If you want a lighter color than you can obtain by removing old paint, apply a ground color. Then apply varnish stain as you would an ordinary varnish. (See pages 339, 340.)

3. On new wood, brush on a base coat of equal parts of raw linseed oil and turpentine. Allow this to dry 24 hours on softwoods, 48 hours on hardwoods. Then with a brush, sponge, or rag, apply a coat of stain in the desired color, wiping off the excess as you proceed. The longer the stain remains before being wiped off, the darker it will be. Because some parts of the surface are more porous than others, the shades will vary unless a thorough undercoat has been applied previously (step 2). Allow it to dry 24 hours.

4. Check surface for any remaining blemishes and repair by filling or sanding as necessary. Sand entire surface with No. 0 paper. Brush off dust.

On open-grained woods (mahogany, oak, walnut, birch, chestnut) apply a transparent wood filler or one of the same color you are using, thinned with turpentine to the consistency of milk. Allow it to dry for 48 hours, and resand.

5. Where necessary, apply a second coat of stain.

6. Varnish or shellac to give a protective coat. (See pages 339, 340.)

One of the simplest and most successful finishes for things you make around the house is a coat of stain followed by several coats of shellac, each rubbed with fine sandpaper, then rubbed with wax.

To shellac over a stained surface, select either white shellac (for light finishes) or orange shellac (for darker finishes). Thin with denatured alcohol. Brush the surface free of dust. Then, using a new brush, apply shellac in long, even strokes, completely and evenly covering the surface. Remember, shellac dries quickly and cannot be retouched. Allow 3 hours for drying. Resand with No. 00 sandpaper and apply a second coat. Repeat with a third coat if necessary.

Shellac dries very quickly and is very hard, but it will not stand up under moisture. When you apply it, you must do so quickly, with long, even strokes. If you fail to cover a single spot, the coating fails, because you cannot go back afterwards and touch it up the way you can with paint. (Shellac is used frequently as a liquid filler underneath varnish or wax polish.)

An oily spot—possibly a fingerprint—may refuse to accept the stain. This should be sanded down immediately.

Special stain brushes should be used. The preferred types are of black china bristles set in rubber. Brushes of 1½-inch and 3-inch sizes are most useful to have on hand. These brushes should be reserved only for staining. After each use, the brush should be cleaned in turpentine and washed with soap and water, rinsed clean, and allowed to dry in open air for 24 hours.

Stains are sprayed with a fast motion, and the stain brushed over while still wet. Spraying permits a heavier coat on the areas that need more color, and some practice is necessary before a fine-quality job can be obtained. A problem often occurs when heartwood and sapwood, with different absorption rates, are side by side in a single surface. More stain must be laid immediately; if the stain dries, a second coat will make the area darker.

Varnishing

Varnish is used principally for outdoor finishing jobs, to preserve wood in a natural state without other finish, to preserve a stain finish, and to preserve and refinish an old finish of stain, paint, or enamel.

Varnish finishes are easy to produce. The wood, of course, must be filled, then shellacked, after which it is ready for a light sandpapering for finishing. The usual varnish finish consists of one or two coats of rubbing varnish followed by a coat of finishing materials.

There are numerous varnishes useful in finishing, both for cabinetwork and for use in the home.

Start with all your equipment at hand and in order:

> duster
> clean varnish pots
> closed brush keeper
> tack rag
> picking stick
> turpentine
> varnish
> sheets of 6/00 split-garnet finishing paper

As in staining and shellacking, the surface must be properly prepared for varnishing because varnish is essentially transparent. Old wood can be washed with laundry soap or kitchen detergent, then sanded lightly with No. 00 paper. Take care not to remove portions of underlying color that are to remain visible. If original paint is cracked or peeled, remove it by sanding or by applying chemicals.

Varnishing must be done in a dust-free room, well ventilated, at a temperature above 65 degrees Fahrenheit. Use only a varnish brush for varnishing.

For a good varnish job—

1. Prepare the surface carefully, filling all holes, removing all blemishes and any undercoating that is not to appear in the final finish. Varnish gives almost no cover to blemishes.

2. Apply a coating of transparent natural-wood-filler paste thinned with turpentine to the consistency of milk. Brush with a strong motion with the grain until the gloss turns flat; then, before it is set, rub across the grain with a clean cloth. Avoid streaks and accumulation of filler in the corners. Allow 36 hours for drying.

3. Sand lightly with No. 00 paper. Brush off the dust.

4. Apply a thin coat of white shellac mixed with 20 per cent denatured alcohol. Brush with long, even strokes, with the grain, covering the entire surface. Allow no brush strokes to remain. Remember that shellac cannot be retouched. Allow 3 hours for drying.

5. Sand lightly with No. 00 paper. Brush off the dust.

6. Apply a thin coat of rubbing varnish. Brush with the grain, then across the grain with an empty brush, then with the grain, before refilling the brush. Allow 36 hours for drying.

Grasp the brush like a pencil at the ferrule, using a short, quick, easy wrist movement, with almost no arm movement; hold the brush lightly so that the brush maintains a chisel shape. The handle is held at a low angle pointing in the direction of the stroke.

Work from the raw to the finished surface to avoid stroke marks. After two or three strokes, remove excess varnish against the strike wire on your paint can and tip out bubbles. Varnish is self-leveling and should require no rebrushing.

On vertical work, begin at the upper right-hand area (if you are right-handed) and work 6-inch strips to the center. Then repeat from the left. Tip off each area as you finish. Check each area from several angles to make sure the gloss is even.

If varnish in the can develops a skin, the material should be strained through cheesecloth that has been dipped in weak shellac solution and dried. Otherwise portions of the skin will blemish the varnish finish as debris.

7. Rub the surface with a mixture of pumice and water with the consistency of a thin syrup. Rub this lightly with a felt pad with the grain. (Never with a circular motion.) Wash the surface with a sponge and water, and dry with a cotton cloth or a chamois. Allow 24 hours for drying.

8. For a high finish, apply a second coat of rubbing varnish and repeat the rubbing process.

9. Apply a coat of finishing varnish. Brush in long, even strokes with the grain, then, with the empty brush, across the grain and with the grain. Allow 72 hours for drying.

10. For a higher finish, use wax or oil polishing.

Make sure that the denatured alcohol you use is pure. Some types, like those used in radiators, contain kerosene which makes shellac gummy.

Some experts feel that shellac (which hardens by evaporation) and varnish (which hardens by oxidation) have no attraction for each other, despite sanding. They suggest that if shellac is used for one coat, it should be used for all coats.

If varnish is to be applied on floors, a good grade of floor varnish should be used. This varnish also can be used for window trim and doors, although special varnishes are made for this work.

In cabinet or wood work, it is necessary to have a rubbing varnish in order to build up a smooth surface before applying the finishing varnishes, which generally contain more oils and require a longer time to dry.

The time required after each of these coats varies with the stains, fillers, and varnishes used, but never should be less than 24 hours, and preferably longer. Each coat must be thoroughly dry before the next coat is applied.

After varnish has been applied and rubbed and allowed to dry, it is rubbed with a felt pad moistened in a water-and-pumice-stone mixture to a smooth finish, being careful not to rub through the coat of varnish. Rubbing should always be done in the direction of the grain, not with a circular motion. Do not rub part of work on same panel in a different direction.

Now wash work off with a sponge and water, making sure to leave none of the pumice. Then wipe with a chamois skin and allow to dry thoroughly before applying the next coat of varnish. If a rubbed effect is desired, it can be done either now or after applying the second coat of rubbing varnish, and proceeding as before. If a gloss effect is desired, a finishing varnish is applied and allowed to dry thoroughly.

On certain work where the varnish film has extremely hard usage, such as on floors, it has been proved that a coat of shellac after the filler is injurious. The shellac coat is extremely brittle, and when a flexible film of varnish is applied over this and this varnish film receives extremely hard service, the shellac coating causes the varnish coat to be loosened from the wood surface. Therefore, varnish should not be applied on floors over shellac.

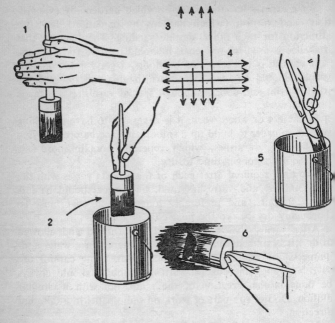

1. *Before using, twirl brush between the hands to remove oil or turpentine.*
2. *Raise the brush from the can like this.*
3. *Stroke up and down with the grain.*
4. *Then stroke across the grain.*
5. *Draw surplus varnish from the brush on the inside of the can.*
6. *Give finishing strokes lightly along the grain.*

Polishing

Rubbing and polishing are important branches of finishing. It is here that the final touches are often added when a dull or polished finish is required.

If a dull finish is required, the finish coat of varnish, after thorough drying, is rubbed down with very finely powdered pumice sprinkled on a felt pad and soaked in water.

On the other hand, if a polished surface is required, the work, after having been carefully rubbed down with pumice stone and water, is then polished with very finely powdered rottenstone and crude or sweet oil.

Very soft cotton waste makes an ideal polishing pad. This pad is moistened with water, then wrung as dry as possible. Rottenstone and a polishing oil, which have been thoroughly mixed together into a thin cream, are then applied to the pad and the polishing is begun. The motion is not the same as polishing, but it is a straight stroke extending from one end of the surface to the other.

After the polish has been brought to the highest point possible, its brilliance can be deepened by rubbing rapidly with the bare hand, using the least possible quantity of oil polish, just enough to prevent the hand from sticking to the finish. This rubbing by hand should be done in a circular motion.

If a greasy appearance persists after polishing, clean the polish off with a soft cloth moistened with alcohol or benzolene. The greatest care must be exercised in doing this. Have but a very small quantity of alcohol on the cloth and go over the surface very lightly, using a circular motion. Do not pause or stop. If there is too much alcohol on the cloth, it is sure to burn into the varnish and destroy the polish.

Waxes are made in paste and liquid form and of different mixtures. They are easily applied with a piece of cheesecloth or a brush, and, after allowing to dry, are briskly rubbed until a smooth polish is achieved. Waxes are used on floors, linoleum, table tops, and the like. Wax polishing can be done over unfilled wood, or over wood filled with a paste filler or a thin coating of shellac. The wax is applied in the form or a brush, and, after allowing to dry, are briskly rubbed vigorously with a piece of cheesecloth to obtain a polish. This must be done several times to secure a good gloss.

A simple oil polish can be used in the same way as a wax polish on filled or unfilled wood. Oil polish is durable and very simple to prepare. Equal parts of linseed oil and turpentine, if applied sparingly, rubbed vigorously, and repeated frequently, will give a beautiful and lasting semi-gloss. This finish is excellent in its resistance to heat and water marks, and is used generally on dining-room tables.

French Polishing

The French polish finish is the finest shellac finish there is. It takes time and care to produce it.

The wood must be made perfectly smooth, then filled and

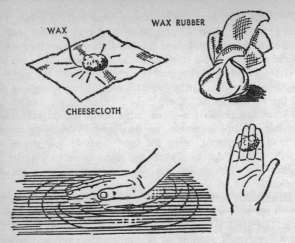

To apply wax by hand, take a little wax on the fingers and rub vigorously.

again smoothed. To bring out the grain, the surface is sometimes oiled. Two or three coats of shellac are applied and rubbed down with No. 00 sandpaper. This forms a body on which to work and prevents the oil from being absorbed by the wood.

Prepare three wads of clean cotton waste and three pieces of clean, soft muslin, free from lint or sizing, in which to wrap the cotton wads. An old linen handkerchief is also good for this. Dip one of the wads in shellac, picking up just enough so that it will squeeze out readily; then wrap it in the cover. The polishing consists of rubbing on the shellac with a circular motion. Do not allow the pad to rest on the work at any time, for this could break the uniformity beyond repair. After the shellac has been applied and is dry, dust a little pumice on the work and also sprinkle on a few drops of linseed oil. Now use the second rubber, continuing the circular motion, and rub until the work presents an even dull surface; then wipe it clean. Continue this three or four times, allowing sufficient time for the work to dry after each rubbing. Finally, with very little alcohol on the third rubber, go over the work quickly and wipe off the polishing marks. Do not have too much alcohol on the rubber, and be careful not to let it stop on the work, or a dull burned spot will show.

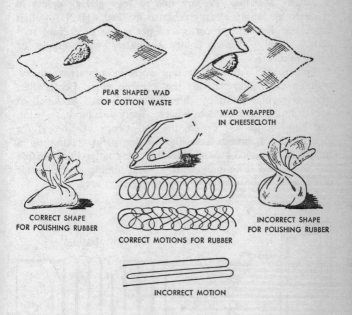

PEAR SHAPED WAD
OF COTTON WASTE

WAD WRAPPED
IN CHEESECLOTH

CORRECT SHAPE
FOR POLISHING RUBBER

CORRECT MOTIONS FOR RUBBER

INCORRECT SHAPE
FOR POLISHING RUBBER

INCORRECT MOTION

The "rubbers" are said to improve with age, and they should be kept in separate, tightly covered bottles to keep them soft. In any case, the muslin cover should be washed in strong borax, then rinsed and dried.

Other Finishes

There are, of course, other special types of finish designed to create special effects.

For *highlighting,* apply bone-white enamel as in ordinary painting. Allow this to dry; then with a cloth apply a glazing compound mixed with burnt- or raw-umber oil, colored to a rich brown. Remove the surplus and allow this to dry.

Scumbling. After base paint has dried, apply a second color. Crumple newspaper into a wad, tightly or loosely, depending on the pattern desired. While the second color is still wet, remove some of it by pressing the paper into the wet paint and removing some of the top color.

Tiffany Blending. Prepare one to four glazing colors in paste form. Apply clear glazing to finished wall. (If wall is hard, add 1 pound of cornstarch per gallon to prevent running.) Apply glazing colors separately with stipple or scumble method.

Spatterdash. After protecting surrounding areas, floors, walls, and furniture, divide the job into areas. For spatter, prepare regular paint by thinning it only half as much as usual, and pour it into a saucer. Apply regular base paint, and allow it to half dry to the consistency of glue. Dip a stiff brush or broom into the spatter paint, taking on a moderate amount of paint. Holding the spatter brush in the left hand, rap it soundly with a stick, aiming at the center of the area to be spattered. Repeat for each area.

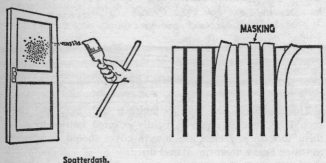

Spatterdash.

Starching. Starch is a protective coating used on walls to reduce gloss. Apply a solution of cold water saturated with laundry starch, thinned with cold water to the consistency of milk, with a flat wall brush.

CHAPTER EIGHTEEN

This Will Be a Bench

Now, roll up your sleeves and get set for the most fun you've had in a long time. You are going to make your first piece of furniture—and an important piece it is.

Your workbench!

It's going to be a good one, too! It should be, for it will be the scene of countless hours of fun and satisfaction for you and your family.

Naturally, you'll need a flat, solid surface on which to work; two or three kitchen chairs, or the kitchen table, or a couple of wooden boxes will do.

There is no fine work required in making a bench. If you make a few mistakes—and you won't have much fun unless you do—it won't seriously matter. What you are actually producing is a big, strong table. Most important, there isn't any easier way to learn to use tools than to start right in on something that you really want.

If you follow through carefully from the beginning of the operation to the completion of the finished product, you will have learned all the basic things about using a saw and a hammer, a plane and a chisel, as well as a brace and bit. You will have seen how a simple joint is made. You will have had the experience of going to your lumber dealer to get the materials, to the hardware store to get the hardware needed to complete the job, experience, adventure, instruction, and a sense of accomplishment—all for the price of one sturdy bench.

As in every carpentry or cabinetmaking project, all there is to do is to cut materials into their proper lengths, widths, and thicknesses, make the necessary joinings, and put the whole group of pieces together. If you do these things one at a time, and do each carefully, you will do a beautiful job.

A good bench for practical use should be about 5 feet long and should stand 32 inches high. It has a vise, and you can add to the top of it various little devices as you wish, such as a bench stop for surfacing boards and a bench hook for holding work while you are sawing or chiseling. As a matter of fact, this will be a bench fine enough for any woodworker. But at the moment of starting don't be burdened with the thought that you're making a piece of shop furniture. All one has to worry about in the beginning is getting some boards.

The first question, of course, is what wood must be bought from the mill or lumber dealer. Your working drawing will really pay off here. From it you can easily determine just how few boards it will take to do the job. Your bench will require only five or six pieces of wood. From these will come all sixteen or eighteen wooden parts.

The bench is going to get some hard wear. That means that you will need a certain amount of hardwood that will stand strain and rough usage. As you probably know, there are basically just two kinds of wood—hard and soft. Hardwood takes a fine polish. Some of the hardwoods are relatively soft; some of the softwoods are relatively hard. But any lumber dealer can tell you the right wood to use for each purpose. Most home carpenters never bother to learn much more than the general classifications, although some home carpenters who make a hobby of craftsmanship can discuss at length the difference between kinds of pine and when to use oak or maple or chestnut.

In the case of a bench, you know what parts of it must be strong. Therefore you use strong, tough wood. You might use oak, which is strong and very hard. But oak has a tendency to split. Mahogany is too expensive. What is best for a job like this is maple. A botanist would tell you that oak is "ring-porous." If you look at the end of an oak board you will see that the rings by which you can count the age of the wood are so porous that you can actually drop water into them. This is what makes oak split so easily, despite its excellent strength and toughness. Maple, on the other hand, is "diffuse-porous." It has small pores of various sizes, but these are scattered irregularly through the rings of growth so that the piece of maple is much harder in actual use.

Almost any lumberyard can supply the maple you need for your bench, but if maple is not obtainable, you can safely use almost any hardwood. Tell your lumber dealer what you want your wood for, so that, if he cannot supply you with maple, he can provide a good substitute, such as birch, beech, or oak. Other woods, such as white pine, yellow pine, whitewood, fir, or spruce, will also serve.

If you decide on one of these, try to get at least one piece of maple for the front board of the top, which is going to get the most hard wear.

What you want are good pieces of wood that are straight and well seasoned, and comparatively free from knots. Knots are the bane of the amateur workman. It is next to impossible to learn to saw, or plane, or chisel a piece of knotty wood, and if the wood is for use in a finished piece of work, a knot presents the disadvantage of being more difficult to finish.

Of course, you cannot buy wood that is absolutely clear unless you go to great trouble and expense. What clever carpenters do is accept lumber that has a few firm knots in it, calculating to saw out their individual pieces in such a way that any large knots do not come where they interfere with nailing or joining.

If you take your carpentry seriously, you may want to go to your local lumberyard and get a small piece of every kind of wood they have. Make a bundle of twenty or thirty sticks and get the lumber man to label each one for you. Then try all of them, making a little memorandum that tells you about the various difficulties and the various points of advantage from your own experience.

What the dealer may have to say about one of the softwoods—Georgia pine—may be more profane than logical. Georgia pine is cheap, usually, but it is full of resin. It is as hard as most hardwoods and very difficult to saw, let alone plane or chisel. Yellow pine (often known as longleaf pine) is halfway between white pine and Georgia pine in this respect. It is very strong and serviceable for things like the legs of a bench.

If you can do so, follow this procedure. Try with your own tools the various woods that your lumber dealer carries.

Here is what the dealer should be asked for on the bench we are describing. (But read this chapter through before you purchase this lumber.)

Pieces	Thick	Wide	Long	Part
*1	2″	8″	12′ D4S	Top
*1	2″	6″	12′ D4S	Top
1	2″	4″	12′ D4S	Legs
1	2″	4″	10′ D4S	Top rails
1	2″	6″	10′ D4S	Bottom rails
1	1″	12″	6′ D4S	Tool rack

(*Any combination of pieces of varying widths can be used.)

D4S means "dressed four sides." Thus, the 2-by-8-inch piece will measure approximately 1¾ by 7½ inches when dressed. The sizes mentioned are stock sizes that almost any lumber dealer will carry, except for the board for the tool rack. In this case he might have a short-length piece, or he might accommodate you by cutting a 12-foot piece in half. You may wonder about the lengths mentioned when comparing them with the finished sizes. Some waste should be anticipated because stock lumber almost always has ends cut unevenly, and there are invariably some short splits, or checks, as they are called.

When buying lumber, it is important to remember that it is measured and sold by the board foot (the amount of lumber in a piece 1 foot by 1 foot by 1 foot). However, when you buy lumber that has been milled down to less than 1 inch thick the lumber dealer charges you for a full inch. Because of milling, 1-inch lumber actually measures 25/32 inch. Lumber that is 2 to 6 inches thick is actually ⅜ inch less than the named dimension. Planks 8 inches or more thick lose ½ inch when dressed.

The stock should be cut to the following sizes and the pieces marked with their proper name:

Pieces	Thick	Wide	Long	Part
*2	1¾″	7½″	5′	Top
*2	1¾″	5½″	5′	Top
4	1¾″	3¾″	30¼″	Legs
2	1¾″	3¾″	35½″	Top front and back rails
2	1¾″	3¾″	16½″	Top end rails
2	1¾″	5¾″	35½″	Bottom front and back rails
2	1¾″	5¾″	16½″	Bottom end rails
1	¾″	9½″	5′	Tool rack
1	¾″	1⅝″	5′	Tool rack

(*Any combination of pieces of varying widths can be used.)

The little waste you will have will probably prove handy later for some repair around the house or for one of your next projects.

You are now ready to start your cutting. Suppose you think first of cutting the four bench legs. Begin by carefully marking a line around four sides near one end of the 2-by-4, using a try square and a pencil. Next you measure off the length of the leg plus 1 inch, and again square a line around the four sides. Do this for all four legs.

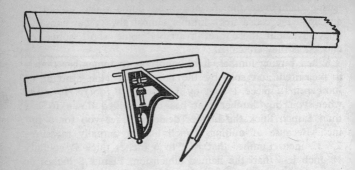

Using a square, mark your board on all sides before cutting.

This is an example of the way you always use a piece of material as it comes from the lumber dealer. Make as many pieces out of it as you possibly can, but always allow extra space for the finishing process. To forget about this necessary extra length and width means that every mistake is irremediable. If you try to cut each piece as if it were a finished piece, you are bound to be short in some place. There really isn't anybody good enough to do that; all of us occasionally make a mistake. Another common trouble arises if you do not mark each piece as you cut it out. You will find yourself with sticks and boards of various sizes when you get all through, and you won't know where half of them belong. It is like putting together a watch and having a couple of wheels left over.

Mark your plan with numbers, or write on each piece of wood as you saw it out exactly what it is for. But don't try to carry the purpose of each piece in your head. No head is that good. Somebody will call you to the telephone or send you down to the grocery store to get some butter, and when you come back you may have forgotten whether you were cutting out a leg or a rail.

Now begin cutting off the legs with your crosscut saw. Be sure to stay on the waste side of the line. If the cut is not perfectly true—and it probably won't be, even if an experienced woodworker is cutting it—you can plane off the end down to the pencil line. Test it with your try square. If in sawing or planing you have gone below the line, the

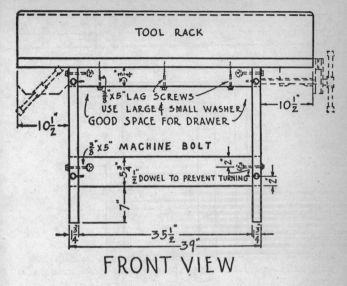

FRONT VIEW

This is the front view of our working drawing.

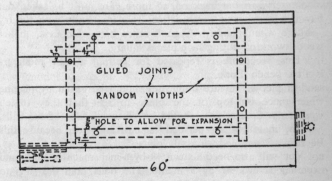

TOP VIEW

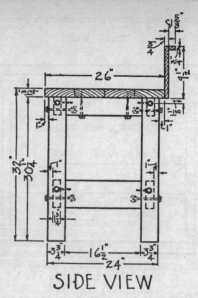

SIDE VIEW

extra inch on the other end will save you from cutting the leg too short. When you are satisfied with the trueness of one end, square a line for the finished length on four sides and saw it to an accurate finished length. Remember to saw on the waste side of the line. On this second end you have no reserve to fall back on, so more care must be taken not to cut below your finished line. Test frequently with the try square when planing. A good mitre box, of course, makes short work of cutting such pieces square.

This procedure is repeated for cutting all the members of the bench frame.

All pieces that are duplicates should be tested by placing one piece on top of the other to see that they match perfectly. Special care should be given all ends of the rails, to see that they are perfectly square and true, because this bench is assembled with butt joints.

You will also need sixteen ⅜-by-6-inch machine bolts and ten lag screws ⅜ by 5 inches. The bolts hold the rails to the legs, and the lag screws fasten the top to the underframing. Note these in the plan. Use a 7/16-inch auger bit

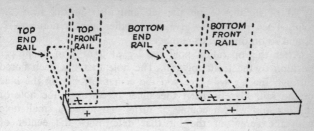

for all the machine bolts and a ⅝-inch for the lag screws. This enlarged hole permits for some expansion and contraction of the top.

Locate the two edge and two side bolt holes on the four legs. Lay them out carefully with the aid of your try square and the marking gauge. Extra squared lines to determine the position of top and bottom rails will be of considerable help.

Lay all four legs alongside each other to check their

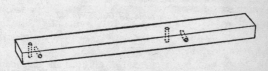

Bolt holes bored in leg.

accuracy. Then follow by boring the holes through the legs.

The next step is to locate the centers for the bolt holes in the bottom and top rails. Give each butt joint a number. For example, the joint for the front top rail would be number

1. Mark number 1 on the leg and the top rail near the joint. Then proceed to give every other joint a number—2, 3, and so on through to number 16.

After this operation hold the leg at joint 1 in its proper position to the front top rail. The hole that has been bored through the leg will give you the center for boring the hole in the rail. Merely insert the auger bit through the hole of the leg and with a couple of turns you make a small hole with the screw of the bit that determines the center of this hole.

By following this procedure for each joint, holes will be located properly even though the hole bored through the leg may be slightly out of line.

With all these centers determined on the ends of the rails, you can proceed to bore the holes.

In the rails all the holes for the bolts should be as deep as the bolts, less the 1¾-inch thickness of the leg for front and back rails and less 3¾ inches for the width of the leg for the end rails. Use the bit gauge to control the depth of holes.

Stanley Adjustable Bit Gauge No. 47

Following these boring operations, lay out the centers on the inside faces of the rails for boring 1-inch holes for the nuts. The bit gauge is again used for boring a 1-inch-diameter hole for the nuts of the machine bolts. Remember that the holes for the machine bolts in the end rails are not as deep as they are in the front rails. Put a bolt through one of the holes in a leg and determine in this manner where the hole should be for the bolt nut.

The bit gauge is again used on the 1-inch bit because you will bore only partway through.

Centers can then be located for the ⅝-inch holes (to allow for expansion) in the top rails for the lag screws to fasten the top to the frame and the holes bored.

Short dowels ⅜ or ½ inch in diameter and 1½ or 2 inches long should be provided in addition to bolts between all the rails and legs, to keep the rails from turning. Your hardware dealer sells dowels in 36-inch lengths, and all you need to do is to cut them off to the length desired. Lay out the centers for these dowel holes carefully and bore the holes to the desired depth, about 1/16 inch deeper than half the length of the dowel.

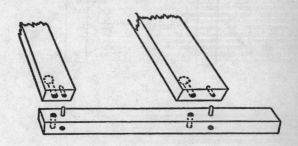

Now the entire bench frame is ready for assembly. Place all four pieces for one end in position on the floor. Put the dowels in place, put a washer on each bolt, and pass it into its hole.

Place a nut through the nut hole and turn the bolt until the leg and the rail are drawn tightly together. When all bolts are in place, assemble the other end unit in the same manner.

Place these end units on edge on the floor with the top and bottom back rails in place between them and assemble the balance of the frame. Go over the entire assembly with a try square or steel square and test it for right angles.

You now come to the preparation of the bench top. This is where you will have some experience in planing the edges

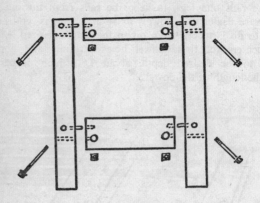

of the top straight and true. Lay out the pieces the way you want them, determining also the top or best side. Number these pieces, then start planing to get them true and straight so that they will fit together perfectly. For this job the longest plane is, of course, the best. The skilled carpenter or cabinetmaker would use his jointer plane or fore plane for this work. These planes are 18 inches, 22 inches, or 24 inches in length, and therefore their long bottom surfaces produce a true surface more easily. Nevertheless, the same result can be accomplished with a little more patience and time with a jack plane. Plane a little and test frequently with the square. If you have a full-size carpenter's square with a 24-inch blade, it will serve as a good testing tool for straightness. The bottom of the plane tilted on its corner is, of course, also a common quick test for trueness.

After all the edges are true and matched to each other they are ready for gluing. If desired, holes can be bored

*Assembling end unit
of work bench*

*Assembling top and bottom
rails to end unit*

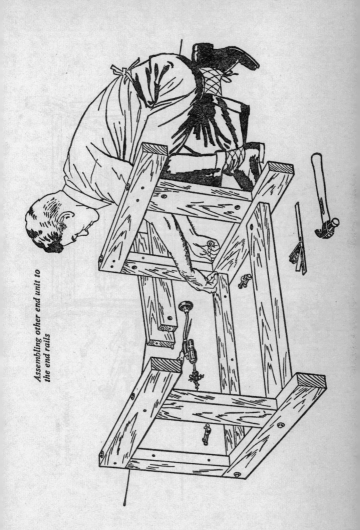

Assembling other end unit to
the end rails

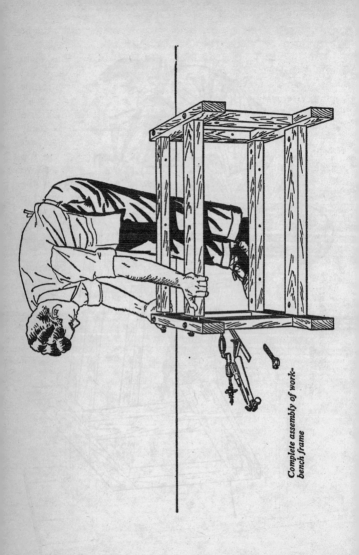

Complete assembly of work-bench frame

for dowels. Dowels will improve such a top and will keep the pieces aligned perfectly.

Gluing is accomplished with clamps, but it can also be performed by wedging on some old boards or planks.

Apply glue to the edges of the boards and clamp them firmly together. Remove excess glue before it hardens. Let the work set overnight, then remove the clamps and scrape off any remaining glue.

The top should now be planed, scraped, and sanded to a good, smooth surface for your fine workbench. It is ready for assembling to the frame. Use the ⅝-inch auger bit again to locate the centers of the holes through the top rails, marking the underside of the top. You can then move the frame of the bench and bore holes in the top for the lag screws. Try boring a ¼-inch hole into a piece of scrap wood and turn the lag screw into it. If you want a stronger drive, perhaps a 3/16-inch hole will be better, depending on the wood that you are using. Do not bore through the top. Set the bit gauge for the depth of hole desired.

Place the bench top flat on the floor with the underframing in proper position on it, as shown in the illustration. Turn the ten lag screws with washers through the rails into the top and drive them tight.

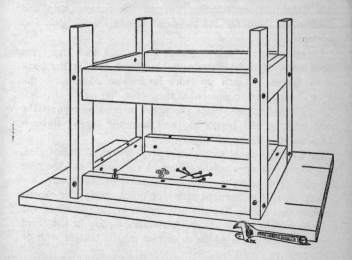

Turn the bench up on its legs and inspect your work. See that all joints are tight and all sharp edges removed, and give it a general cleaning up.

The tool panel or rack is a suggested place to store the most frequently used tools in a handy working position. You may prefer instead, because of necessity, to keep your tools covered or locked up in a tool chest or cabinet. You should in any case have a definite place for each tool, and plan to keep each tool in its place when not in use. Good tools, when so cared for, and occasionally coated with a little oil to keep them from rusting, will last a lifetime.

If the tool panel is your choice, you will want to proceed with the two pieces to make this rack. The narrow top one must be prepared to hold chisels, try squares, screwdrivers, and other small tools. This rack will not hold all the tools recommended. You should decide which you want to place in this handy rack. The picture on page 348 will give you some suggestions. Lay out the various holes and slots required for your tools along this piece, and then bore, chisel, and saw these out. Finish all edges smooth with sandpaper.

The narrow strip is then fastened along the top and at the back of the 9½-inch piece with glue and screws. Use five 2¼-inch No. 10 flat-head wood screws at practical intervals. Drill the screw holes through the narrow strip and countersink them for the flat-head screws. Apply glue and assemble.

Locate a screw hole 3 inches from each end and three more holes at regular intervals along the base at the back of the panel ⅞ inch up from its bottom edge. Drill the screw holes and countersink them for flat-head 1½-inch No. 12 wood screws. Place the panel in position against the back edge of the bench top and turn the screws through the panel into the bench edge.

Go over the panel with sandpaper, remove all excess glue, and round the upper-end corners of the panel, as shown in the plan. This completes the construction of the bench.

Any type of continuous screw or quick-acting vise can be used on this bench, like the one shown in the picture of the finished bench (see p. 348). A retractable dog in the front jaw is a worth-while addition. A vise can be bought with or without it.

An ideal arrangement is to include not only a front vise but another on the right end, although this is not necessary. If you do install an end vise, it should have a dog in the front jaw. Such a vise is useful for holding short boards secure and flat on the bench, which at times is very convenient. This is accomplished with a bench stop. Boards are clamped between the dog of the end vise and the bench stop located in one of the ⅝-inch holes that should be made for it. These holes should be in line with the dog of this end vise.

If your front vise has a dog also, one hole should be directly opposite the dog and in line with the others.

A ⅝-inch hole for the bench stop should be bored near the left front end of the top. The bench stop in this position is of value as a means of holding a piece of wood for many brief planing jobs because it provides a stop against which a person can hold a board.

The bench stop can be removed from the hole when not in use.

The illustration shows the arrangement of holes for the bench stop when the bench has a front as well as an end vise. It also shows how a board can be clamped in place between the bench stop and the dog in the end vise.

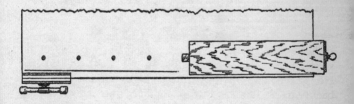

If the expense of this type of vise for the front of your bench seems like a burden, you can manage by purchasing a low-priced woodworking vise. This will hold boards horizontally and vertically, and will serve as a good auxiliary vise on a sawhorse, and the like, if at a later date you install a bench vise as shown.

In an effort to simplify construction for the amateur, the plan does not specify drawers, but one or more can be added under the top. The entire bench can be given two preserving coats of varnish or shellac. The end grain should be well filled to prevent checking or cracking.

CHAPTER NINETEEN

Things around the House

With the knowledge that you already have, you should be able to make almost anything you like, and make any repairs around the house as well. One of the most interesting problems likely to arise is the old one of hanging a door. Now that you know how to make a mortise and how to mark and gauge accurately, the job should arouse no fears in you at all, for those are the problems of door hanging. The bugbear that remains in most minds is that of lining up the leaves of hinges. It is plain that if the hinges do not line up perfectly opening the door would pull off either one or the other of the two. Worse, it might be impossible to open the door at all after you hang it.

Door Problems

A door that you have made yourself or a stock door supplied by the door dealer will come to the job oversize both in width and in height. Door openings in old buildings may be square, with sides perfectly parallel, or they may not be, owing to settling of the building or warping and twisting of the framework. It is important, before proceeding to work down the door to fit the opening, to make sure just what kind of an opening you are dealing with. The edge of the hinge stile should be perfectly square and should be planed down smooth, removing sufficient material so that, when the opposite lock stile is trimmed down, the panels of the door will be about as near the jamb on the lock side as they are on the hinge side. In other words, roughly speaking, it is desirable to have the two stiles of the finished door approximately equal in width.

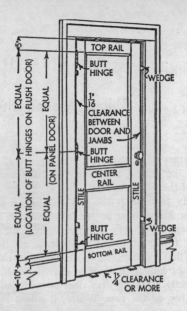

How To Hang A Door:

1. Saw off lugs (*the projecting ends of the stiles*) at top and bottom of door.

2. Plane the butt stile to fit side jamb. Plane to the correct width of the opening at top and bottom after subtracting ⅛ inch for clearance, or 1/16 inch for clearance for each side. The lock stile should be beveled slightly.

3. Plane door to fit at the top, then scribe and plane the bottom, allowing 1/16 inch for clearance at the top and ¼ inch or more at the bottom, for rugs.

4. Wedge the door in place and mark the position of the butt hinges on the door and the jamb at the same time with a knife.

5. Remove the door and square lines with the butt gauge for the length of the butt hinge, or gain. Gauge the width of the gain and the depth of the gain with the butt gauge. Repeat on the jamb.

6. Chisel the gains as illustrated on page 372.

7. *Draw the pins from the butt hinges and screw one leaf to the door and one to the jamb.*

8. *Put the door in position and slip the pins in place.*

9. *If the door hangs away from the jamb, the gains should be deeper. If the door binds against the jamb, place a piece of cardboard between the butt hinge and the bottom of the gain.*

10. *The stop beads should then be nailed in place, allowing clearance.*

After planing the hinge stile, the top should be roughly fitted to the top jamb by sawing or planing or both. In planing down the edge of the lock stile, the cut ordinarily is made at right angles to the face of the stile. You will find in the case of thick doors that it will be beneficial to finish this edge on a slight bevel rather than precisely square with the face of the door, so that the beveled portion will more readily clear the jamb when the door is opened and closed. Sometimes locks are made with beveled faces with this same idea in mind.

The bottom of the door now is trimmed off by sawing, and here it is necessary to consider whether there will be a threshold or not. Where a threshold is used the door can be fitted rather closely, probably so as to swing ⅛ inch over the threshold. Where thresholds are not used, it usually is necessary to cut the door short so as to clear the floor by ¼ to ½ inch so that, if rugs are used on the floor, the door will swing clear of them.

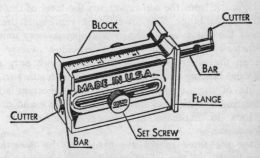

Stanley Butt Gauge No. 95G

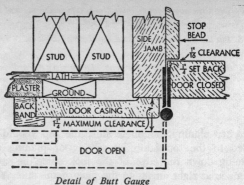

Detail of Butt Gauge

When the door is properly fitted to its opening it should have about 1/16-inch clearance on the hinge side, 1/16 inch to ⅛ inch on the lock side, 1/16 inch at the top jamb, and proper clearance at the bottom. Wedges should then be driven to hold the door in its proper position in the opening while certain measurements are taken. Measuring on the hinge stile down from the top, mark off with a sharp knife from the top jamb on both the door and the jamb. Measuring up from the floor, make a similar mark on the door and jamb. These marks should, of course, exactly register between the door and the jamb, inasmuch as all measurements for mortises are to be taken from them.

The mark from the top represents the level of the top edge of the upper hinge. The lower mark represents the bottom edge of the lower hinge. Doors will operate very much more satisfactorily if a third hinge is provided exactly midway between the other two. This third hinge not only provides additional bearing and wearing areas, thus tending to prolong the life of the hardware, but has the important advantage of resisting warping and springing of the door and of helping the lock to maintain its proper alignment for smooth performance.

After the three marks are made on the door and correspondingly on the jamb, the door is removed from the opening and the proper gains made on the edge of the door and the jamb for receiving the leaves of the hinges. By using a butt gauge the work of laying out the outline of the hinges can be simplified (see page 372). It is customary to cut the mortises in the door to a point ¼ inch from the inside face, except where the door is made of very thin stock, in which case leave ¼ inch of wood beyond the edge of the leaf.

Hinges and Locks

In the case of loose-pin hinges, the pins may be withdrawn and the leaves of the hinges fastened in place separately on the jamb and on the door, after which the door is again put back into place, and the knuckles of the hinges fitted together, whereupon the pins are replaced in the hinges.

If the work has been accurately done and no miscalculations made, the door will swing freely. If, however, you discover a tendency to bind, the trouble can be corrected

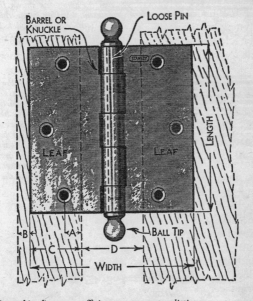

A. Keep this distance sufficient to prevent splitting.
B. Set back enough to prevent splitting when chiseling.
C. Width of the gain.
D. Maximum clearance when door is open.

by loosening one of the leaves and packing with cardboard
or paper, or perhaps by removing one of the leaves and
slightly deepening its mortise.

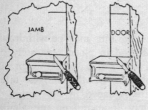

To square lines for the length of the gain, hold the flange of the butt gauge against the side of the door, or the jamb, and use it like a try square as shown in the illustration.

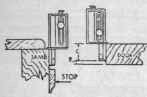

To gauge the width of the gain, adjust the gauge as shown for the dimension C. This is the thickness of the door less the setback B, usually ¼ inch.

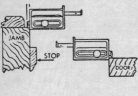

To gauge the depth of the gain, set the gauge for the thickness of the leaf of the butt hinge and mark the door and the jamb. The space between the leaves allows for clearance at the butt edge of the door. Most butt hinges are swaged for this clearance, but some small butt hinges are straight. For straight butt hinges set the gauge for slightly less than half the thickness of the barrel.

LENGTH WIDTH AND DEPTH OF
GAIN LAID OFF

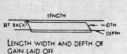

SWAGED   NOT SWAGED

Now comes the time to fasten on the locks. The easiest one, of course, is the rim lock, so called because no mortise is required.

To apply a rim lock, hold the lock in place with the lock face even with the edge of the door. Mark the screw holes, the knob spindle hole, and the keyhole with an awl. Bore the holes and screw the lock into place, insert the knob spindle and attach the knobs. Screw on the escutcheon plate over the keyhole. Close the door and locate the position of the strike plate on the door jamb and screw it in place.

To apply a mortise lock, place it against the edge of the door with the lock face against the edge and locate the knob spindle hole and the keyhole with an awl.

Bore these holes. Draw a line in the center of the edge of the door stile parallel with the face and bore holes centering

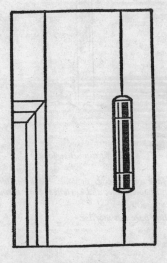

Butts should be recessed one leaf of the hinge in the door and one in the jamb for the best application.

on it for the mortise to receive the box of the lock. Use an auger bit the diameter of the thickness of the lock box.

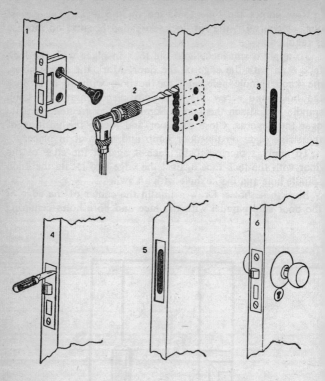

To fit a mortise lock.

1. Hold lock face against edge of door. Mark for length of mortise, knob spindle, and keyholes. Bore them.

2. On center line bore out mortise.

3. Chisel sides of mortise.

4. Insert lock and mark sides of gain with a knife.

5. Chisel out gain for the lock face.

6. Insert lock, screw the lock face fast, insert spindle, attach plates, escutcheons, and knobs.

Trim out the mortise nicely with a chisel to straighten the sides, and insert the lock.

Mark around the lock face with a knife; remove the lock and cut the grain with a chisel deep enough to make the lock face set slightly lower than the edge of the door. Screw the lock fast, insert the knob spindle, attach the knob and the escutcheon plate. It is now necessary to close the door in order to locate the vertical position of the strike plate on the jamb. Locate its horizontal distance from the edge by carefully measuring from the face of the door to the catch. Hold the plate in position and scribe around it. Cut the gain as deep as the plate is thick. The plate can now be screwed in place. With the chisel, cut out the wood back of the openings to receive the catch on the bolt.

Here are some hints about a few other chores you may find to do around the house.

Loose hinges. These may cause a door to sag. To tighten the screws, remove screws, fill holes with sticks and plastic wood, allow to dry before replacing. Use longer screws if necessary. If frame is not uniform, insert "shims" of thin wood or cardboard to even out or raise the surface.

Doors that don't stay closed. Doors sometimes shrink so that they do not reach the frame when closed. Remove the lock and add a thin strip to the lockside edge, then replace the lock. Simpler alternative: Remove strike plate, add strips of wood or cardboard under plate till it can engage lock.

Doors that don't close. Warping and settling may put door or frame out of shape and prevent closing. (1) Check the hinge plates to see if they are fastened firmly. (2) If the door is at an angle, remove the door (bottom first) and add "shim" of cardboard under one hinge and a thinner strip under the center hinge, if there are three hinges; equalize the hinges. (3) If necessary, plane the edge that protrudes. Plane as little as possible, because a door may shrink as it dries. Top and front edge can be planed without removing door.

Doors that stick. To open (1) check to make certain that the door is not locked. (2) Pound top, lock edge, and bottom with a cloth-covered mallet or hammer (so as not to damage the wood). (3) If necessary, remove the hinge pins. (4) If the door remains jammed, call a carpenter. After opening, remove the door from its hinges, plane down protruding edges.

Locked doors. In an emergency, locked doors can be removed from hinges and eased open. This, however, may mar the frame. Almost all locks can be forced open by a skilled locksmith. Spring-cylinder locks can sometimes be opened by forcing a thin piece of metal between the door or the stop and the frame, lifting, and pulling at the bolt simultaneously.

Sprung doors. If a door has sprung or bent at the hinge edge, add a third hinge to keep door straight. Before removing the door from hinges, mark the point where the hinge is to be attached. If a new hinge is not available, move the other hinges closer to the point of pressure.

Sticking windows. Find the parts that stick. Dismount the window and plane lightly. Chalk or soft-pencil the edge of window and replace. If binding still occurs, remove and note the chalk marks at the points of pressure. Sand or plane these points. Repeat as necessary, working gradually. Wait for dry weather. Lubricate with paraffin or graphite solution.

Sagging screen doors. Sometimes a few metal corners will do the job. Otherwise, attach a brace to two corners of the door.

Replacing screens. Remove molding. Carefully pry screening from frame, removing all tacks. Lay the screen flat with the ends resting on blocks. Clamp the center and bend the frame slightly. Replace the screening by tacking the corners to make sure that the screen is taut. Trim screen. Replace molding.

Storm windows. By trapping air between two panes of glass, storm windows insulate at the point where houses lose most of their heat or coolness. They are sometimes heavy and require skilled workers to hang. Proceed as follows: (1) Buy a size larger than needed and plane evenly on both sides to leave 1/16-inch clearance on sides and ⅜ inch at bottom. (2) Plane gradually to ensure that door is perpendicular and that both sides are of equal width. (3) Mark out the space for gain cut for hinge. Cut the gain with a sharp knife narrowing from ¼ inch deep to 1/16 inch at jamb. (4) Screw in hinge. Two 3½-inch hinges are usually satisfactory for an ordinary door.

Floors and Stairs

Squeaky floors. These are due to loose boards, either in the finished floor or in the subflooring. Loosening may be due to warping or loose nails.

If the floor is over the basement and the underside can be seen, it is comparatively easy to locate the trouble between the floor and the beam and to nail the floor board firmly to two or more beams. For the upper floors, it is best to locate the loose beams by sound. (A tap over the beam will not have the hollow ring.) Beams are usually 2 by 8 inches and spaced 16 inches apart.

Creaky stairs. Squeaks are caused by space between the tread and the riser of a stair. Screw down the tread, after drilling a hole large enough to keep the head of the screw below the surface. Drive in the screw, and plug the hole by gluing in a plug and leveling it off with sandpaper. Alternative: nail down the tread.

Sagging floors. Sagging is caused by weakness in joists. On the first floor, reinforce at key point by inserting wedges between beams and floor, or by setting up a metal jack post, well supported at the bottom. If necessary, pour a 6-inch cube of concrete to support the jack.

Sagging floors on upper stories may require new joists or new flooring. This would require skilled help.

Floor cracks. Shrinkage or warping of floors may cause cracks. These can be filled with wood-pulp paste, which resembles wood when dry. Apply with a putty knife, and sand smooth. Cracks more than $\frac{1}{4}$ inch wide should first be filled with thin sticks, cut to fit, and glued in. Floors in bad repair can be used as a base for new flooring.

Drawers, etc.

Sticking drawers. Sticking drawers can be freed by sanding or planing sides or bottom. Apply paraffin, soap, or powdered soapstone to relieve minor sticking. A slight readjustment of the drawer guides may eliminate a great deal of work on a warped drawer. Unpainted parts can be covered with water paint, shellacked, and allowed to dry.

Loose drawer joints. If glue joints at corners show signs of loosening, repair them with glue blocks to prevent dovetail corners from breaking. Do not repair loose corners with brads, as this may split the wood.

Shaky drawers. Screw metal angle brackets inside the drawer, or nail or glue on triangular wood blocks.

Enlarged screw and nail holes. Screw or nail holes often become enlarged, with resultant loosening of hinges, strike plates, latches, handles, and similar fittings. Fill such holes with plastic wood or a softwood plug. Replace the fitting and fasten it securely.

Wear around fittings. If wood surfaces around a fitting become seriously worn, remove the fitting, inlay a new piece of wood in the worn area, and refasten the fitting. If this is not practicable, relocate the fitting. Use the following method to relocate butt hinges for doors or lids:

1. Mortise the door or lid to a depth equal to the double hinge thickness. This eliminates the second mortise and reduces chances of an error in marking or mortising.

2. Fasten the hinges on the door or lid. Cut off one screw just long enough to project about 1/16 inch through the hinge when it is closed and the screw is in place. File a point on this stub and set it in the hinge.

3. Set door or lid in position and press the hinge against frame. Drill screw hole in frame at point marked by stub screw. (Keep stub-screw marker for future use.)

Splits or cracks. Repair lengthwise splits or cracks extending entirely through a piece by forcing glue into the crack, then applying pressure to close it. Maintain the pressure until the glue is dry.

Broken mortise joints. To repair broken mortise joints, butt-glue the broken ends together. Reinforce the joint with a screw or dowel long enough to penetrate at least 1 inch into the tenon member. Do not use this method to repair parts under great stress. Replace such parts completely.

Loose dowels. Dowels sometimes shrink and become loose at one end, allowing the joint to open. If the dowel cannot be replaced, repair it by one of the following methods:

1. Make a saw cut lengthwise through the shrunken end of dowel. Insert a small wedge in the cut, with the wide end of wedge projecting beyond the end of the dowel, and force the dowel back into joint. This drives the wedge deeper into dowel, expanding it and making joint tight.

2. If wedging is not practical because the parts cannot be disassembled, anchor the loose dowel end in the joint with a smaller cross dowel or screw.

Shaky chairs. Unsteady chairs are usually caused by loosening of rungs. (1) Remove loose rungs, remove all glue from both rung and hole, apply new glue, bind firmly with cord until glue has set. (2) Metal "rung fasteners" are available to slip over a rung that is too narrow. (3) Where several legs are to be repaired, use "chair-bracing sets" to keep the legs taut during the drying period. When shakiness is caused by loose slat, apply corner splines.

Cross breaks. Repair cross breaks by splicing, or replace the entire piece. Splicing by scarf joint requires closely fitting contact surfaces. Hand tools can be used with a simple jig, to ensure accurate work. Using Jorgensen or C clamps, fasten jig, guide, and pieces to be spliced to a workbench, and cut a bevel by slicing a hand plane, side down, against the edge of the jig base.

Sagging chair cane. To tighten caning, wet the cane; allow it to dry and shrink. Varnish to add life.

Major furniture repairs can be largely eliminated by making frequent inspections to detect weak spots, wear, and minor scratches or breaks, and repairing them before they become serious.

Surface defects. Sand or plane the surface to remove shallow defects in solid wood tops. If the wood is dented and not chipped, try to expand the wood with a wet pad after removing polish, oil, or wax so that water can penetrate. If possible, apply steam by holding a hot iron over a damp cloth. Be careful to avoid burning.

To repair a scratch, apply a cloth dampened with denatured alcohol if scratch is only shellac-deep, or apply furniture polish containing a wood dye, allowing a day for it to sink in. Rub the surface with flannel cloth and furniture polish. If the scratch does not respond, remove the varnish from the area, rub carefully with fine sandpaper or steel wool, remove the dust, and apply varnish over the surface to be refinished. Build up to the level of the surrounding area. If the new finish leaves a surface shinier than the surrounding area, rub with oil and pumice or fine rottenstone, or with a gauze cloth dampened with alcohol.

Deep defects. If a defect is too deep to be removed by sanding or planing, repair it with shellac filler or a matching color. Clean out the scratch, removing all loose or crushed wood fiber. Enlarge it if necessary and undercut slightly. Apply stick shellac with a hot knife blade, filling the depression to surface level. Smooth the fill.

Extensive defects. If the surface is so damaged that neither of the preceding procedures is practical, cover the entire surface with plywood or tempered Prestwood cemented down with woodworking glue. Remove the finish and sand the old surface until it is smooth and free of irregularities. Cut the edges of the covering flush with the old top edge. If the old edge is marred, use a thin wood banding of the same finish and species as the original surface. Make sure the top edge of the banding is flush with or very slightly under the surface level of the new top. Make the banding wide enough to cover both old edge and surface material. A tempered Prestwood surface need not be finished.

Warped tops. Replace warped tops. To increase stability, use a glued-up board instead of a solid one. For instance, if an 18-by-36-inch top is needed, glue up a top from three 6-inch pieces, or rip an 18-inch piece into three 6-inch pieces and reglue.

Minor defects in veneer. Use stick shellac to repair minor defects in veneered surfaces.

Small defective areas in veneer. If damage is confined to a small area, repair it as follows: (1) Select a patch slightly larger than the damaged section. Apply three or four small spots of glue to the damaged area, press the patch over the glue and allow it to set. (2) With a sharp knife held vertically, cut through both patch and damaged veneer. This cut need not follow a rectangle; it is better to taper it to a point. (3) Detach the patch and clean out the damaged veneer within the cut area. Apply glue, insert patch, and place a weight on it. Remove excess glue from the surface and allow the repair to set.

Extensive damage in veneer. If the damaged area is too extensive for repair by these methods, re-cover the entire surface.

CHAPTER TWENTY

Two Basic Techniques

PANELING

Paneling in wood is a comparatively simple way of creating a distinctive wall treatment that requires minimum care and, as initial construction, saves the cost of plastering. Factory-finished or semi-finished plywood panels are available in a large variety of veneers and treatments. A well-stocked lumberyard may have 48 styles ranging from cherry to Philippine mahogany, from plain pine to rare hardwoods.

If you prefer using solid wood, stock is available in regular or random widths, with factory-made tongue and groove, beveled sidings, or shiplap edges.

The material you will require can be estimated by measuring the wall area, deducting space for doors and large windows, and adding 5 per cent. Lumber should be kiln-dried and left in the area where it is to be used for several days to equalize the moisture content in lumber and room. To provide maximum surface exposure for this drying or damping, narrow strips should be placed between the boards, making a sticker pile. Stock that has not been moisture-conditioned must be sealed on backs and edges if substantial warping is to be avoided.

Random-length boards are usually sold to equal 8-foot lengths and should be kept together. Panels should be arranged with flashiest grain in center, or in some other logical order.

After the stock is prepared, the steps in paneling are simple.

1. Basement walls or other areas subject to dampness are to be covered with tar paper. All walls covered should be moisture-proof.

2. Over a finished plaster wall, locate studs (they are 16 or 24 inches apart), mark them, and fasten furring strips (1-by-2-inch or 1-by-3-inch furring, using 8d nails), leaving

1 to 2 inches of space at top and bottom so that panels overlap.

3. Remove all protruding hardware and electrical receptacles and cut spaces (slightly smaller) in panels to allow proper exposure.

4. Starting from the left corner, nail boards or panels (with 4d nails), first tacking each board or panel, then finishing with nails 6 inches apart. Tongue-and-groove boards are nailed at an angle; rabbeted boards are nailed square in, inasmuch as the heads are covered by the following board. Panels are nailed at grain angles or in serrations.

5. Where the wall area is irregular, shape edges.

6. Measure, cut, fit, and attach casings and jambs for projections, doors, closets, built-ins, and the like.

7. Round edges and shape arrises.

8. Nail strips along the base of the wall to support the bottom of the baseboard ¼ inch off the floor.

9. Cut and nail the baseboard, working from left to right. Leave ¼ inch at bottom over hardwood floors. Mitre the ends at each joining and at corners. For tile floors a plastic base cove can be used.

10. Apply suitable molding at ceiling, corners, and casings.

11. Countersink all nails and cover with plastic wood. Remove excess. Finish panels as desired.

VENEERING

Any ordinary piece of wood can have a beautiful face if a thin sheet of finely grained stock is glued to it. In a simple but carefully done operation, an ordinary table of white pine or gumwood can be made to look like walnut, mahogany, zebrawood, rosewood, cherry, or any of the exotic woods. Plywood sheets are made with many types of veneer coating in raw and finished states.

Veneers can be made or purchased. Simulated veneers are also sold in rolls and sheets in a great many patterns.

Although most veneers are used principally for decorative purposes, some are also used to make a joining stronger. For this purpose ¼-inch plywood is popular.

Poor workmanship in veneering and in pieces underlying veneers fostered a prejudice against this type of carpentry for many years. Modern glues and care in conditioning of wood now avoid the warping and peeling that caused so much trouble years ago.

Ordinarily, veneer is cut from almost all species of trees that have an interesting grain, by saving, slicing, or rotary processes. Veneers are usually 1/28 inch thick.

Sawed veneer is produced in long, narrow strips, usually from flitches selected for figure and grain. The two sides of the sheet are equally firm and strong, and either side can be glued or exposed to view with the same results.

Sliced veneer is also cut in the form of long strips by moving a flitch or block against a heavy knife.

The rotary-cut process produces continuous sheets of flat-grained veneer by revolving a log against a knife. The half-round process, the back-cut process, and other modifications of straight rotary-cutting are used to produce highly figured veneer from stumps, burls, and other irregular parts of logs. In these processes a part of a log, stump, or burl is placed off center in a lathe and is rotary-cut into small sheets of veneer. All rotary-cut veneer has an open and a closed side, although it may be difficult to distinguish one from the other if the veneer is well cut. When rotary-cut veneer is used for faces, the checked or open side should, if possible, be the glue side.

Because veneer usually is not resurfaced before it is glued, it must be cut carefully. If the veneer is well cut, there is no appreciable difference in any property except appearance of wood from veneer produced by any of the three processes. Veneer selected to be glued should be (1) uniform in thickness, (2) smooth and flat, (3) free from large checks, decay, or other quality-reducing features, and (4) straight-grained. For lower grades of plywood, however, some of these requirements may be modified. The veneers are kept in sequence as they are cut and numbered so that they can be matched in the finished panel.

To make a veneered panel or table top, select the wood carefully from clear, straight-grained, thoroughly seasoned wood. If narrow boards are used (even 2 or 3 inches in width), chances of warping are minimized.

The surface must be squared and planed perfectly smooth and flat in all directions with a jack plane. Make sure that the core stock is of equal thickness at all points. Cut the core to size and shape and sand with No. 1 paper.

Onto this core, an inexpensive straight-grained veneer, called crossbands, is first applied. These are glued at right angles to the core strips. These crossbands should first be laid out on the board and joined edge to edge with a veneer tape or other gummed tape.

The veneer is clamped to the edge between two pieces of waste stock on which a protective paper coating has been laid. A ½-inch excess crossband veneer should protrude along each edge.

Spread glue over the face side of the core; lay on crossbands and tack lightly to the core with ¾-inch No. 20 brads. If brads project more than ¼ inch, cut down the heads to this size with pliers. To prevent warping, both sides of the core should be veneered, the second side treated in the same way as the first surface and glued at the same time. Over each set of crossbands place a few sheets of newspaper, then a flat board, or caul. The whole pack—core in the center, with crossbands, paper, and caul—is then placed into a veneer press for 12 hours.

Care must be taken to keep glue off veneers (it causes curling) or the cauls (it causes blemishes). Waxing the cauls or soaping them makes glue removal easy.

When the crossband has dried, remove caul, brads, and veneer tapes. Trim edges of the veneer flush with the core using a veneer saw or a plane, chisel, or knife.

Edges of veneered stock are usually veneered in the same fashion. They should be cut a little wider than required and cut back after they have been tacked and glued. Bar clamps are used to apply pressure to the two edges.

The beauty of the finished grain depends on the artistry with which the final veneer is assembled, cut, and placed. A typical assembly is the diamond match, where four similar pieces are placed in a square in different positions so that the grain appears to form a diamond in the center. Other patterns stress the stripe, a mottled effect, a crotch (where the branch of the tree grew), a burl (from a lump on the tree), and stump wood (from the base). Other effects achieved are interwoven or fiddleback, a cross or X pattern, a herringbone, a repeat pattern, and a woven pattern.

When your proper pattern has been selected and laid out, it is glued over the crossbands, using the same technique as was used for the first veneer. The veneer is allowed to extend ½ inch beyond the core and finished to size after it has been completed.

The veneer press is easily made by attaching handscrews to two flat boards of the proper size. Steel frames are sold commercially.

A relatively new tool, the new veneer trimmer (Stanley 2621), cuts working time and guarantees accuracy for professional craftsmen and home carpenters who do considerable work with veneers.

The trimmer is contoured and can be held comfortably in one hand. It trims flush or bevel, vertically or horizontally, and has a swivel base that can be set up to 45 degrees in either direction for flush or bevel trimming of acute-obtuse, or right-angle laminate edges. A large wing screw clamps the base tightly to prevent movement from point of exact angle setting. This precision tool scribes and trims the back edge of a counter top in one operation. Moving along a partition with the wall guide against the wall and the bit in trimming position, the veneer trimmer duplicates all irregularities on the back edge of the veneer. A smaller base permits trimming up closer to a wall. Tilted, the tool trims right into a corner up to both walls for a custom-fitted job.

A special wall guide bracket, furnished as standard equipment, is substituted for the trim guide when there is no room for the trim guide below the trim edge.

The device has a spring-loaded trim guide, a quick depth adjustment with a base bracket adjustment knob, and a locking knob that locks the adjustment. The base moves up or down along a precise track holding the base in perfect alignment with the motor axis and chuck.

The trimmer can be converted to a high-speed router or shaper with a tilting base for making all kinds of wood joints, cuts, and moldings, by removal of trim guide bracket.

CHAPTER TWENTY-ONE

Working Drawings for 37 Things to Build

MAKING A SCREEN

Making a door or window screen is not a difficult home project, especially if you have a power saw.

The first step is to measure the opening, using the outside edges of the screen stops as margins. Deduct ⅛ inch from each dimension—width and height.

Materials required:

screening (Fiberglas preferred): as measured, less ½ inch from width and height, but include ½ width of any center rails

brass screws: ten No. 12 2-inch flat head

doweling: 8 inches

copper or aluminum nails: ¾ to 1 inch long

paint

lumber: 1 x 2 sufficient for framing

Cut the stock, with stiles full height and rails the width minus 1¾ inches.

Cut a 60-degree angle rabbet ⅝ inch wide along the inside edge of all pieces, using a thin blade. (See illustration.) Salvage the portion of the stock removed, as this will be the molding.

Cut notches in the stiles so that the end rails and the center rails will fit. The center rails should be spaced to be at the same position as the center rail of the window or door.

Drill each corner for a ½-inch dowel in the end rail. This dowel provides a stronger hold for the screw than the end grain. Drill each stile for a No. 10 screw. Insert dowel and screws.

Clean the rabbet with a chisel and mortise the strips that were removed.

Smooth and sand all surfaces and finish wood as desired.

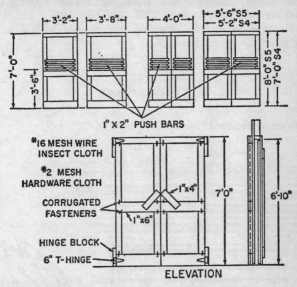

I" X 2" PUSH BARS

#16 MESH WIRE INSECT CLOTH

#2 MESH HARDWARE CLOTH

CORRUGATED FASTENERS

HINGE BLOCK

6" T-HINGE

ELEVATION

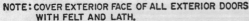

NOTE: COVER EXTERIOR FACE OF ALL EXTERIOR DOORS WITH FELT AND LATH.
LAP STILES AND RAILS TO AVOID THRU JOINTS

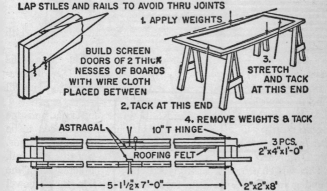

1. APPLY WEIGHTS

BUILD SCREEN DOORS OF 2 THICKNESSES OF BOARDS WITH WIRE CLOTH PLACED BETWEEN

2. TACK AT THIS END

3. STRETCH AND TACK AT THIS END

4. REMOVE WEIGHTS & TACK

ASTRAGAL   10" T HINGE

ROOFING FELT

3 PCS. 2"x4"x1'-0"

5-1½" x 7'-0"

2"x2"x8'

BATTEN DOOR & SCREEN DOOR

Lay on screening. Replace the strips removed in making the rabbet, nailing these from the center toward top and bottom.

Remove protruding screening and strands with a knife or razor. Cover nail heads.

SAWHORSE

Materials required:

>8 feet of fir: 2 by 4 inches
>7 feet of pine: 1 by 8 inches
>6 feet of pine: 1 by 4 inches
>2-inch screws or box nails

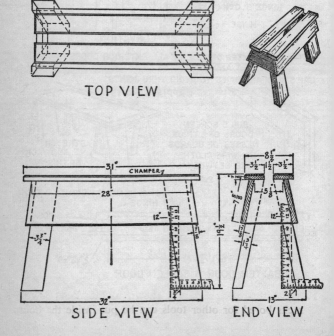

TOP VIEW

SIDE VIEW   END VIEW

To make the sawhorse, first cut one leg, using the square to get the required angles at top and bottom. Then use it as a pattern to saw the other three legs. Nail or screw ends, sides, and top pieces to the legs, in that order.

Making a sawhorse is quite simple if you use standard sawhorse brackets (Stanley No. 362A). With these you can assemble a sawhorse in a minute or less without screwing or nailing. Made of heavy zinc-plated steel, they have a simple hinge design that makes the rigidity increase with the load. The disassembled sawhorse has the important advantage of being a space saver in a basement and handily portable.

When your sawhorse is to be used at a distance from your workbench, it is sometimes handy to make a temporary vise at one end. This is easily done by attaching a large C clamp to one end.

TOOL CABINET

Materials required:

Cabinet Part

- 2 pieces, ends, pine: ¾ by 7 by 28⅜ inches
- 2 pieces, top and bottom, pine: ¾ by 7 by 24⅜ inches
- 4 strips, door sides, pine: ¾ by 1 by 28⅜ inches
- 4 strips, door top and bottom, pine: ¾ by 1 by 12 11/16 inches
- 2 pieces, door fronts, plywood: ¾ by 12 11/16 by 29¼ inches
- 1 piece, back, plywood: ¾ by 25⅜ by 29¼ inches
- 2 pieces, tool racks, plywood: ⅜ by 2⅛ by 24¼ inches
- 1 piece, shelf, plywood: ⅜ by 7 by 24¼ inches
- 2 pieces, shelf supports, plywood: ¾ by 2½ by 6¼ inches
- 2 elbow catches and catch plates
- 4 butt hinges: 1¼ by 3 inches

NOTE: Either saw racks, as shown in the door view, or racks bored for other tools can be put inside the doors.

TOOL CABINET

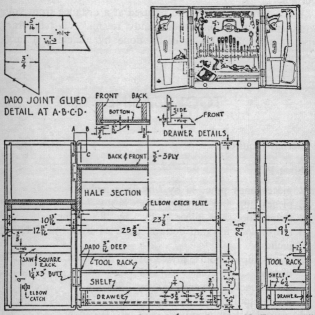

DADO JOINT GLUED
DETAIL AT A·B·C·D·

DRAWER DETAILS

VIEW OF OPEN CABINET & ONE DOOR   SECTIONAL VIEW

A DOVETAIL DRAWER

The strongest and neatest-appearing drawer is put together with a dovetail joint, and the best dovetail joint can be made with electric tools. All four sides of the drawer can be dovetailed with flush joints. The best construction, however, is to make the drawer front with a ⅜-inch lip or overhang. This lip acts as a stop and improves the appearance of the finished project.

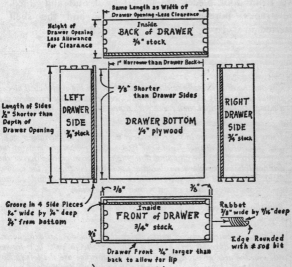

Same Length as Width of Drawer Opening-Less Clearance

Height of Drawer Opening Less Allowance For Clearance

Inside BACK of DRAWER ¾" stock

1" Narrower than Drawer Back

⅜" Shorter than Drawer Sides

LEFT DRAWER SIDE ¾" stock

Length of Sides ½" Shorter than Depth of Drawer Opening

DRAWER BOTTOM ¼" plywood

RIGHT DRAWER SIDE ¾" stock

Groove in 4 Side Pieces ¼" wide by ¼" deep ½" from bottom

⅜"   ⅜"

Inside FRONT of DRAWER ¾" stock

Rabbet ⅜" wide by 9/16" deep

Edge Rounded with #50B bit

Drawer Front ¾" larger than back to allow for lip

If ½" stock is used for sides and back, make drawer bottom ½" narrower than back.

Drawer

2 pieces, sides, plywood: ⅜ by 2½ by 5 15/16 inches
2 pieces, partitions, plywood: ¼ by 2⅛ by 4⅞ inches
1 piece, front, plywood: ¾ by 2½ by 22⅜ inches
1 piece, back, plywood: ⅜ by 2 5/16 by 21⅝ inches
1 piece, bottom: 3/16 by 5 11/16 by 21¼ inches
2 wood knobs: ¾ inch

NOTE: All above sizes are exact measurements.

The sides of the cabinet and doors are joined to the top and bottom by a 5/16-inch dado. The middle sides of each door are recessed ⅜ inch from the center. The back and two front door pieces are joined by a butt and glued. The tool racks, bored for specific tools, and the shelf are inserted in 3/16-inch dadoes, and glued.

Cut out the drawer parts to dimensions shown in the sketch. All pieces should be carefully planed and squared. For smooth, waveless edges use a power plane. Label each piece with a pencil and mark the edges that are to be joined together.

Using a rabbeting bit in the router, cut a rabbet 7/16-inch deep on all four sides of the drawer front. For best results rabbet the ends of the drawer front first. The chipping that might occur in cutting across the grain will be removed when rabbeting the top and bottom of the drawer front. The pilot on the bit follows the edge of the work as a guide so that the bit cuts a rabbet ⅜-inch wide.

Round over the edges of the drawer front using a rounding-over bit in the router.

Set up your router, templet guide, dovetail bit, and dovetail attachment for the large dovetail cut. Make dovetail cuts to join the left drawer side and the drawer back. For uniform appearance use the left side of fixture. Make dovetail cuts to join the right drawer side and the drawer back. For uniform appearance use the right side of fixture.

Using the long-finger templet and locating spacer in the dovetail attachment, make the dovetail cuts in the left drawer side and drawer front. For uniform appearance use right side of fixture. With the same setup, dovetail the cuts in the right drawer side and drawer front.

Rout a ¼-inch groove ¼-inch deep ¼-inch from the bottom of all four pieces to provide for letting in the plywood bottom. Do not extend the groove through the dovetail joints.

Glue and assemble the pieces together.

The drawer front is dadoed 3/16 inch for the bottom, and rabbeted 7/16 inch for the sides. There is a 3/16-inch space between the drawer bottom and the cabinet bottom. The back is joined to the bottom, sides, and partitions by a butt, which is glued and nailed.

LARGE TOOL CHEST

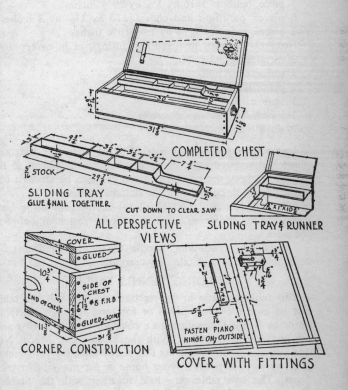

COMPLETED CHEST

SLIDING TRAY
GLUE & NAIL TOGETHER

CUT DOWN TO CLEAR SAW

ALL PERSPECTIVE VIEWS

SLIDING TRAY & RUNNER

CORNER CONSTRUCTION

COVER WITH FITTINGS

FASTEN PIANO HINGE ON OUTSIDE

Materials required:

Chest

    2 pieces, sides, plywood: 9/16 by 5 9/16 by 31⅝ inches
    2 pieces, ends: 9/16 by 5 9/16 by 10¾ inches
    2 pieces, lid sides: 9/16 by 1 by 31⅝ inches
    2 pieces, lid ends: 9/16 by 1 by 10¾ inches
    1 piece, bottom: 9/16 by 11⅞ by 31⅝ inches
    1 piece, top: ½ by 11⅞ by 31⅝ inches

Tray

    2 pieces, sides, plywood: 5/16 by 1¼ by 29⅞ inches
    1 piece, bottom: 5/16 by 3⅝ by 29⅞ inches
    6 pieces, partitions and ends: 5/16 by 1¼ by 3 inches
    2 pieces, runners: 5/16 by 1 by 10¾ inches
    NOTE: Use scraps to make saw fittings, as in cover view.
    2 metal hand pulls
    1 screen-door pull
    2 piano hinges
    1 snap catch
    1½-inch flat-head wood screws
    ¾-inch wire brads

In assembling chest, all butt joints of sides and ends are glued and screwed together. Depending on the weight to be carried in chest, the bottom and top can also be screwed on, remembering to countersink the bottom screws.

The tray is nailed and glued together, again using butt joints, with the ends and partitions fastened between the sides.

Attach the screen-door handle to the top and a snap catch to the lid to facilitate easy carrying.

FOLDING TENNIS TABLE

This table is made in two sections so that half the table can be used for other games or for food serving or display purposes. These tables close to a compact size for storing and are conveniently handled. With the Stanley Leg Braces No. 446 you can readily construct this sturdy table for your recreation or rumpus room in your home or for many other purposes. The two tables are held together with the Stanley Hinges No. 813. To take them apart the Bent Loose Pin of this hinge is simply withdrawn.

BUILD A FOLDING
TENNIS TABLE

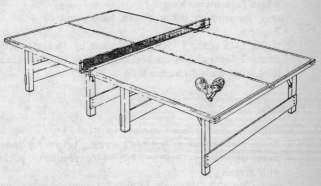

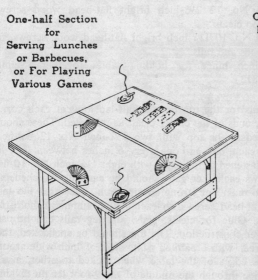

**One-half Section
for
Serving Lunches
or Barbecues,
or For Playing
Various Games**

**One Section
Folded For
Storage**

Materials required:

> 2 pieces plywood made especially for a regulation 5-by-9-foot tennis table: ¾ inch by 4½ feet by 5 feet
>
> 7 pieces D4S pine: 2 inches by 3 inches by 10 feet (D4S means "dressed four sides"); cutting sizes: 6 cleats under top 4½ feet long, 4 cleats under top 5 feet long, 8 legs 28½ inches long
>
> NOTE: Be sure to cut a 5-foot length out of 4 of the 7 pieces.
>
> 2 pieces D4S pine: 1 inch by 7 inches by 16 feet; cutting sizes: 2 leg rails 44 inches long, 2 leg rails 54 inches long, 8 leg pads 20 inches long

Hardware

> 4 2-inch hinges for legs (Stanley No. 814½)
>
> 5 dozen No. 8 ¾-inch flat-head screws, bright for hinges
>
> 4 pairs leg braces (Stanley No. 446, regularly packed with screws)
>
> 1 gross No. 12 2½-inch bright flat-head wood screws, for top cleats
>
> 1 gross No. 10 1¼-inch bright flat-head wood screws, for leg pads and rails
>
> 1 1¾-inch hinge for holding tables together (Stanley No. 813)

All cleats for the top have a half-lap joint at each corner and at the ends of the center cleat, as indicated. These should be fastened to the top with two 2¼-inch No. 12 flat-head screws at each joint and one every 6 inches between. The leg pads are fastened as indicated with eight 1¼-inch No. 10 flat-head screws each. Leg rails should be carefully notched into the legs to make for strong construction. Use three 1¼-inch No. 10 flat-head screws on each leg. Countersink holes for all screws. Glue for cleats, pads, and leg rails can be used for stronger construction. The top should be shellacked, then painted green with a painted white stripe 1 inch wide around all outside edges of the table when locked together, also a 1-inch stripe through the middle of the 9-foot length dividing the 5-foot width equally. Scotch tape for masking will prove handy when striping.

DETAIL DRAWINGS
OF FOLDING TENNIS TABLE

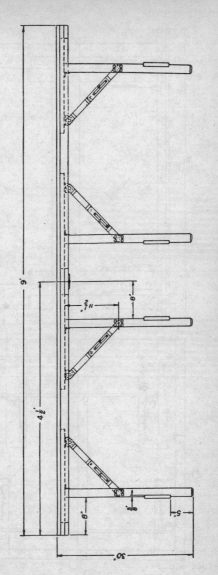

SIDE VIEW

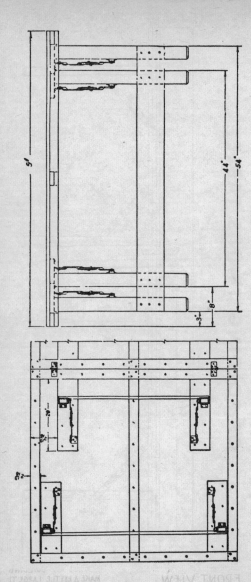

END VIEW

BOTTOM VIEW

FRONT VIEW

UNIQUE SEWING KIT

Materials required:

1 18-inch turning block: 2 by 3 inches
1 piece, bottom, specialty plywood: 3/16 by 7 by 7 inches
1 piece, top, plywood: ⅜ by 7 by 7 inches
1 piece veneer: 3/32 by 7 by 7 inches
1 piece, bird, hardwood: 1 by 4 by 5 inches
1 dowel rod: 3/16 inch
1 dowel: 7/16 by 1 inch
6 yards natural wood strips: ⅛ by 1/28 inch

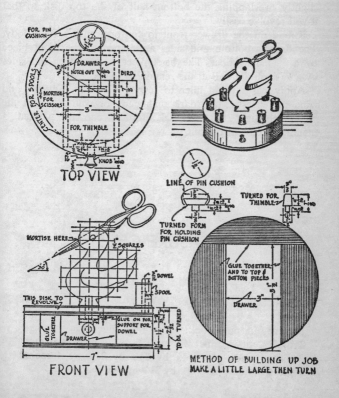

TOP VIEW

FRONT VIEW

METHOD OF BUILDING UP JOB
MAKE A LITTLE LARGE THEN TURN

Drawer

   1 piece, front, hardwood: 1 by 1½ by 3 inches
   2 pieces, sides, plywood: ¼ by 1½ by 5 1/16 inches
   1 piece, back, plywood: ¼ by 2¾ by 1¼ inches
   1 piece, bottom, plywood: ¼ by 2½ by 5 1/16 inches
   1 knob, wood or brass: ⅝-inch

Cut turning block and glue pieces together to form the detailed drawer opening. Turn the piece to a 7-inch diameter. Cut and glue on bottom and veneer top. Make holes on top disk for all dowels. Cut out bird pattern from 1-inch stock, and turn thimble holder and pincushion form from scraps. Glue in all dowels, including a 7/16-inch dowel used to fasten the bird. Glue or staple wood strips or borders, slightly overlapping the bottom half of the top disk so that it will revolve easily.

Round off the drawer front to conform with turned body. The drawer bottom and sides are joined to the front piece by a ⅜-inch rabbet. The back piece is joined to the sides by a ⅛-inch dado. Butt the remaining joints.

Apply paste wood filler to sewing kit body. Let flat and wipe off excess. Stain dark mahogany or walnut. Paint the bird with light blue enamel. Borders can be painted a matching color, if desired.

TREASURE CHEST

Materials required:

   1 piece, lid, pine stock: ¾ by 4 by 8 inches
   2 pieces, sides, pine: ⅜ by 2⅞ by 7¼ by 8 inches
   2 pieces, ends, pine: ⅜ by 2½ by 2⅞ by 4 inches
   1 piece bottom, pine: ⅜ by 3¼ by 7¼ inches

Hardware

    3 hinges, galvanized sheet iron: 1 by 1¾ inches
    1 clasp, galvanized sheet iron: 1 by 1¾ inches
    2 No. 24 black iron handle holders: ½ by 1 inch
    2 galvanized-iron wire handles: 1/16 by 2¾ inches
    1 ½-inch brass screw eye
    1 brass padlock: ¼ by ¾ by 1¾ inches
    4 feet ⅜-inch black iron, copper, or brass strips
    1 foot ⅜-inch black iron, copper, or brass strips
    No. 2 glimp tacks

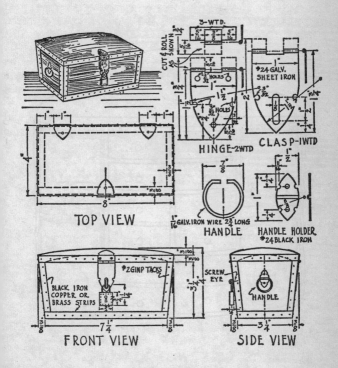

Cut all pieces to size. Butt ends between the sides and attach bottom. The lid is rounded off to effect the ⅜-inch convex shape. Leave off hardware.

Apply a coat of white shellac, thinned 50-50 with alcohol. When dry, sand lightly. Attach all hardware. Spray or brush on lacquer, full strength.

SPICE CABINET WITH SHELVES

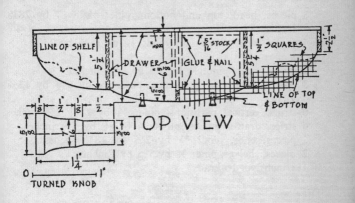

TOP VIEW

TURNED KNOB

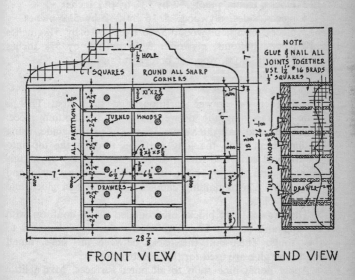

FRONT VIEW

END VIEW

Materials required:

Cabinet part

3 pieces, head, top and bottom, pine: ⅜ by 7 by 28⅞ inches

1 piece, back, pine or plywood: ⅜ by 18⅜ by 28⅛ inches

2 pieces, sides, pine: ⅜ by 5½ by 18⅜ inches

3 pieces, horizontal partitions, pine: ⅜ by 6⅝ by 13⅜ inches

6 strips, vertical partitions, pine: ⅝ by 1 by 2¾ inches

6 strips, drawer guides, pine: ⅜ by ½ by 5⅝ inches

2 pieces, ends, pine: ⅜ by 2½ by 18⅜ inches

2 pieces, shelves, pine: ⅜ by 5½ by 7 inches

1¼-inch No. 16 brads

Drawers

12 blocks, fronts, pine: 1⅝ by 2¾ by 6½ inches

24 pieces, sides, plywood: 5/16 by 2¾ by 5¼ inches

12 pieces, backs, plywood: 5/16 by 2 7/16 by 5⅞ inches

12 pieces, bottoms, plywood: 5/16 by 5¼ by 5⅞ inches

12 ⅝-inch knobs, wood or porcelain

¾-inch brads

Construct the drawer partitions and sides first. This is done by fastening the drawer guide to the bottom piece. Then glue and nail the vertical partition to the guide, using a small brad. Nail the long partition through the top into the vertical strip and attach to both sides. Build up in this manner until the top piece is butted to vertical strip and both sides. The remaining cabinet parts are then glued and nailed in place.

The drawer-front blocks are rounded off to conform with the top and bottom line. Rabbet the sides and bottoms to the fronts. Then butt the backs between the sides. Small brads and glue are used for this construction.

Apply honey-pine stain to all outer surfaces. Mix a little burnt umber with stain and apply along edges and around drawers, blending evenly into undarkened areas. Let dry overnight. Brush on a non-shellac sealer, also sealing the insides of the drawers.

PORTABLE TOWEL RACK

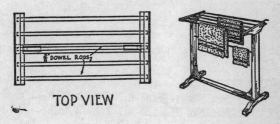

TOP VIEW

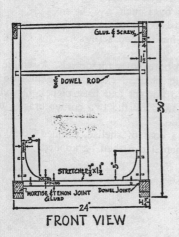

GLUE & SCREW

DOWEL ROD

STRETCHER 2½ x 1½

MORTISE & TENON JOINT GLUED   DOWEL JOINT

24"

FRONT VIEW

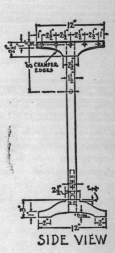

CHAMFER EDGES

SIDE VIEW

Materials required:

    5 feet No. 1 grade fir: 2 by 2 inches
    2 feet No. 1 grade fir: 2 by 4 inches
    2 feet clear pine: 1 by 2 inches
    3 feet clear pine: ¾ by 3 inches
  12 feet dowel rod: ⅝ inch
    4 dowels: ⅜ by 1 inch
  21 ½-inch flat-head wood screws
    2 1-inch flat-head wood screws

Cut pieces to size, and bore holes for dowels. Assemble and glue the dowel rods in place. Next, glue the mortise and tenon joints of the two upright and base pieces. Dowel the stretcher in place, followed by the two corner braces, using dowels, screws, and glue.

Seal the rack with a coat of shellac, thinned 50-50 with alcohol. Varnish or enamel can then be applied.

COMBINATION TRAY

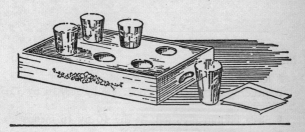

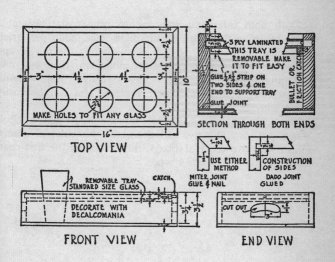

TOP VIEW

MAKE HOLES TO FIT ANY GLASS

3"   4½"   4½"

16"

10"

SECTION THROUGH BOTH ENDS

3 PLY LAMINATED
THIS TRAY IS
REMOVABLE. MAKE
IT TO FIT EASY

GLUE ½×½ STRIP ON
TWO SIDES & ONE
END TO SUPPORT TRAY

GLUE JOINT

BULLET OR FRICTION CATCH

USE EITHER METHOD
MITER JOINT
GLUE & NAIL

CONSTRUCTION OF SIDES
DADO JOINT GLUED

FRONT VIEW

REMOVABLE TRAY
STANDARD SIZE GLASS   CATCH

DECORATE WITH
DECALCOMANIA

3¼"   3½"

END VIEW

CUT OUT

Materials required:

  5 feet clear pine: ½ by 4 inches
  1 piece choice stock plywood: ⅜ by 9 3/16 by 15 3/16
    inches
  1 piece bottom plywood: ¼ by 10 by 16 inches
  42-inch strip: ¼ by ¼ inch
  1 bullet or friction catch

With both sides and ends cut to proper size, assemble them by using the mitre or the dado joint, dado preferred. Remember to cut a 3/16-inch groove along the top of one end. Also glue the ¼-inch strips along two sides and one end, and install the catch, before assembly. Holes should be carefully plotted on the tray piece, and can be easily made with an adjustable hole saw.

Apply a coat of white shellac, thinned 50-50 with alcohol. When dry, sand lightly, and decorate with colorful decals. Finish with two coats of spar varnish, rubbing the first coat, when dry, with fine steel wool.

PLATE RACK

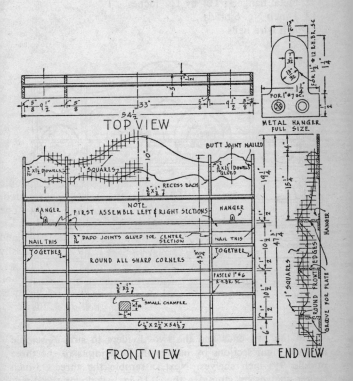

Materials required:

- 4 pieces: ⅝ by 5 by 43¾ inches
- 3 pieces: ½ by 5 by 54½ inches
- 1 piece: ½ by 10 by 54½ inches
- 3 pieces: ½ by 2¼ by 54½ inches
- 3 pieces, strips: ⅜ by ½ by 54½ inches
- 2 metal hangers: 1¼ by 1¼ inches
- 12 1-inch No. 6 brads
- 1-inch wire nails

Cut the two ends and the two dividers to size. Assemble left and right sections by nailing the butt joints of the three middle 9½-inch shelves. Next, assemble the three 33-inch center shelves by gluing in the 3/16-inch dado of the dividers. All back pieces can then be affixed by nailing butt joints at the two ends and the ½-inch recess notches of the two dividers. The ⅜-by-½-inch strips are then nailed across the front and the hangers attached to the back.

Stain pine or walnut. Apply a thin penetrating wood sealer. After rubbing off the sheen with fine steel wool or pumice and oil, apply a good paste wax.

FOOTSTOOL

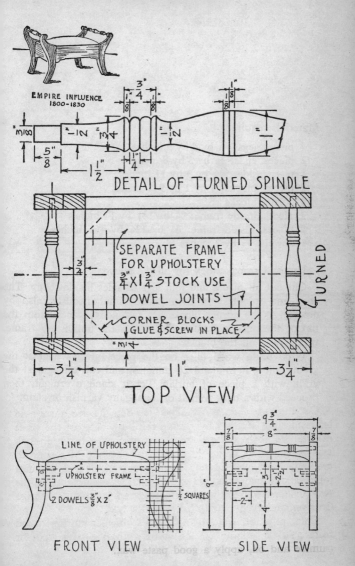

EMPIRE INFLUENCE
1800-1830

DETAIL OF TURNED SPINDLE

SEPARATE FRAME
FOR UPHOLSTERY
¾" X 1¾" STOCK USE
DOWEL JOINTS

CORNER BLOCKS
GLUE & SCREW IN PLACE

TURNED

TOP VIEW

LINE OF UPHOLSTERY

UPHOLSTERY FRAME

2 DOWELS ⅜" X 2"

½" SQUARES

FRONT VIEW

SIDE VIEW

Materials required:

  4 pieces, legs: ⅞ by 4 by 9 inches
  2 pieces, ends: ¾ by 3 by 8 inches
  2 pieces, sides: ¾ by 3 by 11 inches
  2 pieces, blocks: 1 by 1 by 9¼ inches
  4 corner blocks
  2 pieces, inside frame: ¾ by 1¾ by 11 inches
  2 pieces, inside frame: ¾ by 1¾ by 4½ inches
24 dowels: ⅜ by 2 inches

NOTE: Use oak stock for all the above.

Cut out all pieces and join legs to sides by doweling. The ends and spindles are then joined simultaneously, also by doweling. The corner blocks are fastened ¾ inch from the top of the outside frame to allow for the upholstery frame, which rests on the blocks.

Wipe paste wood filler on the piece, always against the grain. Allow it to stand 20 minutes, and rub off against the grain with a piece of burlap. Let it stand overnight, then proceed with a dark walnut or mahogany varnish or stain.

SHOESHINE BOX

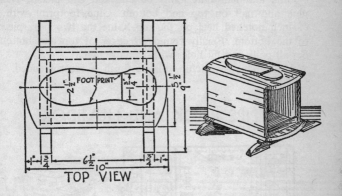

TOP VIEW

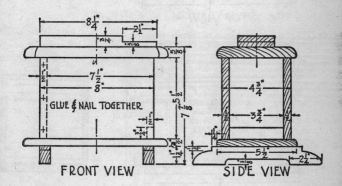

FRONT VIEW   SIDE VIEW

Materials required:

    4 feet pine: ½ by 6 inches
    2 feet pine: ¾ by 4 inches
    1 piece choice stock plywood: ⅝ by 5½ by 10 inches
    1-inch wire nails

NOTE: For increased durability, use oak stock.

Glue and nail butt joints of side and end pieces. Next, glue and nail on top and bottom. Glue footprint with a ⅜-inch notched heel on the top. Glue the two base pieces to the bottom. Finally round off edges of top and bottom. Set all nails and fill holes with wood dough.

A tough non-scratching plastic finish is recommended.

PIPE RACK AND HUMIDOR

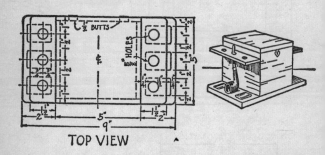

TOP VIEW

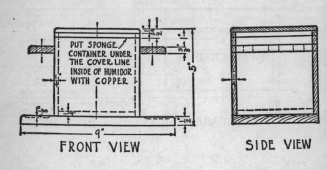

FRONT VIEW   SIDE VIEW

Materials required:

   1 foot pine: ½ by 6 inches
   6 pieces plywood: ¼ by 5 by 5 inches
   2 pieces plywood: ⅜ by 1½ by 5 inches
   1 sponge container
   2 butt hinges: 2¼ by ½ inches
   1 small sheet copper lining
   1 small snap catch
   ½-inch wire brads

Cut and assemble ¼-inch sides and bottom, using glue and brads. After routing bowl depressions, glue on bottom. Next, glue ⅜-inch pieces with stem holes to sides. Mortise cover and side for ½-inch butt hinges, and with sponge container in place, affix cover. Cement in fitted copper lining and put on small catch for cover. Set all brads and fill with wood dough.

Tobacco stain is suggested for this piece. Break up one plug of chewing tobacco in a jar. Add one pint of non-sudsing household ammonia. Place a lid on the jar and allow it to stand for one week. Wipe the piece with a damp cloth and apply the stain after straining it through clean nylon hose. Rub lightly with steel wool after piece has dried 24 hours.

COLONIAL MAGAZINE STAND

Materials required:

   7 feet pine: ½ by 12 inches
   2 feet pine: ½ by 4 inches
   2 feet pine: ¾ by 8 inches
   2 feet pine: 1 by 1 inch
   1 piece plywood: ¼ by 7½ by 16 inches
 26 dowels: 3/16 by 1 inch

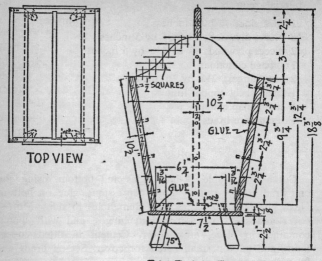

TOP VIEW

END VIEW

½ SQUARES

10¾

GLUE

10½

6¼

GLUE

7½

2⅛

2½

75°

2¼

3"

3½

9¾

12¾

18⅜

GLUE

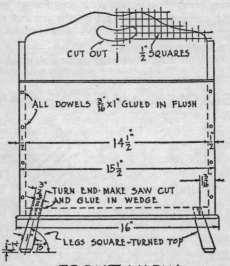

CUT OUT

½ SQUARES

ALL DOWELS 3/16"x1" GLUED IN FLUSH

14½

15½

TURN END·MAKE SAW CUT
AND GLUE IN WEDGE

16"

LEGS SQUARE·TURNED TOP

75°

FRONT VIEW

Glue and clamp some of the ½-by-12-inch and the ½-by-4-inch stock. Let it dry, and cut to form center piece. Cut ends and sides out of remaining ½-inch stock. Dowel both ends to center piece. Glue ¾-inch bottom, with 3/16-inch dado and holes for legs, to center piece. Both sides are then doweled in place. Fasten the ¼-inch bottom, and finally glue in legs. The edges of the ¼-inch bottom and the top part of the center piece are rounded.

Stain antique pine and finish with a penetrating wood sealer. The final coat should be rubbed with pumice and oil for a soft patina.

COLONIAL MAGAZINE CASE

Materials required:

1 piece, bottom, plywood: ½ by 8⅝ by 16⅝ inches
1 piece, back, plywood: ⅜ by 13½ by 16 inches
1 piece, front, plywood: ⅜ by 8½ by 16 inches
1 piece, divider, plywood: ⅜ by 11 by 16 inches
2 pieces, sides, plywood: ⅜ by 7¼ by 12 inches
2-foot block: 1 by 1 inch
24 dowels: 3/15 by ⅞ inch
12 1¼-inch flat-head wood screws

NOTE: With the exception of the 1-by-1-inch wedges, all sizes given are finished measurements.

Make jigs using ½-inch squares and cut pieces to size. Assemble one side and divider, then other side. The front and back can then be doweled in place. With the wedges glued in at a 75-degree angle, the bottom can be screwed on to complete the assembly. All exposed edges should be rounded off before finishing.

Apply pine stain to case. Let it set 15 to 20 minutes, then wipe off excess. If desired, a little burnt umber mixed with the stain can be applied to edges to give antique effect. Let it dry overnight.

Finish with a commercial non-shellac sealer or a thin type of natural penetrating floor sealer.

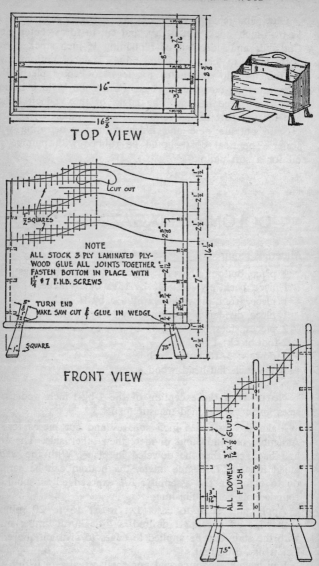

TOP VIEW

NOTE
ALL STOCK 3 PLY LAMINATED PLY-
WOOD GLUE ALL JOINTS TOGETHER
FASTEN BOTTOM IN PLACE WITH
1¼" #7 F.H.B. SCREWS

CUT OUT

2 SQUARES

5" TURN END
MAKE SAW CUT & GLUE IN WEDGE
1" SQUARE

75°

FRONT VIEW

ALL DOWELS 3/16" x 7/8" GLUED
IN FLUSH

75°

SIDE VIEW

KIDNEY-SHAPED COFFEE TABLE

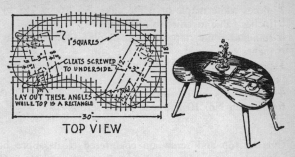

1" squares

CLEATS SCREWED TO UNDERSIDE

LAY OUT THESE ANGLES WHILE TOP IS A RECTANGLE

30"

TOP VIEW

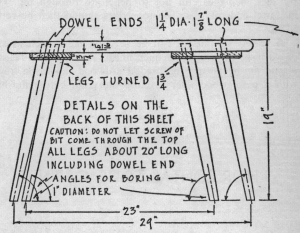

DOWEL ENDS 1¼" DIA · 1⅞" LONG

LEGS TURNED 1¾"

DETAILS ON THE BACK OF THIS SHEET

CAUTION: DO NOT LET SCREW OF BIT COME THROUGH THE TOP

ALL LEGS ABOUT 20" LONG INCLUDING DOWEL END

ANGLES FOR BORING 1" DIAMETER

23"

29"

19"

FRONT VIEW

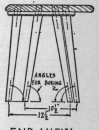

ANGLES FOR BORING 2"

12½" 10½"

END VIEW

Materials required:

3 pieces white maple or white oak: 1 5/16 by 7½ by 26 inches (glue together to form top)

4 standard round tapered legs, maple: 1¾ by 1¾ by 20 inches

1 piece maple or oak: ¾ by 7½ by 24 inches (use for cleats)

4 dowels: 1¼ by 1⅞ inches

6 1½-inch No. 10 flat-head wood screws

Cut out top and screw on chamfered cleats. Bore holes for legs, being careful not to penetrate through top. Glue in dowel ends of legs. The top edges should then be rounded off.

A variety of finishes can be used on table, such as stain or varnish, or a clear lacquer finish. A clear, mar-resistant plastic finish can also be used. Hardwood should be treated with a paste wood filler to close the grain before finishing.

HORIZONTAL SPICE CABINET

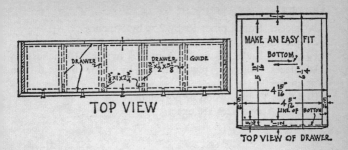

TOP VIEW

TOP VIEW OF DRAWER

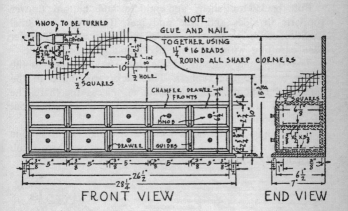

FRONT VIEW

END VIEW

Materials required:

Cabinet part

- 1 piece, back, pine: ⅜ by 15 by 26½ inches
- 2 pieces, sides, pine: ⅜ by 6½ by 10 inches
- 2 pieces, top shelf and middle-drawer support, pine: ⅜ by 6⅛ by 26½ inches
- 1 piece, bottom-drawer support, plywood: ¼ by 6⅛ by 26½ inches
- 1 piece, base, pine: ⅜ by 7 by 28¼ inches
- 8 strips, vertical partitions, pine: ⅜ by 1 by 2¾ inches
- 8 strips, drawer guides, pine: ⅜ by ½ by 5⅛ inches
- 1¼-inch No. 16 brads

Drawers

- 10 pieces, fronts, pine: ½ by 2¾ by 5 inches
- 20 pieces, sides, plywood: 5/16 by 2½ by 5 13/16 inches
- 10 pieces, backs, plywood: ¼ by 2½ by 4 15/16 inches
- 10 pieces, bottoms, plywood: ¼ by 4 15/16 by 6 1/16 inches
- 10 knobs ½-inch wood or porcelain
- NOTE: Above sizes are exact.
- ¾-inch brads

Butt back, top shelf, and middle and bottom drawer supports to sides and glue and nail. Then glue and nail partition strips, along with drawer guides, in place. Chamfer base carefully with cornering tool, and glue on cabinet.

The sides and bottoms of the drawers are joined to the fronts by 5/16-inch rabbets. The backs are butted to the sides and bottoms. Glue and nail all pieces together. The chamfered drawer fronts should extend 3/16 inch in front of the supports and partitions.

After filling all nail holes with wood dough, stain antique pine. Apply non-shellac sealer in a dry atmosphere. Rub down lightly with fine steel wool, and wax if desired.

TELEPHONE SHELF

Materials required:

- 1 piece, head: ⅝ by 5¾ by 12 inches
- 2 pieces, sides: ⅝ by 10⅝ by 14 inches
- 3 pieces, shelves and support: ⅝ by 10⅝ by 12½ inches
- 1 piece, sliding shelf: ⅝ by 10⅝ by 12½ inches
- NOTE: All the above in pine stock.
- 1 strip: ¾ by 1 by 12 inches
- 2 1¼-inch cleats
- 1 dowel: ¼ by ⅞ inch
- 1½-inch brads

Glue two shelves and support to the sides in ¼-inch dadoes. Butt the headpiece to the sides and top shelf using nails and glue. Cut the sliding shelf to fit easily and groove under side, stopping 2 inches from the front and 1 inch from the rear. Then mark and bore a ¼-inch hole and glue in a dowel from the under side of the shelf support. Attach a ¾-inch strip to the wall, using expansion screws. Cleats can be glued to the sides for added support to the sliding shelf.

Stain the piece the tone desired. Seal in stain with non-shellac sealer. Suggested is a durable plastic finish which can be dulled with rubbing felt and a paste of FFF grade powdered pumice. A telephone pad will further protect the surface.

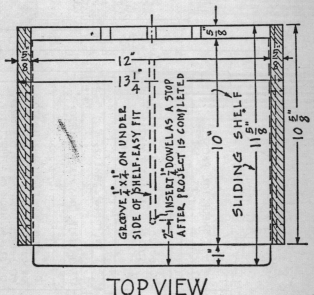

TOP VIEW

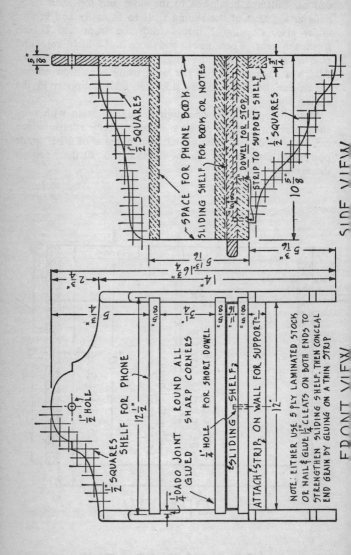

SIDE VIEW

$\frac{5}{8}$"

SPACE FOR PHONE BOOK
SLIDING SHELF FOR BOOK OR NOTES
1" 2 SQUARES
STRIP TO SUPPORT SHELF
$\frac{1}{2}$ SQUARES
$\frac{3}{4}$"
$10\frac{5}{8}$"
$\frac{1}{4}$" DOWEL FOR STOP
$5\frac{3}{16}$"
$5\frac{13}{16}$"
14"
$2\frac{3}{4}$"

FRONT VIEW

$\frac{1}{2}$ HOLE
$\frac{1}{7}$ SQUARES
SHELF FOR PHONE
$12\frac{1}{2}$"
5"
4"
$\frac{5}{16}$"
$\frac{3}{4}$"
$\frac{1}{4}$" DADO JOINT GLUED   ROUND ALL SHARP CORNERS
1" HOLE FOR SHORT DOWEL
SLIDING SHELF
$\frac{5}{16}$" $\frac{1}{16}$" 1" $\frac{5}{16}$"
ATTACH STRIP ON WALL FOR SUPPORT
12"
NOTE: EITHER USE 5 PLY LAMINATED STOCK OR NAIL & GLUE 1$\frac{1}{4}$" CLEATS ON BOTH ENDS TO STRENGTHEN SLIDING SHELF. THEN CONCEAL END GRAIN BY GLUING ON A THIN STRIP

GLOVE CASE

Materials required:

Case

1 piece, head, white pine: ⅜ by 3 5/16 inches

2 pieces, sides, white pine: ⅜ by 7 9/16 by 4⅝ inches

1 piece, bottom, white pine: ⅜ by 5 by 13 inches

1 piece, top, white pine: 5/16 by 4⅝ by 11½ inches

2 pieces, drawer supports, pine: 5/16 by 4⅜ by 11½ inches

1 piece, back, plywood: ¼ by 6⅛ by 12 inches

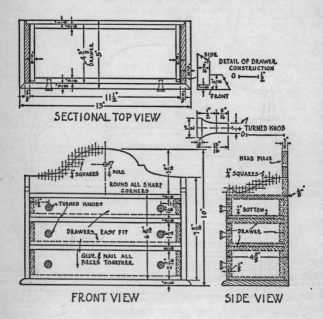

SECTIONAL TOP VIEW

FRONT VIEW

SIDE VIEW

Drawers

   1 piece, front, white pine: ⅜ by 1 7/16 by 11½ inches
   1 piece, front, white pine: ⅜ by 1¾ by 11½ inches
   1 piece, front, white pine: ⅜ by 2 3/16 by 11½ inches
   2 pieces, sides, plywood: 5/16 by 1 3/16 by 4¼ inches
   2 pieces, sides, plywood: 5/16 by 1 15/16 by 4¼ inches
   1 piece, back, plywood: 5/16 by 1 3/16 by 10⅞ inches
   1 piece, back, plywood: 5/16 by 1½ by 10⅞ inches
   1 piece, back, plywood: 5/16 by 1 15/16 by 10⅞ inches
   3 pieces, bottom, plywood: ¼ by 4¼ by 11½ inches
   4 ½-inch wood knobs
 30 nails

NOTE: All dimensions are exact.

Cut out patterns for the headpiece and sides. Assemble the case, using butt joints, small nails, and glue. The back is joined by a 3/16-inch rabbet at the top, a ¼-inch rabbet at the sides, and a butt joint at the bottom.

Both the sides and the ¼-inch bottoms are joined to the front drawer pieces by ¼-inch rabbets. The back pieces are butted to the sides and the bottoms. plywood 5/16 inch thick can be used for drawer construction, since the laminations will not be exposed. The knobs can be turned as in the detailed view or ready-to-finish ½-inch wood knobs can be purchased. The case bottom is rounded off with a cornering tool.

Stain light or dark pine. Apply a non-shellac sealer to the newly stained surface and the insides of the drawers. Rub off the glaze with fine steel wool, and wax.

HANDY MEMO ROLL

Materials required:

1 piece, back: 5/16 by 4⅛ by 10 1/16 inches
2 pieces, sides: 5/16 by 3¾ by 8 inches
1 piece, front: 5/16 by 4⅛ by 3¾ inches
1 piece, lid: 5/16 by 4⅛ by 5 5/16 inches
1 piece, top: 5/16 by 1⅜ by 4⅛ inches

Note: Use pine stock of plywood.

1 piece, base, pine: ⅜ by 4⅝ by 4⅝ inches
2 blocks: 9/16 by 2 by 3¾ inches
    Paper roll: 2¼ inches wide, 3⅜ inches in diameter
1 brass strip: ⅜ by 3 inches
2 butt hinges: ½ by ½ inch
¾-inch brads

Cut all pieces to size. Groove top for pencils and assemble, butting sides between all other pieces. Glue interior blocks in place. Cut lid for detailed fit. Make a 2½-inch slot, and notch for the hinges. Attach lid.

With all nail holes filled, stain antique pine. Apply a coat of non-shellac sealer, and rub off shine when dry. Paste wax can be applied. Lacquer brass cutting strip and attach.

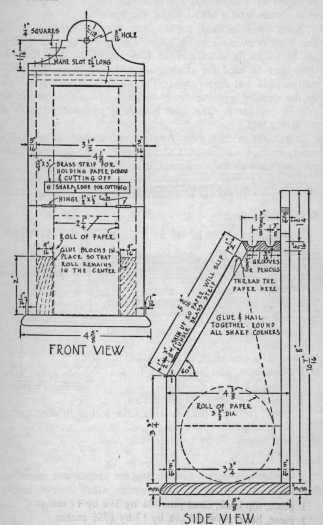

FRONT VIEW

SIDE VIEW

WALL BOOKSHELF

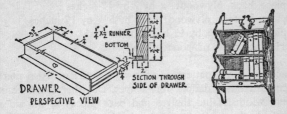

DRAWER
PERSPECTIVE VIEW

SECTION THROUGH
SIDE OF DRAWER

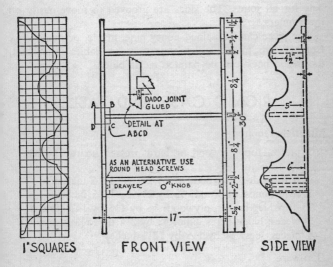

1" SQUARES   FRONT VIEW   SIDE VIEW

Materials required:

Shelf

    2 pieces, sides, clear pine: ½ by 8 by 31 inches
    3 pieces, shelves, clear pine: ½ by 6 by 18 inches
    1 piece, top back, clear pine: ¾ by 3¼ by 17 inches
    1 piece, back, plywood: ½ by 17 by 17½ inches

Drawer

  1 piece, front, clear pine: ½ by 2 by 17 inches
  2 pieces, sides, clear pine: ½ by 2 by 5¾ inches
  1 piece, back, plywood: ¼ by 2 by 17 inches
  1 piece, bottom, plywood: 3/16 by 5¾ by 17 inches
  1 piece lattice: ¼ by ½ by 12 inches
  1 1½-inch brass or wooden knob

Trace the scroll pattern for the sides, and cut. Also mark and cut 3/16-inch dadoes for shelves. Cut shelves for three different widths. Glue shelves and back pieces to the sides. The two back pieces are joined by butts and recessed between the sides. Glue two ¼-by-½-inch runners ¾ inch below the bottom shelf. Construct the drawer, using rabbets for all joints. The sides are grooved to move easily on the runners.

The piece can be stained honey pine, maple, or mahogany. Combination primer-sealer stains are available. If desired, the inside back can be painted a flat blue.

PICNIC CASE AND TABLE

Materials required:

  2 pieces, top, plywood or hard pressed board: ¼ by 17 by 17½ inches
  4 strips, sides, plywood: ½ by 2¼ by 17½ inches
  2 strips, ends, plywood: ½ by 2¼ by 15⅜ inches
  2 strips, leg braces, plywood: ½ by 1½ by 14⅞ inches
  2 pieces, hinge strips, pine: ¾ by 2¼ by 15⅜ inches
  4 pieces, legs: ¾ by 1½ by 12⅛ inches

Hardware

  3 1½-inch hinges (Stanley No. 838)
  4 4½-inch lid supports (Stanley No. 440)—2 right-hand and 2 left-hand
  8 stove bolts or rivets
 12 1¼-inch No. 14 round-head screws, with 8 washers
  2 suit-case catches
  1 handle (Stanley No. 4825, No. 2)
  4 domes of silence

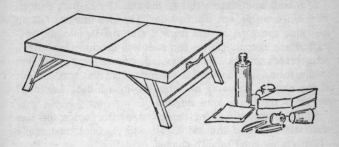

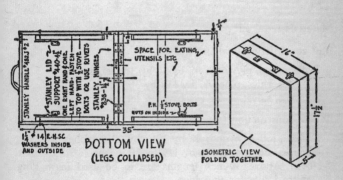

SPACE FOR EATING
UTENSILS ETC

P.H. ½ STOVE BOLTS
NUTS ON INSIDE 2—⅜

STANLEY LID
SUPPORT #40-4½
ONE RIGHT HAND & ONE
LEFT HAND · FASTEN
TO TOP WITH ½ STOVE
BOLTS OR USE RIVETS

STANLEY HINGES
#335—2½"

STANLEY HANDLE #482 ½" 2

1½" × 14 R.H.SC
WASHERS INSIDE
AND OUTSIDE

BOTTOM VIEW
(LEGS COLLAPSED)

35'

ISOMETRIC VIEW
FOLDED TOGETHER

16'

17½'

5'

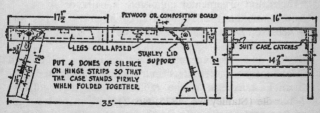

17½'

PLYWOOD OR COMPOSITION BOARD

LEGS COLLAPSED

STANLEY LID
SUPPORT

PUT 4 DOMES OF SILENCE
ON HINGE STRIPS SO THAT
THE CASE STANDS FIRMLY
WHEN FOLDED TOGETHER

75°

35'

FRONT VIEW

16'

SUIT CASE CATCHES

14⅞'

12'

SIDE VIEW

NOTE: Check screws for all hardware.

Join ends and hinge strips to the sides by ¼-inch dadoes. The hinge strips are notched for 1½-inch hinges. Clamp and glue the tops on the frames. Cut the legs to the prescribed angle, rounding the top ends and notching for braces. Affix braces to legs, using glue and screws. Next screw legs to the frame, and fasten lid supports. Join the two sections of the case by screwing on three 1½-inch hinges. Leave off the other hardware until finished.

Apply plastic finish in desired decorator color, or size with white shellac thinned 50-50 with alcohol, and apply two coats of good quality enamel.

FOLDING CARD TABLE

Materials required:

Butt construction (top and sides)

   1 piece, top, plywood: ⅜ by 30 by 30 inches
   2 pieces, sides, pine: ¾ by 1⅛ by 30 inches
   2 pieces, sides: ¾ by 1⅛ by 28½ inches

Rabbet construction (top and sides)

   1 piece, top, plywood: ⅜ by 29½ by 29½ inches
   4 pieces, sides, pine: ¾ by 1½ by 30 inches
   NOTE: Above 30-inch lengths are to be used in making mitre joints for the sides.
   4 tapered legs, hardwood: ¾ by 1¼ by 25¾ inches
   4 card-table braces (Stanley No. 448)
   1 piece leatherette: 34½ by 34½ inches
   Tacks and ornamental upholsterer's nails, or
   4 pieces molding: 5/16 by 1 7/16 by 30⅝ inches and ¾-inch No. 7 oval-head wood screws

Cut top and sides for either butt or rabbet joints, and side lengths for either butt or mitre joints. Clamp and glue together. Fasten legs to the table so that they collapse counterclockwise. A covering can be tacked on to top with either ornamental nails or molding protecting the sides. With the rabbet construction, the top can be left uncovered and molding applied to the sides. In either case, the top edges are rounded off.

Size exposed wood with one coat of shellac thinned 50-50 with alcohol. Sand lightly when dry. Apply two coats of good quality enamel.

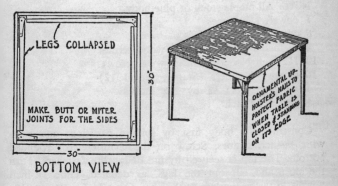

LEGS COLLAPSED

MAKE BUTT OR MITER JOINTS FOR THE SIDES

30"

30"

BOTTOM VIEW

ORNAMENTAL UP-HOLSTERS NAILS TO PROTECT FABRIC WHEN TABLE IS CLOSED & STANDING ON ITS EDGE

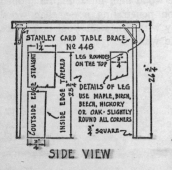

STANLEY CARD TABLE BRACE No 448

1¼

OUTSIDE EDGE STRAIGHT

INSIDE EDGE TAPERED

25¾

LEG ROUNDED ON THE TOP ¾

DETAILS OF LEG USE MAPLE, BIRCH, BEECH, HICKORY OR OAK · SLIGHTLY ROUND ALL CORNERS

¾ SQUARE

26¾

¾

¾

SIDE VIEW

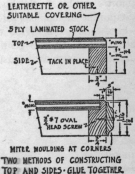

LEATHERETTE OR OTHER SUITABLE COVERING

5 PLY LAMINATED STOCK

TOP

SIDE

TACK IN PLACE

¾

5

#7 OVAL HEAD SCREW

MITER MOULDING AT CORNERS

TWO METHODS OF CONSTRUCTING TOP AND SIDES · GLUE TOGETHER

REVOLVING BOOK STAND AND TABLE

Materials required:

  2 pieces, top and bottom: ¾ by 16 by 16 inches
  1 piece, partition: ¾ by 9½ by 13¾ inches
  6 pieces, partitions and sides: ¾ by 9½ by 7¼ inches
  1 piece, post support: ¾ by 6 by 6 inches
  1 turning block: 3 by 3 by 12 inches
  4 legs: ¾ by 3 by 8 inches
  NOTE: All maple stock or pine body.
  1 dowel: 1¼ inches
  8 dowels: ⅜ by 2 inches
  4 ¼-inch No. 10 flat-head wood screws
  10 1½-inch No. 9 flat-head wood screws
  10 mortise fasteners (Stanley No. 1912)
  1 metal washer: ⅛ by 2½ inches
  1 pin: 3/32 inch

Construct the body first by joining partitions and sides with ⅜-inch dadoes. Screw on the chamfered or rounded bottom. The top is secured by use of mortise fasteners. Turn the post and cut out the legs, as detailed. Glue ⅜-inch dowels to fasten the legs to the post. Cut a ¼-by-2½-by-2½-inch square out of the post support to accommodate the washer and pin, and bore for the dowel. Glue a 1¼-inch dowel in the post top. Place support with washer over the dowel on post, and insert pin through dowel. Then screw the support assembly to the bookcase bottom.

Stain pine or maple. Paste wood filler must first be applied to hardwood parts. Wipe on penetrating non-shellac wood sealer. When dry, rub gently with fine steel wool or pumice and water. Finish with paste wax.

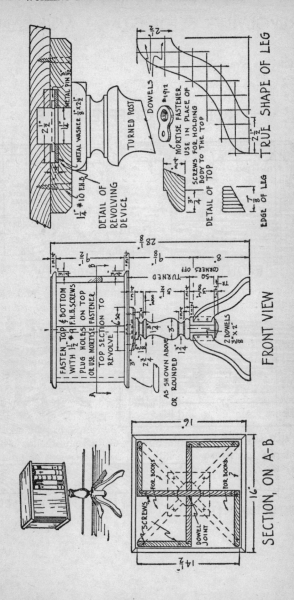

TRUE SHAPE OF LEG

DETAIL OF REVOLVING DEVICE

METAL PIN

METAL WASHER $\frac{5}{8}" \times 2\frac{1}{2}"$

TURNED POST

$1\frac{1}{4}"$ #10 F.H.B.

DOWELS

MORTISE FASTENER. Use in place of SCREWS FOR HOLDING BODY TO THE TOP

#172

DETAIL OF TOP

EDGE OF LEG

FRONT VIEW

FASTEN TOP & BOTTOM WITH $1\frac{1}{2}"$ #9 F.H.B. SCREWS

PLUG HOLES ON TOP OR USE MORTISE FASTENER

TOP SECTION TO REVOLVE

TURNED

CORNERS OFF

AS SHOWN ABOVE OR ROUNDED

2 DOWELS $\frac{3}{8}" \times 2"$

$28\frac{1}{8}"$

SECTION, ON A-B

16"

$14\frac{1}{2}"$

FOR BOOKS

SCREWS

DOWEL JOINT

DROP-LEAF COFFEE TABLE

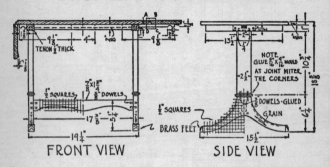

FRONT VIEW

SIDE VIEW

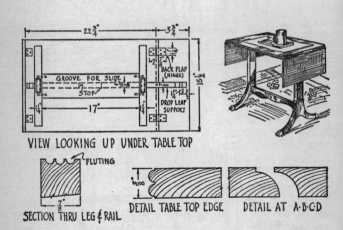

VIEW LOOKING UP UNDER TABLE TOP

SECTION THRU LEG & RAIL

DETAIL TABLE TOP EDGE

DETAIL AT A·B·C·D

Materials required:

1 piece, top, wide Honduras mahogany: ⅝ by 12 by 48 inches

2 pieces, straight legs: ⅞ by 2½ by 11¼ inches

4 pieces, splayed legs: ⅞ by 4 by 7¾ inches

1 piece, stretcher: ⅞ by 1¾ by 17⅜ inches

NOTE: All mahogany stock.

1 piece, slide support: ⅞ by 4 by 17 inches

2 pieces, aprons: 1 by 1¼ by 13½ inches

2 pieces, drop-leaf supports: ½ by ⅞ by 9⅛ inches

Molding: 5/16 by 9/16 by 18 inches

1 ⅜-inch dowel rod

4 back-flap hinges: 1¼ by 2⅞ inches

4 brass ferrules

Cut top board into three 16-inch pieces; glue and clamp them together. Cut off drop leaves, shaping joints as described below. The slide support is dadoed 5/16 inch to accommodate ⅞-inch slides. Glue and dowel aprons and slide support to underside of top. Straight leg pieces are then joined to the aprons by a mortise and tenon. Cut pieces for the splayed legs and firmly dowel together the dowel rail or stretcher to two legs at either end. The splayed section is then joined to the straight pieces by dowels and molding glued on the joints. Attach the leaves and insert the leaf supports.

To enhance the beauty of mahogany, an oil finish is suggested. Prepare the oil by mixing 2 parts boiled linseed oil and 1 part turpentine. Apply to table-top surface and underside of leaves (to prevent warping), rubbing 5 to 20 minutes. Wipe off excess and polish 10 to 20 minutes. Let it stand two days at least, then repeat. Five to twelve coats are needed, and one week should elapse between coats, except between the first and second.

Apply oil and shellac finish to legs and underparts. (Cold oil is used on grooved surfaces.) Rub on one coat of light oil mixture (1 part oil to 2 parts turpentine). Rub until excess oil is removed and let stand two days. Apply 2 or 3 coats of heavy oil mixture (2 parts oil to 1 part turpentine). Let it stand a week between coats, and a week before applying oil and shellac. Apply oil and shellac (2 parts oil to 1 part white shellac). Apply as oil finish and rub to high luster.

THE DROP-LEAF TABLE JOINT

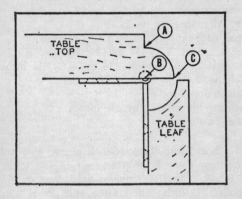

Nearly every woodworker has occasion to make at least one drop-leaf table in his hobby shop. Cutting the joint for the drop-leaf table is a long and painstaking process if hand tools alone must be relied upon. With a portable router, however, the cuts in both the table leaf and the table top can be made in a few minutes.

The convex cut is usually made in the table top, and the concave or cove cut is made in the table leaf. The main reason for this is to provide a freer working joint with little strain on the hinges. It is the more natural way to make the joint, for the leaf drops down, rather than out of the joint when lowered to the side position.

For best results use Stanley table hinges that are designed especially for this type of joint. For the best-appearing joint select the swaged type of hinge, which has the countersinking of the screw holes on the outside of each leaf. The short hinge leaf is to be attached to the bottom side of the table top. The long hinge leaf is to be screwed to the table leaf. It is necessary to cut recesses for the barrels of the hinges. The hinges themselves should not be mortised into the table top. To do so would leave unsightly gaps which would show through the joint.

Trial cuts should always be taken, using two pieces of scrap stock the same thickness as the table leaf and top. After the trial cuts are made, screw one of the hinges to these scrap pieces so that you will be absolutely certain you have made the proper adjustments.

Let us assume, as an example, that we are going to use for the table leaf and top wood that is ¾ inch thick. The Stanley No. 516 rounding-over bit and the Stanley No. 716 cove bit will be required. Both of these bits cut a ½-inch radius. The No. 516 bit makes the cut in the top, the No. 716 bit the cut in the leaf. We will proceed as follows:

1. The first step is to locate the joint on the stock that will be the table top. Chuck the rounding-over bit in the router and hold the router on top of the work with the bit lined up against the end of the table top.

Lower the bit by means of the depth adjustment in the router base so that the distance from A to B (see illustration) is the same as the distance from B to C. This distance is ½ inch when the 516 or 716 bit combination is used. The point C is to be the center line of the hinge pins, so this point should be extended in the form of a line drawn on the bottom side of the work in order to locate the hinges.

2. The next step is to make the cut in the table top. For best results place a piece of scrap stock underneath the table top with the smooth edge in line with the edge of the top. This will provide ample beating surface for the pilot of the bit.

3. The grooves for the hinge barrels can now be mortised. Turn the table top upside down. Replace the rounding-over bit with a core box bit a little larger than the diameter of the hinge barrel—in this case, either a Stanley No. 408 or No. 410 core box bit. Adjust the router base so that the bit extends a little more than the height of the barrel above the short hinge leaf. Mark out with a pencil the location of the barrels along the center line. Attach the straight and circular gauge, using the straight edge against the table top. Drop the router slowly to the work, the straight and circular gauge on the right side. Rout the grooves, feeding the machine away from the body.

4. You are now ready to make the concave cut in the table leaf. Replace the rounding-over bit with a No. 716

cove bit. Place one side of the router on the forward end of the table top so that the bit lines up with the cut. Adjust the base so that the contour of the cove bit matches the contour of the cut you have made in the top. After locking the adjustment, place the table top aside and rout the cut in the table leaf.

5. The hinges can now be assembled to the leaf and top. It is well to allow a little clearance between the two pieces to prevent rubbing the finish off when the leaf is lowered.

BENCH

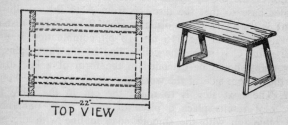

TOP VIEW

22"

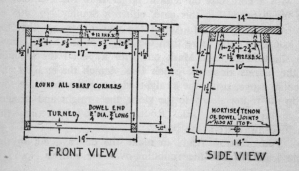

FRONT VIEW

SIDE VIEW

ROUND ALL SHARP CORNERS

TURNED

DOWEL END
¾" DIA. ¾" LONG

MORTISE & TENON
OR DOWEL JOINTS
ALSO AT TOP.

DETAILS & LIST OF LUMBER

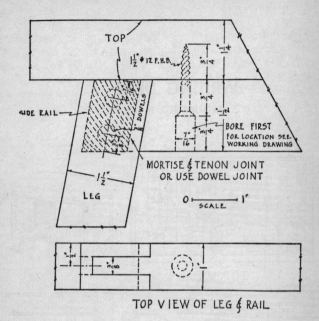

TOP

$1\frac{1}{2}$" # 12 F.H.B.

SIDE RAIL

DOWELS

LEG

$1\frac{1}{2}$"

BORE FIRST
FOR LOCATION SEE
WORKING DRAWING

MORTISE & TENON JOINT
OR USE DOWEL JOINT

0 ⊢————— 1"
SCALE

TOP VIEW OF LEG & RAIL

Materials required:

1 piece, top (glued up): 1¼ by 14 by 22 inches
4 pieces, legs: 1 by 1½ by 17¼ inches
2 pieces, leg rails: 1 by 1½ by 14 inches
2 pieces, leg rails: 1 by 1½ by 10 inches
2 pieces, side rails: 1 by 1¾ by 17 inches
1 dowel for stretcher: 1 by 18½ inches

NOTE: Sizes are finished measurements.

Leg-rail sizes are for mortised joints. Change lengths if
dowel joints are preferred.

WRITING DESK

PROJECT NO. M-13

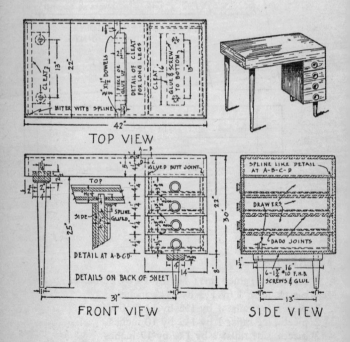

TOP VIEW

FRONT VIEW

SIDE VIEW

(continued on next page)

DETAILS & LIST OF LUMBER

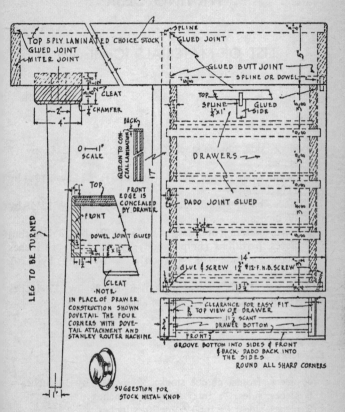

Materials required:

Top section

1 piece, top, choice stock (plywood): ¾ by 21½ by 41½ inches
2 pieces, front and back, choice stock: ¾ by 5 by 43 inches
2 pieces, sides, choice stock: ¾ by 5 by 23 inches
1 piece, cleat: 2½ by 4 by 20½ inches
1 piece, cleat: 1⅛ by 4 by 16 inches
2 pieces, legs: 2 by 2 by 26⅛ inches
2 pieces, legs: 1½ by 1½ by 8¾ inches

(continued on next page)

WRITING DESK

LIST OF MATERIALS (Continued)

Cabinet part for drawer

1 piece, side, choice stock (plywood): ¾ by 21⅝ by 17 inches
1 piece, side, choice stock (plywood): ¾ by 21⅝ by 21¼ inches
1 piece, back, choice stock (plywood): ¾ by 12½ by 17 inches
1 piece, bottom (fir plywood): ¾ by 21 by 13½ inches
3 pieces, partitions (fir plywood): ⅝ by 21 by 13 inches
1 piece, partition (fir plywood): ⅝ by 20½ by 12½ inches
2 pieces, strips, choice stock: ⅛ by ¾ by 17 inches (to be glued to back edges of sides)

Drawers

4 pieces, fronts, choice stock: ¾ by 4¼ by 14 inches
6 pieces, sides: ½ by 3⅝ by 20½ inches
2 pieces, sides: ½ by 3½ by 20½ inches
3 pieces, backs: ½ by 3⅝ by 11¾ inches
1 piece, back: ½ by 3½ by 11¾ inches
4 pieces, bottoms (plywood): ¼ by 20 by 11¾ inches

NOTE: Sizes are finished measurements, except front, back, and sides of top, where allowance is made for mitred corners.

If dovetail construction of drawers is used, add ½ inch in length of backs.

DRESSING TABLE

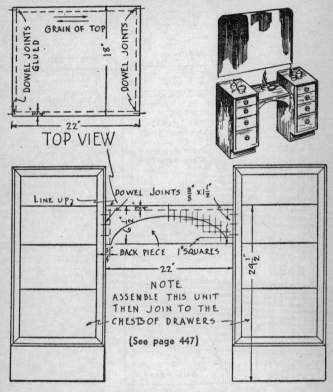

TOP VIEW

FRONT VIEW

Materials required:

1 piece, top, choice stock (plywood): ¾ by 18 by 22 inches

1 piece, front, choice stock: ¾ by 6⅜ by 22 inches

1 piece, back, choice stock (plywood): ¾ by 6⅜ by 20½ inches

2 pieces, side rails: ¾ by 6⅜ by 17¼ inches

NOTE: Sizes are finished measurements.

DRESSING TABLE (Continued)

DETAILS & LIST OF LUMBER

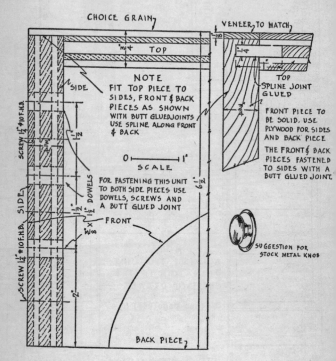

CHOICE GRAIN

VENEER, TO MATCH

TOP

SIDE

NOTE
FIT TOP PIECE TO
SIDES, FRONT & BACK
PIECES AS SHOWN
WITH BUTT GLUED JOINTS
USE SPLINE ALONG FRONT
& BACK

TOP
SPLINE JOINT
GLUED

FRONT PIECE TO
BE SOLID. USE
PLYWOOD FOR SIDES
AND BACK PIECE

THE FRONT & BACK
PIECES FASTENED
TO SIDES WITH A
BUTT GLUED JOINT

SCALE

FOR FASTENING THIS UNIT
TO BOTH SIDE PIECES USE
DOWELS, SCREWS AND
A BUTT GLUED JOINT

FRONT

SUGGESTION FOR
STOCK METAL KNOB

BACK PIECE

DRAWERS

1 piece front ¾" x 5" x 13"
1 piece front ¾" x 6½" x 13"
1 piece front ¾" x 7½" x 13"
1 piece front ¾" x 8" x 13"
2 pieces sides ½" x 5" x 20"
2 pieces sides ½" x 5¾" x 20"
2 pieces sides ½" x 6¾" x 20"
2 pieces sides ½" x 7¼" x 20"
1 piece back ½" x 4⅜" x 12¼"
1 piece back ½" x 5⅛" x 12¼"
1 piece back ½" x 6⅛" x 12¼"
1 piece back ½" x 6⅝" x 12¼"
4 pieces bottom ¼" x 19 11/16" x 12¼"

NOTE: Sizes given are finished measurements except face moldings where allowance is made for mitred corners. If dovetail construction of drawers is used, add ⅝″ in width and ½″ in length of backs.

DETAIL OF DRAWERS

LIST OF LUMBER

Cabinet Part

2 pieces sides choice stock (plywood) ¾″ x 20¾″ x 35¾″
1 piece top choice stock (plywood) ¾″ x 20¾″ x 16″
2 piece side backing (fir plywood) ¾″ x 20½″ x 35¼″
2 pieces top and bottom (fir plywood) ¾″ x 20½″ x 14½″
3 pieces partitions (fir plywood) ¾″ x 19¾″ x 13½″
1 piece toe space choice stock (plywood) ¾″ x 6″ x 16″
1 piece toe space (fir plywood) ¾″ x 3½″ x 14½″
1 piece back (fir plywood) ¼″ x 14½″ x 28½″
2 pieces face molding 1¼″ x 1½″ x 17″
2 pieces face molding 1¼″ x 1½″ x 31″
Strips of veneer as needed

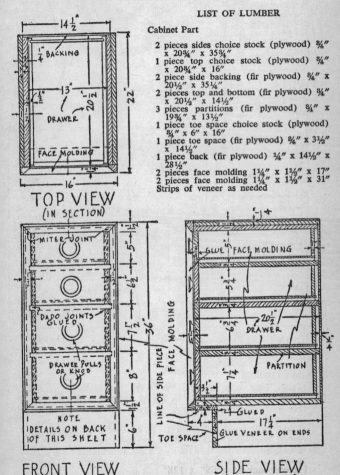

TOP VIEW (IN SECTION)

FRONT VIEW

SIDE VIEW (IN SECTION)

LIVING ROOM CHAIR

PROJECT NO. M-1

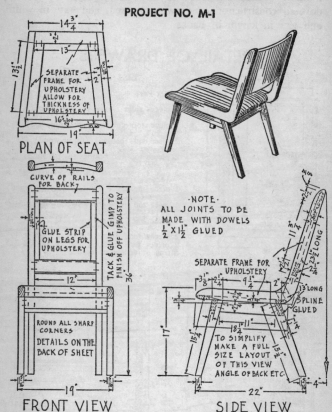

PLAN OF SEAT

FRONT VIEW

SIDE VIEW

· NOTE ·
ALL JOINTS TO BE
MADE WITH DOWELS
½" X 1½" GLUED

Materials required:

2 pieces, seat rails: 1 5/16 by 2¼ by 18½ inches
2 pieces, backs: 1 5/16 by 2¼ by 24 inches
2 triangular pieces: 1 5/16 by 3 by 4 inches (to be glued to back and seat rail)
2 pieces, rails for back section: 1⅛ by 2½ by 12 inches
2 pieces, back legs: 1 5/16 by 2 by 16 inches
2 pieces, front legs: 1 5/16 by 2¼ by 15½ inches
2 pieces, side rails: 1 5/16 by 2¼ by 11 inches
1 piece, front rail: 1 by 2½ by 16½ inches
1 piece, back rail: 1 by 2½ by 13 inches

DETAILS & LIST OF LUMBER

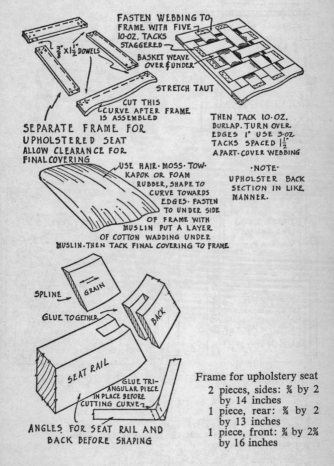

FASTEN WEBBING TO FRAME WITH FIVE 10-OZ. TACKS STAGGERED

BASKET WEAVE OVER & UNDER

STRETCH TAUT

¾" X 1½" DOWELS

CUT THIS CURVE AFTER FRAME IS ASSEMBLED

SEPARATE FRAME FOR UPHOLSTERED SEAT ALLOW CLEARANCE FOR FINAL COVERING

THEN TACK 10-OZ. BURLAP. TURN OVER EDGES 1" USE 3-OZ. TACKS SPACED 1½ A PART. COVER WEBBING

·NOTE· UPHOLSTER BACK SECTION IN LIKE MANNER.

USE HAIR·MOSS·TOW· KAPOK OR FOAM RUBBER, SHAPE TO CURVE TOWARDS EDGES· FASTEN TO UNDER SIDE OF FRAME WITH MUSLIN PUT A LAYER OF COTTON WADDING UNDER MUSLIN. THEN TACK FINAL COVERING TO FRAME

SPLINE   GRAIN

BACK

GLUE TOGETHER

SEAT RAIL

GLUE TRI-ANGULAR PIECE IN PLACE BEFORE CUTTING CURVE

ANGLES FOR SEAT RAIL AND BACK BEFORE SHAPING

Frame for upholstery seat
  2 pieces, sides: ¾ by 2 by 14 inches
  1 piece, rear: ¾ by 2 by 13 inches
  1 piece, front: ¾ by 2¾ by 16 inches

Back section
  2 pieces: 1 by 1 by 11¾ inches

NOTE: Sizes are finished measurements, except pieces to be shaped or cut at angles, where extra stock is allowed.

ARM CHAIR

PROJECT NO. M-2

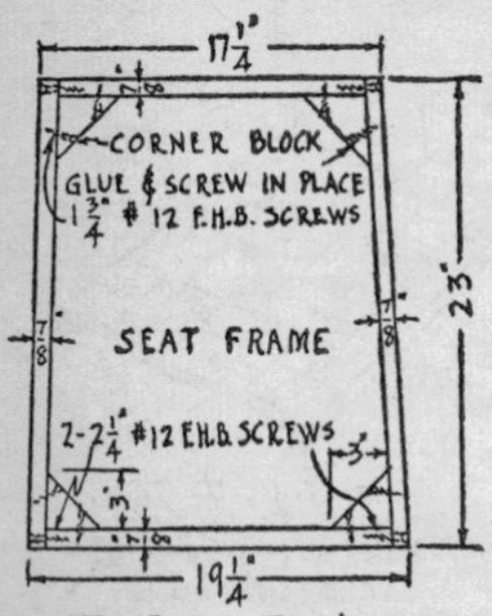
17 1/4"
CORNER BLOCK
GLUE & SCREW IN PLACE
1 3/4" #12 F.H.B. SCREWS
SEAT FRAME
23"
7/8
2-2 1/4" #12 F.H.B. SCREWS
3"
19 1/4"

TOP VIEW

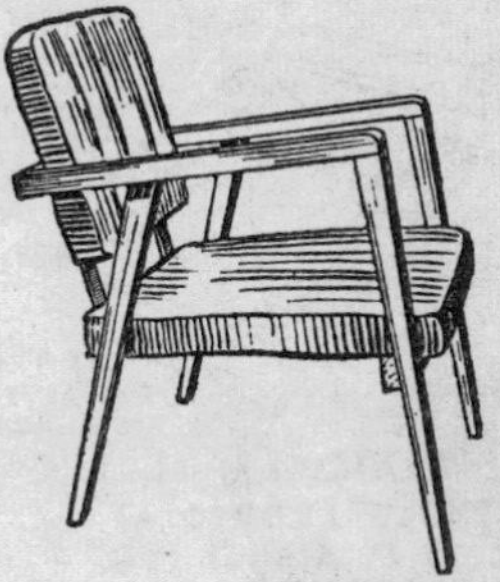

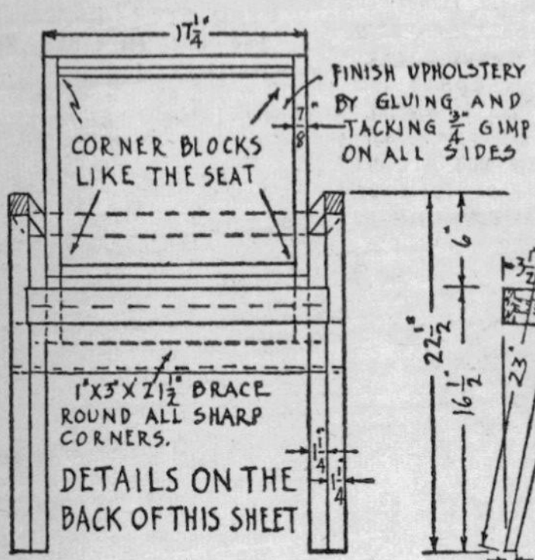
17 1/4"
FINISH UPHOLSTERY
BY GLUING AND
TACKING 3/4" GIMP
ON ALL SIDES
7/8
CORNER BLOCKS
LIKE THE SEAT
1"X3"X21 1/2" BRACE
ROUND ALL SHARP
CORNERS.
DETAILS ON THE
BACK OF THIS SHEET
1 1/4
1 1/4

FRONT VIEW

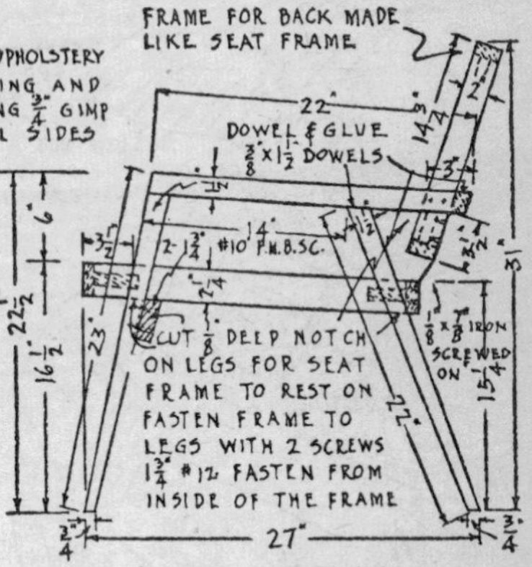
FRAME FOR BACK MADE
LIKE SEAT FRAME
22"
14 3/4"
DOWEL & GLUE
3/8"x1 1/2" DOWELS
14"
2-1 3/4" #10 F.H.B.SC.
22 1/2"
16 1/2"
6"
23"
CUT 1/8" DEEP NOTCH
ON LEGS FOR SEAT
FRAME TO REST ON
FASTEN FRAME TO
LEGS WITH 2 SCREWS
1 3/4" #12 FASTEN FROM
INSIDE OF THE FRAME
1/8"x7/8" IRON
SCREWED
ON
15 1/4"
31"
22"
27"
3/4
3/4

SIDE VIEW

Materials required:
- 2 pieces, back legs: 1¼ by 1½ by 22 inches
- 2 pieces, front legs: 1¼ by 1½ by 22 inches
- 2 pieces, arms: 1¼ by 1½ by 22½ inches
- 1 piece, brace: 1 by 3 by 21½ inches
- 1 piece, back brace for arms: 1¼ by 1½ by 17¼ inches

Frame for seat upholstery
- 2 pieces, sides: ⅞ by 2¼ by 23½ inches
- 1 piece, front: ⅞ by 2¼ by 17¾ inches
- 1 piece, back: ⅞ by 2¼ by 15¾ inches

Frame for back upholstery
- 2 pieces: ⅞ by 2 by 14¾ inches
- 2 pieces: ⅞ by 2 by 15½ inches
- 8 corner blocks: ⅞ by 3 by 3 inches
- 2 pieces scrap iron: ⅛ by ⅞ by 8 inches

NOTE: Sizes are finished measurements, except pieces that are to be cut at angles, where extra stock is allowed.

DETAILS & LUMBER LIST

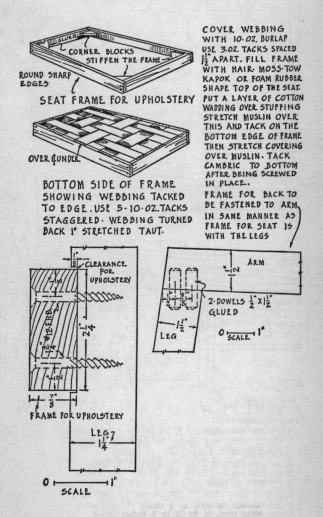

GLUED
CORNER BLOCKS
STIFFEN THE FRAME

ROUND SHARP
EDGES

SEAT FRAME FOR UPHOLSTERY

OVER & UNDER

BOTTOM SIDE OF FRAME
SHOWING WEBBING TACKED
TO EDGE. USE 5·10·OZ. TACKS
STAGGERED · WEBBING TURNED
BACK 1" STRETCHED TAUT.

COVER WEBBING
WITH 10·OZ. BURLAP
USE 3·OZ. TACKS SPACED
1½ APART. FILL FRAME
WITH HAIR·MOSS·TOW
KAPOK OR FOAM RUBBER
SHAPE TOP OF THE SEAT.
PUT A LAYER OF COTTON
WADDING OVER STUFFING
STRETCH MUSLIN OVER
THIS AND TACK ON THE
BOTTOM EDGE OF FRAME
THEN STRETCH COVERING
OVER MUSLIN· TACK
CAMBRIC TO BOTTOM
AFTER BEING SCREWED
IN PLACE.

FRAME FOR BACK TO
BE FASTENED TO ARM
IN SAME MANNER AS
FRAME FOR SEAT IS
WITH THE LEGS

1"/8

CLEARANCE
FOR
UPHOLSTERY

1"/4

#12 FTHD.

2¼"

1"/4

7"/8

FRAME FOR UPHOLSTERY

LEG
1¼"

0   SCALE   1"

ARM

½"N

2·DOWELS ½" X 1½"
GLUED

5"/8

1½"

LEG

0   SCALE   1"

SIDE CHAIR

PROJECT NO. M-3

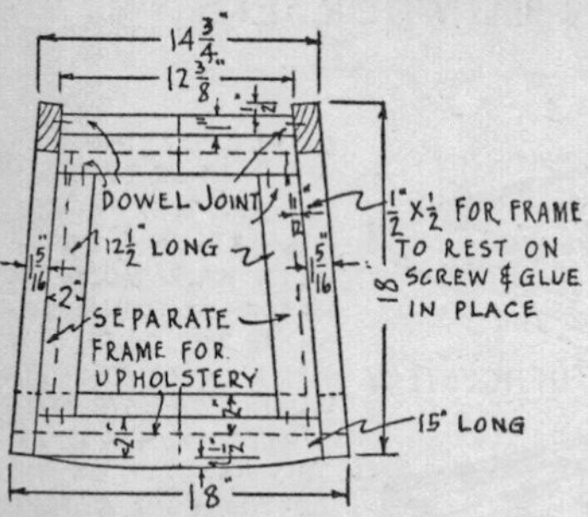
DOWEL JOINT
12½" LONG
½" X ½" FOR FRAME TO REST ON SCREW & GLUE IN PLACE
SEPARATE FRAME FOR UPHOLSTERY
15" LONG
18"

PLAN OF SEAT

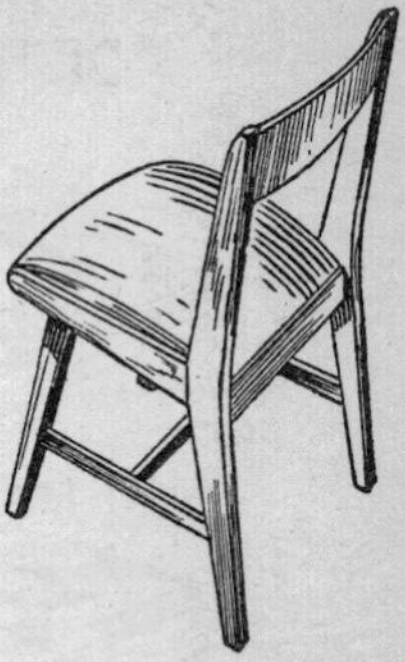

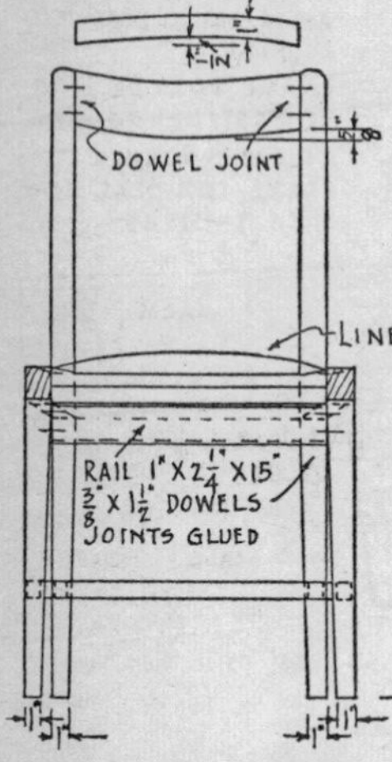
DOWEL JOINT
RAIL 1" X 2¼" X 15"
⅜" X 1½" DOWELS
JOINTS GLUED

DETAILS ON BACK OF THIS SHEET

ROUND ALL SHARP CORNERS

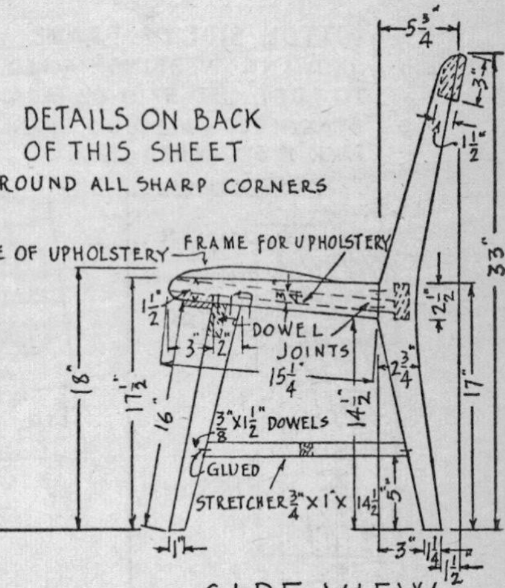
LINE OF UPHOLSTERY
FRAME FOR UPHOLSTERY
DOWEL JOINTS
⅜" X 1½" DOWELS
GLUED
STRETCHER ¾" X 1" X 14½"
33"
18"
17½"
16"
17"

FRONT VIEW

SIDE VIEW

Materials required:

- 2 Pieces, side rails: 1 5/16 by 2½ by 15¼ inches
- 1 piece, back rail: 1 by 2½ by 12½ inches
- 1 piece, brace: 1 by 2 by 18 inches
- 2 pieces, legs: 1 5/16 by 2 by 16½ inches
- 2 pieces, legs: 1 5/16 by 5¾ by 33 inches
- 1 piece, top back rail: 1½ by 3⅜ by 12½ inches
- 1 piece, front rail: 1 by 2¼ by 15 inches
- 2 pieces, stretchers: ¾ by 1 by 15 inches
- 1 piece, stretcher: ¾ by 1 by 16 inches
- 2 pieces, upholstery-frame supports: ½ by ½ by 13 inches

DETAILS & LIST OF LUMBER

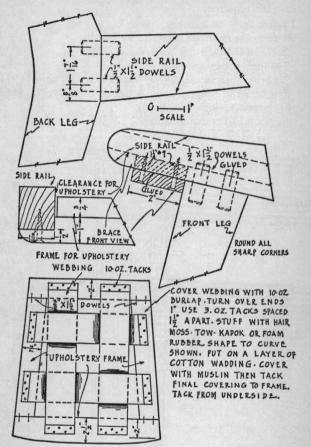

SIDE RAIL DOWELS

$1\frac{1}{2}$ x $1\frac{1}{2}$ DOWELS

BACK LEG

0 |——| 1"
SCALE

SIDE RAIL

SIDE RAIL $1\frac{1}{2}$ x $1\frac{1}{2}$ DOWELS GLUED
$1\frac{1}{2}$ • ?

CLEARANCE FOR UPHOLSTERY

GLUED 2"

BRACE FRONT VIEW

FRONT LEG

FRAME FOR UPHOLSTERY   ROUND ALL SHARP CORNERS

WEBBING   10·OZ. TACKS

$\frac{3}{8}$" x $1\frac{1}{2}$ DOWELS

UPHOLSTERY FRAME

COVER WEBBING WITH 10·OZ. BURLAP·TURN OVER ENDS 1" USE 3. OZ. TACKS SPACED $1\frac{1}{2}$ APART·STUFF WITH HAIR MOSS·TOW·KAPOK OR FOAM RUBBER·SHAPE TO CURVE SHOWN. PUT ON A LAYER OF COTTON WADDING·COVER WITH MUSLIN THEN TACK FINAL COVERING TO FRAME. TACK FROM UNDERSIDE.

Upholstery frame

   2 pieces, sides: ¾ by 2 by 13 inches
   1 piece, front: ¾ by 2½ by 15½ inches
   1 piece, back: ¾ by 2 by 13 inches

NOTE: Sizes are finished measurements, except pieces that are to be cut at angles, where extra stock is allowed.

STURDY VINE SUPPORT

Materials required:

  14 feet fir: 2 by 2 inches
  50 feet pine or lattice stock: ½ by 1 inch
   2 No. 14 3-inch flat-head wood screws
   2 3-inch hooks and eyes
   2 corner braces: 3 by 3 inches (Stanley No. 997PS)
   2 light strap hinges: 3 by 3 inches (Stanley No. Sc900)
  ¼ pound ½-inch wire brads
  ½ pound 3d common nails

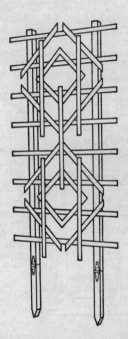

For those vines and ramblers growing next to the house, a strong, properly designed support or trellis greatly enhances the appearance of both vine and home. The support shown is designed to fit in well with most types of home architecture, but may be varied in detail and dimensions if desired. The entire assembly is hinged to tilt forward for convenience in painting and maintaining the house without disturbing the vine. In a few hours, you can build and install the support, using readily available, standard materials.

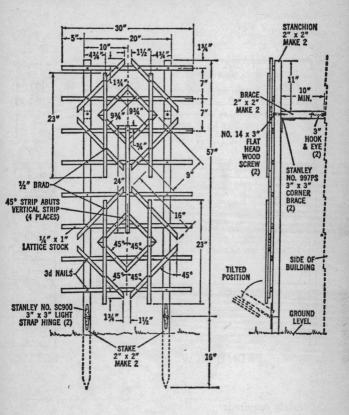

Assemble the support completely, except for the two stakes and hooks and eyes. Attach the upper leaves of the two Stanley No. Sc900 hinges to the stanchions. Cut and shape the stakes, coat them with Cuprinol or other wood preservative, and set in the ground to align with stanchions.

Secure the lower hinge leaves to the stakes and swing the support into position. Assemble the two hooks and eyes so that the brace ends firmly abut the side of the house as shown. Use a good-quality exterior paint on the entire support above the stakes.

HOLLYWOOD HEADBOARD

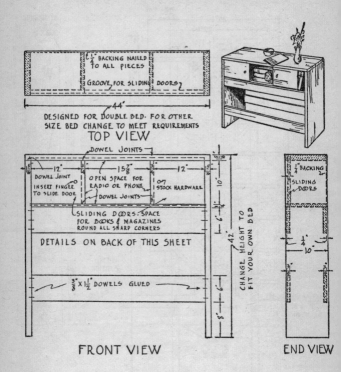

DESIGNED FOR DOUBLE BED. FOR OTHER
SIZE BED CHANGE TO MEET REQUIREMENTS
TOP VIEW

FRONT VIEW   END VIEW

Materials required:

   2 pieces, sides: 1 5/16 by 10 by 40 11/16 inches
   1 piece, top: 1 5/16 by 10 by 44 inches
   1 piece, bottom of cabinet section: ¾ by 9¾ by 41¾ inches
   4 pieces, rails: ¾ by 6 by 41 ⅜ inches
   1 piece, plywood backing: ¼ by 11 13/16 by 43½ inches
   2 pieces, doors: ¾ by 10½ by 12¾ inches
   2 pieces, partitions: ¾ by 8½ by 10 inches

NOTE: Sizes are finished measurements.

DETAILS & LIST OF LUMBER

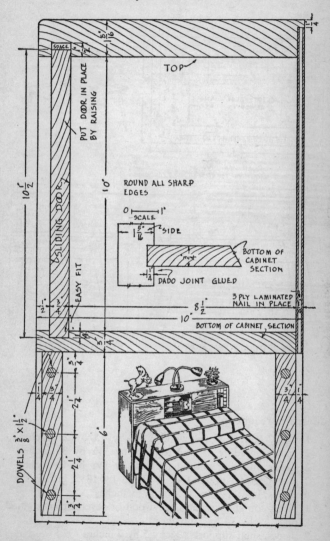

TOP

PUT DOOR IN PLACE BY RAISING

SPACE $\frac{1}{2}$"

$10\frac{1}{2}$"

SLIDING DOOR

10"

ROUND ALL SHARP EDGES

0 — 1"
SCALE

$1\frac{5}{16}$" SIDE

BOTTOM OF CABINET SECTION

$1\frac{1}{4}$" DADO JOINT GLUED

EASY FIT

3 PLY LAMINATED NAIL IN PLACE

$\frac{1}{2}$" $\frac{3}{4}$"

$8\frac{1}{2}$"

10"

$\frac{3}{4}$"

BOTTOM OF CABINET SECTION

$\frac{3}{4}$"

$\frac{3}{4}$" $\frac{1}{4}$"

$\frac{1}{4}$" $\frac{3}{4}$"

$2\frac{1}{4}$"

$2\frac{1}{4}$"

$2\frac{1}{4}$"

$\frac{3}{4}$"

6"

DOWELS $\frac{3}{8}$" x $1\frac{1}{2}$"

$\frac{3}{4}$" $\frac{1}{4}$"

CORNER TABLE

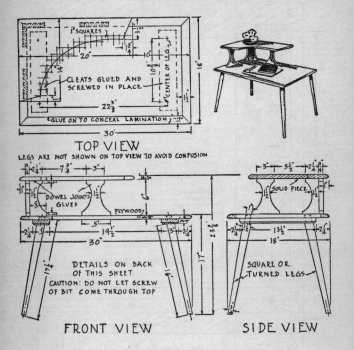

TOP VIEW

LEGS ARE NOT SHOWN ON TOP VIEW TO AVOID CONFUSION

FRONT VIEW

SIDE VIEW

Materials required:

1 piece, table top (plywood): ¾ by 15 by 27 inches
2 pieces, molding around top: ¾ by 1½ by 31 inches
2 pieces, molding around top: ¾ by 1½ by 19 inches
2 pieces, cleats under top: ¾ by 3 by 13½ inches
4 pieces, legs: 1½ by 1½ by 17½ inches
1 piece, top shelf section (plywood or several pieces glued up): ⅝ by 14 by 20 inches
2 pieces, shelf supports: ¾ by 5 by 6 inches

DETAILS & LIST OF LUMBER

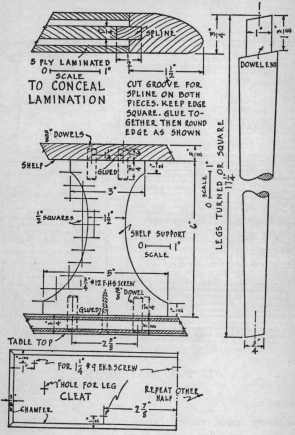

SPLINE

5 PLY LAMINATED
0 |___SCALE___| 1"

TO CONCEAL
LAMINATION

CUT GROOVE FOR
SPLINE ON BOTH
PIECES. KEEP EDGE
SQUARE. GLUE TO-
GETHER THEN ROUND
EDGE AS SHOWN

DOWEL END

$\frac{3}{8}$" DOWELS

SHELF

GLUED

$\frac{1}{2}$" SQUARES

SHELF SUPPORT
0 |___SCALE___| 1"

LEGS TURNED OR SQUARE $17\frac{1}{4}$"

0 |___SCALE___| 1"

$\frac{3}{4}$ #12 F.H.B SCREW

$\frac{3}{8}$" DOWEL

GLUED

TABLE TOP $2\frac{5}{8}$"

$\frac{3}{4}$

FOR $1\frac{1}{4}$" #9 F.H.D. SCREW

HOLE FOR LEG
CLEAT

REPEAT OTHER
HALF

CHAMFER $2\frac{5}{8}$"

1 piece, shelf support: ¾ by 3 by 6 inches
1 piece, shelf support: ¾ by 3¾ by 6 inches

NOTE: Sizes are finished measurements except molding for
top, where allowance is made for mitred corners, and legs,
with ends that are cut at angles.

STUDENT'S HOME DESK

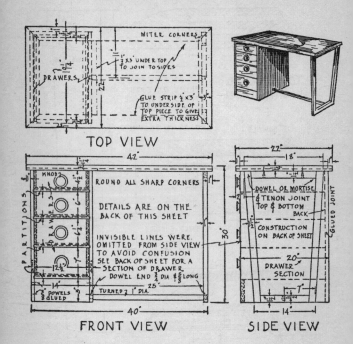

LIST OF MATERIALS

Cabinet part

2 pieces, sides, choice (plywood): ¾ by 20 by 28¾ inches, including ⅛-inch glued strips

1 piece, back, choice (plywood): ¾ by 12½ by 28¾ inches

4 pieces, partitions (fir plywood): ⅝ by 18½ by 13 inches

1 piece, front bottom, choice (plywood): ¾ by 5 by 12½ inches

4 pieces, choice strips: 28¾ by ¾ by ⅛ inches (to be glued on front and back edges of sides)

DETAILS & LIST OF LUMBER

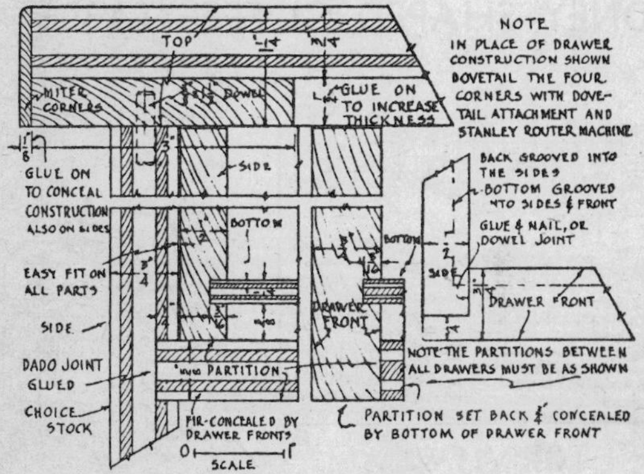
TOP
MITER CORNERS
DOWEL
GLUE ON TO INCREASE THICKNESS
NOTE
IN PLACE OF DRAWER CONSTRUCTION SHOWN DOVETAIL THE FOUR CORNERS WITH DOVE-TAIL ATTACHMENT AND STANLEY ROUTER MACHINE
GLUE ON TO CONCEAL CONSTRUCTION ALSO ON SIDES
SIDE
BOTTOM
BACK GROOVED INTO THE SIDES
BOTTOM GROOVED INTO SIDES & FRONT
GLUE & NAIL, OR DOWEL JOINT
EASY FIT ON ALL PARTS
SIDE
DRAWER FRONT
DRAWER FRONT
DADO JOINT GLUED
PARTITION
NOTE THE PARTITIONS BETWEEN ALL DRAWERS MUST BE AS SHOWN
CHOICE STOCK
FIR-CONCEALED BY DRAWER FRONTS
PARTITION SET BACK ⅛" CONCEALED BY BOTTOM OF DRAWER FRONT
SCALE

CONSTRUCTION OF TOP CABINET PART & DRAWERS

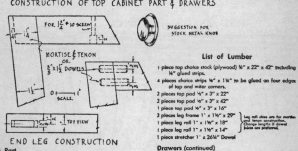

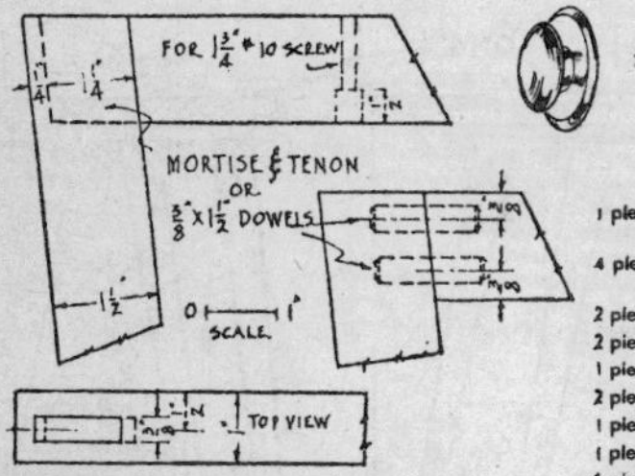
FOR 1¾" #10 SCREW
MORTISE & TENON OR ⅜ x 1½ DOWELS
SCALE
TOP VIEW

END LEG CONSTRUCTION

SUGGESTION FOR STOCK METAL KNOB

List of Lumber

1 piece top choice stock (plywood) ¾" x 22" x 42" including ⅛" glued strips.
4 pieces choice strips ⅛" x 1¼" to be glued on four edges of top and miter corners.
2 pieces top pad ½" x 3" x 22"
2 pieces top pad ½" x 3" x 42"
1 piece top pad ½" x 3" x 16"
2 pieces leg frame 1" x 1½" x 29"
1 piece leg rail 1" x 1½" x 18"
1 piece leg rail 1" x 1½" x 14"
1 piece stretcher 1" x 26¼" Dowel

Leg rail sizes are for mortise and tenon construction. Change lengths if dowel joints are preferred.

Cabinet Part

2 pieces sides choice (plywood) ¾" x 20" x 28¾" including ⅛" glued strips.
1 piece back choice (plywood) ¾" x 12½" x 28¾"
4 pieces partitions (fir plywood) ⅜" x 18½" x 13"
1 piece front bottom choice (plywood) ¾" x 5" x 12½"
4 pieces choice strips 28¾" x ¾" x ⅛" to glue on front and back edges of sides.

Drawers

1 piece front choice stock ¾" x 7" x 12½"
1 piece front choice stock ¾" x 6¼" x 12½"
1 piece front choice stock ¾" x 6" x 12½"
1 piece front choice stock ¾" x 4½" x 12½"

Drawers (continued)

2 pieces sides ½" x 3⅞" x 19"
2 pieces sides ½" x 5⅜" x 19"
2 pieces sides ½" x 5⅝" x 19"
2 pieces sides ½" x 6⅛" x 19"
1 piece back ½" x 3¼" x 11⅞"
1 piece back ½" x 4¾" x 11⅞"
1 piece back ½" x 5" x 11⅞"
1 piece back ½" x 5¾" x 11⅞"
4 pieces bottoms (plywood) ¼" x 18⅜" x 11⅞"

Note: Sizes given are finished measurements.

If dovetail construction of drawers is used, add ⅝" in width and ⅞" in length of backs.

KIDNEY SHAPED COFFEE TABLE

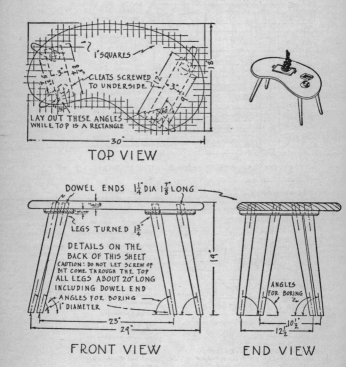

1" SQUARES

CLEATS SCREWED TO UNDERSIDE

LAY OUT THESE ANGLES WHILE TOP IS A RECTANGLE

18"

30"

TOP VIEW

DOWEL ENDS 1¼ DIA 1⅞ LONG

LEGS TURNED 1¾

DETAILS ON THE BACK OF THIS SHEET

CAUTION: DO NOT LET SCREW OF BIT COME THROUGH THE TOP

ALL LEGS ABOUT 20" LONG INCLUDING DOWEL END

ANGLES FOR BORING 1" DIAMETER

19"

23"

29"

FRONT VIEW

ANGLES FOR BORING

12½"   10½"

END VIEW

DETAILS & LIST OF LUMBER

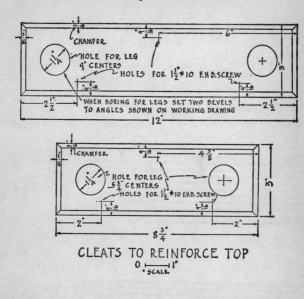

CLEATS TO REINFORCE TOP

0 |———| 1"
• SCALE

LIST OF LUMBER

1 piece top 1 5/16" x 18" x 30"
Made up of several pieces glued together
4 pieces legs 1¾" x 1¾" x 20"
1 piece cleat ¾" x 3" x 8¾"
1 piece cleat ¾" x 3" x 12"

NOTE: Sizes given are finished measurements.

APPENDIX

Working Drawings for Five Things to Build

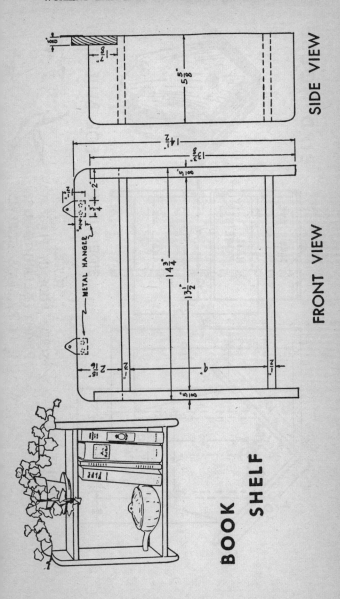

SIDE VIEW

FRONT VIEW

BOOK

SHELF

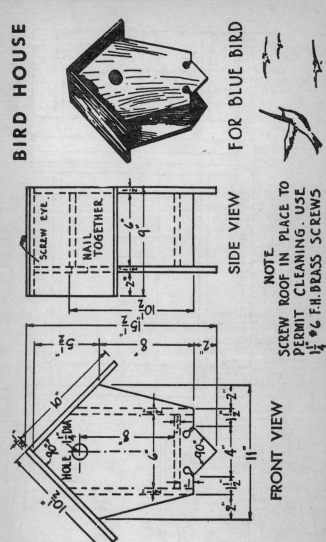

BIRD HOUSE

FOR BLUE BIRD

SIDE VIEW

FRONT VIEW

NOTE

SCREW ROOF IN PLACE TO
PERMIT CLEANING. USE
1¼" #6 F.H. BRASS SCREWS

COFFEE TABLE

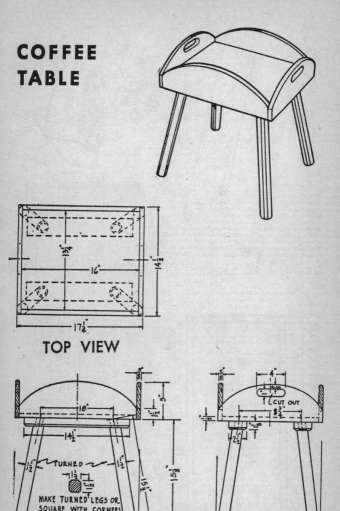

TOP VIEW

13¾

16"

14½

17½"

FRONT VIEW

10"

14½"

5

1½"

TURNED

1½"

1½"

7½"

15½"

15⅛"

MAKE TURNED LEGS OR SQUARE WITH CORNERS CHAMFERED AS SHOWN

SIDE VIEW

4"

CUT OUT

8¾"

1½"
2½"

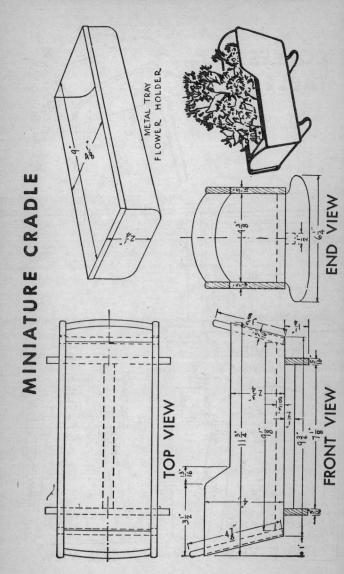

MINIATURE CRADLE

METAL TRAY FLOWER HOLDER

9"

4⅛"

2¼"

TOP VIEW

END VIEW

5/16"

4⅜"

1½"

6¼"

FRONT VIEW

11¾"

3⅝"

9⅛"

9¾"

7⅞"

3½"

4⅛"

4"

2¼"

2"

5/16"

1"

FOOT STOOL

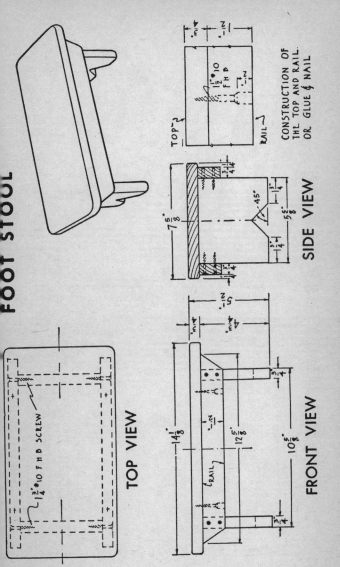

TOP VIEW

CONSTRUCTION OF
THE TOP AND RAIL
OR GLUE & NAIL

SIDE VIEW

FRONT VIEW

INDEX

Abrasives, 279–282, 285–287
Accidents, 107–109
    axes and, 108, 109
    blades and, 107
    causes of, 107
    chisels and, 107–108
    files and, 108
    hammers and, 107, 108
    hatchets and, 108
    knives and, 109
    mallets and, 107, 108
    nails and, 108
    National Safety Council and, 107
    planes and, 108
    pliers and, 109
    punches and, 107
    screwdrivers and, 109
    vises and, 109
    wood handles and, 107, 108
    wrenches and, 109
Adjustments, 49
    of carpenter's level, 103
    of plane, 49–55
    of spokeshaves, 62–63
Adzes, sharpening, 224
Alder, 132
Aluminum oxide, 281, 286
Anchor nails, 212–213
Animal glue, 183, 185
Armchair, 452–453
    materials for, 452
    working drawing for, 453
Ash, 131, 132
Aspen, 132
Auger bits, 3, 22, 93–94
    sharpening, 224–225
Awl, 3, 16, 207
    scratch, 106, 107
    use of, 106
Axes, 108, 109
    accidents and, 108, 109
    sharpening, 224

Back bend chisels, 73, 242
Back saw, 3, 17, 20, 48–49
    care of, 49
    use of, 48–49

Ball-peen hammer, 10
Band clamps, 190, 191
Bar clamps, 190
Basswood, 131, 132
Bastard files, 31
Beading, 237
Beech, 132
Bell faced hammer, 4, 9, 35–36
Bench, 440–441
    materials for, 441
    working drawing for, 440–441
Bench rule, 5
Bench shaper, router as, 312–313
Beveling, 237–239
    crosscut, 238
    curved edges, 238
    sanding, 238–239
    use of, 237
Bill poster's hammer, 12
Binding head screws, 198
Bird house, 469
    working drawing for, 469
Birch, 131, 132
Bit stock drills, 207
Bits, 3, 21–23
    auger, 3, 22, 93–94, 224–225
        construction of, 93, 94
        sharpening, 224–225
        use of, 93
    countersink, 208
    double twist, 22
    expansive, 23
        construction of, 93–94
        use of, 93–94
    Fostner, 208
    power drill, 254–265
        auger, 254
        disc-sander, 257–258
        drill stand, 262
        drum-sander, 258
        electrician's, 254, 255
        flat, 255
        grinding wheel, 260
        hole saw, 255–256
        power bore, 253–254

screwdriver, 256–257
self-feed, 255
sets for, 255
spade type, 256
stirrer, 261
Surform drum, 259
use of, 262–265
wire brush, 259–260
router and, 293–296
beading, 293
chamfer, 293
composition of, 293
cove, 293
grooving, 293
rounding over, 293
screwdriver, 23
construction of, 95–97
use of, 95–98
twist, 208
use of, 85–89, 93–94
auger, 93–94
countersinking screws, 90, 96
diamond point, 94
double thread, 94
dowel, 94
expansive, 93–94
Fostner, 93
Phillips screwdriver, 97
screwdriver, 95–98
single thread, 94
twist, 93, 94
Black walnut, 131
Blacksmith's hammer, 12
Blades, accidents and, 107
Block plane, 3, 24, 26, 56
use of, 56
Blood-albumen, 183, 185
Blueprints, 111–114
detail, 114
dimension lines, 113, 114
extension lines, 113
legend, 114
reading, 114
scale, 113, 114
section lines, 113
title, 114
working lines, 112–113
Board feet, 79–80
Bolts, 200–201
countersinking, 203–204
hardware and, 200, 203, 215–217
replacement of, 205
storage of, 205

Bookrack, 115–123
Bookshelf, 467
working drawing for, 467
Box nails, 208
Brace table measure, 79
Braces, 3, 21
use of, 85–89
chucks and, 87–88, 91, 96
ratchet, 88, 96–97
Brad nails, 37, 39, 210, 212
Brushes, 186
glue, 186
for power tools, 247
storage of, 326
Buckeye, 132
Bung head screws, 198
Butt chisel, 28
Butt joints, 141, 143, 146, 157
Butternut, 132

Cabinet chisel, 28
Cabinet scraper, 29, 62, 64
use of, 62
Cabinetmaker's rabbet plane, 26
Caliper rule, 9
use of, 104
inside, 104
outside, 104
Carpenter's level, 103
adjustment of, 103
aluminum, 103
care of, 103
description of, 103
"line level" and, 103, 105
magnesium, 103
spirit, 103
wood, 103
Carriage maker's clamps, 190
Carving, 241–243
chisels and, 241–242
gouges, 241–243
Carving chisels, 73
Casein glue, 183, 184–185
Cast head hammer, 9
Cedar, 131, 132
Cellulose cement, 183
Chairs, 379
breaks in, 379
sagging, 379
shaky, 379
Chamfering, 237, 238
ends, 238
marking, 238
sanding, 238

Cherry, 132
Chestnut, 131
Chisels, 3
  accidents and, 108–109
  back bend, 73, 242
  butt, 28
  cabinet, 28
  care of, 68
  carving, 73, 241–243
  carving gouge, 73
  construction of, 67, 73–74
  flats, 74
  fluters, 74
  front bent, 73, 242
  gouges, 68, 73–74
  long bend, 73, 242
  sharpening, 219–221
  short bend, 73, 242
  skew, 73, 74, 242
  spade, 73
  use of, 67–74
    for concave corners, 67,
      68, 69
    for convex corners, 68, 72
    for cutting dadoes, 68, 73
    for hardwood, 67
    for horizontal cuts, 68, 71
    for paring a chamfer, 68,
      72
    for paring shoulders, 71
    for softwood, 67
    for vertical cuts, 68, 70, 71
  "V," 73, 74
  veining, 73, 74
Chucks, braces and, 87, 88,
  91, 96
Clamps, 107, 189–190
  band, 190
  bar, 190
  carriage maker's, 190
  column, 190
  glue and, 189–190
  use of, 107
  web, 190
  wood screw, 190
Claw hammer, 9
  curved, 10
  straight, 9
Clinch nailing, 212
Coarse files, 31
Coffee table, 470
  working drawing for, 470
Coilable rules, 105
Cold glue, 185
Colonial magazine case, 417–

418, 468
  materials for, 417
  working drawing for, 418,
    468
Colonial magazine stand, 415–
  417
  working drawing for, 416
Column clamps, 190
Combination square, 8, 78
Combination tray, 407–408
  materials for, 408
  working drawing for, 407
Compass saw, 17, 19
Compression splices, 142, 144
Concave corners, chisels for,
  67, 68, 69
Coniferous wood, 132
Convex corners, chisels for,
  68, 72
Convex-bottom spokeshaves,
  62
  use of, 62
Coping saw, 3, 17, 19, 46
  use of, 46
Corner table, 460–461
  materials for, 460–461
  working drawing for, 460
Corrugated steel nails, 213–
  215
Cottonwood, 132
Countersink bits, 208
Countersinking screws, 90
Crosscut saw, 3, 4, 17, 18,
  46, 47, 48
  use of, 46, 47
Cypress, 131, 132

Dado joints, 179–181
  end, 181
  grained, 179
  housed, 179, 180
  plain, 180
  shoulder-housed, 180
  stopped, 180–181
Dadoes, chisels for cutting, 68
Deciduous wood, 132
Decorative head nails, 210
Depth gauge, 9
Diagrams, 111
Diamond point bits, 93
  bit stock, 207
  hand, 3, 23–24
  power, 205, 248–265
    bits for, 253–255
    brushes for, 259–260

chucks for, 250, 252–253
portable, 248–265
selection of, 248–251
speed for, 251–252
use of, 262–265
twist, 90–93
care of, 93
use of, 90–92
Drive screws, 198
Dividers, 102, 104, 106
wing, 8, 105
Door problems, 367–371
hinges, 371–372, 373, 375
locks, 373–375, 376
Double cut files, 31
Double thread bits, 94
Double twist bits, 22
Douglas fir, 132
Dovetail drawer, 391–393
materials for, 392
working drawing for, 391
Dovetail joints, 170–177
dado, 172–173
half-blind, 173–174
half-lap, 171–172
lap, 173–174
multiple, 172, 175
secret, 174–177
single, 172, 173
stopped lap, 173
Dowel bits, 94
Doweling jig, 154–157
Drawers, 377–378
joints, 377
shaky, 378
Dressing table, 446–447
materials for, 446
working drawing for, 446,
447
Driving nails, 35–39
Drop-forged steel head hammer, 9
Drop-leaf coffee table, 436–
440
working drawing for, 436,
438
Duplex-head nails, 210
Duplex rabbet plane, 26

Edges, planing, 56, 61
Electrician's screwdriver, 16
Elm, 132
Enameling, 334–335
Engineer's hammer, 11
Ends, planing, 56, 58, 60, 62

Essex board measure, 79–80
Expansive bits, 23, 93–94
Extension cords, 247
Extension stick, 105

Fasteners, 206–207
steel corrugated, 213–215
Fiberboards, 137, 140
Fibers, 131–132, 133
diameter, 131
length, 131
lignin and, 131
medullary rays and, 131
rings and, 131–132, 133
vertical grain and, 133
Files, 3
accidents and, 108
bastard, 31
care of, 77–78
coarse, 31
double cut, 31
flat, 31
half-round, 31
round, 31
second, 31
single cut, 31
smooth, 31
square, 31
triangular, 31
use of, 75–78
wood, 31
Fillers, 329–330
Fillister head screws, 198
Finishing process, 322–346
brushes, 325–326
storage of, 326
enameling, 334–335
fillers, 329–330
highlighting, 345
old finish and, 327–328
painting, 330–334
mixing, 331
order for, 333
outdoor, 333–334
preparation for, 330–331
plane and, 55, 56
polishing, 342–345
French, 343–345
rollers, 326–327
sanding, 323–324
scumbling, 345–346
sealing, 328
spatterdash, 346
spraying, 327
staining, 335–338

starching, 346
Tiffany blending, 346
undercoating, 328
varnishing, 338–342
Fir, 132
Fished splices, 142
Flat-bottom spokeshaves, 64
use of, 64
Flat chisels, 74
Flat files, 31
Flat-head nails, 208
Flat head screws, 198
Flexible-rigid steel tape, 6–7
Floors, 377
cracks in, 377
sagging, 377
squeaky, 377
Fluter chisels, 74
Folding card table, 432–433
materials for, 432
working drawing for, 433
Folding rule, 6
Folding tennis table, 394–398
materials for, 396
working drawing for, 397–398
Footstool, 411–412, 473
materials for, 412
working drawing for, 411
Fore plane, 24, 25–26
Fostner bits, 93, 208
Front bent chisels, 73, 242
Furniture, 379–380
deep defects, 379–380
extensive defects, 380
surface defects, 379
veneer defects, 380
warped tops, 380

Gauge, 3
depth, 9
marking, 3, 13–14
Glove case, 425–427
materials for, 425, 426
working drawing for, 425, 426
Glue, 129, 183–189
animal, 183, 185
blood-albumen, 183, 185
brushes for, 186
casein, 183, 184–185
cellulose cement, 183
clamps for, 189–190
cold, 185

hardwood and, 183
heartwood and, 183
heavy wood and, 183
hot, 185–186
light wood and, 183
liquid, 183, 184, 185
pots for, 185, 186
rubber compounds, 183
sapwood and, 183
softwood and, 183
synthetic resin, 183–184, 185
vegetable, 183, 185
Gouges, 68, 73–74
carving, 73, 241–243
sharpening, 221–224
use of, 73–74
firmer, 68, 73, 74
paring, 68, 73, 74
Grades, 135
defects and, 135
lumber, 131–137
Grain, 133, 134
coarse, 133
cross section, 133, 134
edge, 133, 134
fine, 133
flat, 133, 134
vertical, 133, 134
Grinders, 218–219
use of, 98–103

Hack saw, 17, 20, 49
use of, 20, 49
Hackberry, 132
Half-round files, 31
Halved splices, 142
Hammer, 3, 4, 9–12
accidents and, 107, 108
ball-peen, 10
bell faced, 4, 9, 35, 36
bill poster's, 12
blacksmith, 12
cast head, 9
claw, 9
curved, 9, 10
straight, 9
drop-forged steel heads, 9
engineers, 11
handles, 9–10
hickory, 9
hatchet, 12
machinist's riveting, 10
plain faced, 9
riveting, 12

soft-face, 11
  use of, 74–75
upholsterer's, 11
use of, 9, 35, 74–75
  soft face, 74–75
Hand drills, 3, 23
Hand scrapers, 64–67
  care of, 64–65
  use of, 64–67
Handles, 9–10
  accidents and, 107, 108, 109
  hammer, 9–10
  hickory, 9
Handy memo roll, 427–428
  materials for, 427
  working drawing for, 428
Hanger bolt screws, 198
Hardware, 215–217
  bolts and, 200–201, 215–217
Hardwood, 131, 132
  chisels for, 67
  glue and, 183, 184
Hatchet, 12
  accidents and, 108
  sharpening, 224
Headless screws, 198
Heartwood, 132
  glue and, 183
Hemlock, 132
Hickory, 132
Highlighting, 345
Hinges, 215–217, 371–372,
  373, 375
Holders, nail, 36–37, 39
Hollywood headboard, 457–
  458
  materials for, 457
  working drawing for, 457–
    458
Horizontal cuts, chisels for,
  68, 70, 71
Horizontal spice cabinet, 420–
  422
  materials for, 421–422
  working drawing for, 420,
    421
Horseshoe nails, 208
Hot glue, 185–187
Household woodworking, 367–
  380
  chairs, 379
    breaks in, 379
    sagging, 379
    shaky, 379
  door problems, 367–371

  hinges, 371–372, 373, 375
  locks, 373–375, 376
drawers, 377–378
  joints, 377, 378
  shaky, 378
  splits, 378
  worn fittings, 378
floors, 377
  cracks in, 377
  sagging, 377
  squeaky, 377
furniture, 379–380
  deep defects, 379–380
  extensive defects, 380
  surface defects, 379
  veneer defects, 380
  warped tops, 380
stairs, 377
  creaky, 377

Iron vise, 31

Jack plane, 3, 24, 25, 33, 56
  use of, 24, 25, 56
Jointer plane, 24, 25
Joints, 190–193
  classification of, 141
    butt, 141, 143, 146, 157
    mitre, 141, 148, 157–162,
      174–177
    oblique, 141, 147–148
    plain, 141, 146
    square, 141
  conditioning for, 193–194
  dado, 179–181
    end, 181
    grained, 179
    housed, 179, 180
    plain, 180
    shoulder-housed, 180
    stopped, 180–181
  definition of, 141
  dovetail, 170–177
    dado, 172–173
    half-blind, 173–174
    half-lap, 171–172
    lap, 173–174
    multiple, 172, 175
    secret, 174, 176–177
    single, 172, 173
    stopped lap, 173
  dowel-pin method, 149–157
    doweling jig and, 154–157
  durability of, 194
  mitre, 141, 148, 157–162

blind, 174–177
  butt joints and, 157
  halved, 159–162
  mitre box and, 157–159
  slip feather, 159
  tongued, 159
mortise and tenon, 162–170
  barefaced, 168
  blind, 166
  foxtail, 168, 169
  haunched, 166–167
  lock, 170
  open, 169, 170
  pinned, 167, 168
  through, 166
  wedged, 168, 169
rabbet, 177–178
Juniper, 132

Keyhole saw, 17, 19
Kidney-shaped coffee table, 419–420
  materials for, 420
  working drawing for, 419
Knives, 3, 28–29
  accidents and, 109
  sharpening, 224
  utility, 28–29
Knotholes, 48

Lag screws, 196, 200
Laminated wood, 137
Larch, 132
Lentil head screws, 198
Lignin, 131
"Line level," 103–105
Liquid glue, 183, 184, 185
Living-room chair, 448–452
  materials for, 451
  working drawing for, 448–451
Locks, 373–375
Locust, 132
Long bend chisels, 73, 242
Lubrication, power tools and, 246
Lumber, 131–137
  grades of, 135
  purchase of, 131, 135–137

Machinist's riveting hammer, 10
Magnolia, 132
Mahogany, 131
Mallets, accidents and, 107, 108
Maple, 131, 132

Marking gauge, 3, 13–14, 40–42
  panel, 41–42
  use of, 40–42
  zig-zag rule, 42
Materials list, 114
  estimate for, 114
Measuring Tools, 5–9
  bench rule, 5
  caliper rules, 9
  combination square, 8
  depth gauge, 9
  flexible-rigid steel tape, 6–7
  folding, 6
  steel square, 7–8
  try and mitre square, 8
  wing dividers, 8
  zig-zag rule, 5–6
Medullary rays, 131
Metal screws, 196
Miniature cradle, 471
  working drawing for, 471
Mitre box, 20–21, 157–159
Mitre joints, 141, 148, 157–162, 174–177
  blind, 174–177
  butt joints and, 157
  halved, 159–162
  mitre box and, 157–159
  slip feather, 159
  tongued, 159
Mitre squares, 78, 83, 84
  use of, 78, 83, 84
Modified wood, 137–140
  fiberboards, 137–140
  laminated wood, 137
  plastics, 140
  plywood, 137
Moldings, 239–240
Mortise and tenon joints, 162–170
  bare-faced, 168
  blind, 166
  foxtail, 168, 169
  haunched, 166–167
  lock, 170
  open, 169
  pinned, 167–168
  through, 166
  wedged, 168, 169

Nails, 208–215
  accidents and, 108
  anchor, 212–213
  box, 208

brad, 37, 39, 210
  clinch, 212
  corrugated steel, 213–215
  decorative head, 210
  drawing of, 38, 39
  driving, 35–39
  duplex-head, 210
  flat-head, 208
  holders for, 36–37, 39
  horsehoe, 208
  points of, 211
  purpose of, 212, 213
  shanks of, 211
  size, 209, 210, 212
  small, 36, 39
  special, 210–211
  type, 208–211
  use of, 209–211, 212, 213
  wiggle, 39, 213–215
  wire, 208, 209
Nylock screws, 200

Oak, 131, 132
Oblique joints, 141, 147–148
Oiler, 3
Oilstone, 3, 218
  care of, 103
  construction of, 101
  use of, 99–103
Oval head screws, 195, 198

Painting, 330–334
  mixing, 331
  order for, 333
  outdoor, 333–334
  preparation for, 330–331
Pan head screws, 198
Paneling, 381–382
Paring, 68
  chamfer, 72
  gouges, 68, 73
    construction of, 73
    use of, 68, 73
  shoulders, 71
Pencils, use of, 43
Phillips head screws, 196
Phillips screwdriver, 14, 15
  bits, 97
Picnic case and table, 430–432
  materials for, 430
  working drawing for, 431
Pipe rack and humidor, 414–415
  materials for, 415

working drawing for, 414
Pilot project, 115–123, 124–130
  finishing up, 124–130
  working drawings, 115–122
Plain faced hammer, 9
Plain joints, 141, 146
Plain-sawed wood, 133, 134
Plane, 3, 24–27
  accidents and, 108
  adjustment of, 49–55
  assembling of, 50–53
  blades for, 219–221
  block, 3, 24, 26
  fore, 24, 25–26
  inspection of, 49
  jack, 3, 24, 25
  jointer, 24, 25
  parts of, 50–52
  purpose of, 24
  rabbet, 26–27
    cabinetmaker's, 26
    duplex, 26
    side, 26–27
  router, 27
  smoothing, 24
  use of, 24–27, 49–62
    block, 56
    for edges, 56, 61
    for ends, 56, 58, 60, 62
    for finishing, 55, 56
    jack, 56
    smoothing, 56
Plastic wood, 39
Plastics, 140
Plate rack, 409–410
  materials for, 410
  working drawing for, 409, 410
Pliers, 3
  accidents and, 109
Plumb bob, 105
Plywood, 137
Poplar, 131
Polishing, 342–345
  French, 343–345
Portable towel rack, 405–406
  materials for, 405
  working drawing for, 406
Pots, glue, 185, 186
Power drills, 205, 248–265
  auger bits, 254
  bits for, 253–255, 256, 257
  brushes for, 253, 259–260
  buffing wheel, 261

chucks for, 250, 252–253
disc-sander, 257–258
drill stand, 262
drum-sander, 258
electrician's bit, 254, 255
flat bits, 255
grinding wheel, 260
hole saw, 255–256
portable, 248–265
power bore, 255
screwdriver, 256–257, 258
selection of, 248–251
self-feed bit, 254, 255
sets for, 255
spade type, 256
speed for, 251–252
stirrer, 261
Surform drum, 259
use of, 262–265
wire brush, 259–260
Power plane, 316–317
Power sanders, 279–287
abrasives, 279–281, 285–286
aluminum oxide, 281–286
polishing belt, 286
silicon carbide, 281, 286
belt, 279, 282–285, 286, 287
sizes of, 282
use of, 282–285
disc, 279
orbital, 279, 281–282
paper for, 281–282
use of, 281–282
portable, 279–287
sandpaper, 279–281
aluminum oxide, 281, 286
closed-coat, 280, 286
flint, 281
garnet, 281
grit of, 281, 282
open-coat, 280–281, 286
silicon carbide, 281, 286
use of, 285–287
Power saws, 266–278
blades for, 266, 269–270
classification of, 266
crosscuts with, 270
long cuts with, 271
ripping with, 271–272
saber, 275–278
special cuts with, 272–275
use of, 266, 267–275
Power tools, 244–247
bits for, 293–296
brushes for, 247

extension cord for, 247
grounding for, 246
lubrication for, 246
motors for, 245–246
portable, 244–247
drill, 248–265
safety and, 319–321
sanders, 279–287
saws, 266–278
router, 288–318
parts of, 290, 292–293
use of, 296–315
use of, 290–291
"Pull-Push" tapes, 42
Punches, accidents and, 107–108
Putty, 39

Quality tools, 110
Quarter-sawed wood, 133, 134

Rabbet joints, 177–178
Rabbet plane, 26–27
cabinetmaker's, 26
duplex, 26
side, 26–27
Rafter table measure, 79
Rasps, 31
use of, 78
Ratchet braces, 88
use of, 88
Ratchet screwdriver, 15–16, 204–205
Redwood, 131, 132
Revolving book stand and table, 434–435
materials for, 434
working drawing for, 435
Rings, wood, 131–132, 133
Rip saw, 3, 4, 17, 18–19, 47
use of, 47
Riveting hammer, 12
Rollers, 326–327
Round files, 31
Round head screws, 195, 198
Router, 239, 288–318
as bench shaper, 312–313
use of, 312–313
bits for, 293–296
parts of, 290, 292–293
use of, 290–291, 296–315
as bench shaper, 312–313
as power plane, 316–317
as veneer trimmer, 317–318

Routing, 239
Rubber compounds, 183
Rules, 5–7, 9
  bench, 5
  caliper, 9, 104
    inside, 104
    outside, 104
  coilable, 105
  folding, 6
  use of, 43–44
  zig-zag, 5–6, 42, 105

Safety, 107–110
  accidents, 107–110
    axes and, 108, 109
    blades and, 107, 108, 109
    causes of, 107
    chisels and, 107–108
    files and, 108
    hammers and, 107, 108
    hatchets and, 108
    knives and, 109
    mallets and, 107, 108
    nails and, 108
    National Safety Council
      and, 107
    planes and, 108
    pliers and, 109
    punches and, 108–109
    screwdrivers and, 109
    vises and, 109
    wood handles and, 107
    wrenches and, 109
  portable power tools and,
    319–321
Saf-lok screw, 200
Sanders, 279–287
  abrasives, 279–282, 285–287
    aluminum oxide, 282, 286
    polishing belt, 286
    silicon carbide, 281, 286
  belt, 279, 282–285, 286
    sizes of, 282
    use of, 282–287
  orbital, 281–282
    use of, 281–282
    paper for, 282
  power, 279–287
    abrasives, 279–282, 285–
      287
    belt, 279, 282–287
    disc, 279
Sandpaper, 126–128
  grades of, 128
  power sanders, 279–282

  aluminum oxide, 281, 286
  closed-coat, 280, 286
  flint, 281
  garnet, 281
  grit of, 281, 282
  open-coat, 280–281, 286
  silicon carbide, 281, 286
  use of, 285–287
Sapwood, 132
  glue and, 183
Saw, 3, 17–21
  back, 3, 17, 20
  compass, 17, 19
  coping, 3, 17, 19
  crosscut, 3, 4, 17–18
  hack, 17, 20
  keyhole, 17, 19, 20
  power, 266–278
    blades for, 269–270
    classification of, 266
    crosscuts with, 270
    long cuts with, 271
    ripping with, 271
    saber, 275–278
    special cuts with, 272–274
    use of, 267–278
  rip, 3, 4, 17, 18–19
  sharpening, 231–236
  use of, 17–20, 44–49
    back, 20, 48–49
    coping, 19, 46
    crosscut, 17–18, 45–46, 47
    hack, 20
    rip, 18–19, 47
Sawhorse, 388–389
  materials for, 388
  working drawing for, 388
Scraper, 29, 62, 64–67, 226–230
  cabinet, 29, 62, 64, 226
  sharpening, 226–230
  use of, 62–67
    cabinet, 62, 64
    hand, 64–67
Scratch awl, 106, 107
  use of, 106
Screens, 386–388
  materials for, 386
  working drawing for, 387
Screwdriver, 3, 14–16, 95–98,
    206
  accidents and, 109
  bit, 15, 95–97
  electrician's, 16
  Phillips, 14
  ratchet, 15–16, 204–205

sharpening, 230–231
spiral, 15
stubby, 14, 15
"Yankee" spiral ratchet, 204
Z-shaped offset, 14–15
Screwdriver bits, 23, 95–97
Screw-Mate, 205, 258
Screw sinks, 90
Screws, 195–200
    advantage of, 195
    binding head, 198
    bung head, 198
    composition of, 195
    countersinking, 90
    dovel, 198
    drive, 198
    fillister head, 198
    flat head, 195, 198
    hanger bolt, 198
    headless, 198
    lag, 196, 200
    lentil head, 198
    metal, 196
    Nylock, 200
    oval head, 195, 198
    pan head, 198
    Phillips head, 196
    round head, 195, 198
    Saf-lok, 200
    Sems screw, 200
    slots for, 198, 200
        cross, 198, 200
        Freason, 198
        Phillips, 198
        Pozzi, 198
        straight, 198
    slotted head, 196
    Spin-Lok, 200
    Springtite, 200
    starting of, 200, 202
    stove head, 198
    Thredlock, 200
    truss head, 198
    winged, 198
    wood, 195
        construction of, 195
        sizes of, 195–196, 198–199
Scumbling, 345–346
Second files, 31
Sems screw, 200
Sewing kit, 399–400
    materials for, 399, 400
    working drawing for, 399
Sharpening, 218–236
    adzes, 224

auger bits, 224, 225
axes, 224
chisels, 219–221
gouges, 221–224
hatchets, 224
knives, 224
plane blades, 219–221
saws, 231–236
scrapers, 226–230
screwdrivers, 230–231
spokeshaves, 224
twist drills, 224
Shellac, 122, 123, 338, 341
Shoeshine box, 413–414
    materials for, 413
    working drawing for, 413
Short bend chisels, 73, 242
Shoulders, chisels for paring, 71
Shrinkage, 133, 135
Side chair, 453–454
    materials for, 454
    working drawing for, 453–454
Side rabbet plane, 26–27
Silicon carbide, 281, 286
Single cut files, 31
Single thread bits, 94
Skew chisels, 73, 74, 242
Slots, screw, 198, 200
    cross, 198
    Freason, 198
    Phillips, 198
    Pozzi, 198
    straight, 198
Slotted head screws, 196
Smooth files, 31
Smoothing plane, 24
    use of, 56
Soft-face hammer, 11, 74–75
    use of, 74–75
Softwood, 131, 132
    chisels for, 67
    glue and, 183
Spade chisels, 73
Spatterdash, 346
Spice cabinet, 402–404
    materials for, 404
Spin-lok screws, 200
Spiral screwdriver, 15
Splices, 142–144
    compression, 142
    definition of, 142
    fished, 142
    halved, 142
    square, 142–143

tension, 142–144
Spokeshave, 3, 27–28
    adjustment of, 62, 63, 64
    sharpening, 224
    use of, 62, 63, 64
        convex-bottom, 63
        flat-bottom, 64
Spraying, 327
Springtite screws, 200
Square, 3, 7–8, 78–85
    brace table measure and, 79
    combination, 8
    Essex board measure and, 79
    mitre, 78
        use of, 78, 83, 84
    rafter table measure and, 79
    steel, 7–8
    try, 8, 78, 80–81, 82, 83, 85
        use of, 8, 78, 80–81, 82, 83, 85
    try and mitre square, 8
    use of, 7–8, 78–85
        combination, 8, 78
        mitre, 78, 83, 84
        steel, 7, 78, 79
        try, 8, 78, 80, 81, 82, 83, 85
Square files, 31
Square joints, 141, 146
Square splices, 142–143
Squaring, wood, 78–85
Stain, 122–123, 335–338
Staining, 335–338
Stairs, 377
    creaky, 377
Starching, 346
Steel corrugated fasteners, 213–215
Steel square, 7–8, 78, 79–80
Stove head screws, 198
Stubby screwdriver, 14, 15
Student's home desk, 461–463
    materials for, 462–463
    working drawing for, 461–462
Sturdy vine support, 454–456
    materials for, 454–455
    working drawing for, 455–456
Surform Tools, 3, 29–30
    use of, 29–30, 75–78
Sycamore, 132
Synthetic resins, 183–184, 185

Tamarack, 132
Tapes, 6–7

flexible-rigid steel, 6–7
    "Pull-Push," 42
    use of, 42–43
Telephone shelf, 422–424
    materials for, 422
    working drawing for, 423–424
Tension splices, 142
Thredlock screws, 200
Tiffany blending, 346
Tongue and groove joints, 181–182
Tool cabinet, 389
    materials for, 389
    working drawing for, 390
Tool chest, 393–394
    materials for, 394
    working drawing for, 393
Trammel points, 105, 106
    use of, 105, 106
Treasure chest, 400–402
    materials for, 400–401
    working drawing for, 401
Triangular files, 31
Truss head screws, 198
Try and mitre square, 8
Try squares, 8, 78, 82, 83, 85
    use of, 78, 80, 81, 85
Twist bits, 93

Upholsterer's hammer, 11
Utility knife, 28–29

"V" chisels, 73, 74
Varnishing, 338–342
Vegetable glue, 183, 185
Veining chisels, 73, 74
Veneer trimmer router as, 317–318
Veneering, 382–385
Vertical cuts, chisels for, 68, 70, 71
Vise, 3, 31
    accidents and, 109
    iron, 31
    wood, 31

Wall bookshelf, 429–430
    materials for, 429–430
    working drawing for, 429
Walnut, 132
Web clamps, 190
White spruce, 131, 132
Whitepine, 131, 132
Wiggle nails, 39, 213–215

Willow, 132
Wing dividers, 8, 104, 105
Winged screws, 198
Wire nails, 208, 209
Wood, 131–140
  alder, 132
  ash, 131, 132
  aspen, 132
  basswood, 131, 132
  beech, 132
  birch, 131, 132
  black walnut, 131
  board feet in, 79–80
  buckeye, 132
  butternut, 132
  cedar, 131, 132
  cherry, 132
  chestnut, 131
  choice of, 131–140
    coniferous, 132
    deciduous, 132
    defects and, 135
    fibers, 131–132, 133
    grades and, 135
    grain, 133, 134
    hardwood, 131, 132, 138–
      139
    plain-sawed, 133, 134
    quarter-sawed, 133, 134
    shrinkage and, 133–135
    softwood, 131, 132, 138–
      139
  classification of, 132, 138–
    139
    coniferous, 132
    deciduous, 132
    hardwood, 131, 132
    heartwood, 132
    sapwood, 132
    softwood, 131, 132
  cottonwood, 132
  cypress, 131, 132
  Douglas fir, 132
  elm, 132
  fibers, 131–132, 133
    diameter, 131
    length, 131
    lignin and, 131
    medullary rays and, 131
    rings and, 131–132, 133
    vertical grain and, 133, 134
  files, 3, 31
  fir, 132
  grain, 47, 133, 134, 135
    coarse, 133

  cross section, 133
  edge, 133, 134
  fine, 133
  flat, 133, 134
  vertical, 133, 134
hackberry, 132
hammer handles, 9–10, 107
hemlock, 132
hickory, 132
joinery, 144–182
  binding agents, 183–217
juniper, 132
larch, 132
locust, 132
magnolia, 132
mahogany, 131
maple, 131, 132
modified, 137, 140
  fiberboards, 137, 140
  laminated wood, 137
  plastics, 140
  plywood, 137
oak, 131, 132
plastic, 39
poplar, 131
purchase of, 135–137
redwood, 131, 132
screws, 195
  construction of, 195–196
  sizes of, 195–196, 198, 199
squaring, 78–85
sycamore, 132
tamarack, 132
vise, 31
walnut, 132
white pine, 131, 132
white spruce, 131, 132
willow, 132
yellow pine, 131
yellow poplar, 132
yew, 132
Woodworking, 452
  armchair, 452–453
    working drawing for, 453
  beading, 237
  bench, 440–441
    materials for, 441
    working drawing for, 440–
      441
  beveling, 237
    crosscut, 238
    curved edges, 238
    sanding, 238
    use of, 237–239
  bird house, 469

working drawing for, 469
blueprint, 111–114
    detail, 114
    dimension lines, 113, 114
    extension lines, 113
    legend, 114
    reading, 114
    scale, 113, 114
    section lines, 113
    title, 114
    working lines, 112–113
bookrack, 116–122
bookshelf, 467
    working drawing for, 467
carving, 241–243
    chisels and, 241–243
chamfering, 237
    ends, 238
    marking, 238
    sanding, 238
coffee table, 470
    working drawing for, 470
Colonial magazine case,
    417–418
    materials for, 417
    working drawing for, 418
Colonial magazine stand,
    415–417
    materials for, 415
    working drawing for, 416
combination tray, 407–408
    materials for, 408
    working drawing for, 407
corner table, 459–461
    materials for, 460–461
    working drawing for, 460
dado, 179–181
dovetail drawers, 391–393
    materials for, 392
    working drawing for, 391
dressing table, 446
    materials for, 446
    working drawing for, 445–
    446, 447
drop-leaf coffee table, 436–
    440
    materials for, 437
    working drawing for, 436,
    438
finishing process, 322–346
    brushes, 325–326
    enameling, 334–335
    fillers, 329–330
    finishing, 324–326
    highlighting, 345

old finish and, 327–328
    painting, 330–334
    polishing, 342–345
    rollers, 326–327
    sanding, 323–324
    scumbling, 345–346
    sealing, 328
    spatterdash, 346
    spraying, 327
    staining, 335–338
    starching, 346
    Tiffany blending, 346
    undercoating, 328
    varnishing, 338–342
folding tennis table, 394–398
    materials for, 396
    working drawing for, 395,
    397, 398
folding card table, 432–433
    materials for, 432
    working drawing for, 433
footstool, 411–412
    materials for, 412
    working drawing for, 411
glove case, 425–427
    materials for, 425, 426
    working drawing for, 425,
    426
handy memo roll, 427–428
    working drawing for, 428
Hollywood headboard, 457–
    458
    materials for, 457
    working drawing for, 457,
    458
horizontal spice cabinet,
    420–422
    materials for, 421–422
    working drawing for, 420,
    421
household, 367–380
    chairs, 379
    door problems, 367–371
    drawers, 377–378
    floors, 377
    furniture, 379–380
    stairs, 377
joints, 141–182
    classification of, 141
    definition of, 141
    dovetail, 170–177
    dowel-pin method, 149–157
    mitre, 141, 148, 157–162,
    174–177
    mortise and tenon, 162–170

kidney-shaped coffee table, 419–420
  materials for, 420
  working drawing for, 419
living-room chair, 448–452
  materials for, 448–452
  working drawing for, 448–451
materials list, 114
  estimate for, 114
miniature cradle, 471
  working drawing for, 471
moldings, 239–240
paneling, 381–382
picnic case and table, 430–432
  materials for, 430
  working drawing for, 431
pipe rack and humidor, 414–415
  materials for, 415
  working drawing for, 414
pilot project, 115–123, 124–130
  finishing up, 124–130
  working drawing, 116–121
plan for, 111–114
  blueprint, 111–114
  diagram, 111
  materials list, 114
  working steps, 114
plate rack, 409–410
  materials for, 410
  working drawing for, 409, 410
portable towel rack, 405–406
  materials for, 405
  working drawing for, 406
primary tools for, 32, 33–34
rabbet, 177–178
revolving book stand and table, 434–435
  materials for, 434
  working drawing for, 435
routing, 239
sandpapering, 126–128
sawhorse, 388–389
  materials for, 388
  working drawing for, 388
screens, 386–388
  materials for, 386
  working drawing for, 387
sewing kit, 399–400
  materials for, 399, 400

working drawing for, 399
shellac, 122–123
shoeshine box, 413
  materials for, 413
  working drawing for, 413
side chair, 453–454
  materials for, 454
  working drawing for, 453–454
spice cabinet, 403–404
  materials for, 404
  working drawing for, 403
splices, 141, 142–144
stain, 122–123
student's home desk, 461–463
  materials for, 462–463
  working drawing for, 461–462
sturdy vine support, 454–456
  working drawing for, 455–456
telephone shelf, 422–424
  working drawing for, 423–424
tongue and groove, 181–182
tool cabinet, 389–390
  materials for, 389
  working drawing for, 390
tool chest, 393–394
  materials for, 394
  working drawing for, 393
treasure chest, 400–402
  materials for, 400–401
  working drawing for, 401
veneering, 382–385
wall bookshelf, 429–430
  materials for, 429, 430
  working drawing for, 429
wood for, 131–140
  choice of, 131–140
writing desk, 442–444
  materials for, 443
  working drawing for, 442, 444
Workbench, 347–366
  construction, 347–366
    assembly of, 357–362
    boring for, 355–357
    cutting for, 351–354
    finish for, 366
    frame for, 357–363
    glueing of, 363
    tool panel for, 364
    top for, 363–364
    vise for, 364–365

wood for, 348–349
Working drawings, 115–122, 387
  armchair, 452–453
  bench, 440–441
  bird house, 469
  bookshelf, 467
  coffee table, 470
  Colonial magazine case, 417–418
  Colonial magazine stand, 415–417
  combination tray, 407–408
  corner table, 59–60
  dovetail drawers, 391–393
  dressing table, 445
  drop-leaf coffee table, 436–440
  folding card table, 432–433
  folding tennis table, 395–398
  footstool, 411–412
  glove case, 425–427
  handy memo roll, 427–428
  Hollywood headboard, 457–458
  horizontal spice cabinet, 420–422
  kidney-shaped coffee table, 419–420
  living-room chair, 448–452
  miniature cradle, 471
  picnic case and table, 430–432
  pipe rack and humidor, 414–415
  plate rack, 409–410
  portable towel rack, 405–406
  revolving book stand and table, 434–435
  sawhorse, 388–389, 472
  screens, 386–388
  sewing kit, 399–400
  shoeshine box, 413–414
  side chair, 453–454
  spice cabinet, 403–404
  student's home desk, 461–463
  sturdy vine support, 454
  telephone shelf, 422–424
  tool cabinet, 389
  tool chest, 393–394
  treasure chest, 400–402
  wall bookshelf, 429–430
  writing desk, 442–444
Workshop, 31
  expense of, 32
Wrenches, accidents and, 109
Writing desk, 442–444
  materials for, 443
  working drawing for, 442, 444

"Yankee" spiral ratchet screwdriver, 204
Yellow pine, 131
Yellow poplar, 132
Yew, 132

Z-shaped offset screwdriver, 14–15
Zig-Zag rule, 5–6, 105